Professional Examinati

Strategic Level

Paper P6

Management Accounting Business Strategy

Exam Kit

CIMA

KAPLAN PUBLISHING

British Library Cataloguing-in-Publication Data

A catalogue record for this book is available from the British Library.

Published by Kaplan Publishing UK
Unit 2 The Business Centre
Molly Millars Lane
Wokingham
Berkshire
RG41 2QZ

ISBN 978-1-84710-446-5

Printed and bound in Great Britain

Acknowledgements

We are grateful to the Chartered Institute of Management Accountants, the Association of Chartered Certified Accountants and the Institute of Chartered Accountants in England and Wales for permission to reproduce past examination questions. The answers have been prepared by Kaplan Publishing.

INTRODUCTION

We have worked closely with experienced CIMA tutors and lecturers to ensure that our Kits are exam-focused and user-friendly.

This Exam Kit includes an extensive selection of questions that entirely cover the syllabus – this ensures that your knowledge is tested across all syllabus areas. Wherever possible questions have been grouped by syllabus topics.

All questions are of exam standard and format – this enables you to master the exam techniques. Section 1 contains Section A-type questions you will come across in your exam; Section 2 contains Section B-type questions.

May and November 2007 exams are at the back of the book – try these under timed conditions and this will give you an exact idea of the way you will be tested in your exam.

CONTENTS

INDEX TO QUESTIONS AND ANSWERS

Section A-type questions

Section B-type questions

Business Strategy

The Competitive Environment

SYLLABUS AND LEARNING OUTCOMES

Learning aims

This syllabus aims to test the student's ability to:

- identify and evaluate approaches to strategic management;
- explain the place of the enterprise in the broader economic and social environment;
- apply contemporary thinking on strategic management;
- identify and utilise appropriate tools for strategic analysis;
- evaluate appropriate strategic options and make recommendations;
- evaluate the linkages between strategic planning and the implementation of those plans;
- design and recommend appropriate performance measurement systems.

Learning outcomes and syllabus content

A – ASSESSING THE COMPETITIVE ENVIRONMENT – 20%

Learning outcomes

On completion of their studies students should be able to:

- identify relevant stakeholders in respect of an organisation;
- evaluate the impact of regulatory regimes on strategic planning and implementation;
- evaluate the nature of competitive environments, distinguishing between simple and complicated competitive environments;
- distinguish the difference between static and dynamic competitive environments;
- evaluate strategies for response to competition.

Syllabus content

- PEST analysis.
- SWOT analysis.
- Interacting with stakeholders and the use of stakeholder mapping.
- Regulation in major markets (WTO, EU, NAFTA, Asia-Pacific).
- Country analysis and political risk.
- Porter's Diamond and its use for assessing the competitive advantage of nations.
- Porter's Five Forces Model and its use for assessing the external environment.
- Qualitative approaches to competitive analysis.
- Competitor analysis and competitive strategies (both qualitative and quantitative tools of competitor analysis will be used).
- Sources, availability and quality of data for environmental analysis.

B – INTERACTING WITH THE COMPETITIVE ENVIRONMENT – 20%

Learning outcomes

On completion of their studies students should be able to:

- evaluate the impact and influence of the external environment on an organisation and its strategy;
- recommend proactive and reactive approaches to business/government relations and to relations with civil society;
- discuss how stakeholder groups work and how they affect the organisation;
- discuss how suppliers and customers influence the strategy process and recommend how to interact with them;
- evaluate the impact of electronic commerce on the way business is conducted and recommend an appropriate strategy;
- evaluate the strategic and competitive benefits of IS/IT and advise on the development of appropriate strategies.

Syllabus content

- Derivatives of PEST such as STEEP (social, technological, environmental, economic and political factors) and PESTEL (political, economic, socio-cultural, technological and legal factors).
- Approaches to business-government relations and with civil society (Braithwaite and Drahos).
- Stakeholder management (stakeholders to include government and regulatory agencies, non-governmental organisations and civil society, industry associations, customers and suppliers).
- The customer portfolio: customer analysis and behaviour, including the marketing audit and customer profitability analysis as well as customer retention and loyalty.
- Negotiating with customers and suppliers and managing these relationships.
- The impact of IT (including electronic commerce) on an industry (utilising frameworks such as Porter's Five Forces, the Value Chain) and how organisations can use IT (including the Internet) to enhance competitive position.
- Competing through exploiting information (rather than technology), e.g. use of databases to identify potential customers or market segments, and the management of data (warehousing and mining).
- The relationship between current and predicted strategic importance of IS/IT (the applications portfolio).
- Implications of these interactions for Chartered Management Accountants and the management accounting system.

C – EVALUATION OF OPTIONS, PLANNING AND APPRAISAL – 30%

Learning outcomes

On completion of their studies students should be able to:

- evaluate strategic options;
- evaluate the product portfolio of an organisation and recommend appropriate changes to support the organisation's strategic goals;
- prepare a benchmarking exercise and evaluate the results;
- identify an organisation's value chain;
- evaluate the importance of process innovation and re-engineering;

- discuss and apply both qualitative and quantitative techniques in the support of the strategic decision-making function;
- discuss the role and responsibilities of directors in the strategy development process.

Syllabus content

- Mission statements and their use in orientating the organisation's strategy.
- Forecasting and the various techniques used: trend analysis, system modelling, in-depth consultation with experts (Delphi method).
- Scenario planning and long range planning as tools in strategic decision making (including gap analysis).
- Strategic options generation (e.g. using Ansoff's product/market matrix and Porter's generic strategies).
- Audit of resources and the analysis of this for use in strategic decision making.
- Management of the product portfolio.
- Benchmarking performance with the best organisations.
- Value chain analysis.
- Acquisition and divestment strategies and their place in the strategic plan.
- The role of IT in innovation and Business Process Re-engineering.
- The role and responsibilities of directors in making strategic decisions (including issues of due diligence, fiduciary responsibilities).

D – IMPLEMENTATION OF STRATEGIC PLANS – 30%

Learning outcomes

On completion of their studies students should be able to:

- evaluate and recommend appropriate control measures;
- prepare and evaluate multidimensional models of performance measurement;
- identify problems in performance measurement and recommend solutions;
- evaluate and advise managers on the development of strategies for knowledge management, IM, IS and IT that support the organisation's strategic requirements;
- identify and evaluate IS/IT systems appropriate to the organisation's strategic requirements, and recommend changes where necessary;
- discuss the role of change management in a strategic context.

Syllabus content

- Assessing strategic performance (i.e. the use and development of appropriate measures that are sensitive to industry characteristics and environmental factors).
- Non-financial measures and their interaction with financial ones. (Note: candidates will be expected to use both qualitative and quantitative techniques.)
- Multidimensional models of performance (e.g. the balanced scorecard, the results and determinants framework, the performance pyramid).
- Business unit performance and appraisal, including transfer pricing, reward systems and incentives, and agency theory. (Note: Details of agency theory will not be tested.)
- Project management: monitoring the implementation of plans.
- The implementation of lean systems across an organisation.
- Change management in a strategic context.
- Marketing in a strategic context.
- The purpose and contents of IM, IS and IT strategies, and the need for strategy complementary to the corporate and individual business strategies.

- The concept of knowledge management and its role as a key element in an organisation's success.
- Critical success factors: links to performance indicators and corporate strategy, and their use as a basis for defining an organisation's information needs.
- The role of research and development in an organisation, particularly the need to integrate product and process development.

REVISION GUIDANCE

Planning your revision

Begin by asking yourself two questions:

How much time do I have available for revision?

Remember to take into account:

- times of the day when you work most effectively
- other commitments
- time definitely unavailable (e.g. holidays)
- relaxation time.

What do I need to cover during my revision?

Remember to take into account that:

- all syllabus areas are equally examinable
- you need more time when revising areas of the syllabus you feel least confident about
- question practice is the best form of revision.

Make a timetable/plan to remind yourself how much work you have to do and when you are free to do it. Allow some time for slippage.

Revision techniques

- Go through your notes and textbook **highlighting the important points**
- You might want to produce your own set of **summarised notes**
- **List key words** for each topic to remind you of the essential concepts
- **Practise exam-standard questions**, under timed conditions
- **Rework questions** that you got completely wrong the first time, but only when you think you know the subject better
- If you get stuck on topics, **find someone to explain** them to you (your tutor or a colleague, for example)
- **Read recent articles** on the CIMA website and in *Financial Management*
- **Read** good newspapers and professional journals.

THE EXAM

Format of the exam

	Number of marks
There will be a written exam paper of three hours, with the following sections:	
Section A	
A maximum of four compulsory questions all relating to a single scenario.	50
Section B	
Two questions, from a choice of four, each worth 25 marks. Short scenarios will be given, to which some or all questions relate.	50
Total:	100
Total time allowed: 3 hours	

About the exam

- You are allowed **20 minutes' reading time** before the examination begins.
- Where you have a **choice of question**, decide which questions you will do.
- Unless you know exactly how to answer the question, spend some time **planning** your answer.
- **Divide the time** you spend on questions in proportion to the marks on offer. One suggestion is to allocate 1½ minutes to each mark available, so a 10 mark question should be completed in 15 minutes.
- Stick to the question and **tailor your answer** to what you are asked. Pay particular attention to the verbs in the question.
- If you do not understand what a question is asking, **state your assumptions**. Even if you do not answer in precisely the way the examiner hoped, you should be given some credit, if your assumptions are reasonable.
- If you **get completely stuck** with a question, leave space in your answer book and **return to it later.**
- Spend the last **five minutes** reading through your answers and **making any additions or corrections**.
- You should do everything you can to make things easy for the marker. The marker will find it easier to identify the points you have made if your **answers are legible**.
- **Essay questions**: Your essay should have a clear structure. It should contain a brief introduction, a main section and a conclusion. Be concise. It is better to write a little about a lot of different points than a great deal about one or two points.
- **Computations**: It is essential to include all your workings in your answers. Many computational questions require the use of a standard format: company profit and loss account, balance sheet and cash flow statement for example. Be sure you know these formats thoroughly before the examination and use the layouts that you see in the answers given in this book and in model answers.
- **Scenario-based questions:** read the scenario carefully, identify the area in which there is a problem, outline the main principles/theories you are going to use to answer the question, and then apply the principles/theories to the scenario.
- **Reports, memos and other documents**: some questions ask you to present your answer in the form of a report or a memo or other document. So use the correct format – there could be easy marks to gain here.

MATHEMATICAL TABLES AND FORMULAE

Area under the normal curve

This table gives the area under the normal curve between the mean and a point Z standard deviations above the mean. The corresponding area for deviations below the mean can be found by symmetry.

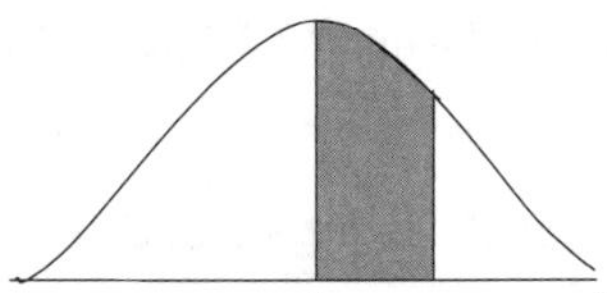

$Z = \frac{(x - \mu)}{\sigma}$	0.00	0.01	0.02	0.03	0.04	0.05	0.06	0.07	0.08	0.09
0.0	.0000	.0040	.0080	.0120	.0159	.0199	.0239	.0279	.0319	.0359
0.1	.0398	.0438	.0478	.0517	.0557	.0596	.0636	.0675	.0714	.0753
0.2	.0793	.0832	.0871	.0910	.0948	.0987	.1026	.1064	.1103	.1141
0.3	.1179	.1217	.1255	.1293	.1331	.1368	.1406	.1443	.1480	.1517
0.4	.1554	.1591	.1628	.1664	.1700	.1736	.1772	.1808	.1844	.1879
0.5	.1915	.1950	.1985	.2019	.2054	.2088	.2123	.2157	.2190	.2224
0.6	.2257	.2291	.2324	.2357	.2389	.2422	.2454	.2486	.2518	.2549
0.7	.2580	.2611	.2642	.2673	.2704	.2734	.2764	.2794	.2823	.2852
0.8	.2881	.2910	.2939	.2967	.2995	.3023	.3051	.3078	.3106	.3133
0.9	.3159	.3186	.3212	.3238	.3264	.3289	.3315	.3340	.3365	.3389
1.0	.3413	.3438	.3461	.3485	.3508	.3531	.3554	.3577	.3599	.3621
1.1	.3643	.3665	.3686	.3708	.3729	.3749	.3770	.3790	.3810	.3830
1.2	.3849	.3869	.3888	.3907	.3925	.3944	.3962	.3980	.3997	.4015
1.3	.4032	.4049	.4066	.4082	.4099	.4115	.4131	.4147	.4162	.4177
1.4	.4192	.4207	.4222	.4236	.4251	.4265	.4279	.4292	.4306	.4319
1.5	.4332	.4345	.4357	.4370	.4382	.4394	.4406	.4418	.4430	.4441
1.6	.4452	.4463	.4474	.4485	.4495	.4505	.4515	.4525	.4535	.4545
1.7	.4554	.4564	.4573	.4582	.4591	.4559	.4608	.4616	.4625	.4633
1.8	.4641	.4649	.4656	.4664	.4671	.4678	.4686	.4693	.4699	.4706
1.9	.4713	.4719	.4726	.4732	.4738	.4744	.4750	.4756	.4762	.4767
2.0	.4772	.4778	.4783	.4788	.4793	.4798	.4803	.4808	.4812	.4817
2.1	.4821	.4826	.4830	.4831	.4838	.4842	.4856	.4850	.4854	.4857
2.2	.4861	.4865	.4868	.4871	.4875	.4878	.4881	.4884	.4887	.4890
2.3	.4893	.4896	.4898	.4901	.4904	.4906	.4909	.4911	.4913	.4916
2.4	.4918	.4920	.4922	.4925	.4927	.4929	.4931	.4932	.4934	.4936
2.5	.4938	.4940	.4941	.4943	.4945	.4946	.4948	.4949	.4951	.4952
2.6	.4953	.4955	.4956	.4957	.4959	.4960	.4961	.4962	.4963	.4964
2.7	.4965	.4966	.4967	.4968	.4969	.4970	.4971	.4972	.4973	.4974
2.8	.4974	.4975	.4976	.4977	.4977	.4978	.4979	.4980	.4980	.4981
2.9	.4981	.4982	.4983	.4983	.4984	.4984	.4985	.4985	.4986	.4986
3.0	.49865	.4987	.4987	.4988	.4988	.4989	.4989	.4989	.4990	.4990
3.1	.49903	.4491	.4991	.4991	.4992	.4992	.4992	.4992	.4993	.4993
3.2	.49931	.4993	.4994	.4994	.4994	.4994	.4994	.4995	.4995	.4995
3.3	.49952	.4495	.4995	.4996	.4996	.4996	.4996	.4996	.4996	.4997
3.4	.49966	.4997	.4997	.4997	.4997	.4997	.4997	.4997	.4997	.4998
3.5	.49977									

Present value table

Present value of one unit of currency i.e. that is $(1 - r)^{-n}$ where r = interest rate; n = number of periods until payment or receipt.

Periods (n)	Interest rates (r)									
	1%	2%	3%	4%	5%	6%	7%	8%	9%	10%
1	0.990	0.980	0.971	0.962	0.952	0.943	0.935	0.926	0.917	0.909
2	0.980	0.961	0.943	0.925	0.907	0.890	0.873	0.857	0.842	0.826
3	0.971	0.942	0.915	0.889	0.864	0.840	0.816	0.794	0.772	0.751
4	0.961	0.924	0.888	0.855	0.823	0.792	0.763	0.735	0.708	0.683
5	0.951	0.906	0.863	0.822	0.784	0.747	0.713	0.681	0.650	0.621
6	0.942	0.888	0.837	0.790	0.746	0705	0.666	0.630	0.596	0.564
7	0.933	0.871	0.813	0.760	0.711	0.665	0.623	0.583	0.547	0.513
8	0.923	0.853	0.789	0.731	0.677	0.627	0.582	0.540	0.502	0.467
9	0.914	0.837	0.766	0.703	0.645	0.592	0.544	0.500	0.460	0.424
10	0.905	0.820	0.744	0.676	0.614	0.558	0.508	0.463	0.422	0.386
11	0.896	0.804	0.722	0.650	0.585	0.527	0.475	0.429	0.388	0.350
12	0.887	0.788	0.701	0.625	0.557	0.497	0.444	0.397	0.356	0.319
13	0.879	0.773	0.681	0.601	0.530	0.469	0.415	0.368	0.326	0.290
14	0.870	0.758	0.661	0.577	0.505	0.442	0.388	0.340	0.299	0.263
15	0.861	0.743	0.642	0.555	0.481	0.417	0.362	0.315	0.275	0.239
16	0.853	0.728	0.623	0.534	0.458	0.394	0.339	0.292	0.252	0.218
17	0.844	0.714	0.605	0.513	0.436	0.371	0.317	0.270	0.231	0.198
18	0.836	0.700	0.587	0.494	0.416	0.350	0.296	0.250	0.212	0.180
19	0.828	0.686	0.570	0.475	0.396	0.331	0.277	0.232	0.194	0.164
20	0.820	0.673	0.554	0.456	0.377	0.312	0.258	0.215	0.178	0.149

Periods (n)	Interest rates (r)									
	11%	12%	13%	14%	15%	16%	17%	18%	19%	20%
1	0.901	0.893	0.885	0.877	0.870	0.862	0.855	0.847	0.840	0.833
2	0.812	0.797	0.783	0.769	0.756	0.743	0.731	0.718	0.706	0.694
3	0.731	0.712	0.693	0.675	0.658	0.641	0.624	0.609	0.593	0.579
4	0.659	0.636	0.613	0.592	0.572	0.552	0.534	0.516	0.499	0.482
5	0.593	0.567	0.543	0.519	0.497	0.476	0.456	0.437	0.419	0.402
6	0.535	0.507	0.480	0.456	0.432	0.410	0.390	0.370	0.352	0.335
7	0.482	0.452	0.425	0.400	0.376	0.354	0.333	0.314	0.296	0.279
8	0.434	0.404	0.376	0.351	0.327	0.305	0.285	0.266	0.249	0.233
9	0.391	0.361	0.333	0.308	0.284	0.263	0.243	0.225	0.209	0.194
10	0.352	0.322	0.295	0.270	0.247	0.227	0.208	0.191	0.176	0.162
11	0.317	0.287	0.261	0.237	0.215	0.195	0.178	0.162	0.148	0.135
12	0.286	0.257	0.231	0.208	0.187	0.168	0.152	0.137	0.124	0.112
13	0.258	0.229	0.204	0.182	0.163	0.145	0.130	0.116	0.104	0.093
14	0.232	0.205	0.181	0.160	0.141	0.125	0.111	0.099	0.088	0.078
15	0.209	0.183	0.160	0.140	0.123	0.108	0.095	0.084	0.079	0.065
16	0.188	0.163	0.141	0.123	0.107	0.093	0.081	0.071	0.062	0.054
17	0.170	0.146	0.125	0.108	0.093	0.080	0.069	0.060	0.052	0.045
18	0.153	0.130	0.111	0.095	0.081	0.069	0.059	0.051	0.044	0.038
19	0.138	0.116	0.098	0.083	0.070	0.060	0.051	0.043	0.037	0.031
20	0.124	0.104	0.087	0.073	0.061	0.051	0.043	0.037	0.031	0.026

Cumulative present value of one unit of currency

This table shows the present value of one unit of currency per annum, receivable or payable at the end of each year for n years $\frac{1-(1+r)^{n}}{r}$

Periods (n)	Interest rates (r)									
	1%	2%	3%	4%	5%	6%	7%	8%	9%	10%
1	0.990	0.980	0.971	0.962	0.952	0.943	0.935	0.926	0.917	0.909
2	1.970	1.942	1.913	1.886	1.859	1.833	1.808	1.783	1.759	1.736
3	2.941	2.884	2.829	2.775	2.723	2.673	2.624	2.577	2.531	2.487
4	3.902	3.808	3.717	3.630	3.546	3.465	3.387	3.312	3.240	3.170
5	4.853	4.713	4.580	4.452	4.329	4.212	4.100	3.993	3.890	3.791
6	5.795	5.601	5.417	5.242	5.076	4.917	4.767	4.623	4.486	4.355
7	6.728	6.472	6.230	6.002	5.786	5.582	5.389	5.206	5.033	4.868
8	7.652	7.325	7.020	6.733	6.463	6.210	5.971	5.747	5.535	5.335
9	8.566	8.162	7.786	7.435	7.108	6.802	6.515	6.247	5.995	5.759
10	9.471	8.983	8.530	8.111	7.722	7.360	7.024	6.710	6.418	6.145
11	10.368	9.787	9.253	8.760	8.306	7.887	7.499	7.139	6.805	6.495
12	11.255	10.575	9.954	9.385	8.863	8.384	7.943	7.536	7.161	6.814
13	12.134	11.348	10.635	9.986	9.394	8.853	8.358	7.904	7.487	7.103
14	13.004	12.106	11.296	10.563	9.899	9.295	8.745	8.244	7.786	7.367
15	13.865	12.849	11.938	11.118	10.380	9.712	9.108	8.559	8.061	7.606
16	14.718	13.578	12.561	11.652	10.838	10.106	9.447	8.851	8.313	7.824
17	15.562	14.292	13.166	12.166	11.274	10.477	9.763	9.122	8.544	8.022
18	16.398	14.992	13.754	12.659	11.690	10.828	10.059	9.372	8.756	8.201
19	17.226	15.679	14.324	13.134	12.085	11.158	10.336	9.604	8.950	8.365
20	18.046	16.351	14.878	13.590	12.462	11.470	10.594	9.818	9.129	8.514

Periods (n)	Interest rates (r)									
	11%	12%	13%	14%	15%	16%	17%	18%	19%	20%
1	0.901	0.893	0.885	0.877	0.870	0.862	0.855	0.847	0.840	0.833
2	1.713	1.690	1.668	1.647	1.626	1.605	1.585	1.566	1.547	1.528
3	2.444	2.402	2.361	2.322	2.283	2.246	2.210	2.174	2.140	2.106
4	3.102	3.037	2.974	2.914	2.855	2.798	2.743	2.690	2.639	2.589
5	3.696	3.605	3.517	3.433	3.352	3.274	3.199	3.127	3.058	2.991
6	4.231	4.111	3.998	3.889	3.784	3.685	3.589	3.498	3.410	3.326
7	4.712	4.564	4.423	4.288	4.160	4.039	3.922	3.812	3.706	3.605
8	5.146	4.968	4.799	4.639	4.487	4.344	4.207	4.078	3.954	3.837
9	5.537	5.328	5.132	4.946	4.772	4.607	4.451	4.303	4.163	4.031
10	5.889	5.650	5.426	5.216	5.019	4.833	4.659	4.494	4.339	4.192
11	6.207	5.938	5.687	5.453	5.234	5.029	4.836	4.656	4.486	4.327
12	6.492	6.194	5.918	5.660	5.421	5.197	4.988	7.793	4.611	4.439
13	6.750	6.424	6.122	5.842	5.583	5.342	5.118	4.910	4.715	4.533
14	6.982	6.628	6.302	6.002	5.724	5.468	5.229	5.008	4.802	4.611
15	7.191	6.811	6.462	6.142	5.847	5.575	5.324	5.092	4.876	4.675
16	7.379	6.974	6.604	6.265	5.954	5.668	5.405	5.162	4.938	4.730
17	7.549	7.120	6.729	6.373	6.047	5.749	5.475	5.222	4.990	4.775
18	7.702	7.250	6.840	6.467	6.128	5.818	5.534	5.273	5.033	4.812
19	7.839	7.366	6.938	6.550	6.198	5.877	5.584	5.316	5.070	4.843
20	7.963	7.469	7.025	6.623	6.259	5.929	5.628	5.353	5.101	4.870

Formulae

Annuity

Present value of an annuity of one unit of currency per annum receivable or payable for n years, commencing in one year, discounted at r% per annum:

$$PV = \frac{1}{r}\left[1 - \frac{1}{[1+r]^n}\right]$$

Perpetuity

Present value of one unit of currency per annum, payable or receivable in perpetuity, commencing in one year, discounted at r% per annum:

$$PV = \frac{1}{r}$$

Growing perpetuity

Present value of one unit of currency per annum, receivable or payable, commencing in one year, growing in perpetuity at a constant rate of g% per annum, discounted at r% per annum:

$$PV = \frac{1}{r - g}$$

Section 1

SECTION A-TYPE QUESTIONS

1 T PLC

Introduction

T plc is a well-established company providing telecommunications services both nationally and internationally. Its business has been concerned with telephone calls, the provision of telephone lines and equipment, and private telecommunication networks. T plc has supplemented these services recently by offering mobile phones, which is an expanding market worldwide.

The company maintains a diverse customer base, including residential users, multi-national companies, government agencies and public sector organisations. The company handles approximately 100 million calls each working day, and employs nearly 140,000 personnel.

Strategic development

The Chairman of T plc stated within the latest Annual Report that there are three main areas in which the company aims to develop in order to remain a world leader in the telecommunications market. He believes that the three main growth areas reflect the evolving nature of the telecommunications market and will provide scope for development.

The areas in which development is planned are:

- expansion of the telecommunications business in the national and overseas markets, both by the company acting on its own and through partnership arrangements with other suppliers
- diversification into television and multi-media services, providing the hardware to permit telephone shopping from home and broadcasting services
- extension of the joint ventures and strategic alliances which have already been established with companies in North America, Europe, India and the Far East.

The Chairman explained that the company is intent on becoming a world leader in communications. This will be achieved through maintaining its focus on long-term development by improving its services to customers, developing high quality up-to-date products and being innovative, flexible and market-driven. His aim is to deliver a world-class service at competitive cost.

Financial information

Comparative statistics showing extracts from the company's financial performance in its national telecommunications market over the last two years are as follows:

	Last year	*Previous year*
	$ million	$ million
Turnover	16,613	15,977
Profit before interest and tax	3,323	2,876
Capital employed	22,150	21,300

The company estimates its cost of capital to be approximately 11%.

The Chairman expressed satisfaction with the increase in turnover and stated that cost efficiencies were now being generated following completion of a staff reduction programme. This would assist the company in achieving a target return on capital employed (ROCE) in this market of 20% over the next three years.

Business opportunities

The Chief Executive of T plc has stated that the major opportunities for the company lie in the following areas:

- encouraging greater use of the telephone
- provision of advanced services, and research and development into new technology, including the internet and systems integration
- the increasing freedom from government control of worldwide telecommunication services.

An extensive television and poster advertising campaign has been used by the company. This was in order to penetrate further the residential market by encouraging greater use of the telephone with various charging incentives being offered to residential customers.

To further the objective of increasing long-term shareholder value, the company is actively considering investment of $200 million in each of the next three years in new technology and quality improvements in its national market. Because of its specialist technical nature, the investment is not expected to have any residual value at the end of the three-year period.

Following the investment, the directors of T plc believe that its rate of profit before interest and tax to turnover in its national telecommunications market will remain constant. This rate will be at the same level as last year for each of the three years of the investment.

Markets and competition

The company is currently experiencing an erosion of its market share and faces increasingly strong competition in the mobile phone market. While T plc is the leader in its national market, with an 85% share of the telecommunications business, it has experienced a reduced demand for the supply of residential lines in the last five years as competition has increased.

The market for the supply of equipment in the national telecommunications market is perceived to be static. The investment of $200 million in each of the next three years is estimated to increase T plc's share of this market to a level of 95%. The full improvement of 10% is expected to be received by T plc next year, and its market share will then remain at this level for the full three-year period. It is anticipated that unless further investment is made after the three-year period, T plc's market share will revert to its current level as a consequence of the expected competitive response.

Industry regulation

The government has established an industry regulatory organisation to promote competition and deter anti-competitive behaviour.

As a result of the activities of the regulator and aggressive pricing strategies, it is anticipated that charges to customers will remain constant for the full three-year period of the new investment.

All cash flows can be assumed to occur at the end of the year to which they relate. The cash flows and discount rate are in real terms.

Required:

(a) Explain the nature of the political, economic, social, and technical forces which influence T plc in developing its business and increasing its market share. **(10 marks)**

(b) (i) Apply Ansoff's Product/Market Growth Vector matrix to assess the extent of the potential market development opportunities available to T plc. **(15 marks)**

(ii) Explain how this matrix may be incorporated into the strategic planning process to determine the extent of the planning gap. **(5 marks)**

(c) Evaluate and comment on T plc's proposed investment in new technology and quality improvements in its national telecommunications market.

Assume that variable costs are 80% of the incremental revenue, and that fixed costs will not increase. Ignore working capital. **(15 marks)**

(d) Assess to what extent the investment in new technology and quality improvements in T plc's national telecommunications market contributes towards the closure of the company's planning gap in respect of its target ROCE. **(5 marks)**

Note: You may assume that the entire capital investment is written off at the end of the three-year period.

(Total: 50 marks)

2 B PLC

Background

Over 20 years ago, B plc was established to manufacture and sell naturally based cosmetics and skin products. The first shop was opened in the United Kingdom (UK). Since then, B plc has successfully expanded and now trades in over 40 countries world-wide through more than 1,000 retail outlets, 75% of which are located outside the UK. The ecologically friendly aims of B plc have not changed since it was first established. The company campaigns against animal testing in the cosmetics industry and for human rights all over the world. It seeks to establish trade relations with overseas countries, and to integrate itself into the local communities in which it trades so that it can be more aware of the specific needs of its customers. B plc prides itself on its achievements in educating staff and customers through providing information on its products and methods of manufacture.

Corporate activities

B plc is intent on preserving the environment by promoting the efficient use of energy, keeping waste to a minimum and using only renewable resources whenever possible. These basic principles have been challenged by some observers who suggest that, in the aggressive corporate climate which currently prevails, B plc will need to abandon its environmentally friendly aims in order to compete. The company's Chairman is determined that this will not be the case and is proud of the fact that B plc was one of the first companies within the UK to publish environmental audit reports. Activities which B plc carries out include sourcing high quality raw materials directly from producers throughout the world and extensive product research and development, both in the UK and Latin America. The results of successful research are converted into innovative products which are manufactured by B plc in its modern production facilities. The products are then transferred to its retail outlets. In addition, B plc is active in health education promotion throughout the world and, some years ago, initiated a newspaper designed to help the homeless, which sells throughout major cities in the UK.

Market share and financial review

The ecologically innovative approach adopted by the founders of B plc resulted in it initially attaining 100% share of what was a niche market in the UK when the company first started. Since then, competition has developed to the extent that B plc now has 90% of the naturally-based cosmetics and hair-care market. In terms of profitability, B plc achieved in the last financial year an operating profit of £26 million (previous year £29 million) on a turnover of £175 million (previous year £154 million). The Chairman of B plc attributed the reduction in profit to difficult trading conditions, particularly in the UK, and an increase in overheads due to the enlargement of its head office facilities. It is clear to B plc's directors that the increasing level of competition is now threatening its niche market domination.

Strategic development

The directors of B plc have considered a number of strategic options and have identified two possible courses of action. They could either invest more in quality improvement and further differentiate the company's products from its competitors, or increase the level of promotion and attract a higher market share. Capital constraints on the company prevent it from doing both in the next year.

Quality improvement

B plc's previous experience of improving quality has resulted in optimism about its potential success. The company estimates that it has obtained good results 70% of the time by following the strategy of quality improvement. Unsatisfactory results have been experienced from the remaining 30% of the time in which the strategy has been applied. The cost of carrying through the improvements in the next financial year would be £50 million. Over a four-year period it is estimated that in present value terms, a net cash inflow of £100 million would be made if the market response was strong, and £60 million if it was weak. (Both of these values are before deduction of the capital cost of the improvements.) To assess the likelihood of a strong or weak market response, the directors have engaged a firm of consultants who have in the past been proved right on 80% of occasions when they predicted a strong market response. The consultants have also been proved right on 90% of occasions when they have predicted a weak market response.

The management accountant for B plc has carried out some decision analysis on this information and has concluded that the most likely outcome is a net cash inflow of £37.996 million. The management accountant's workings to arrive at this value are as follows:

	Higher return £100 million	*Lower return* £60 million
Strong response	$0.8 \times 0.7 = 0.56$	$0.1 \times 0.3 = 0.03$
Weak response	$0.2 \times 0.7 = 0.14$	$0.9 \times 0.3 = 0.27$

Probability of a high return given a strong response is $\frac{0.56}{0.59} = 0.95$

Probability of a low return given a strong response is $\frac{0.03}{0.59} = 0.05$

Probability of a high return given a weak response is $\frac{0.14}{0.41} = 0.34$

Probability of a low return given a weak response is $\frac{0.27}{0.41} = 0.66$

The expected value of the proposal is:

Response	*Return*	*Probability*	*Return* £ million	*Expected value* £ million
Strong	Higher	0.95	100	95.0
	Lower	0.05	60	3.0
				98.0
Weak	Higher	0.34	100	34.0
	Lower	0.66	60	39.6
				73.6

However, there is a 59% probability of a strong response and a 41% probability of a weak response. The expected outcome of the investment is:

Strong	59% of £98.0 million	57.820
Weak	41% of £73.6 million	30.176
		87.996
Less:	Cost of quality improvement	50.000
Expected outcome		37.996

Increased promotion

The directors believe that by investing £10 million in promotional activities in the next financial year, the net cash inflow, before deducting the cost of the initial investment, over a four-year period in present value terms would be £40 million.

Competitive reaction to proposed strategies

B plc's directors believe that the current competitors are likely to react to either of these strategies. The most likely reaction is to increase their own promotion activities; it is also likely that efforts will be made by competitors to identify and exploit areas where B plc is not able to maintain its high standards of ecological protection. It is very clear that improved information on its activities in order to counter this threat is an essential requirement for the directors to maintain customer confidence.

From the start, B plc has grown in size organically. The directors are keen to ensure that the company continues to develop and at the same time maintain its principles of ecological protection. They further recognise that organic growth is not the only route they could take and are seeking other potential forms of strategic development.

Required:

(a) Present a corporate appraisal for B plc. **(10 marks)**

(b) Comment on the two options evaluated. Your answer should:

- include an assessment of the best and worst outcomes from the quality improvement option
- express any reservations you might have about the results, and
- take into consideration the likely potential reaction of competitors if B plc implements either strategy. **(18 marks)**

(c) Recommend what information the management accountant should provide to the directors of B plc to assist them in assessing the company's progress towards the achievement of its strategic environmental aims. **(12 marks)**

(d) By reference to potential future market opportunities and threats, recommend a strategy which B plc may adopt in order to pursue its strategic environmental aims.

(10 marks)

(Total: 50 marks)

3 WG PLC

Introduction

WG plc was formed four years ago in the UK following the merger of two large pharmaceutical companies. Prior to the merger the two companies had been competitors: they believed that by combining forces the shareholders of each company would benefit from increased profits arising from the rationalisation of manufacturing facilities, distribution networks, and concentration of resources towards more focused research and development.

With operating outlets in Europe, Asia, the United States of America and Africa, WG plc regards itself as a global company. It employs approximately 50,000 people worldwide and has developed a wide portfolio of products. Its profits before tax last year increased by 20% and represented approximately 35% of turnover. The company declared that its earnings and dividends per share in the same period each increased by 15% over the previous financial year.

All manufacturers of pharmaceutical products claim that their pricing policies need to be set at a level to achieve high profitability in order to attract funds from investors. They argue that this is necessary to meet their high research and development commitments. In recent years, WG plc and other pharmaceutical manufacturers have encountered public and governmental challenges to their high levels of profitability.

WG plc encounters strong competition from other world-class pharmaceutical manufacturers, but these are few in number. High research and development costs present a major obstacle to potential competitors tempted to enter the industry.

Mission and objectives

The directors of WG plc have defined their overall corporate mission as being to 'combat disease by developing innovative medicines and services and providing them to healthcare organisations for the treatment of patients worldwide'.

The directors have confirmed their main objective is to sustain profitability while achieving the company's overall mission. They have also explained that WG plc aims to work towards eliminating those diseases for which the company is engaged in providing treatments. Achievement of the profitability objective is continually threatened by patents coming to the end of their lives. Patents give the sole right to make, use and sell a new product for a limited period.

Product development

A large proportion of the company's turnover in recent years has been derived from one particular drug. The patent for this drug expires next year and it is expected that its sales at that time will represent no more than 10% of total turnover. Four years ago, the sales of this drug produced almost half the company's entire turnover.

A new product, Coffstop, has now completed its rigorous development phases and is being marketed to pharmaceutical stores throughout the world by WG plc. It is in competition with a similar drug, Peffstill, produced and marketed by a direct competitor of WG plc. Medical research and opinion has concluded that Coffstop is generally more effective than Peffstill in treating the condition for which they are intended. Both drugs are available over the counter from pharmacies. The directors of WG plc are optimistic that Coffstop will become very popular because of its improved effectiveness over other market products.

The retail market price of Coffstop is £1.50 per bottle, compared with £10 per bottle of Peffstill. However, the recommended dosage of Coffstop is 6 times more than that for Peffstill. The bought-in costs per bottle to the retail pharmacist are £0.50 and £7.40 for Coffstop and Peffstill respectively. Initial indications to the management of WG plc are that retail pharmacists tend to prefer to stock Peffstill on the basis that it achieves 2.6 times the level of gross contribution per bottle compared with Coffstop.

It is estimated that the cost to the retailer of holding Coffstop is £0.40 per bottle and £0.80 for Peffstill. The availability of shelf space is a limiting factory for most retailers. The shelf area occupied by each bottle of Coffstop is 18 square centimetres and 60 square centimetres for each bottle of Peffstill. Early indications show that the average weekly sales volume for retail outlets stocking both products are 120 bottles of Coffstop and 20 bottles of Peffstill.

Market development

WG plc has experienced slow growth in its mature markets of Western Europe, North America and Japan. These markets contribute 80% of overall turnover but their governments have reduced expenditure on pharmaceutical products in recent years. The company has encountered a rapid sales increase in its expanding markets of Eastern Europe, South America, the Asia Pacific region, India, Africa and the Middle East. The directors of the company hold the view that increasing population growth in these markets is likely to provide substantial opportunities for the company over the next two decades.

Research and development

Almost 15% of WG plc's turnover last year was spent on research and development. WG plc has the largest research and development organisation of all pharmaceutical companies worldwide.

Much research is sponsored by national governments and world health organisations. A major piece of research which has recently been undertaken relates to new treatments for malaria as the disease is now demonstrating some resistance to existing treatments. WG plc has established a 'donation programme' for the new drug in virulent areas for the disease. This means that the company is donating batches of the drug to the health organisations in these areas. The cost of this programme is offset by the sales of the new drug in other areas of the world by making it available to people proposing to travel to the regions where malaria is widespread.

Required:

(a) Evaluate the nature and importance of the market threat which WG plc would face if it failed to provide sufficient resources for product development. **(10 marks)**

(b) WG plc's main objective is to sustain profitability through developing innovative medicines and services for treating patients worldwide. The company also aims to eliminate disease.

Discuss the nature of the five competitive forces (identified by Porter) which are exerted on WG plc in satisfying both these objectives at the same time. **(12 marks)**

(c) (i) Demonstrate whether Coffstop can provide a higher contribution to the retailer than Peffstill by using:

(1) Cost Volume Profit analysis, taking account of the gross contribution per limiting factor **(4 marks)**

(2) Direct Product Profitability analysis after charging holding costs.

(6 marks)

(ii) Explain how WG plc can market Coffstop to improve its competitive position.

(8 marks)

(d) Discuss the practical issues which the directors of WG plc would need to consider if the company entered a strategic alliance with a competitor for the joint development of future pharmaceutical products. **(10 marks)**

(Total: 50 marks)

4 BSN

Introduction

BSN is a public service radio and television broadcasting organisation. Its Board of Directors stated in its latest annual report that the main objectives of the organisation are to:

- remain a public service broadcaster
- provide a comprehensive range of distinctive programmes and give excellence in providing a public broadcasting service
- make and broadcast television and radio programmes which inform, educate and entertain.

BSN is mainly funded through television licence fees, which are paid by the residents of the country in which it is based. The television signal is currently broadcast through transmitters located on the surface of the land rather than via a remote satellite. The Board of Directors is held responsible by the government for ensuring that best value is obtained by the licence-fee payer.

Competition

The main competition for BSN comes from commercial broadcasters who are funded through advertising revenue. Some of these broadcasters use earth-bound transmission media for both television and radio programmes, and others transmit via satellite. BSN has achieved an improvement in its market share of the viewing the viewing and listening audience in recent years despite this competition. One of the most distinguished services provided by BSN is its world radio service, which is renowned for its unbiased and uncensored news broadcasts relating to national and international events. None of its competitors is able to provide a parallel service of the same quality and reputation.

Accountability and editorial policy

BSN is accountable through its Board of Directors to the licence-fee payers and to the government. It regularly consults with representatives of its audiences for both television and radio programmes and has established independent panels of viewers and listeners to review and advise on programmes.

In terms of editorial policy the Board of Directors tries to ensure that there is as little interference as possible on the creativity of programme makers. Nevertheless, the Board aims to ensure that programmes are fair, accurate and impartial, and meet the highest standards of good taste and decency.

New developments

Recently, BSN has introduced a 24-hour television news service. In addition, the organisation has entered a joint venture with a television subscription channel provider which allows the subscriber to access television programmes at any time to suit themselves rather than when they are broadcast. The additional income earned through subscriptions to this facility is re-invested by BSN in its main public service. Another potential development is the connection of the television to the telecommunications network which would allow greater efficiency in the delivery of programmes.

Financial efficiency

The Board of Directors has entered a four-year licence-fee agreement with the government. The terms of this are that the licence fee will increase at a compound rate of 2% per annum both this year and next year. The licence fee will then remain at this level for the remaining two years of the agreement. The total licence fee income received in the last financial year was $2,147 million. The Board of Directors expects the number of licences sold to remain at the same level as last year for the full four-year period.

The Board of Directors is proud that BSN exceeded the efficiency savings target set by the government by 2% in each of the last three years. Over this period, BSN has out-sourced its financial processing functions and sold its transmission service to an independent company, which has guaranteed the maintenance of a high-quality service at a reduced cost. The Board of Directors has placed much emphasis on the elimination of duplication of effort and reduction in waste from surplus capacity or over-staffing. An internal market has been introduced into BSN with programme-makers given the freedom to buy from producers who may be employed by the organisation or who may be external and completely independent of it. The savings achieved have been re-invested in programmes and services.

Despite these efficiency measures, BSN has experienced a steady average compound rate of growth of 3.7% in its expenditure over the last five years, and this is expected to continue at the same level over the next four-year period.

The following estimated levels of income and expenditure for the four-year period of the licence fee agreement are as follows:

	Income	*Expenditure*
	$ million	$ million
Year 1	2,190	2,114
Year 2	2,234	2,192
Year 3	2,234	2,273
Year 4	2,234	2,357

Future targets and developments

The government has congratulated the Board of Directors on its record of achieving efficiency savings and has set a Return on Capital Employed (ROCE) target of 6% per annum. Its current ROCE is 9%, which has been calculated as follows:

$$\frac{\text{Excess of income over expenditure} \times 100}{\text{Average capital employed}} = \frac{\$108\text{ million}}{\$1{,}195\text{ million}}$$

with average capital employed here equalling $\dfrac{\$1{,}250\text{m} + \$1{,}140\text{m}}{2}$

It is assumed that the value of capital employed by BSN will change only by adjustments in its operating reserve.

There has been continuing debate on the funding mechanism used for BSN through the licence fee. Some members of the government have questioned the fairness of this. They argue that commercial broadcasters cannot rely on a regular and guaranteed source of income and that the licence itself is a form of tax giving no discretion to the fee payer. One suggestion being considered by the government to reduce BSN's dependence on the licence fee is to separate the radio and television services. The radio services may then be financed by advertising revenue but would remain within the overall group alongside the television service. The rationale for this is that the licence fee is charged only on television receivers and therefore BSN does not obtain any direct income to support its radio services.

Financial extracts

Extracts from BSN's accounts reveal an increase in the overall surplus transferred to the operating reserve in the last financial year. Comparative extracts from the accounts over the last two years are as follows:

	Last year $ million	*Previous year* $ million
Income and expenditure account		
Excess of income over expenditure	108	82
Balance sheet		
Total assets less current liabilities	1,355	1,240
Long-term creditors and provisions	105	100
Represented by:		
Capital reserve	700	698
Operating reserve	550	442
	1,250	1,140

BSN's total expenditure in the last financial year was $2,039 million, compared with $1,700 million five years ago. The breakdown of these costs in the last financial year was as follows:

	Last year $ million
Broadcast expenditure:	
Television services	1,265
Radio services	423
Non-broadcast expenditure	351
	2,039

Required:

(a) Describe the contents of a rational planning model which should be applied by BSN when formulating its strategic plan. **(8 marks)**

(b) BSN's major stakeholders are the public, the government, its employees and management. Explain how the Board of Directors can obtain the views of BSN's major stakeholders in determining the future strategic development of the organisation. **(7 marks)**

(c) (i) Calculate BSN's ROCE for each of the four years of the licence fee agreement.

(ii) In the light of your findings, discuss what action BSN's management could take.

(15 marks)

(d) Discuss the implications for BSN's objectives if the television and radio services are separated. **(10 marks)**

(e) Explain what financial and non-financial information should be provided to the Board of Directors of BSN on the performance of the radio subsidiary following its separation from the television service. **(10 marks)**

(Total: 50 marks)

5 P GROUP

Background

The corporate history of the P Group (P) stretches back 30 years. During that time, P has developed internationally and now trades in many diverse areas. Fifteen years ago, the company launched P Airlines, which has proved to be one of its most successful business ventures. Five years ago, the company established P Rail and obtained franchises for running rail services in its home country. However, P Rail has not achieved the success that P had intended and is frequently publicly criticised for providing services which do not run on time.

The Group has a distinctive brand name which was established when P's charismatic founder and Chairman launched the first business venture. The majority of the citizens in its home country have heard of the brand which has over time been applied to many diverse areas of business. The Chairman believes the reputation of the brand name places a heavy burden of responsibility on P not to disappoint its customers. The Chairman himself has impressed his own personality on P by pursuing personal publicity in business ventures and becoming involved in high-profile and sometimes dangerous 'leisure' activities.

P has achieved a reputation for entering markets which are dominated by major companies, and has been successful in taking business from some major competitors by exposing their consistently poor service and complacency.

The principal business approach which has been adopted is that of 'brand stretching' across different products and services. Each company within the group runs its own affairs but they are all encouraged to help each other resolve their particular problems in a kind of family spirit.

Key strategic factors

The Chairman has stated that P is in business 'to be different' and that the P brand name should be clearly associated with this.

It is considered essential by the Directors that any products or services incorporated within the brand must help to build its good reputation, provide an opportunity to add value, and yield an appropriate trade-off between risk and rewards.

The Chairman considers that there are a number of key factors which have contributed to the success of P. The brand name is associated with being the consumer's champion, and has been very successful in delivering what the Chairman refers to as a 'sense of excitement' in most ventures to which it has been applied. In addition, the business contacts which have been established are important and he recognises that his own personality attracts customers and venture partners. P also encourages talented staff within the group to interact with each other in order to solve problems. The management style of P is therefore seen as a major contributory factor in its corporate success. Much weight is placed on its corporate image. The Chairman explains that the quality of a customer's experience when coming into contact with P is the most important item in determining its success.

Management style

The Directors agree that the first priority in being able to achieve success is for P to ensure that the Group employs personnel of the best quality and calibre. Their simple philosophy is that motivated staff lead to satisfied customers which results in repeat and new business and provides benefit to the shareholders.

P has a flat management structure with few authority levels within the hierarchy. The Chairman himself is committed to providing good communication channels within and outside the group. He believes very firmly that managers within the organisation must be prepared to listen both to the customers and also the staff.

Financial performance

The business approach which has been developed is that the brand name is provided by P with a cash injection from a joint venture partner. This has generally proved to be a very successful formula although this has not been the case with the latest venture into the domestic railway market. The Directors consider that the performance of P Rail will improve following a programme to upgrade the infrastructure inherited from the previous nationalised rail network.

Comparative financial information relating to P Airlines and P Rail for the last two years at 31 December is as follows:

	20X3 $m	*20X4* $m
Turnover		
Airlines	570	678
Rail	410	423
Pre-tax profit		
Airlines	60	80
Rail	30	32
Capital employed		
Airlines	750	790
Rail	530	640

Other performance indicators

The following information is provided relating to P's airline and rail businesses:

Airline	*20X3*	*20X4*
Number of passengers carried	1.2 million	1.4 million
Passenger miles travelled	3,000 million	3,300 million
Ratio of cabin staff to passengers (excluding aircrew, i.e. pilots and navigators):		
Economy class	1 to 10	1 to 12
Business and first class	1 to 4	1 to 5
Number of airline routes flown	40	44

- P Airlines sells economy, business and first-class seats to passengers. The prices reflect the level of comfort and service. For example, first-class seats cost double the price of business class seats and ten times the price of economy seats.
- Airline passenger numbers are expected to increase by 3% in the next two years in the long-distance economy-class market from which P attracts most of its customers.
- There is an increasing level of partnerships emerging among airlines whereby each carries the other's passengers as well as its own on designated routes. P is engaged in such partnerships for two of its routes.
- A general survey of satisfaction among airline passengers carried out by independent representatives from the travel industry in P's home country ranks P as being within the top three for most services.

Rail	*20X3*	*20X4*
Number of passengers carried	4.5 million	4.3 million
Passenger miles travelled	160 million	150 million
Ratio of customer attendants to passengers:		
Standard class	1 to 100	1 to 120
First class	1 to 20	1 to 25
Number of routes travelled	25	25

- P Rail sells standard and first-class seats to its passengers. The first-class seat is priced at about double that of a standard priced seat.
- An increase of 5% in total rail passengers is expected over the next four years.
- P operates the railway services under a franchise agreement, which is due for renewal in five years' time.
- The government has established a Railway Regulatory Authority to monitor the quality of the services provided by the P Group and other railway franchisees, and is constantly increasing pressure on the franchisees to improve their services.
- A general survey of passenger satisfaction carried out by the Railway Regulatory Authority was highly critical of P's services with regard to its record relating to punctuality and service on its trains.

Future development

P has enjoyed considerable success in its ventures within its domestic market. However, the Directors believe there is much opportunity to develop the brand name within the emerging highly populated retail markets elsewhere in the world where currently it is relatively unknown.

Required:

(a) Discuss the importance of the external forces which P faces in its worldwide business development. **(10 marks)**

(b) With reference to the comparative financial and other performance indicators, evaluate the performance of the P Airlines and P Rail companies. Recommend ways in which they may increase their individual contribution to the future development of the Group. **(15 marks)**

(c) Advise the Directors of P how their brand extension strategy may be successfully implemented in countries where the brand is relatively unknown at present.

(13 marks)

(d) Explain the main factors which have contributed to P's commercial success so far. Comment on the Chairman's personal responsibilities to the Group's shareholders, employees, joint venture partners and customers. **(12 marks)**

(Total: 50 marks)

6 C

Introduction

C is a large civil engineering company which carries out various building contracts within both its home and overseas markets. Its main area of work, particularly overseas, is in road construction. The company has a strong financial track record and successfully survived a major recession within its home market about ten years ago.

Economic circumstances in overseas markets

During the last three years, the overseas markets in which C has been carrying out building contracts have suffered a serious economic recession. Business confidence in these markets has been seriously weakened over this period. One country, which has been affected by adverse economic circumstances, is Eastlandia. C has been engaged in carrying out contract work in Eastlandia for several years. Government action in Eastlandia to protect its ailing economy has also had an adverse impact on foreign contractors such as C operating in this country.

The concern felt by C's Directors regarding the economic situation in Eastlandia has been increased as a result of recent events involving a large development company (D) which C has worked with in the past. Company D, which is wholly owned by Eastlandian shareholders, had previously received Eastlandian government backing. However, it has recently been allowed to go into receivership without any further government support. The government announced that partial repayment of debts owed by the development company to local investors would take priority over those it owed to foreign investors. The result of this is that foreign investors are unlikely to see any recovery of their loans.

The serious economic situation developing in Eastlandia has threatened to result in an economic recession. There has been a consequent negative effect on related industries within the country, such as steel, building materials and transport. Another major concern for C's Directors is the constant threat posed by currency fluctuations and the possibility of the Eastlandian government being forced into currency devaluation.

Work-in-progress

Currently, C is engaged in the construction of a major road linking two parts of a new Eastlandian city, bypassing the central congested area. C is engaged as a sub-contractor to a major Eastlandian development company – a different company from D which went into receivership recently. The contract was accepted by C after estimating that it would provide a high positive net present value. At the time the investment appraisal calculation was made, the expected currency exchange rate between Eastlands (Eastlandia's currency) and £ sterling (C's home currency) was 7.26 to the £ in the current year and 7.54 to the £ next year. In fact, the current exchange rate is 7.74 to the £ and the forward rate in 12 months', time is quoted at 8.56 to the £.

As far as C's overall business is concerned, the contract represents about 10% of total turnover for the company. The contract commenced three months ago and payment to C is to be in Eastlands. Progress payments for the work done so far have been delayed without any explanation. The contract is about 15% complete and is expected to be finished in another 21 months', which is three months later than planned. This will result in penalty payments being incurred by C.

The Directors of C have expressed to the contract manager for the road development in Eastlandia their concern regarding the need to undertake remedial work on what has been completed so far. This has resulted from the use of faulty materials obtained from an Eastlandian supplier. The remedial work has already consumed the total amount of the financial contingency which was allowed within the contract estimates.

Strategic information and market size

C uses external databases to establish the levels of its own share of the market and overall patterns of market growth and development. In addition, the management accounting department of the company provides internal information on market share and growth and internal capacity to meet its future contractual demands. Over the last two years, there has been a general decline in market opportunities, but C has in fact managed to increase its overall market share. This has been achieved because of its strong reputation for using good quality materials and applying high standards of workmanship.

One of the major criticisms being made in Eastlandia is the poor quality of the civil engineering projects which have been completed quickly. There have been reports of numerous casualties among the site workers during the construction process. Some buildings have partially collapsed after completion and there have been instances where roads have begun to break up shortly after they have been opened. This has caused civilian casualties with some fatalities and resulted in noisy public protest in Eastlandia about the lack of attention to safety in civil engineering and building work.

C is well regarded by the Eastlandian government. It has taken a long time for the Directors of C to build the company's reputation and gain recognition in Eastlandia for its workmanship.

Possible future development

The Eastlandian government has invited C's Directors to tender for other civil engineering work. C has taken the invitation and, if the company is successful in all its tenders, the total commitment in Eastlandia would represent about 40% of its order book.

In recognition of the importance of the Eastlandian market and in order to reduce the potential losses from developers which engage their services becoming insolvent, the Directors of C have proposed that a strategic alliance be formed. It is proposed that this alliance will be established with an Eastlandian civil engineering contractor who, it is expected, will have an insight into the financial integrity of potential customers. The alliance partner would be able to give clear advice as to which of these Eastlandian customers would be suitable for the establishment of contractual arrangements.

Required:

(a) Prepare a corporate appraisal for C in respect of its strengths, weaknesses and opportunities. **(10 marks)**

(b) Discuss the threats posed to C by its involvement with the road-building project in Eastlandia and explain how it can reduce the impact of these threats on its own strategic position. **(25 marks)**

(c) Recommend appropriate sources of information which may be used by C's management accountants when evaluating the potential future demand for its services in its overseas markets. **(10 marks)**

(d) Discuss the strategic logic and practical considerations for C of entering into an alliance with an Eastlandian civil engineering contractor. **(15 marks)**

(Total: 60 marks)

7 S GROUP AND AE DIVISION

Company development

The headquarters of the S Group (S) is located in K, a country which has experienced rapid economic growth in recent years.

S itself has been established for over 100 years. Two brothers first started trading in K and developed the group, which is now a highly profitable international conglomerate company. Its diverse business activities range from capital goods manufacture, through materials handling to operation of airlines and banking. Some of its activities involve the transfer of partly completed goods between manufacturing and assembly plants located in different countries. The group operates a divisionalised structure.

Economic circumstances

Over the last three years the region of the world in which K is located has been subject to serious economic difficulties. K itself has not been affected as much as some of its neighbours, owing to the fact that its independent currency is pegged to the US dollar.

There has been much activity and intervention by the monetary authorities in K to protect the value of the currency, and this has proved to be largely successful, despite the intense pressure exerted by foreign speculators. Nevertheless, the effects of the regional economic difficulties are being felt. This is exemplified by the recent emergence of unemployment after a period of 30 years of full employment and a dramatic fall in property prices.

Organisational economic objectives

Fifty-five per cent of S's holding company shares are held within the families of the original founders. The remaining 45 per cent of the shares are mainly held by international banks and other financial institutions located all over the world. These institutional shareholders maintain constant pressure on the directors to improve earnings per share and increase dividend payments. The directors have stated that their main objective is to increase shareholder value. In satisfying the requirements of the shareholders, the directors are conscious of the need for improved efficiency in the group's operations. Consequently, the holding company's board of directors carefully scrutinises the activities of the constituent subsidiary companies within the group.

Divisional performance measurement

S has always applied a traditional form of measurement to assess the performance of the group's subsidiaries. It uses return on capital employed (ROCE) and defines this as:

$$\frac{\text{Profit before interest and tax}}{\text{Average capital employed}} \times 100$$

(The capital employed value is the average of that shown at the beginning and end of the year.)

The performance of the divisional managers is strictly monitored on this basis and their remuneration increases if they achieve growth in their ROCE, which is measured annually. Inevitably, the divisional managers strive to improve their performance as measured by this method.

The Agricultural Equipment division

The Agricultural Equipment (AE) division, which is not located in K, assembles components into a single product. It receives the components from other subsidiaries in the group which are situated in other countries. The group as a whole has been able to benefit from economies of scale, as a result of other subsidiary divisions, which have long experience in manufacturing, supplying AE. Following assembly, AE ships the product to various customers throughout the world. The geographical location of the country in which AE is situated enables the product to be easily exported, but the division is subject to high levels of corporation tax.

The transfer prices of the components transferred to AE are set centrally by group head office located in K. The divisional manager of AE has no influence over them at all. The group head office may vary the transfer prices during the financial year.

Comparative results for the AE division over the last two years (translated into K's currency) are as follows:

	Last year		*Previous year*	
	K$m	K$m	K$m	K$m
Sales		800		750
Components transferred	600		400	
Assembly costs	100		75	
		700		475
Gross profit		100		275
AE Division Head Office (all fixed)		75		75
Net profit before interest and tax		25		200
Average capital employed		2,020		2,000

Selling prices over the two years remained stable.

It may be assumed that the variable costs of the supplying division, relating to the transferred components, were neutral in respect of AE division's profitability over the two years.

The budgeted and actual selling price per unit was K$50,000 in each of the two years. The budgeted production and sales level for each year was 18,000 units. It can be assumed that there were no opening and closing inventories of finished goods or work in progress in either of the years.

The budgeted cost per unit for each of the last two years was as follows:

	Last year	*Previous year*
	K$	K$
Assembly	6,000	5,000
Components transferred	35,000	25,000
	41,000	30,000

It can be assumed that there was no change in the currency exchange rate between the AE division's host country and K$ in the last two years. There have been discussions at S Group headquarters regarding the deteriorating performance of AE and there is growing pressure to close it down. The AE divisional manager believes there is little that he can do in the circumstances, as he only controls a small proportion of the total costs of the division.

Potential for growth in AE division

Despite the reduced profitability in the last financial year, the divisional manager of AE believes there is potential for growth. He has put forward plans to group headquarters to take over a competitor company in the country in which the division is situated. This would result in an increase for the division in world wide market share and provide the capacity to increase the range of agricultural equipment supplied in accordance with the divisional manager's perception of demand. To do this AE will need to obtain funds which will be secured against group assets.

Required:

(a) State the sources from which the board of directors of S may obtain information relating to the group's business environment and explain how it might use that information for strategic management purposes. Explain how the board of directors might assure itself of the quality of that information for strategic management purposes. (You are not required to consider the ecological environment in answering this question.) **(12 marks)**

(b) Making use of the information contained in the case, produce a critical appraisal of the method applied by S Group's directors to assess the performance of the AE division. **(16 marks)**

(c) Discuss the factors that should be taken into consideration by the directors of S in deciding whether the strategic development proposals put forward by AE's divisional manager should be pursued. **(10 marks)**

(d) Assume that the AE division makes the acquisition as proposed by its divisional manager.

Recommend how S Group's directors should improve the methods of measuring the performance of the AE division in order to assess its contribution to the group's strategic requirement to increase shareholder value. **(12 marks)**

(Total: 50 marks)

8 FNJ AND WT MERGER

Background

FNJ is a company which has developed business interests in the very competitive music industry. It produces and sells compact discs (CDs) and traces its history back to when it manufactured vinyl records. It is contracted to product CDs for many famous recording artists which it is able to distribute through its own worldwide chain of retail music stores.

A new Chief Executive (CJ), who came from an unrelated business, was appointed to run FNJ about 12 months ago. The financial situation for the company has become perilous with falling worldwide sales and difficult trading conditions. The company has issued a number of profit warnings and experienced severe management disputes which have been made public. The result of these factors has been a low share price. CJ implemented cost reductions at FNJ and developed a strategy which focuses the company's attention on the provision of music to customer via the Internet, with the eventual aim of replacing CDs with Internet sales in the years to come.

WT is a large entertainments group which has growing business interests in producing motion pictures (movies) and retail outlets (trading under its own brand name of WT). The company is well regarded worldwide within its industry. It has augmented the product range with, for example, soft toys (related to its popular movie characters) which are sold through its retail outlets.

The merger

A merger deal has recently been agreed between the directors of FNJ and WT. This has yet to be ratified by both sets of shareholders, but it is expected to be accepted. The new group (FW) aims to achieve a high market share of total worldwide music sales. Following the merger, it is expected that the two companies will shed jobs throughout the world in the interests of improving efficiency. The contracts for some of the recording artists who are not achieving high sales will not be renewed.

Financial summary of the merger

The following details highlight the main points relating to the merger:

(i) The merger is worth $10 billion in terms of total asset value.

(ii) WT has eight seats while FNJ has seven seats on the new board of FW.

(iii) CJ will be the Chief Executive of FW.

(iv) Shares in FW will be allocated in proportion to the current shareholdings. This will result in each company's shareholders holding 50% of the shares.

(v) Directors' share options come to fruition on completion of the merger.

(vi) The share price of FNJ rose by 11% after the merger was announced.

Selected details relating to FNJ and WT before the proposed merger

CDs (FNJ):

	Last year	*2 years ago*
Actual sales	$90 million	$95 million
Budgeted sales	$100 million	$100 million
Average actual price per CD	$20	$20
Average actual cost per CD (1/3 of this is variable cost)	$12	$12
Average budgeted price per CD	$22	$20
Average budgeted cost per CD (1/3 of this is variable cost)	$15	$10.5

The average annual sales of CDs over the last five years were $100 million. The trend of changes in sales levels for CDs which has been apparent over the last two years is expected to continue.

Motion pictures (WT):

	Last year	*2 years ago*	*3 years ago*	*4 years ago*
Total revenue	$2,000 million	$1,800 million	$1,400 million	$1,000 million
Total costs	$1,900 million	$1,600 million	$1,100 million	$700 million

Retail music stores (operated by FNJ):

	Last year	*2 years ago*	*3 years ago*	*4 years ago*
Total revenue	$140 million	$138 million	$136 million	$135 million
Total costs	$136 million	$131 million	$134 million	$135 million

The resale value of FNJ's retail music stores is reducing because of the increasing popularity of alternative methods of shopping.

Strategic development of FW

CJ has forecast that next year sales of music will be available through the Internet with digital downloading to the customer's own personal computer. At the moment, most of the FNJ retail music store's revenue is generated by the sale of FNJ-produced CDs. He believes that, by supplying customers through the Internet, overall sales revenue (combining Internet sales with CDs), will increase by 20%. The average variable costs for Internet sales will reduce by 25% on that currently incurred in CD production. This cost reduction is expected as a result of not needing to employ expensive recording studios which are currently required to produce a CD. The average selling price and average variable cost of a CD are expected to remain at $20 and $4 respectively throughout next year. The average selling price of each Internet sale is also expected to be $20.

Independent research has revealed that the market for digitally downloaded music is forecast to grow next year. Customers will have the opportunity to create their own 'do it yourself' compilation albums.

Some of FW's competitors have already made effective use of the Internet to distribute CDs and videos, undercutting high street retailers on price. However, digital download through the Internet is still experimental.

Required:

(a) Discuss the dynamic nature of the business environment experienced by FNJ and WT, and explain the rationale for the merger. **(10 marks)**

(b) (i) Analyse the business performance of CDs, motion pictures and FNJ's retail music stores over the period contained in the scenario. Include calculations on the projected change in contribution each year for CD and Internet sales if CJ's forecast is accurate. **(16 marks)**

(ii) Calculate and analyse the contribution volume variance relating to CD sales for last year and two years ago. **(5 marks)**

(iii) Recommend ways in which the directors of FW should pursue the strategic development of the CD, motion pictures and FNJ's retail music store businesses. **(10 marks)**

(c) Briefly explain the theory of shareholder value and discuss how shareholder value may be increased by the merger. **(9 marks)**

(Total: 50 marks)

9 Y-LAND FE

Introduction

The Y Corporation is based in the United States of America (USA). It was founded in the early part of the last century when Mr Y produced cartoon films. These soon proved very popular as a form of family entertainment and the characters in the films became household names.

The Corporation established a theme park (based around the film characters) in the southern USA, where there was a warm and mainly dry climate. The theme park, known as Y-land, proved to be an immediate success, attracting millions of visitors each year. A whole range of family entertainment flourished, based on the original theme of the cartoon characters. These included shops, restaurants, hotels and amusement rides.

Following the success of Y-land in the USA, the directors of the Corporation established another Y theme park based in Northern Europe. The rationale behind this was that, although many Europeans visited Y-land in the USA, the cost of travel made visiting the attraction very expensive. The directors believed that establishing a Y-land in Northern Europe would enable European people to visit the attraction without incurring high travel expenses. Y-land Europe was built in a highly populated area of Northern Europe which is easily accessible. A factor which differentiates Y-land Europe from the theme park in the USA is that it is located in a region which is frequently affected by rain and it does not enjoy a guaranteed warm climate. Y-land Europe did not in fact attract the volume of visitors that were expected and almost went bankrupt before receiving a massive cash injection from a wealthy donor who took part shares in the theme park.

Further strategic development

The Y Corporation is now considering building another theme park, this time in a tropical area in the Far East. Y-land FE will be part-funded by the host government in the Far East, which will take a 60% share in the park. The Y Corporation will fund the remaining 40%. Profits and losses will be shared in direct proportion to the shareholding of each of the joint venture partners. It is believed that local tourism and related sectors of the entertainment industry will benefit from the development as the theme park will attract more visitors to the region. Similar to the other two Y-land theme parks, the development will include many facilities such as hotels, bars and restaurants as well as the entertainment attractions.

It will take two years to build Y-land FE before any paying visitors enter the park. The Y Corporation has based its estimates of visitors in the first year of operation (that is, after the two years of construction) on the following probabilities:

	Visitors	*Probability*
Optimistic	8 million	0.25
Most likely	3 million	0.50
Pessimistic	2 million	0.25

After the first year of operation, it is expected that the number of visitors will increase by 50% in the next year. The Y Corporation directors consider that this number of visitors will be the maximum and after that the theme park will suffer a reduction in the number of visitors (marketing decay) of 5% compound each year for the next two years. After two years, the directors expect the number of visitors each year to remain constant at this level.

The host government believes that the theme park will create about 15,000 new jobs in the area through servicing the facilities. It expects the construction of the park to create about 5,000 jobs in addition to the 8,000 who will be employed in land reclamation and other necessary infrastructural work associated with the project.

Cost and revenue estimates

It is expected that the overall capital cost of the theme park will be $2,200 million. This sum will be spread evenly over the construction period and, for the purposes of calculation, the actual cash outflow may be assumed to arise at the end of each of the two years. The Y Corporation will be responsible for raising 40% of this sum.

In any year, the visitors are expected to be in the proportion of 40% adults and 60% children or people who will obtain a concession (reduction) on their entrance fees. For simplicity, the entrance charges will be set at a flat rate of $50 for each adult and $30 for each child or concession. There will be no further fees for entertainment after the entrance charge has been made to the visitor.

Past experience has shown that running expenses of the theme park show a certain level of consistency. In terms of labour, the costs follow the pattern of a 90% learning curve which applies on average to every 1 million visitors. This lasts for the first two years, after which the labour costs for each visitor become constant. The cost of labour at the time the park will open is expected to be $3 for each visitor. The effects of this are that the cumulative average direct labour costs in the first year of operation (that is, year 3 of the project) are estimated to be $9.72 million (after being multiplied by the number of expected visitors in that year). The cumulative average labour costs for both the first and second years of operation (that is, years 3 and 4 of the project) are expected to be $21.14 million (after being multiplied by the total number of visitors for the first two years of operation). After this point the learning effect is expected to cease.

The other direct costs, which are not subject to learning, can be assumed to be incurred at the rate of $2 for each visitor. Attributable fixed running expenses are estimated to be $100 million each year in cash terms.

In addition, the Y Corporation expects that its joint venture with the host government will earn an average net contribution of $10 from the sale of souvenirs and refreshments and $100 from accommodation charges for each adult, child or concessionary visitor each year.

The cost of capital for the whole project is expected to be 15%.

Shareholder value

The Y Corporation believes that its main objective is to increase the wealth of its owners. The Corporation requires a gross return on investment of 22% after eight years of income generated from the venture. It has been recommended to the directors of the Y Corporation that the return is calculated by taking the net present value of the project after eight years of operation and dividing this by the gross initial undiscounted capital outlay of $2,200 million.

Ignore taxation, inflation and variations due to exchange rates.

Required:

(a) Evaluate the usefulness of Porter's Diamond Theory (the Competitive Advantage of Nations) in helping the directors of the Y Corporation to determine whether or not it should proceed with establishing Y-land FE. **(10 marks)**

(b) (i) Produce a discounted cash flow (DCF) calculation for Y-land FE from the start of building work in the first year until eight years of cash inflows have been generated (that is, ten years in total), and calculate the return on investment in accordance with the method recommended. **(15 marks)**

(ii) Analyse and critically appraise the DCF calculation and the resulting return on investment as defined by the method recommended to the directors of the Y **Corporation**, and advise the directors as to whether they should proceed with Y-land FE. You should consider financial and non-financial factors in providing your advice. **(15 marks)**

(c) Discuss how the directors of the Y Corporation can use shareholder value analysis to determine the development of its portfolio of products and services. **(10 marks)**

(Total: 50 marks)

10 ICS

Assume that 'now' is May 20X8.

ICS was established ten years ago. The company began by providing computer software programs to local businesses. This is an industry which is dynamic. Rapid technological development constantly causes fast changes within the industry.

The demand for ICS's services grew. After two years of operation ICS had almost doubled its turnover and had taken on more staff. In addition to software programming, ICS then diversified into providing emergency computer data retrieval services. This necessitated obtaining some specialist equipment and hiring specifically trained staff. Rapid growth in turnover continued for the first four or five years, but has reduced in recent years.

ICS is managed by a board of directors, and the company is financed by equity (mostly held by private investors) and debt. The current gearing ratio is in the proportion of 60% equity to 40% debt. Shareholders are becoming concerned about ICS's recent poor performance.

Financial results

The financial results for the last five years of trading are shown below.

Year ended 31 December	*20X3*	*20X4*	*20X5*	*20X6*	*20X7*
	$000	$000	$000	$000	$000
Sales	6,300	6,400	6,600	6,500	6,300
Variable costs	4,621	4,732	4,881	4,891	4,778
Fixed costs	1,481	1,489	1,730	1,750	1,900
Capital employed	2,400	2,500	2,500	2,600	2,600

Turnover provided in percentage terms each year to different types of customer sector:

	20X3	*20X4*	*20X5*	*20X6*	*20X7*
% retail	70	65	65	55	50
% industrial	23	26	26	30	33
% other	7	9	9	15	17

Comparative figures for each of the three sectors served by ICS for the years 20X3 and 20X4 are as follows:

20X3	*Retail*	*Industrial*	*Other*	*Total*
	$000	$000	$00	$000
Contribution	1,323	290	66	1,679
Profit before interest charges and tax	221	0	(23)	198

20X4	*Retail*	*Industrial*	*Other*	*Total*
	$000	$000	$000	$000
Contribution	1,249	333	86	1,668
Profit before interest charges and tax	209	0	(30)	179

Developments

ICS is looking to develop the services it provides. It has the opportunity to place a bid for a contract with a customer in the industrial sector which will initially have a probationary period of one year. The contract will take effect from 1 January 20X9 and may be renewed after the first year for a further five years. If the bid is successful, it will be necessary for ICS to obtain some new capital equipment which it will rent for the probationary year at a hire charge of $100,000. This sum will be paid at the beginning of the contract.

It is anticipated that the contract will increase turnover by 40% over the **Industrial Sector** level for the year ended 31 December 20X7 in each year of its operation. The variable cost ratio for the contract will be slightly lower than for 20X7. It is estimated that the variable cost ratio for the contract will be **77.5% of the 20X7 level** in the Industrial Sector. Fixed costs, however, are expected to increase by a total of 20% over the amount incurred on the Industrial Sector for the year ended 31 December 20X7, directly as a result of taking the contract.

Z, the Managing Director of ICS, is very keen to place a bid for the contract as he has recognised the decline in profitability in recent years. He believes that the only way to return to profitability is to continually expand the company's service provision.

Management information systems

ICS has never made any provision for management information. Z uses a local accountancy firm, Y & Partners, which produces only the statutory information and returns. It was A, an accountant from Y & Partners, who provided the financial and turnover percentage information given above.

While it is not possible to be fully accurate, A estimates that the variable costs and fixed costs as a proportion of turnover for each type of service provided were:

	Variable costs: % of turnover	*Fixed costs: % of turnover*
Years	20X3 to 20X7	20X3 and 20X4
Retail	70	25
Industrial	80	20
Other	85	20

A calculates the fixed costs in each of these sectors over the last three years to have been as follows:

Year ended 31 December	*20X5*	*20X6*	*20X7*
	$000	$000	$000
Retail	1,070	890	790
Industrial	470	590	800
Other	190	270	310

For some years, A has tried to explain to Z the necessity for ICS to be provided with regular management information, in particular management accounting information. However, Z has always rejected this advice, saying that it would be too expensive and that the board of ICS should not 'waste its time on detail'.

'In any case', Z says, 'I know the business we are in. I am able to see what work we should be taking on. I know the way to be successful and profitable is to expand the services we provide. This worked before several years ago and will work again.'

A has expressed concern to Z over ICS's cash flow.

Note: Net present value calculations are NOT required in answering this question.

Required:

(a) Discuss how setting corporate objectives can help and/or obstruct ICS in satisfying the demands made by its shareholders. **(10 marks)**

(b) Discuss the relevance of the provision of management information to a company such as ICS when the business environment is always changing so fast. **(10 marks)**

(c) Provide an analysis of the turnover and costs for the years 20X5 to 20X7 over the three sectors which ICS services. Comment on the results of your analysis and advise what management accounting information should be provided for ICS. Your advice should identify the priorities which should be addressed, given the **current** financial circumstances of ICS. **(20 marks)**

(d) Advise Z whether ICS should bid for the new contract. Include any reservations you may have about whether or not the bid should be made, and support your answer with calculations. **(10 marks)**

(Total: 50 marks)

11 THE WORLDAIR ALLIANCE

Introduction

PC Airlines was founded nearly 60 years ago by two pilots. The airline began flying from its home base in Asia to local destinations. It soon grew and now has acquired routes to many worldwide locations. The company was listed on its home stock exchange 15 years ago. Now a conglomerate group holds 45% of the airline's shares while a further 25% are held by an Investment Corporation.

Four years ago, PC Airlines entered an alliance with other airline companies. The alliance took the name 'Worldair' as this reflects its composition, which is made up of airlines based in the USA and Europe, as well as Asia. The three airlines in the alliance are PC, AB and US. They operate out of the following geographic regions of the world:

PC Asia	AB Europe	US USA

Aims of Worldair

The Worldair Alliance was formed in response to increasing competition from other airline alliances. These competing alliances threatened to attract customers (passengers) from the Worldair members. The Worldair Alliance members have agreed to co-operate with each other on route destinations. The members also enjoy economies of scale in satisfying their customers' demand by reducing the overall number of flights and increasing the seat occupancy of member airlines. This means that a customer may book a seat with one member of the Alliance and be allocated to another member's flight which is travelling to the same destination. Senior managers of the members of the Alliance claim that by rationalising the number of flights, they are able to pass on economies to customers in terms of seat prices and also reduce aircraft traffic congestion and pollution emissions.

The financial aim of Alliance members is to increase their shareholders' wealth by providing a better service than their competitors. To achieve this aim, it is essential that all members improve profitability by increasing their popularity with customers. All senior managers of the Alliance have agreed that it is very important for the members to establish consistent policies and that each must not deviate from these in any way. In order to coordinate the activities of the Alliance, a Worldair management team, drawn from senior managers of the members, has been appointed.

Recent bad publicity

Much publicity has recently been given to lack of passenger space associated with travelling in economy-class seats on long distance (known as 'long-haul') flights. (Short distance flights are known as 'short-haul'.) The publicity has centred on the fact that many economy-class passengers feel discomfort on long-haul flights because the seats are too close to each other.

An expected level of growth of 5% in passenger numbers for Alliance members next year was anticipated by senior managers of the Alliance airlines. However, as a result of the recent bad publicity, they do not now think there will be any growth next year in long-haul economy-class passenger numbers. Turnover levels from long-haul economy-class passengers of Alliance members are expected to remain at the current year's level. There is also expected to be a depressing effect on the rate of growth of short-haul passenger numbers for next year, but this is not thought by the senior managers to be as severe as for long-haul passenger forecasts.

In a measure to counter the potential threat resulting from the bad publicity, all members of the Alliance have established a programme to increase the amount of space available for each economy-class customer. This will be achieved by reducing the number of this type of seat in its aircraft which undertake long-haul flights. AB favoured delaying this and waiting to see whether the bad publicity actually resulted in reduced customer numbers. The other Alliance members, however, were not willing to wait. They wanted to assure customers of their serious concern for customer safety and comfort while on a long-haul flight. Additionally, it was felt prudent to take some positive action on restricted leg room to calm possible fears among customers and before legislation was passed forcing airlines to comply with minimum space requirements between economy-class seats on long-haul aircraft.

Financial and customer information relating to the Alliance

(Last year actuals and current year forecasts)

	PC	*AB*	*US*	*Total*
Last year:				
Passengers carried	2 million	5.5 million	7 million	14.5 million
	$ million	*$ million*	*$ million*	*$ million*
Turnover	1,000	2,500	3,000	6,500
Gross profit	200	350	450	1,000
Net profit	25	30	50	105
Current year:				
Passengers carried	2.3 million	5.4 million	7.5 million	15.2 million
	$ million	*$ million*	*$ million*	*$ million*
Turnover	1,200	2,540	3,300	7,040
Gross profit	350	330	500	1,080
Net profit	30	15	56	101

Other information for current year:

	PC	*AB*	*US*
	%	%	%
Gross contribution to sales ratios:			
Economy class	25	10	17.5
Other classes	70	85	80
Proportion of total turnover from economy-class seats	75	50	80
Proportion of economy-class turnover coming from long-haul passengers	70	80	60

All aircraft within the Alliance currently fly on average at 95% of passenger capacity.

Impact of bad publicity

For each Alliance member, the net contribution levels for next year which were expected to result if the effects of the bad publicity had not been felt by the airlines are as follows:

PC	*AB*	*US*	*Total*
$ million	$ million	$ million	$ million
456.75	1,266.8	1,039.5	2,763.05

Information for next year

- A marketing forecast for the Alliance has predicted that customer numbers will grow on average by 5% for each Alliance member next year for all classes except long-haul economy-class.
- Turnover from long-haul economy-class passengers for Alliance members next year is expected to be at the current year's level.
- It may be assumed that customer growth will be the sole cause of a change in turnover next year.
- The possible effect of the bad publicity has also been estimated as having a depressing effect on short-haul economy-class marketing growth forecasts for next year, as follows:

  10% reduction on growth forecast – probability of 0.3

  20% reduction on growth forecast – probability of 0.4

  30% reduction on growth forecast – probability of 0.3
- Senior managers of the Alliance estimate that it will be necessary to reduce the number of economy-class seats in long-haul aircraft operated by all Alliance members by 5% from the current average of 400. Next year the cost of this refit will be:

  PC $30 million AB $50 million US £80 million

  In other classes, seating will be unchanged.
- Research and development (R&D) and publicity costs into customer preferences on long-haul flights are estimated to be $50 million and $20 million respectively next year. This will be charged to each Alliance member in proportion to current year turnover.

Required:

(a) Discuss the benefits and disadvantages of Worldair Alliance membership to PC Airlines in determining its future aims and objectives. **(10 marks)**

(b) Discuss what action the Worldair Alliance management team should take regarding the potential threat from the bad publicity. Explain the possible implications for members of the Alliance of not taking any action. In answering this question, you should consider the availability and quality of data provided in the scenario on space between seats in economy-class on long-haul flights. **(10 marks)**

(c) Produce an analysis of the net contribution for next year for each of the Worldair Alliance member airlines. The net contribution should be calculated after the deduction from total gross contribution of costs relating to seat conversion, R&D and publicity. Explain the value of such an analysis for strategic decision making by the Worldair senior management team. **(20 marks)**

(d) Discuss the different attitudes of Worldair Alliance members towards the implementation of an operational policy to address the bad publicity and discuss how disagreements between Alliance members on operational policy issues may be reconciled. **(10 marks)**

(Total: 50 marks)

12 SYNFIB AND THETFIB

Introduction

C is a company which is engaged in synthetic fibre production. It is situated in Home country where it operates two production plants. C pipes raw material from an oil refinery (which it does not own) to its own production plant where it manufactures a single product which is a special grade of polymer. The polymer is then transferred to a second production site which produces two products, 'Synfib' and 'Thetfib'. As the polymer is of a special grade and manufactured specifically for the production of Synfib and Thetfib, there is no intermediate market for it. The transfer price for the polymer has been set at $40 per litre.

Mission and objectives

C's Chairman has declared that the firm's mission is to 'provide its customers with the highest quality product at a reasonable price'. The organisational objectives are to satisfy the demands of the shareholders, reduce pollution to a minimum, maintain secure employment and to sell a product of high quality which satisfies customer requirements. The objectives also make reference to maximisation of shareholder wealth while at the same time keeping the shareholders' exposure to financial risk to a minimum. Approximately 75% of the shares are held by large financial institutions. The remainder are held by individual investors including employees and the Directors.

The final products

While Synfib and Thetfib are both produced at the second production site in Home, they are produced in different processes. There is strong demand for both of these specialist products worldwide and C is the only producer. However, substitute products are available and may be used in place of them. The following schedule shows the monthly demand for each product at various selling prices.

Synfib		*Thetfib*	
Litres (millions)	*$ per litre*	*Litres (millions)*	*$ per litre*
75	200	200	70
100	175	400	60
125	150	600	50

The Divisional Manager (M) of the second production site has autonomy to choose the level of output, and always selects that level of output which maximises divisional contribution.

Output of Synfib is produced in batches of 25 million litres. The minimum monthly quantity produced is 75 million litres. Thetfib is produced in batches of 200 million litres with the minimum monthly quantity being 200 million litres. Sales of each product are made in these batch quantities and it can be assumed that they are indivisible. The maximum monthly demand is 125 million litres for Synfib and 600 million litres for Thetfib, and these are the maximum quantities of each product that can be produced each month.

As a result of its production processes, Thetfib emits waste products which pollute the atmosphere. The government of Home has introduced strict regulations in recent years to control waste emissions and C estimates that the firm incurs a fixed monthly cost of $2,000 million in order to comply with these regulations.

Transfer of production of Thetfib to another plant in Foreign country

The directors of C are considering transferring production of Thetfib to another plant which the firm owns in Foreign. The plant is already established in Foreign and could produce Thetfib in the quantities required without any other costs being incurred except for those shown in the first table. Foreign is a developing country which encouraged the directors of C to build a plant there by offering grants and loans at a very attractive interest rate. Foreign's government also takes a more relaxed view of pollution and, while it does have regulations in place, these are less strict than those which apply in Home. The directors of C estimate that compliance with the regulations applying in Foreign would cost the company $600 million per month.

Information relating to Synfib and Thetfib

	Synfib *$ per litre*	*Thetfib in Home* *$ per litre*	*Thetfib in Foreign* *$ per litre*
Transfer price of polymer	40	40	to be decided
Costs			
Direct labour	12	8	3
Direct processing	2	2	2
Additional materials	6	3	3
Transport	4	2	14

The marginal costs of C's plant which supplies the polymer are $12 per litre. The corporation tax rate in Home is 35% and in Foreign it is 20%. Foreign tax neutrality applies between Home and Foreign. This means that C would pay tax at the rate of 35% on net contribution generated by its production in Home and 20% on its contribution from production in Foreign.

Output of the receiving plant in Home

Recently, M has argued that the transfer price which is charged is too high at $40 per litre. She believes that a transfer price set at the supplying division's marginal cost would result in increased contribution for C as a whole. M has presented the following schedule relating to Synfib to support her view.

Output of Synfib and total contribution per month at a transfer price of (i) $40 per litre and (ii) $12 per litre.

Output of Synfib	*(i) Transfer price of Polymer at $40 per litre*			*(ii) Transfer price of Polymer at $12 per litre*		
	Total revenue	*Marginal costs*	*Total contribution*	*Total revenue*	*Marginal costs*	*Total contribution*
Litres (million)	$ million	$ million	$ million	$ million	$ million	$ million
75	15,000	4,800	10,200	15,000	2,700	12,300
100	17,500	6,400	11,100	17,500	3,600	13,900
125	18,750	8,000	10,750	18,750	4,500	14,250

M has produced the following statement indicating the after-tax increase in contribution if the transfer price was set at $12 and production increased from 100 million litres to 125 million litres.

Synfib	*Revenue*	*Marginal costs*	*Contribution*
	$ million	$ million	$ million
Transfer price $12 (125 million litres)	18,750	4,500	14,250.0
Transfer price $40 (100 million litres)	17,500	6,400	11,100.0
Increase in total contribution			3,150.0
Less tax liability at 35%			1,102.5
Increase in after-tax contribution			2,047.5

Required:

(a) Produce a critical appraisal of the content of the mission statement and objectives of C as they are presented to you in the scenario. Recommend what changes should be made to their content. **(10 marks)**

(b) (i) Produce an analysis of the contribution from Thetfib which would be made in Home by using the existing transfer price of $40 per litre. Show, with supporting calculations, whether contribution could be increased by changing the transfer price and/or varying the level of output. **(12 marks)**

(ii) Compare the expected profitability for C if production takes place in Home or alternatively in Foreign after your recommended transfer price has been applied. **(8 marks)**

(c) With reference to the results of your calculations in requirement (b), discuss the effect transfer pricing would have on C's management accounting systems in helping it to achieve its organisational objectives. **(10 marks)**

(d) Advise the directors of C what action they should take to establish appropriate measures for the assessment of overall divisional performance in order to meet the organisational objectives.

Note: The actual measures which C could use are NOT required. **(10 marks)**

(Total: 50 marks)

13 MW AND FS

Background

MW and FS are both supermarket chains which operate in different parts of a country. Both are listed on the country's Stock Exchange. MW operates in the north of the country while FS stores are located predominantly in the south. Recently the Chairman of FS has approached the Chairman of MW and suggested that MW may wish to present a takeover bid for FS. The Chairman of FS has indicated that such a bid would be favourably received by his Board of Directors and would pre-empt a bid being made by other less desirable predators in the industry. According to the Chairman of FS, there would need to be some staff rationalisation and about 10% of the total number of stores of the combined group would need to be sold as a result of demands which would be made by the country's competition regulatory organisation. However, he believes that there would be increased profitability for the combined group as a whole which would lead to improved shareholder value. At this stage, no public announcement of the possible takeover has been made and all the information relating to it is being treated as strictly confidential.

MW

MW was established over 100 years ago by Mr W. His son (KW), who is now over 70 years old, is the Chairman of the company. The W family has maintained strong control over the business and still owns nearly 40% of its shares. The main principle established by Mr W was that of offering quality products at a reasonable price and this principle has been rigidly maintained throughout the company's history. Organisationally, MW stores are split into two operating areas – the North West and the North East – although it is controlled from its Head Office by KW and his management team. Each individual store is managed locally by a Store Manager and an assistant. In addition, there are supervisors, till checkout staff, store keepers and shelf stackers working in each store. Other skilled trades staff are also employed including butchers, bakers and fishmongers.

Recent results have shown that MW has increased its sales by 8% and its net profit by 15% over the previous year. MW has become a popular share as a result of the company's ability to cut its operating costs and increase its profitability each year. MW's current share price is $3. Its market capitalisation is $4,500 million. Two years ago its price/earnings ratio was 10.

KW follows the sound principles of business development established by his father. He prefers to rely on a capital structure which is low geared and has generated organic growth rather than undertaking large takeovers. The last time MW undertook a takeover was 25 years ago when it bought six supermarkets. If a bid is made for FS then it is most likely that KW will wish to offer a share exchange rather than pay any cash. He is acutely aware of competition in the industry within the country and has been advised by the Finance Director that there are two other main competitors which may put forward counter-bids if MW makes an offer for FS.

FS

FS's stores operate within the South West and South East of the country. Approximately 55% of its shares are held by ten major institutional shareholders which have been disappointed in recent performance. These institutional shareholders have been impressed by the success of MW and instructed the Chairman to begin takeover negotiations with KW. FS's share price currently stands at $2 with a market capitalisation of $4,000 million. Two years ago its price/ earnings ratio was 30.

Performance of both companies for the last financial year

For simplicity, the data supplied below represents the average for each store in the relevant area. All stores for each company are built to a standard layout. On average, FS stores are 20% smaller in terms of area than MW stores.

	MW		FS	
	North West	*North East*	*South West*	*South East*
	$ million	$ million	$ million	$ million
Turnover	10.0	8.0	6.0	5.0
Cost of sales (excluding wages)	4.0	3.0	2.0	1.8
Overheads:				
Managers' and Supervisors' salaries	1.0	1.0	0.7	0.6
Non-supervisory staff wages	1.0	0.7	0.7	0.6
Other overheads	1.0	1.1	1.1	0.9
Local taxes	1.0	0.8	0.7	0.6
Net profit	2.0	1.4	0.8	0.5

Additional information

	MW		FS	
	North West	*North East*	*South West*	*South East*
Total square metres per store	6,000	6,000	4,800	4,800
Average number of customer visits per store	0.3 million	0.2 million	0.15 million	0.1 million
Managers and supervisors per store	15	12	14	12
Total staff per store	69	56	56	51

The profit attributable to ordinary shareholders in the last financial year was $225 million for MW and $200 million for FS. Inventory is held centrally by each company in its own secure warehouse. It is issued on a daily basis to each store. On average, each MW store has a inventory turnover of 2 days while each FS store has a inventory turnover of 3.5 days.

MW's strategy

KW has recognised the need to obtain support from shareholders and therefore will need to maintain enhanced shareholder value. The Finance Director has acquainted him with the seven value drivers which Rappaport believes affect shareholder value. These are as follows:

(i) sales growth rate

(ii) operating profit margin

(iii) the planning period

(iv) the rate of cash income tax payments

(v) incremental fixed capital investment

(vi) working capital investment

(vii) the cost of capital.

Required:

(a) (i) Produce a SWOT analysis for MW.

(ii) Explain how such an analysis can assist the company in achieving its organisational objectives. **(13 marks)**

(b) Discuss the usefulness of Rappaport's seven drivers to the directors of MW in helping the company to improve its shareholder value. **(10 marks)**

(c) In your capacity as Management Accountant for MW, produce a report to KW which outlines the benefits and risks of acquiring FS. Your report should include:

- an analysis of the data provided in the scenario by making whatever calculations you think appropriate

- an analysis of the potential impact of the takeover on shareholder value
- a statement regarding any strategic issues which you think should be considered by the Board of MW before a bid is made. **(27 marks)**

(Total: 50 marks)

14 ACEP (PILOT PAPER)

ACEP plc (ACEP) is a UK listed company which started as a publishing business over 50 years ago and has grown into a company involved in consumer magazines, radio broadcasting, television production and recorded music production. The company is currently based exclusively within the UK. Each industry is represented by a separate division within the company, each of which has been added, and grown, by a series of acquisitions of small companies. All have been successful with the exception of the music business, which was acquired six years ago.

ACEP entered the music industry believing that the music division would grow to rival the larger companies, despite continuing to focus on less well-known artists and groups who had a specialist following of fans. Although there have been successful court cases against the suppliers of file-sharing software, illegal music copying is still a big issue for the industry. The losses of royalties are claimed to be considerable.

The regulation of the broadcasting industry has, traditionally, focused on audience size but over the past ten years there has been considerable deregulation and consolidation. ACEP has the maximum number of radio licences possible, as have the other two major industry players. This division regularly runs concerts at popular tourist venues where its target market tends to spend its summer vacation.

The magazine publishing industry structure is similarly concentrated and, although there is no equivalent regulation based on audience size, it is unlikely that further acquisitions of companies would be allowed on competition policy grounds. The development of new titles by organic growth would, however, be permitted. ACEP has been successful with this approach and has two titles in the top five lifestyle magazines and six in the top ten teenage titles. Both magazines and radio earned 70% of their revenue from advertising in 1999 and 2000. Across the industry, advertising revenue has been depressed for the past two years.

The television production division produces music programmes for satellite and cable television under the Masthead (collective brand name) of '*Taste*', which is the same name as that used for the radio stations and some of the magazines. Although this presents cross-marketing opportunities in the market segment of 13 to 30 year olds, who have considerable spending power, the division is a relatively small player within the industry.

With the exception of the finance director, who was recently brought in from a commercial radio station, each member of the board has a publishing background and has been with the company for a number of years. These individuals have a reputation within that industry for achieving major post-acquisition cost savings.

There are five institutional shareholders, all with significant holdings, who have become more publicly critical of both the share price of the company, which has been falling, and the size of the dividend which has been maintained at its present level for the past four years. They have said that both television and music should be sold off; these could realise £20 million and £10 million respectively. The balance of the shares in issue are broadly held. The results for the past four years are shown in **Appendix A**.

Since the company is market leader in its target market, it has been considering expanding magazine publication into mainland Europe. A potential acquisition has been identified at a cost of £10 million. It is felt that, in the first year only, contribution would increase by £3 million and fixed costs would rise by £1 million.

Alternatively the company is considering an approach from a significantly larger European publisher and broadcaster, whose organisation is privately owned, to form a joint venture in the latter's country. Discussions have suggested that an initial investment by ACEP of £20 million would give rise to an increase in contribution to ACEP of £4 million. Fixed costs for ACEP would again rise by £1 million for the first year. In both cases, ACEP's Board feels that there would be considerable opportunities for cross marketing to its existing market.

The company has also had discussions with a firm which supplies equipment to be installed in retail outlets which downloads music to CD on demand. In addition to the cover charge for the CD advertising, revenue is earned depending on the number sold. A major retail chain has expressed an interest in installing the equipment in its 50 stores across the country. The equipment could be hired by ACEP for a cost of £2 million for the 50 sites. The board is impressed that the project, based on figures supplied by the equipment vendor, has an expected annual net profit of £1.182 million. This option will not be viable if the music division is sold off. A marketing research exercise by the equipment supplier has provided the projections shown in **Appendix B**.

Appendix A

£ millions	*2002*	*2001*	*2000*	*1999*
Sales				
Publishing	425	500	523	419
Radio	350	375	380	320
Television	65	75	80	70
Music	20	30	40	44
Total	860	980	1,023	853
Profit before interest & tax	166	256	281	205
Capital employed	900	900	870	805
Variable costs/sales ratio				
Publishing	0.49	0.45	0.45	0.45
Radio	0.26	0.25	0.25	0.25
Television	0.18	0.25	0.25	0.26
Music	0.20	0.20	0.20	0.20
Fixed costs/sales ratio				
Publishing	0.38	0.32	0.31	0.37
Radio	0.43	0.40	0.39	0.40
Television	0.62	0.53	0.50	0.50
Music	1.50	1.00	0.80	0.73

Appendix B

With promotional costs per month of £12,000 and a CD retail price of £2.00 it is expected that monthly sales will have the following pattern.

probability	*sales (units)*
0.4	10,000
0.5	12,000
0.1	14,000

For sales up to and including 11,000 units, advertising revenue is predicted to be £17,000 per month. If sales are over 11,000 units, advertising revenue is predicted to be £18,000 per month. Combined monthly fixed costs of production and distribution will be £16,000 and variable costs will be £0.45 per CD. Retailers will receive a 25% margin on sales.

Required:

(a) Regarding the proposal to download CD's in retail outlets, demonstrate how the equipment supplier has calculated the expected annual net profit, and evaluate whether it gives a complete picture of the project. **(10 marks)**

(b) Discuss the concept of portfolio planning models and, in the light of the comments of the institutional shareholders, analyse the portfolio managed by ACEP. **(8 marks)**

(c) (i) Evaluate the risks involved in entering the magazine publishing market in mainland Europe. **(8 marks)**

(ii) Discuss the merits of each of the two proposed methods for entering the mainland Europe market. **(9 marks)**

(d) The Board of Directors has asked you, as Financial Controller, to prepare a report which produces:

(i) recommendations regarding the options to purchase the CD download equipment, move into Europe and/or dispose of the television and music divisions

(ii) a response to the institutional shareholders explaining how these recommendations will contribute to sustained business growth for ACEP, recognising any concerns these shareholders might have. **(15 marks)**

(Total: 50 marks)

15 PIPECO (MAY 05 EXAM)

Pipeco, a wholly owned subsidiary of an international chemical company (the parent group), has for the past 20 years manufactured, by an extrusion process, large bore plastic pipe for use in water, sewage and gas piping systems. (Extrusion is a process whereby hot plastic is forced through a die and takes the shape of the die.) Based in Western Europe, Pipeco has been the major supplier to the infrastructure building projects in most surrounding countries. Pipeco has operated from a single site. All projects, which typically last three or four years, are won by competitive tender and Pipeco has had a success rate, for many years, of over 80% of the contracts for which it has bid. Large bore, extruded pipe, is a commodity product sold, by the tonne, on price. Pipeco's dominant position, in a very competitive industry, has been achieved by its cost effectiveness and the high technical skill of its sales engineers.

In the last three years, revenue and profits have declined as existing building programmes have neared completion and no new projects have become available from current markets.

The directors of Pipeco feel that they cannot maintain the dividend to the parent group at the present levels beyond the current year. The parent group has made available to Pipeco a budget of $2 million for investment and has suggested a hurdle rate of 10% on any project undertaken. Although the parent group takes a strategic, long term view it is currently under pressure from the shareholders to at least increase the overall profitability of the group and maintain the dividend.

The parent group is particularly concerned about profitability over the next five years because of the cost of the expansion plans in other subsidiaries.

There are a number of possibilities which Pipeco wishes to consider including:

Option 1

Pipeco could expand geographically to countries that are beginning to improve their infrastructure. The recent expansion of the European Union is considered to be an opportunity over the coming years.

Preliminary investigations have identified two possible countries to which some of the existing extrusion plant and equipment could be relocated leaving sufficient capacity to finish existing orders.

Country A would involve an initial capital investment of $1·5 million and Country B would involve an initial capital investment of $2.0 million. Sales volumes, in tonnes per year, are as follows;

Years	*Country A Tonnes*	*Years*	*Country B Tonnes*
1 to 5	42,000	1 to 8	63,000
6 to 10	64,000	9 to 14	51,000
11 to 15	20,000		

Each tonne of product would sell for $90 and there would be variable costs of $85 per tonne.

Option 2

Pipeco could move into other areas of plastics, producing pipework and fittings for use within buildings. The manufacture of fittings would involve moulding, a very different manufacturing process. There are a number of established firms in that industry, although this is considered to be a strong growth industry within Western Europe, particularly at the prestige design end of the business where gross margins of 55% are quite common. Sales within the industry are made to retail outlets or, for larger building projects, by presentation to the architect.

Pipeco recognises that this is a different business model to that currently used and the approach used by some departments, notably marketing, will need to change. Research has shown that Pipeco could enter the market by investing an initial $1,450,000 in plant and equipment followed by a further $425,000 for plant and equipment payable at the end of the first year of operation. The market entry would be achieved by buying a small, underfunded company from the owner who wishes to retire. The purchase price is included within the total of $1,875,000. This company is based in Pipeco's current home market.

Research has shown that the project would give the following projected probabilities and cash contributions from sales per year for the next ten years:

Year	$000	$000	$000
1 – 10	300	435	265
Probability	0.5	0.3	0.2

These figures will only be achieved if the investment in plant and equipment outlined above is carried out and do not reflect the level of performance under current ownership. The directors recognise that Pipeco will need to market more proactively and have decided to consider adopting relationship marketing for this option should it be selected. Pipeco realises that the adoption of relationship marketing would represent a significant change to the way the company operates.

Summary

Whichever option is chosen, Pipeco believes that, with the exception of depreciation, which is based on gross capital expenditure, there would be no increase in fixed costs. All capital expenditure is depreciated on a straight line basis over ten years.

Pipeco has a good employment record, with low staff turnover, and would prefer to retrain and possibly relocate (depending on the option selected) staff rather than make them redundant. It believes the staff would welcome this approach.

Required:

As the Management Accountant of Pipeco:

(a) Make reasoned recommendations on the selection of options 1 and 2.

Note: Up to 16 marks will be awarded for calculations. **(29 marks)**

(b) Identify the additional information that would need to be gathered to compare and contrast the suitability of the two countries identified for possible relocation in option 1. **(6 marks)**

(c) (i) Briefly describe relationship marketing and explain how the approach would benefit the company. **(6 marks)**

(ii) Advise how the changes associated with the introduction of relationship marketing and the acquisition should be implemented if option 2 is adopted.

(9 marks)

(Total: 50 marks)

16 S COMPANY (NOV 05 EXAM)

S Company provides transport by sea and air between a country's mainland and a small group of islands 30 miles off shore. The company operates two ships, which make daily return trips to the islands. One ship carries only freight and provisions while the other transports freight and passengers. The islands are a popular holiday resort.

In addition to the ships, S operates some aircraft which convey passengers to and from the islands on a daily basis. While other airlines also fly to the islands, S is the only operator of ships to the islands, though some tourists visit in their private yachts. During the winter months the ships are repaired and maintained. However, the two ships are never out of service at the same time. The only other time the ships do not sail to the islands is in extreme weather conditions when it is considered unsafe to make the voyage. Major aircraft repairs are undertaken by S itself.

The islands

The main industries on the islands are agriculture and tourism. Due to their location, the islands enjoy a climate that enables them to successfully cultivate crops ready for market much earlier than can be achieved on the mainland. The islands have established a reputation for growing flowers and vegetables, which they supply to retailers on the mainland. Some of these flowers and vegetables are exported to other locations throughout the world. Much of the produce is transported from the islands on board the ships operated by S.

A strong tourist industry has developed on the islands, peaking during the months of July and August. Most islanders are engaged in tourism, either by providing accommodation, boat trips, catering or retailing. The tourist trade declines sharply after September of each year until the following April. During this period the islanders are mainly engaged in agriculture.

The company

S has 750,000 ordinary shares in issue, which are owned by the directors and employees of the company.

Over the years the company has established a good reputation for reliability and safety in its passenger services. The passenger ship operated by S was launched in 1979. It can carry a capacity of 200 passengers and can accommodate some cargo. The company charges the same price of £120 per person for a return trip irrespective of whether the passenger is an islander or visitor. This charge per passenger has increased steeply in recent years and considerably reduced the difference that, at one time, existed between the fares for travel by air and sea. Similarly, the other airlines operating to and from the islands do not differentiate between visitors and islanders in their charging policies.

S has secured mooring rights at ports on the mainland and on the islands. However, these are negotiated on a periodic basis and are due for renewal in one year's time. In the last financial year, the company achieved an after-tax profit of £120,000 on a turnover of £4.8m. S has experienced a gradual reduction in profit over time, as it has not been able to cover all its continually increasing operating costs by increasing its passenger and freight charges.

S owns the two ships, which had a net book value of £1.6m at the end of the last financial year. At the same point in time, S had in its accounts a net book value of £2.9m for all property, plant and equipment.

Potential development

A few years ago, a mainland holiday company (M) applied to the government of the country and islands for permission to build a holiday complex on one of the uninhabited islands. The complex was planned to accommodate a maximum capacity of 500 people constantly throughout the year, and intended to incorporate numerous entertainment facilities associated with water and beach sports. In addition, the complex was planned to have indoor swimming facilities as well as its own golf course and bars. The application was refused by the government on the basis that the development would be out of character with the local environment. This decision was well received by the local island communities.

Since the application was made, residential holiday accommodation has been built on two of the other uninhabited islands. This has been in the form of high quality hotels and apartments. Since these developments have taken place, the government has undertaken an initiative to increase the revenue generated by tourism, and has indicated to M that it would now view its development proposals more favourably. If the development was in a similar style to the other accommodation, the government would not oppose the scheme. M has indicated to the government that it wishes to proceed with a development similar to that previously proposed (that is, for 500 guests). M is preparing to invite quotations, from S and others, for the transport of building materials from the mainland to the site and the subsequent transport of tourists once the complex is operational.

Implications for S

The directors of S are aware that M intends that its visitors would travel to the complex by both air and sea. In order to prepare for a quotation, the directors have recognised that they would need to be willing to increase their sea passenger capacity. They would need to replace their existing passenger ship if they were awarded the contract. A replacement ship with sufficient capacity would cost £7 million and would be bought in two years' time. The scrap value of the existing ship would be £250,000. The directors estimate that the cash running costs of the replacement ship would be £12 per passenger, the same as for the existing ship.

In order to moor the new ship, extensive building works would be required at the major port on the mainland. S's directors expect that this will cost approximately £1 million and will take one year to complete. These works will commence immediately upon the contract being agreed with the holiday company, which is expected to be in one year's time. There will be no increase in passenger numbers until the new ship is bought in two years' time.

If awarded to S, the contract for the transportation of passengers will be for a duration of five years. It is expected that 90% of the visitors attending the complex will go by the sea route rather than by air. On average, the visitors travelling to the holiday complex will each remain there for two weeks and, due to the extensive entertainment provision at the complex, there will be constant demand throughout the year. There is sufficient capacity available for the existing airlines servicing the islands to carry the extra passengers who wish to travel by air.

If awarded the contract for the conveyance of passengers, the directors of S expect that S will obtain an additional contribution of £2 million for transporting the materials necessary to build the holiday complex. This contribution can be assumed to arise two years from now.

The contract terms (for the conveyance of passengers only) will be that S will receive from M an equal payment each year over the life of the actual contract. Payments to the successful bidder will commence in three years' time and run for a period of five years. It may be assumed that S will also charge each passenger £120 for a return trip throughout the period of the contract.

S requires a return of 20% on this project, to reflect the degree of risk involved. The directors believe that the value of the new ship will have fallen to £4 million by the end of the contract. All cash flows can be assumed to arise at the end of the year to which they relate unless otherwise stated.

Required:

(a) Explain the threats to S from changing market conditions. **(10 marks)**

(b) Identify what price per year the directors of S should quote to M for the contract to convey the additional passengers. You should use the annuity approach to determine the equivalent annual value required. **(15 marks)**

(c) Discuss what financial and non-financial control measures could be implemented by S during the bid process and the operation of the contract to convey passengers to the holiday complex. **(15 marks)**

(d) Identify how S could develop its business in the long term by extending its operations beyond the transport services it provides. **(10 marks)**

(Total: 50 marks)

17 CCC CAR MANUFACTURER (MAY 06 EXAM)

CCC is a specialist car manufacturer, based in Y, a country in Europe. Three ex-employees of a major car manufacturer founded CCC in 1992 as a private limited company. CCC has never required further finance to aid its expansion, and remains a private company owned by the three founders. The three, who are all engineers, decided to leave their former employer in order to establish a business producing hand-built high performance sports cars for wealthy customers. The major car manufacturers are not able to supply such vehicles, as their systems are all based on the assumption that they will produce each car model in sufficient numbers to benefit from significant economies of scale.

CCC has always been profitable, and has grown significantly in recent years. It is now the second largest specialist car manufacturer in Europe and employs 300 staff at its head office and factory near the capital city of Y.

The specialist car industry

The customers who buy specialist cars are very status-conscious, and want a car that is totally unique. They are prepared to pay a very high price for their new car, in comparison to 'top of the range' models from the major manufacturers, but require extremely high quality and service levels in return. At present there are fewer than twenty specialist car manufacturers in Europe, and only six of these (including CCC) produce sports cars. The others specialise in off-road vehicles, armour-plated cars or limousines. As the cars are produced to customer order, there has historically been little price competition between the various specialist sports car manufacturers.

CCC, in common with other specialist car manufacturers, has invested a significant sum in creating the design of its two car models. It also spends a large proportion of its annual budget on sales promotion and marketing. This includes placing expensive advertisements in upmarket car magazines, and attending many car shows and exhibitions. CCC also has a reputation for paying higher than average salaries to its senior designers and production staff. As a result, staff turnover at CCC is virtually non-existent.

Customers, who are often loyal to a particular manufacturer, can specify modifications to the basic design, such as minor changes to the body shape of the car, or major changes to the engine performance and driving characteristics of the car. The directors of CCC have always assumed that their customers are not particularly price-conscious, as they are often wealthy individuals with high disposable incomes. For these customers, the alternative to buying a car from CCC might be to purchase a yacht or go on a round-the-world cruise.

CCC manufactures most of the components of its cars in-house. The main exceptions are electrical and control equipment, wheels and tyres. The only major bought-in component is the car's engine, which CCC buys from a major car manufacturer and then sends to SSS (a subcontractor) for modification and performance upgrades. While the engine is relatively expensive, it is the work of SSS that represents the single most significant cost of producing each car. CCC has, on occasion, paid SSS the equivalent of 25% of the final sales price of a car.

The board meeting

At the most recent board meeting of CCC, the directors discussed the worsening financial position of the organisation. Having spoken to the Sales Manager they came to the conclusion that, with the economies of Y and neighbouring countries in recession, customers had recently become more aggressive in negotiating down the purchase price of their cars. This had put pressure on the profit margin of CCC for the first time in its history. The directors therefore felt it was necessary to commission an independent review of their industry.

The Finance Director provided the following summary of CCC's performance:

€million	*2005*	*2004*	*2003*	*2002*
Revenue	11.75	11.12	10.06	10.10
Pre-tax profit	0.88	1.43	1.55	2.01
Dividend paid	0.08	0.50	0.50	0.50

The directors were particularly alarmed that SSS, the engine modification sub-contractor, seemed to be making almost as much profit on one of the engines as CCC was on the whole car. The Purchasing Manager of CCC said that it was impossible to negotiate a lower price with SSS, as most of CCC's customers specified that their car must have its engine prepared by SSS. The Sales Manager agreed that one of the 'unique selling points' of CCC's cars was the work done by SSS. At present, SSS does not supply engine modification services to any of CCC's competitors, but there is no contractual obligation to prevent it from doing so. The Purchasing Manager reported that CCC has no long-term supply contract with SSS, and the owner-manager of SSS had declined the offer of such a contract, believing that to enter into such an agreement would not be in the best interests of himself and his seven staff.

SSS

The Purchasing Manager has obtained the following information relating to SSS:

Extracts from the financial statements of SSS:

	2005
	€000
Revenue	2,455
Cost of sales	1,398
Other costs	867
Profit before tax	190
Profit after tax	133
Dividend paid	65

	At 31 Dec 2005
	€000
Non-current assets	894
Inventories	232
Receivables	146
Cash	32
Payables	244
Equity share capital	100
Retained earnings	960

Information obtained from the Motor Trade Association:

Automotive component and service suppliers:

Average P/E ratio (for those suppliers with quoted share prices)	7.5
Average annual growth rate in reported post-tax profits (1995 – 2005)	2.5%
Average pre-tax profit margin	4.3%
Average pre-tax return on capital employed	11.2%
Average receivables days	65
Average payables days	28
Average revenue per employee	€128,500

Required:

(a) Using Porter's 'Five Forces Model' as a framework, evaluate the competitive environment in which CCC operates. **(15 marks)**

(b) Evaluate the financial position and performance of SSS, as at 31 December 2005.

Note: There are up to 12 marks available for calculations in this part of the question.

(25 marks)

(c) Advise the directors of CCC how the organisation might overcome the bargaining power of SSS. **(10 marks)**

(Total: 50 marks)

18 AAA AND BBB

Introduction

AAA is a large manufacturing company that specialises in the design and manufacture of televisions. It was formed in 1985, following the merger of two rival companies, and is now one of the three largest TV manufacturers in Asia. AAA employs over 2000 staff at its head office and four manufacturing plants, which are all in the same Asian country, Jurania. AAA is listed on the Juranian stock exchange.

The production system

TV manufacturing is a mass production industry, with high volumes of identical or similar products being made on a production line basis. The products are generally made to order for customers, who are either other electrical manufacturers (who put their name on the product and re-sell it) or large electrical retailers. The manufacture of televisions is still a relatively labour-intensive process, as many of the components need to be assembled in a precise way. Most of the electrical components used in AAA's process are bought in from suppliers, as is the TV screen and cabinet (the plastic case in which the screen and components are contained). The staff who assemble the components are mainly semi-skilled, and have been trained by AAA to perform fairly simple, repetitive operations. When completed, quality assurance staff test the TV sets, and any that are found faulty are returned to the production line to be re-worked.

Components received from suppliers are also tested by the quality assurance staff of AAA. As they do not have the time to test every component, they test a sample of components from each batch delivered. If they find more than one faulty component in every 20 tested, the whole batch is rejected and returned to the supplier.

Business performance

The following is a summary of the performance of AAA last year. AAA reports its performance in the currency of its home country, the Juranian dollar (J$):

	Last year	
Financial performance	*Actual*	*Budget*
	J$ millions	J $ millions
Sales revenue	1,793	1,941
Gross (factory) profit	1,177	1,320
Pre-tax profit	652	790
Capital employed (average)	2,835	2,550
Cash (closing)	179	485
Finished goods inventory (average)	38.2	20.0
Raw material inventory (average)	11.4	9.5
Work in process (average)	0.8	0.3

Other performance indicators	Last year Actual	Last year Budget
Share price (closing) (J$)	334.50	400.00
Earnings per share (J$)	46.00	50.00
Number of employees (average)	2,259	2,128
Sales (million units)	2.35	2.40
Number of finished units re-worked	54,000	30,000
Percentage of purchases from suppliers rejected (by value)	4.25	3.00
Average production cost of sales per unit (J$)	262	259
Average sales price per unit (J$)	763	809
New product lines developed	12	10
New product lines successfully launched	1	4
Products returned from customers as faulty (per 1,000 units sold)	28	20
Warranty claims (per 1,000 units sold)	56	30
Number of working employee-days lost to industrial disputes	2,500	3,200

The board meeting

At the most recent board meeting of AAA, the Chief Executive Officer asked for suggestions as to how the management of AAA might be improved. One of the non-executive directors suggested that the use of the balanced scorecard might assist in controlling the business, as it had in another company of which she is also a non-executive director. The marketing director mentioned that he had compiled some information about another organisation in the television manufacturing industry, BBB, and asked if that might be of use. The purchasing director mentioned that he had recently been at a conference where a speaker had suggested that the introduction of 'knowledge management' was improving the performance of many organisations. As far as the other directors present at the board meeting were aware, this was not an approach used commonly in their industry.

BBB

BBB is a major rival of AAA, and is based in a neighbouring Asian country, Mesnar. BBB is a private company, owned by a wealthy industrialist. BBB compiles its accounts in the local currency of Mesnar, the Mesnari Riyal (RM). Both the Mesnari Riyal and the Juranian Dollar are freely traded currencies, and the current spot exchange rate between the two is J$1:RM2.50. There is free and unrestricted trade between Jurania and Mesnar.

The following information has been obtained from BBB's filed accounts from last year, and from the trade association of which both AAA and BBB are members.

	Last year
Sales revenue (RM million)	1,400
Total production cost of sales (RM million)	435
Profit before tax (RM million)	557
Capital employed (RM million)	1,589
Closing inventories (RM million)	17
Number of employees (closing)	740
Number of units sold	780,000
Number of warranty claims in the year	19,800

Required:

(a) Prepare a balanced scorecard appraisal of the performance of AAA last year.

Note: There are up to 10 marks available for calculations in this section. You are not required to compare the performance of AAA with that of BBB in this section.

(25 marks)

(b) As the Management Accountant of AAA, prepare a benchmarking report for the directors that compares the performance of AAA last year with that of BBB for the same period. You should refer to your answer to part (a) in making your comparison.

Note: There are up to 8 marks available for calculations in this section, and up to 2 marks for the use of an appropriate report format. You are not required to reproduce the calculations from your answer to part (a) in this section, but may do so if you wish.

(15 marks)

(c) Advise the directors of AAA how the introduction of knowledge management might lead to AAA developing a sustainable competitive advantage over BBB. **(10 marks)**

(Total: 50 marks)

Section 2

SECTION B-TYPE QUESTIONS

BUSINESS STRATEGY

19 N

N Ltd is a small family-controlled manufacturing company. In its 40-year history, the company has grown to the extent that it now employs 35 staff, producing a wide and diverse range of household goods and utensils. The company has increased in size from its small original base. However, it has never employed a strategic management approach for its development and has relied on operational decision making to determine priorities. N has never gathered any information relating to its markets. In recent years, the company has experienced a reduction in turnover and profitability and is assessing how it might redress the situation.

Required:

(a) Explain how strategic management differs from operational management. **(10 marks)**

(b) The directors of N have now decided to introduce a strategic management approach, which will assist in the selection of appropriate strategies for future development of the company.

Discuss the cultural and organisational changes which N will need to implement in order to successfully introduce strategic management. **(15 marks)**

(Total: 25 marks)

20 MISSION STATEMENT

(a) In recent years, many organisations have developed mission statements. It has become increasingly common for such statements to be published within the organisation and also externally.

Required:

Contrast the viewpoints that a mission statement is either an embodiment of the prevailing organisational culture or an attempt to change it. Explain other motives for publishing these statements. **(14 marks)**

(b) In discussing not-for-profit organisations, Bowman and Asch state '.... Even if the goals are clear but achievement of them is not measurable, then assessing the performance of the organisation becomes extremely difficult'.

Strategic Management, Bowman & Asch (MacMillan)

Required:

Explain how the performance of a not-for-profit organisation could be assessed. **(11 marks)**

(Total: 25 marks)

21 SPK

There are several different methods of strategy formulation. Most strategists would argue, for instance, that public sector organisations mainly favour a logical, rational approach. The senior partners of the world famous private sector management consultancy firm SPK are presently considering both the issue of their own strategy formulation and making some changes to direction of the company. SPK only deals with traditional "blue chip" companies. SPK is renowned for networking and has access to key decision makers through the personal contacts of its partners and senior managers. These contacts are felt to be at the heart of its business success. SPK places a lot of trust in the decisions made by its relatively small core of partners and senior managers who foster close relationships with clients and identify consultancy opportunities. These individuals draw together and then lead teams of (normally) freelance consultants and academics to fulfil their consultancy briefs. Partners and senior managers are judged on the client profile and profitability levels within their personal portfolios. Individually, they are highly skilled but tend to have definite fixed opinions and to be strong willed. In addition, they work independently when deciding which business areas to target and the nature of work undertaken.

Required:

(a) Discuss the main approaches to strategy formulation and recommend the most appropriate for SPK. **(15 marks)**

(b) Analyse the reasons for public sector organisations generally adopting a logical rational approach to strategy formulation and suggest how, in the absence of profitability, they can measure performance. **(10 marks)**

(Total: 25 marks)

22 CTC TELECOMMUNICATIONS (NOV 06 EXAM)

CTC, a telecommunications company, has recently been privatised by the government of C after legislation was passed which removed the state monopoly and opened up the communications market to competition from both national and overseas companies – a process known as deregulation.

Prior to the deregulation, CTC was the sole, protected, supplier of telecommunications and was required to provide 'the best telecommunications service the nation can afford'. At that time the government dictated the performance levels required for CTC, and the level of resources it would be able to bring to bear to meet its objectives.

The shares were floated on the C Stock Exchange with 80% being made available to the population of C and up to 20% being made available to foreign nationals. The government of C retained a 'golden share' to prevent the acquisition of CTC by any foreign company. However, the privatisation meant that many of the traditional ways in which the industry had operated would need to change under the new regulations. Apart from the money received from the flotation, the government privatised CTC in recognition of both the changing global environment for telecommunications companies, and the overseas expansion opportunities that might exist for a privatised company. The government recognises that foreign companies will enter the home market but feels that this increased competition is likely to make CTC more effective in the global market.

You have recently been appointed as the management accountant for CTC and have a background in the commercial sector. The Board of Directors is unchanged from CTC's preflotation days.

Required:

(a) Explain to the Board of Directors why the objectives of CTC will need to change as a result of the privatisation of CTC and the deregulation of the market. **(10 marks)**

(b) Produce two examples of suitable strategic objectives for CTC, following its privatisation and the deregulation of the market, and explain why each would be an appropriate long-term objective. **(4 marks)**

(c) Advise the Board of Directors on the stages of an appropriate strategic planning process for CTC in the light of the privatisation and deregulation. **(11 marks)**

(Total: 25 marks)

THE COMPETITIVE ENVIRONMENT

23 WATER SUPPLY

A company engaged in the supply of water for public and industrial consumption operates in a service industry. It is subject to external influences when establishing its objectives and formulating strategy. The nature of this industry is that new technology is constantly being developed in treating and supplying water of sufficiently high quality for customer use. The organisational culture of such a company needs to reflect the nature of the industry in the provision of a reliable service to the public.

You are required, as a member of the company's strategic planning team, to advise the board of directors on the extent to which external influences may affect the formulation of organisational objectives and strategies. Your advice should recognise the public service nature of the industry and the way this affects the company's organisational culture. **(25 marks)**

Note: No specific knowledge of the water supply industry is required to answer this question.

24 DON MAC

Don Mac is the world's largest and best-known food service retailing group with more than 30,000 'fast-food' outlets in over 120 countries. Currently half of its restaurants are in the USA, where it first began 50 years ago, but up to 1,000 new restaurants are opened every year worldwide. Restaurants are wholly owned by the group (it has previously considered, but rejected, the idea of a franchising of operations and collaborative partnerships).

As market leader in a fiercely competitive industry, Don Mac has strategic strengths of instant global brand recognition, experienced management, site development expertise and advanced technological systems. Don Mac's basic approach works as well in Kandy or Kuala Lumpur as it does in Kansas: although the products are broadly similar, menus are modified to reflect local tastes. Analysts agree that it continues to be profitable because it is both efficient and innovative.

The group's vision is to be 'the world's favourite' through service, cleanliness and value, and it is following three main strategies:

1 To achieve profitable growth by building on key strengths.

2 To 'delight' every customer in every restaurant.

3 To be a good employer in each community in which it has a restaurant. (Despite this, some critics claim staff are mainly unskilled and lowly paid.)

Don Mac's future plans are to maximise global opportunities and continue to expand markets. Don Mac has long recognised that the external environment can be very uncertain and consequently does not move into new locations or countries without first undertaking a full investigation.

You are part of a strategy steering team responsible for investigating the key factors concerning Don Mac's entry for the first time into the restaurant industry in the Republic of Borderland.

Required:

(a) Justify the use of a PEST framework to assist your team's environmental analysis for the Republic of Borderland. **(8 marks)**

(b) Discuss the main issues arising from applying this framework, and highlight what more information is needed by Don Mac on Borderland. **(17 marks)**

(Total: 25 marks)

25 FIVE FORCES

E, a well known cosmetics manufacturer, obtains worldwide sales for its global branded products. The directors pride themselves on having a clear understanding of E's consumer market which consists of both men and women. Its products mainly comprise deodorants, perfume, after-shave lotions, facial and body washes.

In carrying out an analysis of its competitive environment, the Marketing Director has applied Porter's Five Forces model and analysed the factors which affect E under each heading as follows:

- *Threat of entry:* Little threat as although major competitors exist, the size of E presents a large entry barrier.
- *Power of buyers*: Very important as the customers worldwide have much choice from different competitors' products.
- *Power of suppliers:* Little threat as most suppliers of materials are small scale and E could easily source from other suppliers if necessary. Labour is relatively cheap in E's production facilities in developing world locations.
- *Substitute products:* There are many alternative products offered by competitors but there is little by way of a substitute for cosmetics, and therefore this poses little threat.
- *Rivalry among competitors:* There is strong competition in the cosmetics market with new products constantly being developed, and therefore this is a major threat.

The Marketing Director is reasonably confident that he has judged the impact of these competitive forces correctly as they apply to E. However, he would like some reassurance of this. He has asked you, as Management Accountant, to provide some appropriate performance indicators by which the strength of the five competitive forces as they apply to E can be judged.

Required:

Recommend to the Marketing Director suitable performance indicators which could be used to judge the strength of the five competitive forces as they apply to E. Discuss why you consider your recommendations to be appropriate. Include in your discussion consideration of whether or not you agree with his judgement regarding the impact of each force on E.

(25 marks)

26 UNCERTAINTY AND THE FIVE FORCES MODEL

Professor Michael Porter developed the 'Five Forces Model' in order that it may be used by profit-orientated organisations for the purposes of environmental appraisal.

Required:

Produce a critical appraisal of the value of the Five Forces Model to profit-orientated organisations *when it is used in a period of uncertainty in the business environment.*

(25 marks)

27 2XA (MAY 05 EXAM)

2XA is an established light engineering manufacturer operating in a single country within the European Union (EU). With 300 employees, the majority of whom are employed in the manufacturing processes, the company is run like a large family business. 2XA supplies components to specialist car manufacturers and manufacturers of light aircraft, all of which are small companies. 2XA has had the same customers for a number of years and there are many personal friendships between the senior management of 2XA and those who own or manage those customer companies.

Since most of 2XA's sales are a result of repeat business it does not actively market its products. What marketing it currently does consists of an occasional advert in trade magazines and attendance at trade fairs where the Sales Director, and a few office staff, offer light refreshments to their existing customers and anyone who stops at their stand.

In the past two years 2XA has started to lose customers to more aggressive suppliers from neighbouring countries, which have entered 2XA's home market. The board of directors is concerned at the loss of business and is not really sure why it has happened. It has decided that it is time to become more proactive in its approach to the market and feels the need to know more about both the competitive environment and the competitors themselves.

Required:

As the Management Accountant you have been asked to:

(a) explain what is meant by industry analysis using any models you consider appropriate **(5 marks)**

(b) describe the information that 2XA might include in such an analysis **(10 marks)**

(c) advise the directors as to the possible sources of the information which 2XA could use in performing an industry analysis. **(10 marks)**

(Total: 25 marks)

28 D4D (MAY 05 EXAM)

D4D is a politically stable, developing country enjoying a temperate climate and a young, educated population, many of whom are educated to graduate level. Those who have studied at this level have tended to do so abroad since there are limited opportunities to do so in D4D.

The economy is mixed, based on agriculture and some light manufacturing but has enjoyed considerable revenue from oil exploration and production which is based offshore in its territorial waters. Some of this revenue is generated by providing services for the oil industry but the majority comes from a tax on every barrel of oil which the foreign oil companies extract.

The Government has used the revenue to keep personal and property taxes low and to support the largely uneconomic local industry. It now recognises that, although politically popular, this decision might not have been in the best long term interests of the country.

The Finance and Trade Minister of D4D is aware that the oil revenue may only last a further ten years. He wishes to build competitive advantage over the neighbouring countries. The Prime Minister is sceptical and has made the observation that 'companies have competitive advantages not countries'.

As a Management Accountant within the Ministry of Finance and Trade you have been asked to produce a number of documents, for both the Prime Minister and the Finance and Trade Minister, considering how competitive advantage could be achieved for D4D and examining the possibilities of attracting inward investment from foreign companies.

Required:

(a) Using any models you consider appropriate, explain the factors which lead to competitive advantage being present in particular countries. **(7 marks)**

(b) Identify the aims that D4D should try to achieve in attracting appropriate investors into the country. You should also compare and contrast those aims with the likely aims of any company investing in D4D. **(10 marks)**

(c) Explain the steps that D4D should take to make the country more attractive to appropriate inward investment. **(8 marks)**

(Total: 25 marks)

29 FIVE FORCES MODEL (NOV 05 EXAM)

In the 'Five Forces Model', one of the conclusions reached by Porter is that firms or strategic business units (SBUs) compete with their customers and suppliers.

The same model can be used to evaluate the competitive environment of the SBUs of large complex organisations. In such organisations, some of the SBUs may be customer and supplier to one another. This leads to management accountants becoming involved in negotiations leading to the agreement of appropriate transfer prices between these SBUs.

Required:

(a) Explain how the forces exerted in a customer-supplier relationship led Michael Porter to conclude that firms compete with their customers and suppliers.

Note: You are NOT required to explain the whole of Porter's model or draw the diagram. **(10 marks)**

(b) Discuss the issues to be considered when negotiating and agreeing transfer prices between SBUs within a large, complex organisation. You should make reference to Porter's model, and your arguments in part (a) where appropriate. **(15 marks)**

(Total: 25 marks)

30 FFF COMMUNICATIONS (NOV 06 EXAM)

FFF is a manufacturer of specialist portable communications equipment, which is designed for use in hazardous and dangerous conditions. Developments of new technology in recent years, such as wireless mobile telephony, infra red thermal imaging and global positioning has allowed FFF to create new products.

The market for such equipment has grown significantly over the past five years. The customer base includes fire services, oil and chemical companies and the government. FFF now recognises that, during this period of rapid growth, the market has attracted a number of new entrants and may even be reaching a level of overcapacity.

The directors feel that they do not know as much as they should about the existing, and new, companies in the industry. The market is now maturing and, although FFF is managing to maintain its margins and leading market share (45%), it is likely that the characteristics of the industry will change.

Required

As Management Accountant you are required to:

(a) advise the Board of the advantages of adopting a formal approach to competitor analysis **(10 marks)**

(b) advise the directors of the stages in a formal competitor analysis process and identify any information that would need to be gathered at each stage for FFF. **(15 marks)**

(Total: 25 marks)

REGULATION IN MAJOR MARKETS

31 DF

DF has been engaged in exporting from its home base for many years. Rising shipping costs have led DF to increase its prices. The Board of Directors is also aware of the view held by many customers that the company is too remote from its overseas market. Reduced turnover and profitability in DF's overseas market have resulted from these two factors.

In order to address this steady decline in its foreign customers, DF is now seriously considering the establishment of a manufacturing and distribution base overseas rather than relying on exporting. The new overseas manufacturing and distribution base will be located in the country to which DF currently sends most of its exports. It would operate as a subsidiary of DF with the parent company continuing to service its home market.

Required:

Discuss the strategic issues of organisational management, finance and potential government regulatory requirements that must be considered by the Directors of DF in converting from an exporting company to one which operates an overseas subsidiary. **(25 marks)**

32 CLOTHING COMPANY

A clothing company based in the United Kingdom believes that its domestic market is limited and is proposing to expand by the manufacture and sale of its products abroad. At this stage it has not identified where it will locate its manufacturing facility. The company believes that there are major advantages to be gained by setting up a factory in a country with a low-wage economy.

The company recognises the need to understand the marketing environment of the country within which it establishes its manufacturing facility. It appreciates that besides labour, there are other local environmental issues which need to be fully considered before entering negotiations to build a factory.

Required:

(a) Compare and contrast the environmental factors which apply in both the UK and the other country. **(15 marks)**

(b) Explain the possible cultural influences on the effectiveness of the workforce in respect of local education and training, technology, working hours and domestic amenities. **(10 marks)**

(Total: 25 marks)

33 SOCIAL RESPONSIBILITY

An increasing number of companies have expressed their willingness to consider their wider social responsibilities. This often involves them in voluntarily undertaking extra responsibilities and costs, for example:

- In order to reduce pollution, they may decide to treat waste products to a higher standard than required by legislation.
- They may decline to trade with countries whose governments they find objectionable.
- They may pay wages above minimum levels.

Required:

(a) Discuss:

(i) whether the pursuit of a policy of social responsibility necessarily involves a conflict with the objective of shareholder wealth-maximisation

(ii) the extent to which the existence of a conflict between a company's objectives is acceptable. **(9 marks)**

(b) Discuss the extent to which it is feasible for a company to 'operationalise' its social responsibility aspirations, that is, whether it is possible to bring these considerations to strategic decision making in a programmed or systematic way. **(9 marks)**

(c) Discuss whether it is feasible for companies to include the requirements of their stakeholders when they seek to recognise their wider social responsibilities. **(7 marks)**

(Total: 25 marks)

34 DROSSWAITE PLC

(a) Braithewaite and Drahos see business regulation as 'a process in which different types of actors use various mechanisms to push for or against principles'.

Required:

Explain this statement. **(12 marks)**

(b) Drosswaite plc is considering expanding its activities into various developing markets in Africa and India and has asked your firm to carry out country analyses of the countries and regions in question.

Required:

(i) What is country analysis and what kind of information would be collected? **(7 marks)**

(ii) What protectionist measures may Drosswaite plc come up against and how might governments justify these? **(6 marks)**

Note: You are NOT required to display knowledge of any specific country, region or market. **(Total: 25 marks)**

35 MTM GROUP (NOV 05 EXAM)

The MTM Group (MTM) is a major tobacco products manufacturer. As a global organisation, MTM has production facilities on every continent, and a highly sophisticated distribution network. MTM uses the 'rational planning model' to produce a strategic plan for each country in which it operates. The plan states any assumptions about the business environment in that country, then forecasts retail price levels, the market size and market share of MTM for each of the next five years. This plan is then used as a basis for next year's budget for that country. The budget is fixed at the beginning of the year, and used for control and reporting for the year.

The directors of MTM are currently formulating the organisation's strategy relating to a small Asian country (referred to as the SAC) where the government is known to be considering the introduction of a ban on all tobacco advertising. At present, the probability of such legislation has been estimated at 40%, and the marketing department has estimated that the effect of the ban would be to reduce MTM's profits in the SAC by 20%. Such a reduction would be significant enough to threaten the viability of MTM's operations in the SAC. The marketing manager has therefore suggested that the strategic plan should assume an 8% reduction in profits from the SAC (40% × 20%).

Required:

(a) Discuss the limitations of the use of the expected values technique in the context of a single strategic decision such as this. **(6 marks)**

(b) Recommend how the planning processes of MTM, for the SAC, should be modified to take account of the possible new legislation. **(12 marks)**

(c) Evaluate different methods that MTM might use to influence the government of the SAC. **(7 marks)**

(Total: 25 marks)

STAKEHOLDERS

36 DIGWELL EXPLORATIONS

Eastborough is a large region with a rugged, beautiful coastline where rare birds have recently settled on undisturbed cliffs. Since mining ceased 150 years ago, its main industries have been agriculture and fishing. However, today, many communities in Eastborough suffer high unemployment. Government initiatives for regeneration through tourism have met with little success as the area has poor road networks, unsightly derelict buildings and dirty beaches.

Digwell Explorations, a listed company, has a reputation for maximising shareholder returns and has discovered substantial tin reserves in Eastborough. With new technology, mining could be profitable, provide jobs and boost the economy. A number of interest and pressure groups have, however, been vocal in opposing the scheme.

Digwell Explorations, after much lobbying, has just received government permission to undertake mining. It could face difficulties in proceeding because of the likely activity of a group called the Eastborough Protection Alliance. This group includes wildlife protection representatives, villagers worried about the potential increase in traffic congestion and noise, environmentalists, and anti-capitalism groups.

Required:

(a) Discuss the ethical issues that should have been considered by the government when granting permission for mining to go ahead. Explain the conflicts between the main stakeholder groups. **(12 marks)**

(b) By use of some (mapping) framework, analyse how the interest and power of pressure and stakeholder groups can be understood. Based on this analysis, identify how Digwell Explorations might respond to these groups. **(13 marks)**

(Total: 25 marks)

37 SHAREHOLDER VALUE ANALYSIS

The chairman of your group, which is large and diversified, has expressed concern at the inadequacies of the present voluminous monthly reporting package. He acknowledges that it compares actual and forecast results for all operations with the budget, and that it contains extensive reporting of non-financial indicators of customer satisfaction and quality, and of factory performance towards attaining JIT (just-in-time manufacturing) and TQM (total quality management). However, he regards much of this as operational detail, and considers that the board should place more emphasis on the shareholders' interests. This would be in accord with the declared group aim of maximising shareholder value in the long run.

As part of a response to the chairman's concerns, the finance director has asked you to prepare a report on certain aspects of the problem.

You are required to write to the finance director:

(a) explaining what is meant by shareholder value, and how it can be assessed **(8 marks)**

(b) explaining what measure or measures of divisional performance would enable the management of a diversified group to assess divisional performance against the group objective of maximising shareholder value. Include in your report appropriate commentary on the role of non-financial indicators, and a possible approach to changing the reporting to the board. **(17 marks)**

(Total: 25 marks)

38 SCHOOL

A school operated by a local administrative authority provides educational opportunities for teenage pupils within an area in a city. The school has achieved varying levels of success in public examinations and, in terms of examination results, is performing neither better nor worse than other comparable schools serving the city. Its teaching and administrative staff are conscientious and committed to providing quality education to the pupils. The head teacher is required to improve the school's success in respect of examination performance, but the local administrative authority is unable to provide any resources beyond those which are already available.

The head teacher works within the following parameters:

- there is a maximum number of pupils that the school can admit each year
- the budgets for the school's teaching activities are allocated in accordance with the subjects which are taught
- the pupils admitted to the school study some core subjects and they may also choose to study some subjects from a range of options, which can be extended, or reduced.

The head teacher has an industrial background and has attempted to apply Boston Consulting Group analysis to the situation of the school. He has concluded that 'market growth' could be regarded as relating to the numbers of pupils within certain segments such as socio-economic group and ethnicity. He thinks 'market share' relates to how much of the local market for pupils the school obtains in comparison with other schools in the area.

Required:

(a) Identify the stakeholder groups that the school is seeking to serve within its 'customer' portfolio and briefly outline their requirements. Discuss ways in which the head teacher and staff can determine the requirements of these stakeholders. **(12 marks)**

(b) Discuss how far analysis of market growth and relative market share as defined by the head teacher can help him and his staff to determine the best way to meet the requirements of the school's stakeholders within its 'customer' portfolio. **(13 marks)**

(Total: 25 marks)

39 DOCTORS WITH WINGS (PILOT PAPER)

'*Doctors with Wings*' is a registered charity that raises funds to send volunteer doctors and nurses to medical emergencies around the world. Those emergencies can arise for any reason, ranging from famine to war or major outbreaks of disease. Funding primarily comes from Government agencies and corporate donations, although the charity seeks donations from the public, as well as medicines and other supplies from manufacturers. The majority of volunteers are recruited, often with the support of teaching hospitals, immediately after qualification. These new doctors are often persuaded to donate their time to the charity during presentations made by volunteer doctors who have just returned from a medical emergency.

Bryson, in his 1995 book, *Strategic Planning for Public and Non-profit Organisations*, makes the following statement:

'I would argue that if an organisation has time to do only one thing when it comes to strategic planning, that one thing ought to be a stakeholder analysis.'

Required:

(a) Critically discuss the components and process of such an analysis and the benefits that 'Doctors with Wings' would gain from the exercise. **(10 marks)**

(b) Evaluate the principal stakeholders in the organisation and analyse the nature of the influence and importance that they hold in their relationship with the charity.

(15 marks)

(Total: 25 marks)

40 5E INTERNET UPGRADE (MAY 06 EXAM)

5E is a management consultancy practice. It is a limited liability partnership with eight equal partners. Over the past ten years, 5E has invested heavily in the development of knowledge management. It now has a very large knowledgebase, with over half a million documents that have been produced by 5E staff. These range from internal memos, emails and research reports to major client project reports and articles that have been published in professional journals. The knowledgebase is stored on, and accessed through, 5E's Intranet. The Intranet is currently managed by X, a facilities management company which owns all the necessary hardware and software. PCs and laptops are all owned by 5E and maintained by X.

5E also has a website containing contact details for all of 5E's offices, and detailed descriptions of the products and services offered to clients. It also has mini-case studies of successful 5E consultancy projects. These case studies have each been approved by the relevant client, as some of the content could have been perceived as commercially sensitive. The website is hosted by an Internet Service Provider (ISP). The same ISP also handles all incoming and outgoing email traffic on behalf of 5E.

Ms Y, the Chief Knowledge Officer (CKO) of 5E, has proposed a major upgrade to the Intranet. This would involve a significant investment, and the major aspects of the planned upgrade are as follows:

- to bring web hosting and the management of the Intranet in-house
- to redesign the website so it gives clients of 5E password-protected access to the knowledgebase.

Required:

(a) Recommend the information technology hardware and software that would be required by 5E in order to complete the Intranet upgrade project. **(10 marks)**

(b) Using Mendelow's stakeholder mapping model, identify FIVE major stakeholders of the Intranet project. Explain the classification you have given, within the model, to each stakeholder. **(15 marks)**

(Total: 25 marks)

41 EEE FLAVOURINGS (NOV 06 EXAM)

EEE is an established chemical company extracting flavours and oils from plant materials and supplying them to the flavours and fragrances industries. The shareholders include institutional investors (20%), employees and pensioners of the company (20%) and the descendants of the family (30%) who founded the business approximately 100 years ago. The remainder of the shares are in public ownership. The company is reasonably successful but, recently, there has been pressure on margins and its future is not guaranteed.

The majority of the Board of Directors are members of the founding family who have always taken an active part in the management of the business.

When the company was originally started, the surrounding area was mainly used as agricultural land but, over time, a residential area has developed around the factory. Although many of the workers in the factory live locally, some of the housing is quite expensive and has attracted affluent residents from the local city.

The chemical engineers at EEE have recently developed, and patented, a new process which would allow EEE to extract onion oil and garlic oil at far better yields than those obtained by existing processes. The market for these oils is very profitable and presents a significant opportunity for EEE to gain a real competitive advantage in its industry.

Unfortunately, as with all extraction processes, there will be some leakage and, although perfectly safe and compliant with all safety legislation, the smell of the oils will offend some of the more affluent residents who have complained to local government officers.

There is very little other industry in the area and EEE is a large contributor to the local economy. One of the trade union representatives working in EEE is also an elected council member serving in the local government.

Required:

As Management Accountant you have been asked to:

(a) advise the Board of Directors of the advantages to EEE of conducting a stakeholder analysis in the context of the proposed investment decision **(5 marks)**

(b) analyse the principal stakeholders in EEE in the context of the proposed investment in the new process **(15 marks)**

(c) recommend an acceptable course of action to the Board of Directors in the light of the stakeholder analysis conducted in (b). **(5 marks)**

(Total: 25 marks)

CUSTOMERS AND SUPPLIERS

42 VIRTUAL ORGANISATIONS

For an organisation to successfully achieve its strategies it will need to give adequate consideration to both structure and support systems. Similarly, it should consider the issue of relationship management, as all organisations are reliant on relationships with others. In varying degrees, organisations explore their boundaries of responsibility with others and many have taken the decision to outsource activities, some to the extent that they operate as 'networked organisations'.

The term 'virtual organisations' has been used to describe an extreme form of networked organisation that has minimal owned resources and activities. Here the emphasis is almost solely upon partnership and collaboration rather than permanent staff, physical sites and formal structures. Critics feel that such organisations are unable to operate beyond the short term, citing as evidence the number of 'dot com' companies that have gone out of business.

Required:

(a) Discuss the key strategic issues that will lead to potential strategic strengths or weaknesses for a virtual networked organisation. **(12 marks)**

(b) Discuss the benefits and difficulties of conducting an environmental analysis in an organisation that is highly networked. **(13 marks)**

(Total: 25 marks)

43 V

V is a company which supplies quality floor-covering materials. These materials attract a high market price and are extremely hard-wearing. They have been developed mainly for use within industry rather than in homes.

V pays its sales staff a basic salary plus a commission based on the volume of sales made. This has resulted in some of its sales staff achieving very high earnings.

M is the Sales Director and has become concerned recently at the number of retail shops that have been supplied with materials by V which have then returned large quantities of unsold inventories and requested a refund. These shops are mainly engaged in supplying homes rather than industrial customers.

M has turned to you, as Management Accountant, for advice. He thinks that an alternative method of paying the sales staff will help to overcome the problem of the material being sold to inappropriate retail outlets. In the future, he proposes that the sales staff be paid on the basis of basic salary with the addition of a commission based on repeat customer purchases.

Required:

(a) Explain why V is experiencing demands for refunds from many retail shops, and the implications of this on the attainment of increased shareholder value. **(10 marks)**

(b) Discuss how Customer Account Profitability (CAP) analysis could be used to provide information on which to base the commission payment to the sales staff and how this change would affect their sales practices. Include consideration of repeat customer orders within your discussion. **(15 marks)**

(Total: 25 marks)

44 BXA (MAY 05 EXAM)

The insurance industry is characterised by large organisations producing, packaging and cross-selling a number of different 'products' to their client base. Typical products include life insurance, health insurance, house insurance and house contents insurance. Therefore, cost efficiency, repeat business and database manipulation are of significant importance.

BXA is a medium-sized insurance company that has grown over the past 50 years by a number of relatively small mergers and acquisitions. Its business is focused on life, automobile and private property insurance. Over the last few years the insurance industry has undergone significant change with increasing consolidation and the squeezing of margins.

The Board of BXA recognises that it is quite old fashioned in its approach to business, particularly in its attitude to information technology. Much of the computing is done on personal computers, many of which are not networked, using a variety of 'user written' programs. There are a number of different computer systems in the organisation that have been inherited from the companies that have been acquired in the past. However, these computer systems have not been fully consolidated. It is recognised that this lack of compatibility is causing efficiency problems.

BXA has recently been approached by CXA, an insurance company of a similar size, with a view to a merger. Although BXA has never combined with an organisation of this size before, the Board recognises that this merger could present an opportunity to develop into a company of significant size but that this may also present further problems of system incompatibility. BXA has decided to proceed with the merger, but the Board recognises that this might only make the situation worse with regards to information management strategy of the resulting combined company.

The Finance Director has asked you, as project accountant, to investigate the potential of outsourcing the information technology function as part of the post-merger consolidation process.

Required:

(a) Discuss the advantages and disadvantages of outsourcing the IT function for the merged organisation at each of the strategic, managerial and tactical levels of the organisation. **(15 marks)**

(b) Briefly describe the characteristics of the supplier that BXA will be looking for in the selection of the contractor to take on the outsourcing. **(5 marks)**

(c) Identify the factors which should be included in the service level agreement with which the contractor will be expected to comply in achieving the levels of performance that BXA will require. **(5 marks)**

(Total: 25 marks)

45 EXTRANET (NOV 05 EXAM)

C is a large multinational car manufacturer. It has factories in five countries and sells its products through networks of independent dealerships throughout the world. As part of its strategy of reducing unit costs and improving quality, C has entered into a number of 'sole supplier' agreements. This means that, on a worldwide basis, C buys all of its requirement for a specific material or component from a single supplier organisation. Such contracts are normally for a five-year period.

S is a specialist manufacturer of safety equipment. It has recently been invited, by C, to submit a tender to supply all of the 'airbag' safety devices to be installed in C's cars. This will be the biggest order for which S has ever tendered and, if won, would require a 200% increase in production capacity (that is, to three times its present scale) for S. In return for this large order, S would have to agree to deliver the required parts to each C factory twice a day. Any failure to deliver on time would lead to S being liable for the cost of lost production.

As part of the contract, C would allow S access to its extranet. This would mean that S was able to see C's forecast production schedules on a real-time basis. C maintains detailed forecasts of the number of each model of car being produced in each factory. This information is available on an hour-by-hour basis for the next month, on a day-by-day basis for the following five months, and a week-by-week basis for the subsequent 18 months. This means that S would be able to view detailed production forecasts for a two-year period. The extranet also has a 'virtual trading room' where suppliers bid for new contracts. It also contains a lot of car industry information, some of which is not available to organisations that do not supply C.

Required:

(a) Discuss the advantages and disadvantages, to S, of the sole supplier arrangement described. **(15 marks)**

(b) Evaluate the benefits, to S, of access to the C extranet. **(10 marks)**

(Total: 25 marks)

IT AND COMPETITIVE POSITION

46 SERVICE SECTOR STRATEGY

Required:

(a) Evaluate the need for an IT strategy in a business operating in the service sector (such as a large international firm of accountants). Assume that the primary method of customer contact is face-to-face or by telephone. **(15 marks)**

(b) Explain the information intensity matrix of Porter and Millar and discuss its relevance to a service sector business such as an accounting firm. **(10 marks)**

Note: You may refer to any appropriate service sector business in answering this question.

(Total: 25 marks)

47 KN COMPANY

The KN Company manufactures a wide range of plastic mouldings. The mouldings are used in such diverse products as motor vehicles, garden furniture and children's toys. As a result of this variety, there are six different sales departments, a single manufacturing department and an ordering department. There is a separate IT service department which provides basic IT services to all the other departments.

The company has established its IT systems within each individual department. Each department has its own computerised records and databases. The IT department of KN has been very successful in previous years in meeting IT systems requirements and in providing a high quality of service to each user department.

KN now wishes to set up one central sales database that can be used by all departments. The database will include, amongst other things, details of goods, customers and debtor analysis. This will mean that the individual databases in each department will be amalgamated into this central database.

Required:

(a) Explain the relative merits of the KN Company concentrating its data and information on individual departments compared with centralising its database. **(17 marks)**

(b) Evaluate the problems that the IT department may experience in amalgamating the company's data into one central database.

Note: Your answer must concentrate on the data held by the company. Comments concerning hardware or the physical location of the database are NOT required. **(8 marks)**

(Total: 25 marks)

48 DATA COLLECTION

(a) Evaluate the use of Intelligent Agents with specific reference to their benefits and limitations in data mining. **(10 marks)**

(b) The government of Xanadu, a country with an extensive road network, has recently introduced a road-pricing scheme. This means that car drivers are charged for using certain main roads and bridges in the country. Roadside scanners collect information on road usage by 'reading' the number plate of each car as it passes a scanner. Scanners have been placed on all roads and bridges where a charge is to be made. As car number plates are unique, and the scanning system is extremely accurate, use of roads can be determined. Information collected from the scanners is stored on a central database.

The system has been operational for eight weeks. Car owners are expressing significant concern about the system. They now realise that the central database contains details of their exact locations and times they were at those locations.

As well as using the database for charging car owners for use of the roads, citizens suspect that the government might use this data for purposes other than road pricing (scanners have been placed on approaches to the country's three main assembly and concert halls).

Required:

Discuss the strategic benefits to the government of collecting data on vehicle movements and explain the limitations of the data being collected. **(15 marks)**

(Total: 25 marks)

THE INTERNET AND ELECTRONIC COMMERCE

49 WEBSITE

SK Products was established 65 years ago by two entrepreneurs to distribute tools and spare parts to the then small electronics industry. Since that time the company has expanded its product range to just over 100,000 items and supplies electronic and computer components to many major organisations. The components supplied range from small fuses and computer chips to complicated electrical assemblies requiring specialist knowledge to install.

The current directors pride themselves on the organisation's attention to the specific requests of customers and the personal and friendly service that all staff provide. Recent customer surveys show that a significant amount of repeat business is generated by good customer care, even though SK Products's prices can be higher than those charged by competitors.

The organisation is planning its first website. A review of competitors' sites shows that the information provided is little more than an electronic catalogue. Repeat visits to the site are greeted with the same 'home page' whilst most of the information provided appears to be out-of-date.

SK Products currently supplies a catalogue every four months in paper format.

Required:

(a) Explain the advantages and disadvantages of SK Products providing information on a website rather than in a paper-based catalogue. Ensure that your answer shows how a website can provide a more user-friendly presentation system than a paper-based catalogue. **(18 marks)**

(b) Explain what information SK Products can provide on its website to help customers install and use its products. **(7 marks)**

(Total: 25 marks)

50 DLN

DLN manufactures a range of standard parts for domestic products such as washing machines, refrigerators and freezers. The parts manufactured include motors, gears, cooling elements and standard doors for different manufacturers. The company has 12 main customers who assemble the products prior to selling them to shops and consumers.

The company has been in existence for 75 years and has remained profitable during this time. The directors pride themselves in keeping up-to-date with recent technological change. They have implemented a range of systems within the company including computerised stock control, sophisticated accounting systems and on-line ordering systems for customers via Electronic Data Interchange (EDI). DLN does not maintain a website because no sales are made to the general public.

However, DLN's main customer, GKR, has now decided to start using an electronic trading room to order parts. Rather than place orders direct with manufacturers, GKR will now offer the contract to any supplier via a restricted website. Any manufacturer can bid for the order, and, after a specified period of time, the contract will be awarded to the lowest bidder. Bidders such as DLN will have no knowledge of other bids, which will significantly reduce the likelihood of DLN obtaining contracts.

Trade journals suggest that other companies will also start using a similar system within the next six months.

Required:

(a) Discuss the effects that the electronic trading room is likely to have upon DLN.

(13 marks)

(b) Identify and explain the information that will be required and where this will be obtained, in order for managers in DLN to ensure that bids are placed into the trading room on an appropriate timescale. **(12 marks)**

(Total: 25 marks)

51 SDW (PILOT PAPER)

The SDW Company has been trading for one year. It provides rail travel services between three major cities in the country in which it operates.

Mr M, the majority shareholder and Managing Director, is keen to expand its operations and, in particular, to use the Internet as the major selling medium. He has discovered, for example, that doubling sales on the Internet usually results in no additional costs. However, doubling sales using a call centre normally results in a doubling of staff and an increase in costs.

All tickets are currently sold via the company's call centre. The company has an Internet site although this is used for publicity only, not for sales or marketing. Competitors currently use a mixture of selling media, although detailed information on the success of each medium is not available to the SDW Company.

Mr M has asked you, as a qualified management accountant, to assist him in upgrading the company's Internet site and, in particular, showing how this will help to reduce operating costs.

Required:

(a) Advise Mr M on how to establish and implement an appropriate Internet strategy for the SDW Company. **(13 marks)**

(b) Discuss the key customer-orientated features of an Internet site, showing how these can be used to meet the objective of cost reduction required by Mr M.

(12 marks)

(Total: 25 marks)

52 JURANIA (NOV 05 EXAM)

Introduction

The 222 Organisation (222) is a large information systems consultancy, based in the southern African country of Jurania. 222 was founded in 1987 and has become very successful, both within Jurania and in neighbouring countries, due to growth in the economies of those countries and the highly developed technology sector of the Juranian economy. 222 advises organisations on the development of Intranet and knowledge-sharing systems, and has many clients among the top 100 companies in Jurania.

222 employs over 500 staff in its very impressive modern office building on a business park near the capital city of Jurania. Also based on the business park are several IT hardware and software companies, and the country's largest internet service provider (ISP), JuraWeb. Many of 222's staff were trained at Jurania's university, which has an excellent reputation. Whenever 222 advertises for additional staff, it receives a large number of applications from suitably qualified applicants.

The internet strategy

Recognising that the growth of 222 is limited by the size of the local market for its services, the directors of 222 are considering the further development of its rather basic website. At present, the 222.com website only contains a description of the organisation and contact details. The site was designed by employees of 222 and is hosted by JuraWeb. The directors hope that a better website will allow the organisation to develop new business in other parts of Africa, but have no desire to become a global business at this stage.

The directors are considering using the services of a local specialist web design company to develop a sophisticated website with case studies of previous 222 contracts, and detailed descriptions of staff and services. The directors also believe that 222 should be hosting the website itself, and are considering the purchase of a powerful web server. They also want to upgrade the telecommunications infrastructure of the organisation by investing in a new fibre-optic broadband service, which is available from a recently formed company that has just opened its office on the business park.

Required:

(a) Evaluate whether the 222 Organisation might gain a competitive advantage as a result of being based in Jurania. **(13 marks)**

(b) Evaluate the risks to 222 if it decides to pursue its internet strategy as the directors have suggested. **(12 marks)**

(Total: 25 marks)

STRATEGIC OPTIONS

53 GAP ANALYSIS

Most organisations recognise that continuing as at present, sometimes referred to as the 'do nothing' option, is rarely advisable as it is likely to lead to a performance shortfall against objectives. Even new policies may not guarantee meeting organisational objectives.

The planning technique 'gap analysis' is a means by which an organisation can assess whether proposed policies are likely to achieve their objectives or the degree to which they might fall short.

Required:

(a) Typically, an organisation might construct and then respond to a gap analysis as part of an overall (rational) approach to strategic management. Evaluate the usefulness of the 'gap analysis' technique as part of such a system and the main criticisms of this rational approach. **(10 marks)**

(b) Some people feel that gap analysis has declined in popularity, particularly within the private sector. Discuss why this should be the case and, using examples, explain how gap analysis could be particularly helpful to public sector organisations. **(15 marks)**

(Total: 25 marks)

54 PA POSITION AUDIT

The PA company supplies professional homecare support services to elderly people. The company has been in business for 20 years and has expanded from its local base to become a national organisation. The services undertaken in the home include provision of meals, domestic cleaning and linen washing.

The services provided by PA were initially undertaken by local administrative public authorities but over the years such activities have been privatised and PA now has numerous contracts with authorities throughout the country.

Two years after PA was formed, it began to enjoy rapid growth. The market then began to mature after six years of growth and remained static for a further ten years. Over the last two years, PA has lost some contracts from local administrative authorities, causing the turnover and profitability to decline.

The Managing Director of PA has turned to you to provide advice as to how to carry out what she calls 'an examination of the state of the entity'. The purpose of this is to determine what action should be taken to halt the decline in turnover and profit. In carrying out this review, the Managing Director instructs you to look at the firm's resources, markets, service, operating systems, internal organisation, results and returns to shareholders.

You have carried out some preliminary research and established that there exists the Ms model. This indicates that a position audit can be carried out using headings beginning with the letter M, as follows:

Men, Money, Management, Make-up, Machinery, Methods, Markets, Materials and Management Information.

Required:

Recommend to the Managing Director how a position audit should be carried out for the PA company and discuss, with reasons, the issues that need to be addressed under each heading using the Ms model. **(25 marks)**

55 ENVIRONMENTAL UNCERTAINTY AND SCENARIO PLANNING

Strategy involves planning ways in which the long-term objectives of the organisation can be achieved. An important part of such a process is the analysis of the external environment to determine future potential factors that are most relevant to the organisation.

Some believe that the external environment within which organisations operate has become increasingly uncertain and therefore wholly unpredictable. This raises important issues for strategy development, with some questioning the value of past approaches.

Required:

(a) Discuss how environmental uncertainty might affect strategic thinking within organisations. **(12 marks)**

(b) Assess the usefulness of scenario planning in strategy formulation, particularly under conditions of extreme uncertainty. **(13 marks)**

(Total: 25 marks)

56 NO-FRILLS AIRLINES (PILOT PAPER)

Over the past few years the major airlines have suffered a decline in profitability and some have even filed for bankruptcy. At the same time, some budget airlines have shown considerable success offering a 'no frills service' to an increasing number of passengers at heavily discounted fares.

The traditional airlines have, in the main, a vertically integrated service with many activities such as baggage handling, ticketing and maintenance delivered by their own subsidiaries. Additionally, they have continued to offer a variety of classes ranging from luxury to economy thus catering for all segments of the travelling market from business to tourist. These airlines compete fiercely for landing rights at city centre airports and have formed into two main alliances to share routes giving them global coverage. The traditional airlines tend to purchase their aircraft directly from the manufacturers whereas budget airlines tend to use leasing to source their fleet.

By contrast, the budget airlines have concentrated on the short-haul market and have heavily promoted low-cost flights to secondary airports with no service other than the flight. These low costs have been partially supported by subsidies provided by the secondary airports. An additional advantage of these airports is the rapid turnaround of aircraft on the ground since they are handling fewer flights. Aircrew, at minimum permitted staffing levels, are responsible for aircraft cleaning. The budget price includes only the flight; passengers have no in-flight services and book their tickets directly via the Internet. The budget airlines spend heavily on advertising in all popular media.

Required:

(a) Using an appropriate model of the competitive environment, discuss the difference in performance between the traditional airlines and the budget airlines and the business models they are operating. **(20 marks)**

(b) Evaluate the business model operated by the budget airlines as a source of sustainable competitive advantage. **(5 marks)**

(Total: 25 marks)

57 QUALISPECS

Qualispecs has a reputation for quality, traditional products. It has a group of optician shops, both rented and owned, from which it sells its spectacles. Recently, it has suffered intense competition and eroding customer loyalty, but a new Chief Executive has joined from one of its major rivals Fastglass.

Fastglass is capturing Qualispecs' market through partnership with a high street shopping group. These shops install mini-labs in which prescriptions for spectacles are dispensed within an hour. Some competitors have successfully experimented with designer frames and sunglasses. Others have reduced costs through new computer-aided production methods.

Qualispecs has continued to operate as it always has, letting the product 'speak for itself' and failing to utilise advances in technology. Although production costs remain high, Qualispecs is financially secure and has large cash reserves. Fortunately the country's most popular sports star recently received a prestigious international award wearing a pair of Qualispecs' spectacles.

The new Chief Executive has established as a priority the need for improved financial performance. Following a review she discovers that:

(i) targets are set centrally and shops report monthly. Site profitability varies enormously, and fixed costs are high in shopping malls

(ii) shops exercise no control over job roles, working conditions, and pay rates

(iii) individual staff pay is increased annually according to a pre-determined pay scale. Everyone also receives a small one-off payment based on group financial performance.

Market analysts predict a slowdown in the national economy but feel that consumer spending will continue to increase, particularly among 18 to 30 year olds.

Required:

(a) Produce a corporate appraisal of Qualispecs, taking account of internal and external factors, and discuss the key strategic challenges facing the company. **(16 marks)**

(b) Corporate appraisal offers a 'snapshot' of the present. In order to focus on the future there is a need to develop realistic policies and programmes. Recommend, with reasons, strategies from your appraisal that would enable Qualispecs to build on its past success. **(9 marks)**

(Total: 25 marks)

58 STATUTORY TRANSPORT AUTHORITY

A statutory transport authority is committed to the provision of rural passenger transport services in an area between two large cities. It has received applications from operators as follows:

(a) M Ltd offers to operate a limited stop service between the two main cities in the authority's area. Buses would be timed at hourly intervals from 7 am until 9 pm on condition that the authority would authorise no other operator to service this route or any part of it. M Ltd also requires that district councils would grant the required permission to allow on-board catering.

(b) N Ltd is willing to operate 'social-service' vehicles for disabled passengers and others between the urban areas. Services would operate half-hourly from 6.30 am until 10.30 pm at a cost to the authority of £4,000 per week for the service. All fares would go to the authority. It is estimated that total fare income could eventually amount to £2,400 per week but would initially be between £800 and £1,500 per week. Six months' notice of termination would be required from the authority or the operator, should it be found that some other service is more appropriate to travellers' needs.

(c) O Ltd proposes to operate dial-a-bus rural services (a service by which intending passengers can telephone for a bus). Travellers from within the rural area between the two cities would be able to make use of these out-of-town services to and from either centre at reasonable cost. The authority would need to subsidise the cost of this service by regular weekly payments of £3,000 and all fare income would be retained by O Ltd.

Required:

(a) Discuss the criteria which should be applied to evaluate the three proposals, taking account of the authority's need to seek out the best value-for-money. **(10 marks)**

(b) Discuss how such an authority can quantify the value of a social service such as a public passenger transport facility to a community. **(8 marks)**

(c) Describe and assess other sources of funding that might become available for the successful operation of a rural passenger transport facility other than revenue earned from passenger fares and public funds. **(7 marks)**

(Total: 25 marks)

59 DDD CHEMICALS (NOV 06 EXAM)

DDD is a relatively small, specialist manufacturer of chemicals that are used in the pharmaceutical industry. It does not manufacture any pharmaceutical products itself since these are made by different processes and under different conditions. DDD obtains its raw materials, which are quite simple, from large chemical companies, and modifies them by a number of patented processes before selling them on to a few pharmaceutical companies. DDD makes significantly higher margins than its suppliers, which manufacture in bulk.

Several patents are due to expire in the next three years.

The large pharmaceutical companies, which are DDD's customers, are suffering reduced profits as governments reduce the price they are prepared to pay for drugs. As a result, the pharmaceutical companies are pressuring DDD to reduce its prices.

The majority of the shares are owned by members of the family which started the business some years ago and who still take an active part both as managers of the business and as development chemists. There is a share option scheme for the employees and this is well supported.

Required:

As management accountant for DDD you have been asked to:

(a) advise the Board of Directors of the possible threats related to the patent expiries **(10 marks)**

(b) evaluate suitable courses of action that DDD might take to maintain its profits in the face of the threats identified in (a) **(12 marks)**

(c) from your analysis recommend, with a brief justification, the most appropriate course of action for DDD. **(3 marks)**

(Total: 25 marks)

PRODUCT PORTFOLIO EVALUATION

60 SPORTS CENTRE

A local administrative authority allowed a supermarket development to go ahead providing that the company concerned built an extension to the authority's sports centre on an adjoining site.

In recent years the sports centre has encountered a growth in competition from local commercial recreational organisations. Simultaneously, the authority has experienced a reduction in its central funding and has steadily increased its charges for the use of its sports centre facilities.

In reviewing its services at the sports centre, the authority has applied the product life cycle (PLC) model. It has identified the stage within the life cycle at which each of its sports centre services is positioned, as follows:

Introductory stage: Martial arts, with little take-up as yet.

Growth stage: Squash playing facilities, which have required capital investment from the authority and on-going maintenance costs of the courts and equipment.

Demand for the facilities is increasing rapidly.

Maturity stage: Gymnasium facilities, which require little maintenance expense and experience steady demand which generates surplus cash.

Swimming, which incurs a continual increase in maintenance and water purification costs.

Decline stage: Badminton, with a continual reduction in demand.

Required:

(a) Recommend how the local authority could market its sports centre services. **(8 marks)**

(b) Comment on the strategic resource allocation implications of each stage of the product life cycle (PLC) when applied to the sports centre facility. You are NOT required to describe or draw the PLC model. **(12 marks)**

(c) In the light of your answer to Parts (a) and (b), and paying particular attention to the increasing competitive threat, recommend what services the authority should offer in the future within its sports centre. **(5 marks)**

(Total: 25 marks)

61 GC CONGLOMERATE

GC is a conglomerate which comprises five strategic business units (SBUs), all operating as subsidiary companies. Information relating to each SBU (and the market leader or nearest competitor) is given in the following table:

	Current market share			*Market growth expected by GC*
	GC %	*Market leader* %	*Nearest competitor* %	
Building brick manufacturer	3	25		Small
(Declining profitability)				
Parcel carriage service	1	6		Nil
(Long established, faces strong competition. Turnover and profitability over last three years have been stable but are expected to decline as competition strengthens.)				
Food manufacturer producing exclusively for household consumption	25		5	Slowly declining
Long established with little new investment. High levels of turnover and profitability which are being sustained.)				
Painting and decorating contracting company *(Established three years ago. Continuous capital injections from Group over that period. Currently not making any profit.)*	0.025	0.5		Historically high but now forecast to slow down
Software development and supply company	10		8	Rapid
(Acquired two years ago. Market share expected to increase over next two years. Sustained investment from Group but profitability so far is low.)				

Required:

(a) Comment on GC's overall competitive position by applying the Boston Consulting Group Growth matrix analysis to its portfolio of SBUs. **(10 marks)**

(b) Discuss how GC should pursue the strategic development of its SBUs in order to add value to the overall conglomerate group. **(15 marks)**

(Total: 25 marks)

62 BCG

The Boston Consulting Group (BCG) Growth Share Matrix is a model which plots Strategic Business Units (SBUs) market growth and market share relative to their largest competitors.

The models were established to analyse the balance of a company's product portfolio and has been adopted by many commercial organisations.

Many public sector organisations are now experiencing increasing levels of competition for the supply of their services. This competitive environment has resulted in the need for such public sector organisations to develop analytical techniques which previously operated mainly within the private sector.

Required:

(a) Explain how the BCG Growth Share Matrix could be used to analyse, for the purpose of improving overall market share, the cash flows expected from the activities of different SBUs. **(12 marks)**

(b) Discuss whether application of the BCG Growth Share Matrix can make an effective contribution to the strategic development of a public sector service which is mainly government-funded, but is subject to increasing levels of competition. You may refer to any public sector service with which you are familiar. **(13 marks)**

(Total: 25 marks)

63 3C PHARMACEUTICALS (MAY 06 EXAM)

3C is a medium-sized pharmaceutical company. It is based in Asia, but distributes and sells its products world-wide.

In common with other pharmaceutical companies, 3C has a large number of products in its portfolio, though most of these are still being developed. The success rate of new drugs is very low, as most fail to complete clinical trials or are believed to be uneconomic to launch. However, the rewards to be gained from a successful new drug are so great that it is only necessary to have a few successful drugs on the market to be very profitable.

At present 3C has 240 drugs at various stages of development; being tested or undergoing clinical trials prior to a decision being made whether to launch the drug. 3C has only three products that are actually 'on the market':

- Epsilon is a drug used in the treatment of heart disease. It has been available for eight months and has achieved significant success. Sales of this drug are not expected to increase from their current level.
- Alpha is a painkiller. It was launched more than ten years ago, and has become one of the leading drugs in its class. In a few months the patent on this drug will expire, and other manufacturers will be allowed to produce generic copies of it. Alpha is expected to survive a further 12 months after it loses its patent, and will then be withdrawn.
- Beta is used in the hospital treatment of serious infections. It is a very specialised drug, and cannot be obtained from a doctor or pharmacist for use outside the hospital environment. It was launched only three months ago, and has yet to generate a significant sales volume.

The directors of 3C meet every month to review the product portfolio and to discuss possible investment opportunities. At their next meeting, they are to be asked to consider three investments. Due to a limited investment budget, the three investments are mutually exclusive (that is, they will only be able to invest in ONE of the options).

The three options are as follows:

- The directors can invest in a new version of Alpha, Alpha2, which offers improved performance. This will allow 3C to apply for a new patent for Alpha2, and maintain the level of sales achieved by Alpha for an additional five years. Alpha2 has successfully completed all its clinical trials, and can be launched immediately.
- The directors can invest in a major marketing campaign, to promote the use of Beta to specialist hospital staff. While this investment should lead to a significant growth in the sales of Beta, 3C is aware that one of its competitors is actively promoting a rival product with similar performance to that of Beta.
- The directors can invest in the final stage of clinical trials for Gamma. This is a 'breakthrough' drug, as it has no near rivals on the market. Gamma is used in the treatment of HIV, and offers significantly better success rates than any treatment currently available. The team of 3C specialists managing the development of Gamma is confident it can successfully complete clinical trials within six months. The team also believes that Gamma should be sold at the lowest price possible, to maximise the benefits of Gamma to society. However, the marketing department of 3C believes that it would be possible to earn very large profits from Gamma, due to its success rate and breakthrough status.

Required:

(a) Briefly explain how the product life cycle model can be used to analyse the current product portfolio of 3C (that is, BEFORE the planned investment). **(8 marks)**

(b) Evaluate the potential impact of each of the three investment options (Alpha2, Beta and Gamma) on the product portfolio of 3C, referring to your answer to part (a) above. **(9 marks)**

(c) Discuss the social responsibility implications of each of the three investment options, for the directors of 3C. **(8 marks)**

(Total: 25 marks)

BENCHMARKING AND VALUE CHAIN ANALYSIS

64 COMPETITOR ANALYSIS AND COMPETITOR BENCHMARKING

Organisations are reporting a growth in the sophistication, volume and nature of data that is regularly collected and interpreted for strategic purposes. This data collection supports a number of strategic approaches. Some firms regularly monitor customer expectation and market conditions for instance, while others prefer to attempt to stay in touch with their competitors' methods of doing business, strategies and future intentions.

Required:

(a) Compare and contrast competitor analysis and competitor benchmarking, and evaluate the importance of each process. **(17 marks)**

(b) Discuss how benchmarking might be successfully applied in the public sector. You may use examples drawn from any area of the public sector to illustrate your answer. **(8 marks)**

(Total: 25 marks)

65 PAL

PAL is a banking group specialising in loans for home purchase. It has a network of shops, cash machines and other outlets in and around the capital city (where it has its headquarters) with all outlets within 70 miles. It monitors interest rates offered by competitors and strives to match or better the lowest rates. This strategy has been successful, but in order to compete more fully, it has introduced a range of additional customer services, including home insurance. A dedicated unit was established to extend existing benchmarking of price to other aspects of customer requirements.

Following a survey, the following factors in addition to price have emerged as being relevant to customers:

- delivery
- technical content of literature
- customer service and correspondence.

Required:

(a) Discuss the use of appropriate performance measures which home insurance could use as part of the proposed competitor benchmarking exercise. For each measure, advise on ways in which subjectivity might be dealt with. **(12 marks)**

(b) Analyse the strategies followed by PAL so far and evaluate the possible effects of actions arising from benchmarking in supporting these strategies. **(13 marks)**

(Total: 25 marks)

66 SUPERMARKET

A supermarket company employs you as management accountant. The organisation is undertaking a comprehensive analysis and evaluation of its product and customer portfolio. You have been asked to help because of your knowledge (through study) of value chain analysis.

Required:

(a) Using the example of a supermarket (or similar large mainly food-retailing organisation), discuss the main components of the value chain. You should refer to the particular skills that you as management accountant can bring to an analysis of the value chain. **(17 marks)**

(b) Discuss the contribution of value chain analysis in the effective implementation of generic strategies. **(8 marks)**

(Total: 25 marks)

67 E5E (MAY 05 EXAM)

E5E is a charity concerned with heart disease. Its mission statement is:

To fund world class research into the biology and the causes of heart disease.
To develop effective treatments and improve the quality of life for patients.
To reduce the number of people suffering from heart disease.
To provide authoritative information on heart disease.

E5E obtains funding from voluntary donations from both private individuals and companies, together with government grants. Much of the work it does, in all departments, could not be achieved without the large number of voluntary workers who give their time to the organisation and who make up approximately 80% of the workforce.

E5E does not employ any scientific researchers directly, but funds research by making grants to individual medical experts employed within universities and hospitals. In addition to providing policy advice to government departments, the charity's advisors give health educational talks to employers and other groups.

The Board recognises the need to become more professional in the management of the organisation. It feels that this can be best achieved by conducting a benchmarking exercise. However, it recognises that the introduction of this process may make some members of the organisation, particularly the volunteers, unhappy.

Required:

As Financial Controller:

(a) discuss the advantages and disadvantages of benchmarking for E5E **(8 marks)**

(b) provide advice on the stages in conducting a benchmarking exercise in the context of E5E **(13 marks)**

(c) provide advice on how those implementing the exercise should deal with the concerns of the staff, particularly the volunteers. **(4 marks)**

(Total: 25 marks)

68 2B VALUE CHAIN (MAY 06 EXAM)

2B is a medium-sized retailer of sports equipment and leisure clothing. 2B was established in 1987, and currently operates from three retail shops in town centre locations.

The management team of 2B is very careful about how it recruits staff. In addition to the specific skills required to do the job, any applicant must also have a 'passion' for sport. This has resulted in 2B gaining a reputation for excellent customer service and enthusiastic staff. A large proportion of staff time is also devoted to training, both on the product range and customer service techniques. According to a recent survey conducted by the store managers, the customers believe that 2B employees are 'helpful and knowledgeable'. The customers also praised the 2B shops for being 'well designed' and said that it was 'very easy' to find what they were looking for.

Another feature of 2B that is appreciated by the customers is the range of goods stocked. By developing close relationships with the major manufacturers of sports goods and clothing, 2B is able to stock a far wider range of items than its rivals. Control of this inventory was made easier, last year, by the development of a sophisticated computerised inventory control system. Using the system, any member of staff can locate any item of stock in any of the shops or the warehouse. If the required item is not 'in stock' at 2B, it is also possible to automatically check the availability of stock with the manufacturer.

At a recent management meeting, one of the store managers suggested that 2B could consider developing its very basic website into one capable of e-retailing. At present, the website only gives the location of stores and some very basic details of the range of inventory carried. Although the development of the website would be expensive, the managers have decided to give the suggestion serious consideration.

Required:

(a) Using the value chain model, explain those activities that add value in the 2B organisation, BEFORE the e-retail investment. **(10 marks)**

(b) Identify those activities in the value chain of 2B that may be affected by the e-retail investment, explaining whether the value added by each of them may increase or decrease as a result of the e-retail investment. **(15 marks)**

(Total: 25 marks)

ACQUISITION AND DIVESTMENT STRATEGIES

69 DIVERSIFICATION POLICY

(a) Draw Ansoff's 'product/market expansion grid'. Explain how this might be used in the formulation of corporate strategy. **(5 marks)**

(b) Describe the categories of diversification available to an organisation. **(5 marks)**

(c) Discuss the advantages and disadvantages of using the process of merger to effect diversification. **(8 marks)**

(d) Appraise the validity of a company pursuing a policy of diversification in an economy which has free capital markets. **(7 marks)**

(Total: 25 marks)

70 OBJECTIVES

OB is a trading company which has been in existence for five years. It achieved such high market growth and profitability that the founder (F) was able to quickly repay the bank loan which was taken out to start the business. The growth was achieved through F's creative and imaginative style of undertaking business. However, two years ago the company encountered a crisis of leadership. This resulted in F recruiting managers to co-ordinate the activities of the business.

F still had the final word in strategic decisions affecting the business. More operational employees were recruited and the buildings extended to satisfy the increasing market demand.

F found that the initial enthusiasm displayed by the managers began to reduce. As they became more confident in their roles, the managers became frustrated and sought more autonomy in decision-making. F also found it more difficult to maintain full control and, as a consequence, delegated more responsibility for decision-making to the managers. OB is now in phase 3 of Greiner's organisational life-cycle model and the company is achieving growth through delegation.

It is clear to F that more capital needs to be injected in order to sustain the current level of growth. This will have to be obtained from an outside source as retained earnings are insufficient to finance this development. F has now appointed two of the managers to the respective positions of finance director and operations director to assist him with the strategic management of the company.

Required:

Compare and contrast the likely approaches to establishing organisational objectives for OB at the beginning of its life, with its position now as an expanding business entity. List methods that OB can use to monitor and control progress towards the achievement of its objectives. **(25 marks)**

71 DIVERSIFICATION

Diversification may be achieved by internal growth or through pursuing a policy of acquisition and mergers. Whether the diversification is related or unrelated to the organisation's existing business activities, it is a high-risk strategy for closing the planning gap because it takes the organisation into the development of new products and markets simultaneously.

Required:

(a) Explain why diversification may be adopted as a strategy to close the planning gap. **(6 marks)**

(b) Discuss the potential advantages of diversification to a company in pursuing the strategic management of markets. **(8 marks)**

(c) Explain and discuss the statement that 'diversification is a high risk approach to closing the planning gap'. **(11 marks)**

(Total: 25 marks)

PROCESS INNOVATION AND RE-ENGINEERING

72 INVENTION AND INNOVATION

Given that one important way of gaining competitive advantage is through the processes of invention and innovation, explain:

(a) the distinction between these two processes in respect of both products and manufacturing techniques **(10 marks)**

(b) how organisations can encourage the creative acts required for both invention and innovation. **(15 marks)**

(Total: 25 marks)

73 WOWR ORGANISATION

The WOWR organisation produces books and magazines. It employs 560 staff in 7 different locations. The organisation has been using IT in various departments as follows:

Production – stock control including real-time stock and finished goods levels

Sales – historical record of books and magazines sold for the last 15 years

Finance and administration – maintenance of all ledgers, cash book and wages details

Human resources – factual information on employees, such as rate of pay, department, home address and date of birth.

In other words, most of the basic transaction systems within the organisation have been computerised. Additional investment in IT has been limited, partly as a result of the success of the organisation's core businesses, and partly from a lack of desire for change on the part of existing managers.

Recent changes in the senior management of the organisation now mean that additional appropriate IT investment is seen as being a key success criterion.

Required:

(a) Explain a framework that can be used by managers to help assess the priority for investment in competing IT systems within the WOWR organisation. **(10 marks)**

(b) (i) Explain the difference between Process Innovation (PI) and Business Process Reengineering (BPR). **(5 marks)**

(ii) Explain the reasons why PI and BPR are important in an organisation, making reference to the situation in the WOWR organisation where appropriate. **(10 marks)**

(Total: 25 marks)

74 EXPERIENCE CURVE

The theory of the experience curve is that an organisation may increase its profitability through obtaining greater familiarity with supplying its products or services to customers. This reflects the view that profitability is solely a function of market share.

You are required to discuss the extent to which the application of experience curve theory can help an organisation to prolong the life cycle of its products or services. **(25 marks)**

75 4D TEACHING HOSPITAL (MAY 06 EXAM)

4D is a large teaching hospital. While it offers a full range of hospital services to its local community, it also has a large staff of professors and lecturers who teach and train all kinds of medical students. 4D has a very good reputation for clinical excellence.

One of the areas in which 4D is very highly regarded is the training of surgeons. Three of the nine operating theatres in the hospital can be observed from a gallery, though only a limited number of students can watch any operation due to space constraints. This allows the students to watch an experienced surgeon carry out a procedure and then ask questions of their lecturer or the surgeon. Later in their training, students can use the same facilities to carry out operations while being observed by experienced staff and fellow students.

The IT department of 4D has just developed a new Information System for use in operating theatres. This system (OTIS – the Operating Theatre Information System) uses web technology to allow students anywhere in the world to videoconference with a lecturer during an operation. The students can observe the operation and the surgical team, and discuss the procedure with the surgeon and their lecturer. The system also works 'in reverse' so a surgeon at 4D can watch a student perform an operation elsewhere in the world, and provide guidance and support. The OTIS system is currently being tested, prior to introduction.

Required:

(a) (i) Distinguish between Business Process Re-engineering (BPR) and Process Innovation (PI), and explain the role of information technology in each of these techniques. **(6 marks)**

(ii) Discuss whether, in your opinion, the Operating Theatre Information System (OTIS) implementation is an example of BPR or PI. **(4 marks)**

(b) Evaluate THREE benefits to 4D and TWO benefits to society, of the Operating Theatre Information System (OTIS). **(15 marks)**

(Total: 25 marks)

THE ROLE AND RESPONSIBILITIES OF DIRECTORS

76 MIELAIDE REMEDIES

Mielaide Remedies is a company that produces a variety of antibacterial, anti-inflammatory and anti-allergenic honeys and other natural products for medical purposes.

Extensive testing has shown that the products are highly effective in treating conditions such as dermatitis, gum disease and so on, and particularly effective at protecting wounds from infection and aiding healing. They have been found to be successful against so-called superbugs such as MRSA that have become resistant to the antibiotics in common use.

The governments of most developed countries, including the US and the UK, have almost completed clinical trials and it is almost certain that the products will be approved for distribution.

Mielaide Remedies is currently a 100% family-owned company, but demand for the products is likely to be so high that it will be necessary to raise substantial capital to fund the expansion of production facilities and worldwide marketing and distribution.

The directors favoured option is to issue 40% of its share capital to the public and obtain a listing for its shares on the London Stock Exchange. Your firm has been employed as consultants to guide them through the process.

Ian Candy, the founder and chairman of the board/managing director, is particularly concerned to know about how a public listing will change his own and his fellow directors' responsibilities. Besides Ian Candy, the board comprises a production director, a marketing director, a finance director and a director of human resources. There are no other directors in legal, formal terms, but family members with substantial shareholdings often attend board meetings and express their opinions.

You are required to write a report to the board outlining the consequences, in terms of corporate governance, of obtaining a listing on the London Stock Exchange.

(25 marks)

77 CONFLICT

Scientists from various countries in the world have researched into and achieved success in mapping the genetic code of human beings. It is considered that this research may identify how serious life-threatening diseases develop. It is believed that this will lead to improved treatments and, in time, removal of these diseases altogether. Eventually this may result in the directors of world-class pharmaceutical suppliers facing a conflict of interests. These conflicts may arise because of the need to satisfy the demands of their shareholders in terms of maximised long-term wealth and also the need to discharge social responsibilities by developing treatments which eventually may render its products redundant.

Required:

Discuss the ethical implications of this research for major world-class pharmaceutical companies. In your discussion, comment on how the directors might reconcile conflicts between satisfying the demands of shareholders and discharging their social responsibilities.

(25 marks)

MEASURING PERFORMANCE

78 SCANDALOUS MEASURES

Over the past few years, there have been a number of high profile financial scandals surrounding the reporting of company performance, and the associated role of accountants. As a consequence, organisations have been urged to consider future practice carefully. Some feel that an overemphasis by a company on market expectations and profitability may be detrimental to its long term well-being. Such thinking has implications for the objectives of a company and the range of performance measures used both externally and internally.

Required:

(a) Discuss the functions that organisational objectives should fulfil strategically and the main disadvantages of using only profit related performance measures. **(12 marks)**

(b) The balanced scorecard approach has been described as relating an assessment of performance to choice of strategy through four categories of measurement. It is used by many organisations in monitoring performance. Evaluate the use of the balanced scorecard in meeting stakeholder needs and determining objectives. **(13 marks)**

(Total: 25 marks)

79 MULTINATIONAL AND LOCAL AUTHORITY

All organisations have objectives in some form or another. The methods of setting these objectives vary depending on the nature of the organisation. After they have been set an appropriate period of time has elapsed, organisations should assess to what extent their objectives have been achieved.

Two organisations with very different characteristics set strategic objectives and evaluate their achievement. The two organisations are:

- a publicly-funded local administrative authority which provides housing, education, social and road maintenance services for an area within a country, and
- a multi-national conglomerate company (MNC).

Required:

(a) Explain the differences between how the local administrative authority and the MNC should set their strategic objectives. **(10 marks)**

(b) Discuss how each organisation should assess how well it has performed in respect of the attainment of its strategic objectives. **(15 marks)**

(Total: 25 marks)

80 PUBLICLY FUNDED DEPARTMENT

A publicly funded department within a local administrative authority provides a health advisory service to its local community. This is not a hospital. Its function is purely advisory in respect of preventive medicine and focuses on good health promotion and prevention of accidents and illness.

In recent years, the funding for this service has been reduced in real terms, requiring greater levels of efficiency to be provided. The manager of the service has recognised the need to make economies. Despite receiving criticisms and complaints from the local administrative authority's elected representatives, the manager has reduced the level of service provision in an attempt to remain within budget. However, there has been no reduction in the staffing level which accounts for about 80% of expenditure.

Last year, an independent public audit report criticised the management of the service. The report focused on the fact that the service overspent its budget, was considered to be inefficient in its methods of delivery, and wasted resources allocated to it. The report went on to state that, according to annual performance indicator statistics, there is a decline in the numbers of people using the service. It concluded that the service was failing to operate economically, efficiently or effectively. The result of this was that the local administrative authority reduced the funding still further and gave the manager a warning that the whole service would be reviewed if there were not an improvement in this financial year. The manager has responded by making further cuts to the service, but has protected the staffing levels. It is projected that the service will remain just within its budget allocation this year.

Required:

Discuss the reasons why the service has received criticism.

Explain how the manager can improve the effectiveness and efficiency of the service while ensuring that it remains economic and within its allocated budget. **(25 marks)**

81 ROYAL BOTANICAL GARDENS (PILOT PAPER)

The Royal Botanical Gardens has been established for more than 120 years and has the following mission statement:

'The Royal Botanical Gardens belongs to the Nation. Our mission is to increase knowledge and appreciation of plants, their importance and their conservation, by managing and displaying living and preserved collections and through botanical and horticultural research.'

Located toward the edge of the city, the Gardens are regularly visited throughout the year by many local families and are an internationally well-known tourist attraction. Despite charging admission it is one the top five visitor attractions in the country. Every year it answers many thousands of enquiries from Universities and research establishments, including pharmaceutical companies from all over the world and charges for advice and access to its collection. Enquiries can range from access to the plant collection for horticultural work, seeds for propagation or samples for chemical analysis to seek novel pharmaceutical compounds for commercial exploitation. It receives an annual grant in aid from Central Government, which is fixed once every five years. The grant in aid is due for review in three years' time.

The Finance Director has decided that, to strengthen its case when meeting the Government representatives to negotiate the grant, the Management Board should be able to present a balanced scorecard demonstrating the performance of the Gardens. He has asked you, the Senior Management Accountant, to assist him in taking this idea forward.

Many members of the Board, which consists of eminent scientists, are unfamiliar with the concept of a balanced scorecard.

Required:

(a) For the benefit of the Management Board, prepare a briefing on the concept of a balanced scorecard, which also analyses its usefulness for The Royal Botanical Gardens. **(10 marks)**

(b) Discuss the process you would employ to develop a suitable balanced scorecard for The Royal Botanical Gardens and give examples of measures that would be incorporated within it. **(15 marks)**

(Total: 25 marks)

BUSINESS UNIT PERFORMANCE

82 TRANSFER PRICES

P plc is a multi-national conglomerate company with manufacturing divisions, trading in numerous countries across various continents. Trade takes place between a number of the divisions in different countries, with partly-completed products being transferred between them. Where a transfer takes place between divisions trading in different countries, it is the policy of the Board of P plc to determine centrally the appropriate transfer price without reference to the divisional managers concerned. The Board of P plc justifies this policy to divisional managers on the grounds that its objective is to maximise the conglomerate's post-tax profits and that the global position can be monitored effectively only from the Head Office.

Required:

(a) Explain and critically appraise the possible reasoning behind P plc's policy of centrally determining transfer prices for goods traded between divisions operating in different countries. **(13 marks)**

(b) Discuss the ethical implications of P plc's policy of imposing transfer prices on its overseas divisions in order to maximise post-tax profits. **(12 marks)**

(Total: 25 marks)

83 DIVISIONAL ACTIONS

Within a large group, divisional managers are paid a bonus which can represent a large proportion of their annual earnings. The bonus is paid when the budgeted divisional profit for the financial year is achieved or exceeded.

Meetings of divisional boards are held monthly and attended by the senior management of the division, and senior members of group management.

With the end of the financial year approaching, there had been discussions in all divisional board meetings of forecast profit for the year, and whether budgeted profit would be achieved. In three board meetings, for divisions that were having difficulty in achieving budgeted profits, the following divisional actions had been discussed. In each case, the amounts involved would have been material in determining whether the division would achieve its budget:

Division A had severely cut spending on training, and postponed routine re-painting of premises.

Division B had re-negotiated a contract for consultancy services. It was in the process of installing Total Quality Management (TQM) systems, and had originally agreed to pay progress payments to the consultants, and had budgeted to make these payments. It had re-negotiated that the consultancy would invoice the division with the total cost only when the work was completed in the next financial year.

Division C had persuaded some major customers to take early delivery, in the current financial year, of products originally ordered for delivery early in the next financial year. This would ensure virtually nil stock at year end.

Required:

Discuss the financial accounting, budgeting, ethical and motivational issues which arise from these divisional actions.

Comment on whether any group management action is necessary. **(25 marks)**

84 HOSPITAL

(a) Briefly explain how the measurement of divisional performance differs when assessing the achievement of strategic targets as distinct from operational targets.

(7 marks)

(b) J is a hospital that supplies a wide range of healthcare services. The government has created a competitive internal market for healthcare by separating the function of service delivery from purchasing. The government provides funds for local health organisations to identify healthcare needs and to purchase services from different organisations which actually supply the service. The service suppliers are mainly hospitals.

J is a service supplier and has established contracts with some purchasing organisations. The healthcare purchasing organisations are free to contract with any supplier for the provision of their healthcare requirements.

Previously, J was organised and controlled on the basis of functional responsibility. This meant that each specialist patient function, such as medical, nursing and pharmacy services, was led by a manager who held operational and financial responsibility for its activities throughout the hospital. J now operates a system of control based on devolved financial accountability. Divisions comprising different functions have been established and are responsible for particular categories of patient care such as general medical or general surgical services. Each division is managed by a senior medical officer.

J's Board recognises that it exists in a competitive environment. It believes there is a need to introduce a system of divisional appraisal. This measures performance against strategic as well as operational targets, using both financial and non-financial criteria. The Board is concerned to develop a system which improves the motivation of divisional managers. This will encourage them to accept responsibility for achieving strategic as well as operational organisational targets. In particular, the Board wishes to encourage more contractual work to supply services to healthcare purchasing organisations from both within and outside its local geographical area. It is a clear aim of the Board that a cultural change in the management of the organisation will result from the implementation of such a system.

Required:

Discuss the issues which the Board of J should take into consideration in establishing a system of performance measurement for divisional managers in order to ensure the attainment of its strategic targets. **(18 marks)**

(Total: 25 marks)

LEAN SYSTEMS, R&D AND PRODUCT AND PROCESS DEVELOPMENT

85 INDICATORS

The introduction of indicators to measure operational and managerial performance has grown within organisations over recent years. It has been argued that managers will concentrate only on the indicators upon which their performance is measured. As a consequence of this, they disregard the impact on quality of service which is not subject to a performance indicator.

Required:

(a) Discuss the view that managers will pay attention only to the indicators upon which their performance is measured to the detriment of quality of service. State, with justification, whether you agree or disagree with this argument. **(8 marks)**

(b) Many organisations believe that the introduction of total quality management (TQM) is a method of achieving distinctive competitive advantage.

Discuss the possible impact of performance indicators on the behaviour of operational managers when introducing TQM as a competitive strategy. **(8 marks)**

(c) In the light of your answers to Parts (a) and (b), explain how an organisation can ensure that TQM is successfully implemented. **(9 marks)**

(Total: 25 marks)

86 HOT-SPOTS MULTIMEDIA

Hot-Spots Multimedia is a company that provides publishing services both in traditional media and in digital form.

Hot-Spots employs a number of full-time writers who are experts in various fields. Work that requires expertise which is not available in-house is contracted out to freelancers and then edited in-house. The company also employs a number of editorial staff and project managers, and a studio for production of written material and graphics and for basic web-design work. Expert programmers are employed to handle the more complex multimedia applications and database-driven work.

The company has an excellent reputation in the industry for delivering high-quality work using the very latest technologies available. However, it frequently over-runs the deadlines set by its customers.

Hot-Spots is considering tendering bids for work producing educational and public information material for a number of local and central government bodies in its country of operation. One of the criteria for a successful bid appears to be ISO 9001 certification.

The managing director, Dr Bob Ball, is a sceptical about this. He worked for a firm that was ISO 9001 certified in the early 1990s and as a result of that experience he takes the view that ISO 9001 is only about rules and procedures. He feels it will stifle creativity and hinder rather than help the quality of the work of his staff.

He has heard, however, that ISO 9001 has been considerably revised since its introduction (though he is not aware of the details), and he is now willing to consider ISO 9001 certification if it will help his firm obtain new work.

You are required to prepare a report for the managing director outlining the issues that will need to be addressed before the company can consider attempting to obtain ISO 9001 certification. **(25 marks)**

87 RUS PLC

RUS plc operates a chain of hotels. Its strategy has been to provide medium-priced accommodation for business people during the week and for families at weekends.

The market has become increasingly competitive and RUS plc has decided to change its strategy. In future, it will provide 'a high-quality service for the discerning guest'.

You are required:

(a) to explain the relevance of a programme of 'total quality management' for RUS plc in the implementation of its new strategy **(10 marks)**

(b) to summarise the financial and organisational implications of RUS plc's new strategy **(5 marks)**

(c) to discuss the contribution that RUS plc's management accountant could make to the new strategy. **(10 marks)**

(Total: 25 marks)

KNOWLEDGE MANAGEMENT

88 XYZ PARTNERSHIP

The XYZ Partnership is a firm of surveyors operating from seven locations in one country. Each of the 72 partners produces detailed plans for new buildings ranging from individual houses through to small factories and large office blocks. There are 250 support and administration staff distributed evenly around the different offices. The partners and staff use a variety of software ranging from basic word processing and spreadsheets through to specialist computer-assisted drawing and project management packages.

The normal work method within each office has been to implement and use software required in that office with little or no regard for the use of common software. Communication between each office has been limited to typed memos.

After gaining some significant contracts in the last few months, partners and staff have found themselves working from more than one office. One specific difficulty that has arisen is the inability to use the different computer systems because of a lack of standard software. Many partners and staff are also using the Internet at home. The senior partners are now realising that there are synergies to be gained from networking all offices using a Wide Area Network and are considering the implementation of this system.

Required:

(a) Explain how knowledge of the Internet may have helped the senior partners identify deficiencies in the IT systems at XYZ. **(10 marks)**

(b) Discuss the problems involved in implementing a suitable information-sharing system in XYZ. **(15 marks)**

(Total: 25 marks)

89 VNS CHARITY

The VNS charity monitors and collects information on various diseases affecting the brain. It was established in 1960 to provide hospitals with detailed statistical information concerning the effects of these diseases and provide recommendations for treatments. This information is generally well received by hospitals and has led to a fall in mortality rates. Over the years, the charity has established a large database of information, including numerous case studies from people showing how they have learnt to live with the different diseases.

The charity is now receiving over 250 telephone calls each day from hospital staff and members of the public requesting information. Staff within the charity are becoming over-worked trying to provide this information. Other important activities such as updating the database of cases and supplying statistical information on the diseases to hospitals are also not being carried out in a timely fashion. A few members of staff are actually retaining information deliberately because they see power in retaining access to the information rather than sharing the information with colleagues through a database.

To try to alleviate these issues, the management of the charity has decided to implement an extranet, and allow registered users of the charity full access to the database of information. This solution will involve diverting over 25% of the charity's budget to the production and maintenance of the extranet and associated hardware. Existing staff will be required to re-input information in specific formats for internal statistics collation and extranet use. The extranet database will be updated daily and staff will be responsible for vetting applications for access to the extranet.

Required:

(a) Evaluate the potential use of an extranet within the VNS charity. **(15 marks)**

(b) Identify and evaluate other information-sharing systems that the VNS charity could implement to provide information to third parties. **(10 marks)**

(Total: 25 marks)

90 AHM COMPANY

The AHM Company manufactures luxury sports cars in three factories located within one country. Each factory manufactures a specific model of car and maintains its own production, administration, sales and research departments. Although this effectively replicates all the company systems in each factory, the directors consider that the benefits of local control far outweigh the tangible costs of maintaining those systems.

There is very little communication between the three factories and there are no direct computer links.

The research staff at each factory have recently queried the overall policy of the directors regarding the communication infrastructure. At their first joint staff meeting for five years, the research staff found that many of the projects they were working on were duplicated in the company's other factories. They also found that some useful ideas from the directors and workers had been ignored because they had not been brought to the attention of research staff. Finally, the group discussion also identified four separate potential improvements to models that individual research workers had not found.

Required:

(a) Discuss the organisational, social and technological barriers to sharing of knowledge in the AHM Company, commenting on the impact of these on the efficiency of information transfer within the organisation. **(13 marks)**

(b) Evaluate the different systems that could be used to facilitate the sharing of knowledge between the three groups of research staff. **(12 marks)**

(Total: 25 marks)

91 JN INTERNATIONAL BANK

Required:

(a) Compare and contrast explicit and tacit knowledge, explaining any problems in sharing each type of knowledge.

You should provide examples to illustrate your answer. **(10 marks)**

(b) JN is an international banking organisation with 2,583 branches located across 128 countries. A separate information system is maintained in each country. Each system includes:

- corporate accounting and credit control
- publishing research (within extranet access for specific clients)
- ordering IT equipment
- customer profiling
- informing staff of regulatory changes.

This has given JN a distinct advantage over its competitors as the bank has been able to focus on the requirements of the national rather than international markets.

However, the international Board of JN has started to notice some weaknesses in this method of development, particularly regarding system incompatibility and comparative weaknesses in information provision in some countries compared to others. The Board has noted that some countries have implemented particularly useful systems or have personnel highly skilled in some areas, but these systems and skills are not shared for the benefit of JN as a whole.

The Director of Information Systems has recommended to the Board that standardised information systems based on a Groupware product are implemented throughout JN. These will allow distinct benefits of sharing information on a global basis and enable the Board to obtain organisation-wide information on a more timely basis.

Required:

Evaluate whether the use of Groupware will assist information transfer and sharing within JN. **(15 marks)**

(Total: 25 marks)

INFORMATION STRATEGY AND IMPLEMENTATION

92 SYSTEMS, TECHNOLOGY AND MANAGEMENT STRATEGY

(a) Explain what Information Systems strategy, Information Technology strategy and Information Management strategy are, and the link between them. **(10 marks)**

(b) The Information Systems strategy within the MG organisation has been developed over a number of years. However, the basic approach has always remained unchanged. An IT budget is agreed by the Board each year. This budget is normally 5% to 10% higher than the previous year's to allow for increases in prices and upgrades to computer systems.

Systems are upgraded in accordance with user requirements. Most users accept that the IT systems are there to perform tasks such as recording day-to-day transactions and providing access to accounting and other information as necessary. There is no Executive Information System (EIS). Benchmarking and similar comparisons with other companies are not performed.

The Board tends to rely on reports from junior managers to control the business. While these reports generally provide the information requested by the Board, they are focused at a tactical level and tend to contain some annoying errors and occasional omissions.

Required:

Evaluate the Information Systems strategy of the MG organisation, recommending any changes that you consider appropriate. **(15 marks)**

(Total: 25 marks)

93 DS

DS's main activity is the delivery of parcels. It aims to deliver parcels within 24 hours of collection to any place in the country in which it operates. It maintains 27 distribution warehouses – one in each of the major population centres of the country. Each warehouse has a fleet of delivery vans as well as warehouse, administrative and distribution staff. The company's head office is located in the capital city.

Current computer system

DS's current computer system is described below:

The main network is a Wide Area Network (WAN), with each distribution warehouse being linked to a central database via a dedicated landline. Each warehouse itself runs a Local Area Network (LAN) with a central minicomputer maintaining up-to-date files for that location.

The central database is updated from each warehouse every three hours on average. Update is hindered by the low baud rate of the data transmission equipment. At the same time that the central database is updated, the LAN at each warehouse receives the current copy of the database. There are 27 sites and about 6 minutes' processing data transmission time is required per site for full update of the database.

Input at each warehouse is by keyboard and VDU to the local database. Data are validated on input. Errors normally occur when packages are received from other warehouses, within a 50-kilometre radius, before the local database has been updated to receive details of those packages in transit.

Treatment of packages

Each package in the system is treated as follows:

When the package is collected from the dispatch point, the customer signs a three-part package receipt set to confirm the collection of the package. One part of this receipt is attached to the package, the customer retains the top copy and the van driver keeps the third copy. The package is taken to the local warehouse where the package receipt slip is checked against the list of expected collections for that day. Any non-collections are noted and investigated by 11.00 am the following day.

The destination for the package, taken from the package receipt slip, is entered into the company's computer. The computer works out the optimum method of transferring the package to the warehouse, which is closest to the delivery address. It then prints out a transfer list showing the proposed shipping methods and estimated timings for that package. The transfer list is attached to the package. Each transfer list has a unique reference number on it; this reference number will be input to the computer system at various stages throughout the journey of the package. This will assist the company in ascertaining where individual packages are located.

Each transfer list is read manually and the package placed on the appropriate lorry for forwarding to the distribution warehouse from which the package will be delivered to the customer. Where the package is routed via more than one warehouse, the package will be placed on the lorry for the intermediate warehouse for onward transmission to the final warehouse.

Upon receipt at each distribution warehouse, packages are again sorted using the transfer list attached to each package. Packages for other distribution warehouses are forwarded, whilst packages for local delivery are further sorted by hand into area codes for the city. The driver is given packages for his own area code, and is then expected to deliver the packages after organising his own route.

Customers sign for packages upon delivery. The goods delivery note is left with the customer, and a copy is taken back to the warehouse where details are input to the computer.

Packages are tracked through the system at each warehouse. The unique transfer list code is input to the computer as each package is dispatched or arrives at the warehouse. The computer master files are updated every three hours with this information.

The company is actively investigating the use of hand-held bar-code readers as an input device, which will be linked to a computer terminal located in each of the company's vehicles.

Required:

(a) Analyse and explain the information problems facing the company. **(10 marks)**

(b) Identify the Critical Success Factors (CSFs) that apply to DS. State the data sources that will be required to ensure that these CSFs have been met. Indicate the data that will be obtained from each source by the systems analyst to ensure that each CSF has been met. **(15 marks)**

(Total: 25 marks)

94 PR UNIVERSITY

The PR University provides tuition to degree level to 12,000 students, both on campus and by distance learning courses. The University has 34 different departments, each of which specialises in one specific area, such as economics, geography or astronomy.

Over the past 10 years, information systems have been developed in each department to meet the specific needs of that department. However, the systems are incompatible with each other and use a wide range of software applications.

The information systems are becoming expensive to operate, as well as requiring duplication of input where students study in more than one department. Additional duplication occurs when student details have to be entered into the central University database, which is used for monitoring total student numbers.

The Board of Management of the University has decided that the University should develop and implement an integrated database for future information requirements and place all existing data into a single data warehouse.

Moreover, any new system must meet the information requirements of the central database as well as those of the individual departments.

Required:

(a) (i) Evaluate the use of data within the University. **(7 marks)**

(ii) Explain how the Board of Management should use Critical Success Factors (CSFs) in revising the current information system. **(8 marks)**

(b) Discuss the disadvantages of data warehousing with specific reference to the situation at the PR University. **(10 marks)**

(Total: 25 marks)

95 PRECISION PARTS

You have recently been appointed to lead the management accounting department of W, which is a small engineering company engaged in the manufacture of precision parts. The market in which the company sells its products is small and W faces severe competition. Due to the production facilities available, the company is able to undertake only small-scale engineering work. Large-scale engineering jobs are turned away as the company does not possess the manufacturing facilities to undertake them. At best, it can act only as agent for another contractor to do the work.

The board of W is aware that the volume of work which is being turned away is increasing. This is particularly frustrating as the company is unable to utilise its capacity to the fullest extent all the time. W has achieved a steady increase in profit over the last few years. Nevertheless, the board of the company believes that it could increase profitability still further by expanding and thus being able to carry out the larger scale work which is currently being turned away.

Budgetary control and standard costing information has, for many years, been provided as the sole output of the management accounting department. The previous management accountant prided himself on the punctuality and comprehensiveness of the reports produced. Each job is priced by adding a percentage to its total cost calculated in accordance with the company's standard costing procedures. The annual cost budget is split into monthly parts and flexed to take account of a particular period's actual production. Monthly cost variances – comprising those for direct materials, direct labour, variable and fixed production overheads – are produced and provided to the relevant manager. In addition, sales price and volume variances are produced by the management accounting department each period.

The company does not have a marketing department although new customers are obtained from advertising within professional engineering journals and by attendance at trade shows. At one such recent trade show, the managing director was introduced to the concept of benchmarking. He believes that there may be advantages in W undertaking benchmarking.

Required:

(a) In consideration of the need for the board of W to be provided with information which assists its strategic decision making, comment critically on the management accounting reports currently provided. **(6 marks)**

(b) State and justify what changes you, as management accountant, would make in providing information which facilitates strategic planning in the company.

Within your answer, describe what financial and non-financial information you would supply which is different from that already provided. **(12 marks)**

(c) Explain the concept of benchmarking AND suggest how it might be applied to information for strategic planning in W. **(7 marks)**

(Total: 25 marks)

96 Q

Q is a successful company which sells computers to personal and business purchasers.

The company used to operate a structure where each sales representative was responsible for his or her own customers, with commission being paid on all sales made. Representatives maintained their own database of information to which only they had access. The system worked well; the only complaint from customers was that, when their sales representative was not available, information about their particular requirements could not be obtained. About a year ago, it was found that some orders were being lost to a major competitor because customers were refusing to wait for their sales representative to be available to provide information before an order could be placed.

Six months ago, Q implemented a new Information System based on a company-wide Intranet. The system was designed to enable all sales representatives to share information on customers; the main aim of the system was to enable any representative to access any customer details and so limit loss of orders.

The system was implemented after obtaining user input to try to ensure that the system was appropriate to the needs of most users. However, the system was implemented in some hurry, so final user acceptance and validation was not possible. In fact some last-minute changes were made by the programmers who made the programs run faster on the computer at the expense of some of the user-friendly interfaces. Because of scheduling problems with annual holidays, most users also missed being trained on the new system.

Unfortunately, the system was not particularly well received by staff. In fact, six months after implementation, it is rarely used and most representatives have reverted to using their own individual databases.

Required:

(a) Explain the reasons why representatives may have stopped using the new system. **(10 marks)**

(b) Explain the actions that can now be taken to try to persuade representatives to use the new system. **(15 marks)**

(Total: 25 marks)

CHANGE MANAGEMENT

97 GVF – ORGANISATIONAL CHANGE

Great Value Foods (GVF) is one of the country's leading supermarket chains.

Early development and growth

The company began business bottling wine in the 1940s and gradually expanded into a producer and distributor of a wide variety of products in the west of the country. In 1955 it became a limited company and in 1960 it purchased the first of two large food discount stores complete with ample parking space. By adapting strong financial control techniques, GVF managers were able to bring the stores which had been failing back into profit.

Perhaps without realising it, GVF had stumbled on to the concept of the modern out-of-town supermarket with ample parking space. Until the 1960s, car ownership in the country had been limited to the well off, but a growing economy and the increasing affluence of working people led to a wider spread of car ownership. This development contributed significantly to the success of GVF's first stores. Customers came not only from the immediate area, but included a growing body of new car owners ready to drive miles to buy low-cost groceries. Encouraged by this success, GVF began to buy up abandoned mills and warehouses in the west of the country and to offer to the public a limited selection of produce at the lowest possible price.

By 1972, GVF had 50 supermarket stores with plans to open new stores every year. In the ten years from 1972 to 1982, turnover rose from £150 million to £1,560 million, and pre-tax profits from £7.3 million to £71.6 million. At this time, GVF ranked sixth in the supermarket league. As the number of supermarkets increased, GVF embarked on a diversification programme into the non-food sector. The first move was into discount clothing, which it displayed in a section of each of its larger supermarket stores. Later, consumer electrical goods were added and then, as the success of the company continued, GVF purchased carpet and furniture retailing businesses.

Problems leading to decline

Unfortunately, in the years immediately following these acquisitions, the economy fell into recession and there was heavy price discounting in the furniture sector and increased competition. In 1983, GVF closed its furniture division at a substantial cost to the company. The carpet business managed to make a small profit even in the recession and, when the recession ended, bounced back with substantial earnings.

During the late 1970s and early 1980s, it became fashionable for families to do one major shopping trip per month to large out-of-town superstores and GVF, like the other supermarkets, prospered. But competitors were expanding, especially in the affluent east of the country. GVF also continued to open new stores, but these were in the less well-off western regions of the country. It also became clear as time progressed that GVF was losing customers to its competitors even on its own territory. The main reason for this seemed to be the competition's improved store design with its wider aisles and improved presentation of products. Shoppers evidently liked to shop in pleasant surroundings as well as to be able to buy groceries at discount prices. GVF's old formula of high-volume, low-price goods with no frills came to look outdated.

By the mid 1990s GVF superstore development was floundering, especially in the east, and its older stores were in need of refurbishment to bring them in line with consumer expectations. The organisation also needed a more efficient distribution system. Competitors had already developed their nation-wide systems with state-of-the-art technology, and this gave them a competitive edge over companies like GVF. It was not only the food side of the company's business that suffered but also the own-label clothing that had once done so well. The electrical appliance side of the business did so badly that it had to be sold off. Furthermore, while GVF had once been cheaper, this was no longer the case. Competitors had developed a much larger percentage of own-brand products and this gave them much larger gross margins than the branded goods that all the supermarkets were obliged to stock.

Though fierce competitive activity had reduced the major players in the industry to half a dozen large chains in the years since 1970, the competitive pressures and large-scale capital investment required had not deterred new entrants to the market. A few foreign competitors seeking new markets had managed to secure a foothold by offering unbranded goods at rock-bottom prices. These companies kept costs to a minimum by displaying a limited range of grocery necessities on pallets in large warehouses and offering only minimal service. This development only served to increase the pressure on GVF since the new entrants nibbled away at what had been part of GVF's traditional customer base.

A golden opportunity?

In the midst of all this pain, GVF was suddenly confronted with what seemed to be a golden opportunity. One of its competitors was experiencing trading difficulties and offered GVF the chance to purchase 60 of their stores in the east of the country. This proposition was seemingly too attractive for the management of GVF to pass by. The purchase of these stores would enable the company to double its number of superstores at a stroke and enable it to obtain the store locations in the affluent east that it had been trying to develop for a period of years. The magnitude of this opportunity can only be appreciated when account is taken of the difficulties of finding large enough sites in suitable locations in the east of the country. Many of the better locations had already been snapped up by eager competitors, and stricter planning controls imposed on local authorities by government legislation made the finding of profitable sites even more difficult and expensive. The opportunity was too much to resist and GVF borrowed the £800 million demanded and thereby doubled its outlets.

As GVF took over the management of its new clutch of eastern superstores, however, the directors realised that considerable time and funds would be required to convert them to GVF's own distinctive format and to the modern standards now expected by consumers. This not only delayed the expected revenue stream from the new outlets; it also required additional borrowing and raised the level of gearing to an uncomfortable level. As if GVF did not have enough problems, the threat of inflation forced government to raise interest rates and so the burdens on GVF increased yet more.

During all this activity, GVF had been seeking to catch up on competitors in a number of ways. It had, for instance, managed to increase its number of own-label products significantly and had just developed a new central distribution system that experts agreed was amongst the best in the country. This should have enabled GVF to supply its stores anywhere in the country efficiently and cheaply. Unfortunately, the team of directors responsible for implementing the new distribution system had been less than effective in co-ordinating the new operation and there were delays in distribution of supplies to some stores during the run up to the country's most important festive season. This resulted in a considerable loss for the company and three of the directors considered responsible for the problems were sacked.

These problems, together with an accompanying decline in profits, resulted in a fall in the share price and a general loss of confidence in the company by the stock market. There was general agreement that GVF had paid too much for its 60 eastern stores and that a rights issue would be necessary for the company to reduce its debt burden. These problems came to a head when the major institutional shareholders pressed for changes in senior management. Eventually the chief executive/chairman was forced to resign and a non-executive director ran the company until a new chief executive was appointed.

A new beginning

When the new Chief Executive Officer, Mrs B Bilder, took up her appointment, she found that the company had too many layers of management, narrow functional attitudes and a controlling bureaucratic head office culture. Furthermore, the business was no longer responding to customer needs.

Required:

(a) In the light of the information available from the case scenario, summarise the actions required to turn the company around. **(9 marks)**

(b) In order to make the company competitive again, a considerable amount of organisational change will be required in GVF. In the light of this, describe:

  (i) the most likely sources of resistance to change for a company facing similar circumstances to GVF **(6 marks)**

  (ii) any model of organisational change, and explain how it might be used by the new Chief Executive Officer as a guide for implementing change in GVF. **(10 marks)**

(Total: 25 marks)

98 CC PLC

CC plc is a company employing 2,560 staff in 20 different offices within one country. The company offers a wide range of specialist consultancy advice to the building and construction industry. This includes advice on materials to be used, relevant legislation (including planning applications) and appropriate sources of finance.

The information to meet client requirements is held within each office of the company. Although most clients are serviced by a single office, a lot of the information used is duplicated between the different offices. This is not surprising given that legislation and other standard information such as details of materials used are the same for the whole country.

In the past there has been no attempt to share data because of the cost of transferring information and the lack of trust on the part of staff in other offices. Some senior managers tend to keep part of client data confidential to themselves.

The company has recently provided all employees with e-mail for communications within CC plc and to clients. Software with Internet access is also available so that staff can obtain updated planning information from appropriate websites. The hardware in the company is quite old and only just meets the minimum specification for these purposes.

The Marketing Director has suggested that an intranet should be established in the company so that common information can be shared rather than each office maintaining its own data. This suggestion is meeting with some resistance from all grades of staff.

Required:

Comment on the organisational and human reasons why information may not become more widely available in CC plc, and suggest methods for overcoming these problems.

(25 marks)

99 CITYGO

The CityGo Bus company is currently one of the subsidiary companies and a regional operating division of a public corporation – The City Bus Corporation. As part of the privatisation strategy of the national government all the operating divisions of the City Bus Corporation have been separately sold by tender-based offer for sale. Some divisions have been acquired by private transport operators while the CityGo division has been acquired through a management buyout (MBO) led by the existing general manager of CityGo, Jim Ryan.

The MBO team comprises Jim Ryan, John Smith the engineering manager, Geoff Rodriguez the operations manager and six second tier managers. The MBO team have each subscribed for share capital using personal savings and borrowings and the balance of the equity finance has been raised through venture capitalists. The MBO team have raised the remainder of the acquisition price through a medium-term bank loan secured against the assets of CityGo. The employees of CityGo have not been offered shares in the new business.

The management buyout contract covers all the assets of CityGo. These comprise a small office building, five garage depots from which the 20 CityGo bus routes operate, 150 buses and all engineering and maintenance equipment at the garages. CityGo's existing bus routes are contracted to it for a period of two years after which other operators will be allowed to run services over the routes. The newly privatised CityGo will have the freedom to extend its route network nationally if it wishes and to expand into commercial operations such as coach hire and coach holidays. A structure chart of CityGo can be found in Exhibit 1.

Exhibit 1

Jim Ryan
General Manager

John Smith	Geoff Rodriguez	Rita Moran
Engineering Manager	Operations Manager	Finance and administration
Garage operations	Bus drivers	Accounting
Bus maintenance	Bus conductors	Personnel
Stores	Inspectors	Secretarial services
Building services	Operations planners	Catering
170 staff	320 staff	100 staff

In early September 20X5, following the announcement of the successful tender bids, the CityGo MBO team had the first post buyout meeting. Jim Ryan was both delighted and deeply concerned. The management team had a little over three months before the transfer date of assets and the start of privatised operations on the first day of January 20X6. Jim Ryan opened the meeting.

'Well we won the tender but the price was very tight and the competition will be intense as soon as the routes become fully competitive in January 20X8. As I see it our strengths are our first class experience of bus operations but we have a number of weaknesses that have to be attended to immediately. I believe that these fall into four main areas.

First, we do not have a marketing department or any marketing expertise as we have never had to sell our services or compete over routes. Now however we can fix our own prices, bid to win other route operations and move into commercial activities.

Second, our computing systems are totally integrated into the City Bus Corporation's systems. Our internal management accounts are almost non-existent and most management reports are directed at the corporation's management team, not at CityGo's management. In fact we have never been able to devolve budget responsibility down to our key line managers in operations and maintenance.

Third, we are overstaffed, completely unionised and with a workforce who in general do not support the government's bus privatisation initiative. Our tender bid assumed that we would be able to increase productivity by at least 25 per cent over the next two years.

Finally, what about the culture of the business? Few, if any, of our managers, supervisors or employees have any real idea about customer care, quality or competitive advantage. In fact there has been very limited formal management training and development.'

After the meeting Jim Ryan approached Rita Moran, the finance and administration manager. Rita had only been with CityGo for six months since leaving a medium-sized manufacturing division of an international group. Jim informed Rita that he expects her to play an important role in the fundamental changes, which he sees as being needed over the next few months. She is the only member of the senior management team with experience outside the bus operations industry. Jim Ryan is seeking Rita's help in a number of areas: setting up a marketing unit, implementing new systems, training managers in finance and changing the prevailing culture.

Required:

Explain why you think that Jim Ryan believes that organisational culture is so important to the success of his plans and suggest a strategy for creating and maintaining the culture changes, which he feels are needed at the CityGo Bus Company.

(25 marks)

Section 3

ANSWERS TO SECTION A-TYPE QUESTIONS

1 T PLC

Key answer tips

This case study requires a detailed application of three strategic planning tools: PEST analysis, gap analysis, and Ansoff's product/market growth vector. You must provide a commentary on the proposed investment project described in the scenario.

(a) The following external factors are relevant to T plc:

Political factors

T plc currently dominates its national telecommunications market with an 85% share of the market. The company will be under political pressure from the national government to reduce its dominance by opening up the national telecom market to competition and reducing prices for telecom products charged to consumers.

The government has appointed an industry regulator to be directly involved in the control of the telecom industry and T plc no doubt will be under close scrutiny. Political forces will be a major factor affecting the operations and plan of T plc.

Economic factors

There are three main economic elements that T plc needs to consider. These are:

- Shareholder wealth

  T plc's shareholders are a major stakeholder group who will have economic objectives of profit maximisation and rising share value.

- The contribution of the telecommunications industry to the national economy

  The telecommunications industry plays a major role in contributing towards economic growth and prosperity. T plc has a responsibility to develop new technology and to provide a reliable, value for money service to its users.

- The economies of foreign countries

  The economic conditions in each foreign country T plc operates in should be considered e.g. foreign currency exchange rates and national economic boom and slump cycles.

Social factors

Telecommunication products are social products used by people for many reasons. The company should ensure that it understands the social role of the industry and provides a reliable service. The company should also portray itself as socially responsible, have a set of social objectives and keep in close contact with the consumers e.g. by producing a range of services for elderly citizens who are more dependent on telephones for obtaining help when needed.

Technical factors

The telecommunications industry is a high-tech industry that is currently very dynamic. T plc is the market leader in the industry and must be innovative to maintain its competitive advantage. The company must invest in research and development to ensure it has a constant supply of new products in the years ahead to replace those going into the decline stage of their product life cycle.

(b) (i) By relating products to markets, Ansoff identified four main strategies for achieving long-term growth. The following diagram shows this:

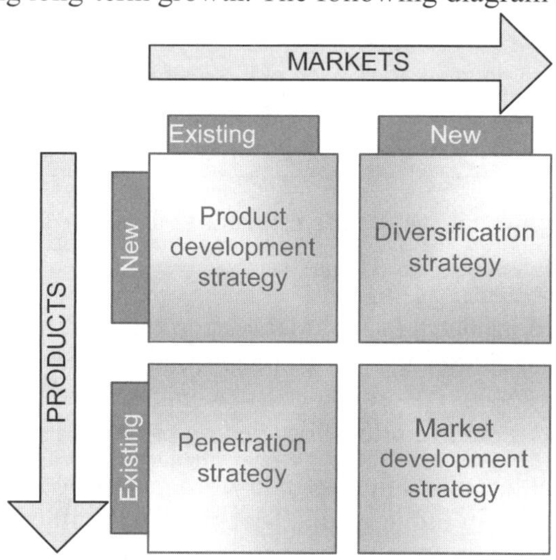

Using this model the potential market opportunities are as follows:

Market penetration strategies

T plc currently has 85% of its national market. There is little scope for obtaining any growth by increasing its market share. Most households and businesses will have a conventional telephone line so some of the company's products will be at the maturity stage of their life cycle offering little prospect of growth. Some market growth might be achieved by getting existing customers to use the telephone more.

A market penetration strategy only offers limited growth prospects.

Product development strategy

This strategy involves introducing new products in existing markets. T plc has already achieved a good track record for new product development and with continued investment in research and development should maintain its momentum. There is a lot of market opportunity in the industry for this strategy e.g. further developments in mobile phone and Internet technology.

Market development strategy

T plc has pursued a successful strategy of expanding into foreign markets with existing products. It currently has operations in North America, Europe, India and the Far East. In T plc's latest annual report, the Chairman refers to developing these markets further. Tremendous opportunities exist in additional developing countries such as those in Africa where the company currently has operations.

Diversification strategy

This involves introducing new products to new markets and is a high-risk strategy. T plc is a large profitable company with a prospector (innovative) culture. The company should evaluate carefully the risk of any diversification strategy and if opportunities exist they should be considered e.g. digital television technology.

The company should pursue all four strategies with the main emphasis on product development and market development, as these exploit the company's main strengths of expertise in research and development, and growth in foreign markets.

(ii) The planning gap can be defined as the difference between:

- the stakeholder's long-term expectations for the undertaking

and

- results from following existing policies and plans

expressed on a quantified scale such as profit, sale or ROCE.

Ansoff's product/market growth model can be used to show four strategies that can fill the planning gap. It is important to appreciate that all, one or any of the four strategies can fill the gap, depending on the situation. This can be shown by the following illustration:

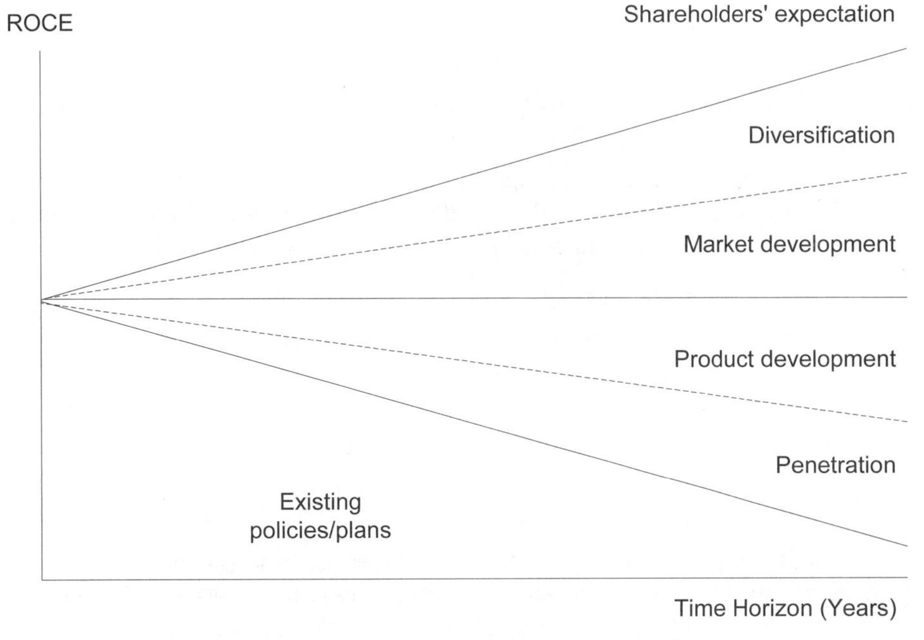

(c) T plc's planning gap can be calculated as follows:

	£m
Target Return	
Capital employed £22,150m × 20%	4,430
Less Profit before interest and tax	(3,323)
Planning gap (shortfall in profit)	1,107

The planned investment project will increase the company's market share from 85% to 95%, i.e. 10% increase.

This will achieve an increase in sale revenue of:

£16,613m × 10/85 =	£1,954m
Variable costs will be £1,954 × 80% =	(£1,563m)
Annual contribution =	£391m
Deduct the annual expenditure on the project of	£200m
Then increase =	£191m

The entire investment will be written off over the three-year period with no residual value.

Over the three-year period the project will have an NPV at an 11% cost of capital of:

Net annual cash flow £191m × annuity factor of 2.444 = £467m

The project's annual ROCE is $\frac{\text{£191m}}{\text{£200m}} = 95.5\%$

(d) Assuming the information provided is accurate, the project will reduce T plc's planning gap by £191m per annum for the next three years.

This will leave (£1,107m – £191m) = £916m remaining to be filled using other strategies.

The investment project appears to be very attractive as it provides a very high ROCE and will increase T plc's overall performance. Before a final decision is made, T plc's management should consider the potential risks. These appear to be:

- forecasting error
- the possible reaction of the industry regulator if the company's market share rises above its current 85%.

2 B PLC

Key answer tips

Part (a) of the question requires a corporate appraisal in which you should try to give equal consideration to strengths, weaknesses, opportunities and threats. Part (b) requires the evaluation of two possible strategic options which should include an assessment of likely competitor responses. Part (c) requires recommendations to be made regarding management accounting information relating to the environmental aims. Energy usage, waste levels, the use of recoverable resources wherever possible, and the replacement of non-renewable resources (if applicable) should be included here. Part (d) concerns strategic options and could be answered by reference to Ansoff's Growth Vector model.

(a) Corporate appraisal is a critical assessment of the strengths and weaknesses, opportunities and threats (SWOT) analysis in relation to the internal and environmental factors affecting an entity in order to establish its condition prior to the preparation of the long-term plan.

Strengths

The company has been operating in the cosmetics and skin product sector for more than 20 years, so the management will have accumulated significant experience of operating in this business area in the UK and overseas.

The company still has 90% of the naturally-based cosmetics and hair-care market. Even after 20 years of being open to competition, competitors still only amount to a 10% market share. B plc is seen as being the obvious choice as the place to go to buy environmentally friendly cosmetics, a message that has been maintained through working to offer high quality products and good customer service.

The company is still highly profitable, earning operating profits last year of £26 million on sales of £175 million, an operating profit percentage of 15%.

The company's sales are increasing rapidly, rising from £154 million two years ago to £175 million last year. This is a 14% rise in sales from year to year.

Weaknesses

Some observers have suggested that the company will need to abandon its environmentally friendly aims if it is to compete in the current aggressive corporate climate. However, the Chairman is adamant that this shall not be the case. Thus the company seems to be pursuing mutually inconsistent objectives; to grow and prosper, while at the same time to be true to good environmental principles.

It has to be said that, in the eyes of many customers, the company's environmental principles are a key strength, so the management of B plc should think long and hard before they change the company's strategy in this area.

Opportunities

The public internationally are becoming more concerned with the impact that companies have on the environment, so B plc's leadership and reputation in operating responsibly will prove increasingly beneficial. Initiatives such as campaigning against animal testing in the cosmetics industry will also attract customers, providing the company with a significant competitive advantage over other companies.

Since 75% of the company's retail outlets are located outside the UK, managers will already have experience of operating abroad, which will help in continuing a successful overseas expansion programme.

Threats

Competition is increasing, with B plc's share of its core market having declined from 100% to 90% over the past 20 years. The increased competition, together with difficult trading conditions generally, has led to a reduction in reported profit last year. The enlargement of the head office facilities has increased the burden of overheads and must be made to pay for itself.

Environmentally responsible retailing may go out of fashion, particularly if the economic downturn continues. Consumers may no longer be willing to pay premium prices for natural products if they are short of disposable income. The Chairman seems to have pinned the company's colours to the mast and insists that, no matter what happens elsewhere, the company's 'green' credentials will be maintained. Such a lack of flexibility may prove costly if the market-place changes.

Some experts believe that products which have not been tested on animals are inherently less safe than conventional cosmetics which have been so tested. It might only take one widely publicised health scare for the public to change its attitude toward the testing of cosmetics on animals, which would have serious implications for the company's future.

The company's external activities such as campaigning for human rights and helping the homeless cost money, which has to be recovered through sales of products. The company may find that it has a higher cost base than its competitors and so cannot compete on price terms, which become more important as the economic downturn continues.

(b) The two possible strategic options to be evaluated are:

(i) invest in quality improvement, or

(ii) increase the level of promotion to attract a higher market share.

Consider first the most likely outcomes:

Quality improvement

An investment of £50m next year would result in an expected net benefit of £37.996m arising over a four-year period. This equates to a benefit of £0.76 per £ invested.

Increased promotion

An investment of £10m next year would result in an expected net benefit of £30m arising over a four-year period. This equates to a benefit of £3m per £ invested.

It thus appears from considering the most likely outcomes that the company should invest £10m next year in boosting the promotional activities.

Considering the best and worst outcomes from the quality improvement option, the investment of £50m could lead to a gross return of £100m over four years if the market response were strong, or £60m over four years if the response were weak. These results can be presented more clearly in a table.

	Investment		*Net benefit over four years*
	£m		£m
Quality	50	Expected	37.996
		Lowest	10
		Highest	50
Promotion	10	Expected	30

Which of these options the management should choose depends on the managers' attitude to risk. A strongly risk-adverse management would choose the promotion option, to avoid the possibility of earning a benefit as low as £10m. A risk-seeking management would choose the quality option, being attracted by the possibility of earning a net £50m. A risk-neutral management would probably choose the promotion option for the argument given above, that it earns a net £3 for each £ invested in the plan as well as to avoid the possibility of earning only £10m from a £50m investment in quality improvement.

The most important reservation that one should have concerning the above analysis centres on the inevitable inaccuracy of the forecast numbers. In practice it is impossible to forecast accurately the results of improving quality or increasing promotional activity. The estimated costs of each option are likely to be reasonably accurate, but the estimated cash inflows will be no more than educated best guesses.

So in the real world, managers will take such decisions on the basis of their 'gut instincts' after having studied the quantitative analysis. These gut instincts will include them taking account of the uncertainties inherent in the figures and their attitude to risk, as well as their bias towards one of the options. Production managers would unconsciously favour the quality option, while sales managers would favour the promotional option. At the end of the day a decision must be taken, and it might be taken as much on the political muscle of the individual managers in the company as it is on the basis of computational analysis.

The potential reaction of competitors to either option must also be taken into consideration. If B plc chooses the quality option, competitors will most likely try to match the new higher quality levels, though this will take some time to achieve. If B plc chooses the promotional option, competitors will most likely increase their own promotional spend to negate B plc's advantage. Thus the difference in reaction arises because of the time lag involved in competitors recruiting new skilled employees or implementing new processes to achieve the higher quality levels.

The manager at B plc must consider competitor's likely reactions as part of the managers' process of reaching a decision between the two possible options. Some sort of scenario planning in advance would be valuable, so that any areas of vulnerability to counter-attack have been identified before the main option is implemented.

(c) To a company like B plc, which uses its green credentials as a key selling point, environmental areas will feature strongly among the company's strategic aims. Therefore the management accounting function of the company must monitor this area and provide regular reports to the directors to assist them in assessing the company's progress in this area. These reports should highlight both the costs and the benefits of following an environmentally responsible line. Topics that could usefully be covered include the following.

The efficient use of energy

B plc is committed to promoting the efficient use of energy, so the various energy costs incurred at each of the company's sites should be identified and reported clearly. In order to drive down energy costs, budgets could be set with each year's energy usage lower than the previous year. Managers are then free to develop their own methods of meeting the budgets, by insulating against heat loss, by using low energy lighting, by not heating warehouse areas, etc.

Keeping waste to a minimum

The actual volume and cost of waste materials should be reported and compared with budgeted figures. For example, expensive packaging should be refused from suppliers and not provided to customers. Once customers have been educated not to expect flashy packaging, this will become an attraction for the company's products which also saves the company money. Special investigations into the company's activities could be carried out to identify further possible cost savings in this area.

Using recoverable resources where possible

All the company's brochures and published statements should be printed on recycled paper; any output not on such paper should be reported to senior managers together with any special reason why this was so.

The company could sell liquids (e.g. shampoo, bath oil, etc) by volume by inviting customers to bring empty bottles to the shop to be filled with the product they want. Again, this will save the company money and boost the company's green image. Managers should be provided with reports of what proportion of the company's products are sold in this way.

Legislation

A large body of environmental legislation now exists with which the company must comply. Managers could be presented with reports of the extent to which the company is meeting these rules, together with comparative data of the extent to which competitor companies are complying.

Other matters

Since there is a fear that the costs of the company's environmentally-friendly objectives may render products uneconomic, management accountants should report the unit cost of the green policy as part of each product line. That way, management are aware of the implications of the policy in their pricing and investment decisions.

Attention to environmental matters should be seen as pervasive to all the company's operations, rather than being a separate topic for reporting to management. For example, even though a potential new project has a positive net present value, it could still be rejected if it contravenes the company's environmental aims. Similarly a new product line might be rejected even though it is forecast to generate a positive contribution, because it is inconsistent with the company's aims.

Finally, management accountants could be responsible for establishing a reward structure for employees and managers that reflects the importance of environmental matters to the company. Therefore, the usual sort of scheme to award bonuses based on growth in sales or profits may not be appropriate. Internal bonuses might be given to staff members who propose successful ideas for the company to act more responsibly towards the environment.

(d) B plc has decided to remain true to its environmental responsibilities, so managers must make the best of this strategy. There will be costs involved in following this strategy (e.g. paying to process waste into safe inert materials or recycling it wherever possible). However, there will also be benefits as B plc will earn a competitive advantage in the market place as a result of its reputation for responsible environmental behaviour.

B plc should therefore publicise its green behaviour as widely as possible, stressing for example that no animals suffered during testing of the company's cosmetics. This will be a powerful message among the shop's customers (mainly young and female) who can sympathise with the message.

The company's strategic options for the future can be summarised in Ansoff's product-market growth vector as drawn below:

	Existing product	*New product/service*
Existing market	Internal efficiency Market penetration	Product development
New market	Market development	Diversification

Market penetration involves continuing to sell naturally-based cosmetics in existing markets, so looking for increased sales of current products in the existing shops.

Market development involves selling the current products in new markets; we know that the company has embarked on this option since 75% of the retail outlets are outside the UK and the company is still expanding.

Product development depends on the company's research and development activities which are described as being extensive, both in the UK and Latin America. This should lead to new products being offered in the company's shops.

Diversification involves the company moving outside the area of cosmetics sales and entering new markets. However, the company can still trade on its reputation for greenness. Perhaps a clothing company could be bought so that eco-clothes could be sold, or a travel company could be bought so that eco-tours could be offered. Diversification offers the riskiest strategic way forward.

The turnover of B plc increased last year, so there is still an appetite for the company's goods in the market. It is the responsibility of management to translate this appetite into economic success in the future that meets the company's growth aspirations while remaining true to the long-standing environmental responsibility that has been the company's hallmark.

3 WG PLC

Key answer tips

This question requires a demonstration of knowledge from across the syllabus – as will many case study questions. In Part (a) you need to assess the nature of market threats that would face the organisation given the lack adequate funds for product development. In Part (b) you should give consideration to the fact that there is conflict between the two objectives of WG plc. Part (c)(i) requires a demonstration of Cost-Volume-Profit analysis and Direct Product Profitability analysis, using relatively simple figures. In Part c(ii) you could apply the 4Ps model to improve the marketing mix. Part (d) focuses upon the practical considerations of strategic alliances, which could easily be included as part of a future case study. Note the importance of a knowledge of techniques from earlier studies.

(a) For any company to retain its position as market leader, it must introduce a continual stream of new products, services or ideas to replace those that are declining. WG plc holds a position as one of the leaders in the global pharmaceutical industry, so it is important that it is able to introduce new products to replace existing ones when patents expire. Because the development phase in the pharmaceutical industry is very long and very risky, it is important that WG plc invests regularly in a programme of research and development (R&D). This will help to ensure that it has new products and services that will meet both its profitability objective and its aim of developing innovative medicines and services.

It has been a well-established idea for many years that products and services follow a '**life cycle**' that affects the current rate of sale and, more importantly, has significant implications for the strategic options for the future. The theory breaks the economic life of a product into a number of stages. The following diagram shows six stages.

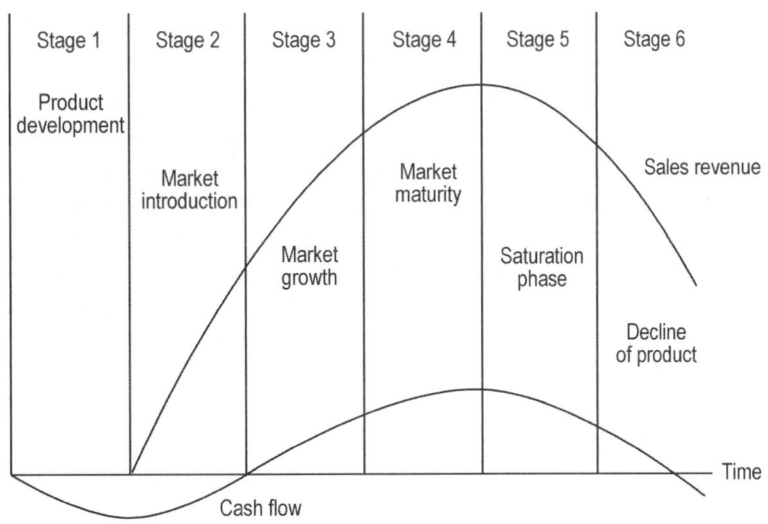

Being aware of the fact that a product has a life cycle can become the foundation for policies and practices aimed at building up the market. The best advantage it gives is in the launching of a new product.

The **Boston matrix** attempts to relate critical strategic issues to the different phases of the product life cycle. Using the rate of market growth and relative market share, the matrix classifies products as either cash cows, stars, problem children or dogs. It is likely that, at any time, companies will have products in all these categories. The position of the product or service within the matrix has implications for the cash flows of the company and it is therefore important that the managers monitor the position continuously. They must recognise that products that are currently classified as cash cows will eventually become dogs and cease to generate cash. To avoid having too many products in a low growth and low market share category, it is essential that steps are taken to ensure that the company is always developing new products that have the potential to become stars. For companies like WG plc it is imperative that adequate resources are allocated to R&D in the strategic plan.

An example of the effects of the stages in the life cycle and in the Boston matrix can be illustrated by one of WG plc's products. Four years ago one particular drug produced almost half of its turnover. Because the patent expires next year, it is expected that sales will drop to represent no more than 10% of turnover. This type of problem makes the company vulnerable to competition in the dynamic environment of the pharmaceutical industry. It is essential for WG plc to be continually developing new products, if it is to retain its dominant position in the industry.

Almost 15% of WG plc's turnover last year was spent on research and development. They have the largest research and development organisation of all pharmaceutical companies worldwide. It is clear that the managers have taken a decision to allocate resources to research activities to ensure that the company retains its competitive advantage. They are also determined to produce and develop new and innovative medicines and services worldwide to enable the company to achieve its corporate mission and objectives.

If the company did not provide the necessary resources to fund R&D, it is likely that the number of new products would not keep up with demand and the company would lose its dominant position in the pharmaceutical industry. This could lead to competitors enjoying increases in their sales, market share and, possibly, profits at WG plc's expense. R&D is evidently the source of WG plc's competitive advantage and so sufficient resources must be allocated to this activity if the company is to retain its current dominance in the pharmaceutical industry.

(b) The main objective of the company is to sustain its profitability through developing innovative medicines and services for treating patients worldwide. The company also aims to work towards eliminating those diseases that they are currently providing treatment for. These objectives are likely to involve the company both in allocating considerable resources to R&D and providing subsidies so that medicines are available to patients worldwide. Obviously, this expenditure will reduce profitability and cause a conflict between the company's objectives of profitability and performance. However, this is really a difference between short-term profitability and the long-term performance of the company and, by using resources at the present time to establish WG plc as a major player in the pharmaceutical market, it is likely that the long-term profits will increase.

Porter's Five Forces Model is used to gain insights into the competitiveness of the firm's industry. These are:

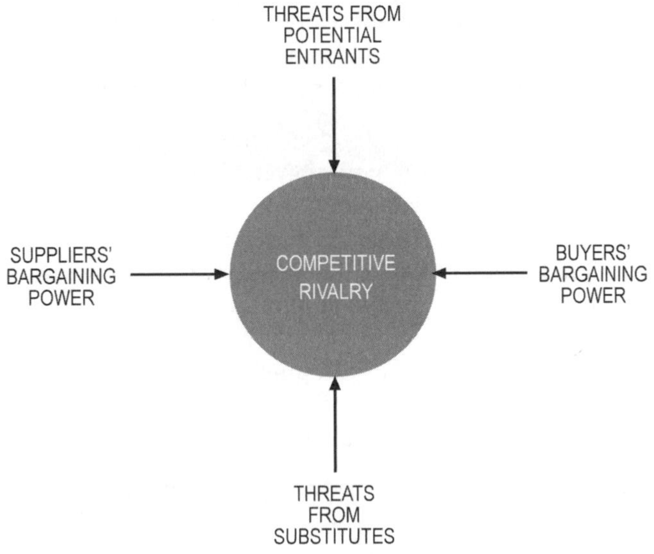

These five forces can form a framework to use when considering the objectives of WG plc:

Competitive rivalry – in the pharmaceutical industry, there are only a few large companies that compete worldwide. Patents mean that certain companies will enjoy a monopoly position for a limited period, but there is always the possibility that a substitute will be developed that will reduce the benefits to the holder of the patent rights. Conflict among existing competitors takes some form of offensive strategy. Tactics commonly used to implement an offensive strategy include product innovations and improvements, price competitions, advertising battles and increased customer services. Rivalry occurs because one or more companies feels threatened or sees a market opportunity to improve its position, although competitive moves by the initiator company usually result in counter-defensive strategies from its competitors. This interactive pattern of offensive and defensive strategies may not leave the initiating company and the industry better off, and on the contrary may leave all the companies in the industry worse off than before. WG plc must ensure that its research activities are at least as effective as its competitors, even if it reduces the company's short-term profitability, because a successful R&D programme will increase the probability of the company's long-term success.

Threats from potential entrants – increasing the extent of competition in an industry may make it more competitive in three ways: by expanding capacity without necessarily increasing market demand; by building market share to include product and marketing innovations; and by increasing costs as they bid for factors of production.

It is in the interest of WG plc to deter new entrants. There are seven main barriers to entry, two of which – capital requirements and economies of scale – affect WG plc. The long-lead, high-cost, high-risk business cycle of the pharmaceutical industry, where the number of successful products reaching the market is relatively small, has deterred all but the largest new companies from entering the market. (In fact with the exception of Janssen and Syntax no totally new company to this market has succeeded, from start up, in becoming medium-sized in the last 40 years.)

There are situations where WG plc might wish to encourage new entrants:

- They might allocate resources to develop the emerging markets although the profit generated in these countries will not be significant immediately. Additional costs will also be incurred if local management is engaged in these countries and products are modified to meet the local demand.
- It is possible that individuals, universities or small companies may make innovations, but it would probably be necessary to collaborate with a major pharmaceutical company, like WG plc, if the new product were to be marketed successfully. This means that WG plc must have funds available to recognise and develop products that emerge from these sources and current costs will increase by the expenditure on research collaboration with other companies and universities throughout the world. However, these ventures will mean that WG plc is aware of the developments that are taking place in all these institutions and will be able to benefit from any successful projects that result from the research that is undertaken.

Threats from substitute products – although patents provide a period during which the company has the sole right to make, use and sell the product, these benefits are only for a limited period. After the expiry of the patent, the competition will be expected to be fierce. The example provided in the case study shows that the sales are expected to decrease from almost 50% to no more than 10% of the company's turnover within a period of about five years. The main threat posed by substitutes is that they limit the price that a company can charge for its products. There is also a danger that the threat of a substitute may not be realised until it is too late to arrest their entry. Substitute products that warrant most attention are those that are subject to an environment that improves their price-performance trade-off with the industry's product, or produced by industries earning high profits and who have the resources available to bring them rapidly into play. Any substitute can have a major effect on the profitability of the company, and it is essential that a stream of new products is being developed continuously to provide alternatives.

Buyers' bargaining power – in an industry makes it more competitive in three ways. They can force down prices, bargain for higher quality or improved services and play competitors off against each other. All three of these will be at the expense of industry profitability. After the expiry of the patent the availability of substitutes will allow buyers to purchase medicines based on the perceived effectiveness, the pricing policy adopted and the success of the promotional activity of the company. It is, therefore, necessary for WG plc to focus attention on marketing its products successfully and drawing attention to its donation programmes. These tactics will increase its costs, especially in the short-term, but would be expected to increase the long-term profitability of the company.

Suppliers' bargaining power – suppliers can exert bargaining power over companies within an industry in two main ways. They can threaten to raise their prices and/or threaten to reduce the quality of their goods and services. The effect of this power will be to squeeze profitability out of an industry unable to recover cost increases by raising its own prices. This competitive force would not appear to be a significant factor for WG plc because they have access to supplies throughout the world. However, the importance of the R&D department within the company does mean that the company needs excellent researchers who are innovative and able to provide the stream of new products that are essential for the success of the company.

The managers of WG plc must strike a balance between the conflicting objectives of profitability and combating disease worldwide. Their decision to allocate resources to R&D expenditure is likely to ensure that the company regularly produces new products. This will assist in retaining WG plc's position as a leading company in the pharmaceutical industry and should ensure the sustained profitability of the company. Spending on R&D and collaborating with institutions outside the organisation that are researching new treatments and medicines, mean that WG plc will be able to benefit from any successful projects that result. These strategies will lead to a reduction in the short term profitability of the company whilst developing both new products and new markets, but will provide the company with the means of sustaining its profitability and also retaining its competitive advantage in terms of innovations and being a leader within this industry in the long term. If the company is successful, it will be able to allocate resources to meet the company's objective to combat disease worldwide.

(c) (i) **Cost Volume Profit analysis**, using the space (square centimetres) as the retailers' limiting factor:

	Coffstop	*Peffstill*
Net selling price per bottle	£1.50	£10.00
Buying-in cost per bottle	£0.50	£7.40
Gross contribution per bottle	£1.00	£2.60
Shelf area per bottle	18 cm^2	60 cm^2
Contribution per sq. cm	£5.56	£4.33

This chart shows that Coffstop generates the higher contribution per unit of limiting factor for the retailer.

If the **Direct Product Profitability** of both products is determined, the results are as follows:

	Coffstop	*Peffstill*
Net selling price per bottle	£1.50	£10.00
Buying-in cost per bottle	£0.50	£7.40
Gross contribution per bottle	£1.00	£2.60
Other direct costs per bottle	£0.40	£0.80
Contribution per bottle	£0.60	£1.80
Average sales in bottles	120	20
Shelf area per bottle	18 cm^2	60 cm^2
Total shelf area	2,160 cm^2	1,200 cm^2

Direct product profitability is determined by the following calculation:

$$\frac{\text{Contribution per bottle} \times \text{Average bottles sold}}{\text{Area occupied}}$$

$$\text{Coffstop} = \frac{£0.60 \times 120}{2{,}160} = £3.33$$

$$\text{Peffstill} = \frac{£0.80 \times 20}{2{,}100} = £3.00$$

Both the Cost Volume Profit and Direct Product Profitability analyses show that retailers will prefer to stock Coffstop.

(ii) The marketing plan for Coffstop to improve its competitive position should describe the specific combination of marketing elements used to achieve the objectives and satisfy the target market. The plan consists of four major factors: product or service; distribution; promotion; and price. One of the most common ways of presenting the marketing mix is by **McCarthy's Four Ps: Product, Promotion, Price and Place**.

Product includes the quality of the product as perceived by the potential customer. It involves an assessment of the product's suitability for its stated purpose, its aesthetic factors, its durability, brand factors, packaging and associated services. WG plc should emphasise its reputation in the pharmaceutical industry and the branding should link Coffstop with the other products in their portfolio. The specific qualities of the product that are likely to appeal to the consumer should be included in the marketing plan.

Promotion includes the advertisement of the product, its sales promotions, the company's public relations effort and salesmanship. The details of the Cost Volume Profit and Direct Product Profitability analyses should be used in the promotional material made available to the stockists as this provides Coffstop with a major competitive advantage over Peffstill. Because WG plc enjoys a favourable reputation as the supplier of quality products, the promotional campaign should make sure that potential consumers link the product to the company. It may be useful to target doctors, clinics and pharmacists to inform them about the qualities of Coffstop. Assuming these professionals could be suitably convinced of the medicinal properties of the product, it could lead to the product being prescribed or recommended for purchase to the consumers. Promotional activities in pharmacies and clinics could be arranged to raise the public's awareness of Coffstop and help it to become well known as an effective medicine.

Price includes the prices to the ultimate customer, discount structures for the trade, promotion pricing, methods of purchase, alternatives to outright purchase. There is a significant difference in the selling price per bottle of Coffstop, which will sell at £1.50, and its rival Peffstill, which will be priced at £10. Despite the difference in dosage, this should make Coffstop more attractive to consumers, as it will enable them to try the product at a lower price. It should also provide WG plc with an advantage over its competitor's product.

Place includes distribution channel decisions, location of outlets, position of warehouses, stock levels, delivery frequency, geographic market definition and sales territory organisation. We know that Coffstop and its rival Peffstill are being sold over the counter from pharmacies, but future developments may make it possible to use alternative outlets such as supermarkets, assuming they are appropriate for the product image.

Market research is not mentioned in the above market mixes. This does not imply that market research is unnecessary. On the contrary, market research can be regarded as the source of information that is used in setting all the variables in the marketing mix.

(d) Strategic alliances play an important part in global strategies where competitors lack a key success factor for some market. It may be distribution, a brand name, a selling organisation, the technology, R&D capability or manufacturing capability. The pharmaceutical industry requires large inputs of both technical expertise and resources, as R&D activities are crucial to the success of the companies. There are many practical issues that the directors of WG plc would need to consider if the company entered a strategic alliance with a competitor for the joint development of future pharmaceutical products.

If the strategic alliance is an informal arrangement it can be implemented faster and be more flexible. As conditions change and people change, the alliance can be adjusted. The problem with this type of arrangement is that with low exit barriers and commitment, there may be a low level of strategic importance and a temptation to pull out when difficulties arise.

A formal joint venture involving equity and legal documentation, on the other hand, has a different set of problems. When equity sharing is involved, there are issues about control, return on investment and achieving a fair percentage of the venture. A major concern is whether or not such a permanent relationship will be equitable in the face of uncertainty about the relative contributions of the partners and the eventual success of the venture. Before the commencement of the strategic alliance it is important that an equitable and agreed method of contributing to and sharing the venture's outputs is finalised.

Basically there are usually two sets of systems, people, cultures and structures that need to be reconciled, so it is essential that the control and management of the venture is discussed and finalised to minimise the possibility of serious disputes during the collaboration. It may be necessary to allocate special managers to the collaboration, but there will still be issues that arise in relation to the fundamental loyalty and commitment of the staff that participate in the venture. The main areas for the directors of WG plc to consider are the extent of the alliance in terms of markets and products and the sharing of costs and expenses between the two participants. It is important that these are agreed so that the position is clear to both parties.

One of the main issues facing the directors of WG plc is likely to be the input of resources, both intangible and physical. The intangible assets such as skill, expertise and patents are likely to be the cause of more disputes than the capital and machinery in an organisation. It may be necessary to share confidential and sensitive information that might prove to be difficult before trust is built up between the parties involved at both the personal and corporate levels. To enhance the chances of a successful strategic alliance, both sides must gain. They should protect and enhance the assets and skills being contributed and not let a partner take over.

The directors should also consider the effect on competitors and regulatory bodies to avoid any legislation or regulations that will affect the alliance adversely. By recognising that there may potential problems in this area, it may be possible to minimise the impact of them.

All of these practical issues will need to be agreed by the directors from the outset if the alliance is to be successful. However, if the companies are able to manage this effectively, a strategic alliance provides the potential of accomplishing a strategic objective or task quickly, inexpensively and with a high prospect for success. It should result in major benefits.

4 BSN

Key answer tips

This question requires a description of the stages of strategic planning. You should explain ways of communicating with BSN's major stakeholder groups. Calculate BSN's ROCE for four years and suggest alternative ways BSN can achieve its financial targets. Explain the impact of a major structural change on BSN's existing objectives and suggest what information the Directors can be provided with after the restructuring relating to the radio division. You are not required to give a description of any strategic planning tool, nor a detailed description of the stakeholder groups, nor financial and non-financial information relating to the television service division.

(a) When formulating a strategic plan BSN should use a structured model which breaks the planning process up into a number of stages, as follows:

Setting a mission and objectives

BSN should produce a mission statement and define clear objectives that it wants to achieve. It will then have a clear purpose in society. Examples of BSN's formal objectives will be to provide an excellent service and to produce programmes that inform, educate and entertain.

External environmental analysis

BSN operates in a dynamic environment and needs to know the current and future external forces it will face. A continuous study should be undertaken of the external environment using PEST analysis and competitor analysis.

Internal analysis

Analysis needs to be undertaken to establish BSN's internal resources at present and in the future. Internal strengths and weaknesses will be established during this stage.

Corporate appraisal

A full corporate appraisal will be undertaken using SWOT analysis. This will enable BSN to analyse its current and future position.

Strategic choice

The options available to BSN will be identified and evaluated at this stage. Each option indicates a strategic pathway that BSN can follow e.g. whether to introduce a divisional structure or not.

Develop and implement the strategy

The best strategy for BSN will be agreed and implemented to a long-term timetable.

Review

The strategy implemented must be continuously monitored and updated whenever the need arises, e.g. when the external environment changes. Once introduced strategic planning is a continuous development.

(b) BSN is a public sector organisation providing radio and television broadcasting services. Its main stakeholders are the government, the public, employees and management. Like other 'not for profit' organisations no one stakeholder group dominates, so the directors of BSN need to consult with all its stakeholders to determine its future development. The following ways of communicating with stakeholders can be used:

- The present system of using independent panels of viewers and listeners should continue. Checks should be carried out to verify the independence of panel members and to ensure they are representative of the views of the general public.
- Questionnaires can be sent out to licencees to obtain feedback on their views of BSN and the services it provides.
- Feedback on individual programmes can be obtained from members of the public by asking for their comments and providing internal addresses and telephone numbers.
- Members of the government can be consulted by using formal committees and working parties, and setting up informal discussion procedures.
- The directors should establish formal and informal communication procedures with employees and management. Many methods can be used including working parties, work groups, committees and staff suggestion schemes.

(c) (i) BSN's ROCE for the four years of the licence fee agreement is calculated as follows:

	Year 1	2	3	4
	$m	$m	$m	$m
Income	2,190	2,234	2,234	2,234
Expenditure	(2,114)	(2,192)	(2,273)	(2,357)
Surplus/(deficit)	76	42	(39)	(123)
Capital employed				
Bal b/f	1,250	1,326	1,368	1,329
Surplus/(deficit)	76	42	(39)	(123)
Bal c/f	1,326	1,368	1,329	1,206
Average capital Employed	1,288	1,347	1,348.5	1,267.5
ROCE	76/1,288	42/1,347	(39)/1348.5	(123)/1,267.5
	= 5.9%	= 3.1%	= (2.9%)	= (9.7%)

The government has set a target ROCE of 6%. In years 2, 3 and 4 BSN will fail to reach this target. A planning gap is opening and will need to be filled.

(ii) BSN's management will need to take action to achieve the target ROCE of 6% by finding ways of filling the planning gap. The options available are as follows:

Increase revenue

The government has stipulated that no further increase in the licence fee can be allowed. Other ways of obtaining revenue should be considered, such as:

- advertising
- obtaining sponsorship of programmes
- selling programmes to other broadcasting companies
- copyright fees charged to video recording companies.

Cost reduction

BSN should investigate ways of reducing costs without compromising programme and service quality. The best way to achieve this would be to find further ways of increasing efficiency. The directors have a good track record over the last three years of initiating improvements to efficiency within BSN.

Reduction in capital employed

BSN's management should investigate ways of reducing the organisation's capital employed. The need to maintain quality might make this difficult.

Using other performance measures

The management of BSN should try to persuade the government to use other performance indicators to assess its performance as the ROCE ignores many factors such as providing a world service, which generates no income, and public satisfaction.

(d) At present, users of the radio service do not pay a licence fee and are subsidised by television licence payers. Separating the television and radio services will result in major changes occurring including:

- Separate charges can be made for using the television and radio services. Making a separate charge to radio users will be difficult to apply unless radio owners are registered. Registering radio owners will be costly and will meet with opposition from the public. A one-off charge added to the selling price of a new radio might be practical.
- BSN could turn its radio division into a commercial radio station raising revenue from advertising and merchandising. The objective of public service broadcasting will have to be changed. To maximise income BSN will then have to maximise audiences by supplying popular programmes so the objectives of providing programmes that inform, educate and entertain will also have to be changed.
- Each division will have to pay for itself. The radio division will have to set new performance criteria for each service provided. Unless the government pays for loss-making services, such as the world service, they will have to be discontinued.
- The perceived quality of programmes by many current radio listeners will be seen to deteriorate if BSN adopts a populist approach to its radio division.

Before a decision is made to separate the services BSN's managers should consult with stakeholder groups and consider the long-term implications.

(e) The following information should be provided to BSN's directors relating to the radio division following its separation from the television service:

Financial information

- Budgets should be produced for the division. Actual results should be compared with the budgeted figures and variances reported.
- Costs should be analysed by programme and operation. This will enable the directors to see where costs are being incurred.
- Analysis of revenue by source. It is important that the directors know the amount and source of revenue.
- For decision making purposes, the contribution earned by each programme should be repeated.
- The net present value of each capital investment project being planned for the division should be reported before a decision to proceed is made.

Non-financial information

- Reports should be produced giving the number of listeners analysed by programme, day and time.
- The radio services market share should be reported together with competitors' market share.

- Feedback should be obtained on listener satisfaction and reported.
- An analysis of listeners as a proportion of the total population in each area would also be useful information.

The management accountant should play an important role in providing this information.

5 P GROUP

Key answer tips

Again, a sound answer can be based on standard models and concepts. Part (a) can be answered by using Porter's Five Forces Model – but you must use the scenario. In Part (b) ensure that you use financial and other performance indicators in your evaluation of the performance of each company. In Part (c) you should emphasise the importance of assessing the prevailing culture in 'target' countries and show an awareness of the demand for additional financial, physical and human resources that would be necessitated by the expansion. In Part (d) remember to consider each stakeholder referred to in the question, i.e. shareholders, employees, joint venture partners and customers. As always, apply the theories to the situation given.

(a) If a business is to be successful it must not only establish but also maintain competitive advantage. During the last 30 years the P Group has developed internationally and has a trading presence in many diverse areas. This inevitably means that the company is likely to encounter many external forces which will make it much more difficult for P Group to meet its objectives not to disappoint their customers with any of the product and services that they provide.

The external forces, to which P Group is subject in developing its business, can be analysed using Michael Porter's 'Five Forces Model':

Power of the buyers

Management must have knowledge of the needs of their customers and also information of the conditions that subsist in the different markets in which they have a presence. Such information assumes critical importance if P Group is to be successful in different sectors. The conditions in the market place will invariably differ and thus if P Group is to be successful then due consideration should be given to the political, legal and social environments which exist within each market place. It is possible that the buyers may benefit from the entry of the P Group, as it is likely that the existing suppliers may have become too self-satisfied, however this situation could well change and become a threat to the P Group.

Power of suppliers

The management of P Group must be certain that there are available suppliers who can provide them with the materials and services needed. The quality and reliability of suppliers could potentially become a major issue; hence managers should take steps to ensure that supplies of materials, services and appropriately skilled personnel can be obtained.

Industrial competitors

In attempting to enter new markets P Group will be faced with competitors who are already established and have acquired market knowledge. It will be difficult to compete effectively in these markets and thus it is essential that P Group acquired skilled managers in order to improve the likelihood of attaining the objectives of the organisation.

Availability of substitutes

P Group is involved in different businesses and it is probable that the tastes and life style of customers within each business will differ. It is therefore essential that products and services of the P Group be adapted in order to be able to meet the requirements of different types of customer. By the same token it is essential that such differences are incorporated into the strategic and marketing plans of the organisation. If P Group is to be successful it is vital that its product and service offerings represent 'value for money' and satisfies the needs of its customers.

Entry barriers

The structure and business conditions may vary considerably within each industry and information should be obtained in order for P Group to be able to operate in an effective manner. If the management of P Group are able to introduce new ventures which, are innovative and 'exciting' within particular industries, then it is possible that they are simultaneously creating barriers to entry of those industries.

Each time P Group mounts a challenge to major companies will probably require the commitment of significant resources. It is therefore of paramount importance that the external forces be evaluated prior to any major decisions are made.

(b) During 20X4, the turnover of the Airline business increased by almost 19%, whilst the turnover of the rail business only increased by just over 3%. There were marked differences in the performance of these respective divisions of the P Group:

	20X3	*20X4*
Airline	%	%
Pre-tax profit as percentage of turnover	10.5	11.8
Return on Capital Employed	8.0	10.1
Turnover/Capital employed	76.0	85.8

	20X3	*20X4*
Rail		
Pre-tax profit as percentage of turnover	7.3	7.6
Return on Capital Employed	5.7	5.0
Turnover/Capital employed	77.4	66.1

P Airlines

A comparison of the results of the two years reveals that no significant change has occurred in any of the ratios, however some of the trends may become significant in the future. The profitability of the Airline division has improved and the ROCE has increased by over 2%. However, the ROCE of the Rail division has declined and this will surely cause anxiety within the management team.

As regards the Airline division the management need to review the current strategy to ensure that the company is able to cope with the competition and the problems faced by those companies within this volatile industry which is subject to international influences. The company should undertake a review of its cost structure and its selling prices, as it is vital that these aspects are closely monitored in order to ensure that the Airline division does not become uncompetitive. The development of overseas business should be given serious consideration, as this is critical to the development of those organisations within the airline industry.

Whilst airline traffic in terms of passengers, passenger miles travelled and the number of routes flown have increased it is possible that the management of the P Group should consider investing additional funds to ensure that these favourable trends continue. P Group should take steps to ensure that they benefit from the 3% projected growth in the long-distance economy market from which P attracts most of its customers. In order to ensure that the customers are given good service it may be necessary to improve the ratio of cabin staff to passengers in both the economy class. P Group must take steps to ensure that the good reputation it has earned and which has become a source of competitive advantage is not lost, hence it is essential to ensure that service levels provided to passengers are maintained and preferably enhanced.

A review of all routes and alliances with other airlines should be undertaken in order to ensure that P Group is operating efficiently and effectively. It is possible that expanding into too many routes could cause fragmentation and this could be injurious to the overall success of organisation. P Group should ascertain the profitability attached to each route and try to focus upon the most profitable routes.

It is likely that price competition may become fierce as competitors attempt to take market share from P Group. It is necessary for the Airline division to protect its strength in the economy class markets where by the customers are very aware of prices charged by P Group and its competitors.

P Rail

A comparison of the two years shows that the profitability of the division is static and this makes it essential for management to review its strategic options. Perhaps ways could be devised which may permit management to increase the level of fares currently being charged, decrease operating costs and reduce the level of capital employed. Of paramount importance is the need for management to successfully address the operating problems which have precipitated a loss of customer confidence. If such problems persist it is quite possible that these could have a seriously detrimental effect on every division of the P Group. Punctuality is probably the most significant issue that needs to be addressed. The management of P Group should give consideration to the fact that the reduction in the number of attendants could be impacting adversely upon customers' perception of the service being offered.

Passenger traffic has decreased in terms of both the number of passengers and the passenger miles travelled and management should attempt to ascertain the reason for this as soon as possible. There has been a significant fall in the turnover to capital employed ratio and a solution to this problem will be required if the objectives of the organisation are to be met.

Unless P Group is able to improve the services it offers, it may not be able to take full advantage of the projected growth of the market over the next four years.

The Regulator poses another threat that the management of the P Group need to address. The loss of the franchise would be a major problem for the organisation. The results of the passenger survey were not good and thus it is vital that punctuality and the services provided improve quickly. The reduction in the number of attendants should be investigated as this could well be a partial cause of customer dissatisfaction.

(c) It is possible that P Group could use the **strong brand name** to enter new markets by virtue of the fact that it is very well known and recognised. It will be possible for P Group to launch a new product under a strong brand using fewer resources than would otherwise be needed had the brand not been one which would be recognised immediately. The fact that fewer resources are consumed in the launching of a new product would constitute a significant competitive advantage for P Group, as they would be able to launch their products at a much lower cost than competitors whose brands were less well known.

The entry of P Group into new markets is made easier by the use of a **brand extension strategy**. It is possible to diversify into both new products and markets and success can be achieved much sooner than might otherwise be the case. However there exists the potential danger that the brand name could be damaged if the development is unsuccessful and this could impact adversely upon the reputation of the entire operation of P Group. Management must ascertain that the brand is recognised in the country which is under consideration as a target for investment. P Group should also undertake a campaign of brand awareness to ensure that they gain competitive advantage.

The **availability of resources** will restrict the extent to which P Group can expand. In circumstances where an organisation such as P Group has extensive plans to enter new markets, then there will be a need for financial, physical and human resources if products are to be launched successfully. Whilst it is probable that P Group has these resources it is essential that the entry into new markets is the subject of detailed planning. P Group undertake market research in order to assess product quality, price and distribution channels. In addition market research should be undertaken in order to assess the likely success of the intended marketing approach.

Managers must also consider the implications of the **prevailing culture in each country** in which P Group intends to have a presence. This could well prove to be a significant factor that ultimately determines the success of any overseas investments. In this respect the products to be promoted and the effects of the methods used to raise brand awareness are of particular importance.

In every country that P Group wishes to enter there will be **a need for additional investments** in fixed assets and working capital. Thus, in order to undertake such an expansion programme, significant capital will be required and it is quite possible that P Group will have to increase borrowings. This increase in the debt burden will need to be carefully evaluated by the management of P Group.

The management of P Group must take into account that having the financial and physical resources must be accompanied by having the **necessary management skills** that will be required in order to manage new businesses. Thus at the outset the management of P Group must ensure that these skills are available either within the organisation or that trained personnel can be recruited.

(d) The personality and charisma of the Chairman is an important factor as regards the success of P Group. The activities of P Group are kept in the public eye via his dominant personality and activities, which generate 'personal publicity'. However, these personal attributes do not guarantee long-term company prosperity, since the organisation must satisfy the expectations of their customers if it is to be a successful business. Other important strategic factors are:

- the development of a culture which enables employee to interact successfully and to contribute fully towards the overall organisational aims and objectives
- the association of the brand with high levels of customer value
- the importance that is attached to the creation and maintenance of a progressive corporate image
- the concern of the Chairman to be 'exciting' and the relaxed management style may increase and sustain the level of motivation of the employees of the organisation.

The Chairman dominates P Group and should consider the interests of all stakeholders. The shareholders, the participants in any management buy-out and any joint venture partners have expectations of returns on their investments. The Chairman, together with other members of the board of directors, needs to ensure that these stakeholders are satisfied. The Chairman should also be cognisant of the fact that employees will identify with him and that he must help provide an environment wherein they can develop and realise their full potential thereby benefiting not only themselves but also P Group.

Whilst the customers will be aware of the public activities of the Chairman, the management need to ensure that the quality of the products and services offered to the customers satisfy their expectations.

The fact that the Chairman deliberately keeps himself in the public spotlight raises his profile as Chairman of P Group. Each stakeholder group must remain convinced as to his ability to satisfy their expectations.

6 C

Key answer tips

Perhaps the most demanding aspect of the question is Part (b). Your answer should demonstrate a good appreciation of the very real threats that exist with regard to undertaking contracts overseas. In particular, you should address the issues of default on payment and the strategic issues, which can arise due to significant fluctuations in exchange rates. In Part (c) you should think in terms of both internal and external information that may be of assistance to management. In Part (d) you should consider why such alliances have become increasingly popular, e.g. shared risk, local knowledge, good reputation for quality of local company, awareness of current developments and local legislation. Note again the role that SWOT often plays in examinations – here split over Parts (a) and (b).

(a) When preparing a corporate appraisal of the organisation, the strengths, weaknesses, opportunities and threats of the organisation should be analysed in such a manner that both internal and external factors are taken into account in the development of C's strategic plan.

Strengths

C is a well-established company that 'has a strong track record'. It has successfully survived a major recession, albeit 10 years ago, and this would give its shareholders more confidence. These factors would indicate that the company has an experienced team of managers and also adequate resources which enable it to grow. C has a strong reputation as an organisation that has successfully undertaken major contracts and is recognised as an organisation 'using good quality materials and applying high standards of workmanship'. It is probable that the success of the organisation has derived from the resources it has developed and retained.

Weaknesses

C has specialised in one activity only, i.e. the building of roads. The company is engaged as a sub-contractor to a major Eastlandian development company. The Board of Directors of C are aware that another development company in Eastlandia 'had been allowed to go into receivership without any further government support'. In the event that this happened to the development company that has engaged C on a subcontract basis, C could be faced with major problems. Of vital importance therefore is the need for C to monitor the financial position of any such parties with which it has a similar relationship.

At present there is possibility that C will lose significant amounts on the contract to construct a major road in Eastlandia. These losses might be precipitated by either the foreign exchange position, or penalty payments that might be imposed as a result of late completion of the project. C's reputation within Eastlandia will have been injured by the failure of the supplier to provide high quality materials. Since it is possible that work in Eastlandia might comprise around 40% of C's order book, the problems in that country might have a significant adverse impact upon C.

Opportunities

C benefits from the lack of confidence in local civil engineering contractors since C itself has a good reputation within Eastlandia. This is a source of competitive advantage for C as it is has become associated with work of a high quality. This is of particular significance due to the fact that other contractors have been responsible for constructions that have collapsed. Confirmation of the good reputation established by C in Eastlandia lies in the receipt of the invitation to tender. C could use its established reputation in order to diversify into related areas of civil engineering.

(b) As a subcontractor to the Eastlandian development company, C faces a number of different threats as a result of its involvement in the road-building project in Eastlandia. The serious economic situation developing in Eastlandia has threatened to result in an economic recession and this may have serious consequences for C. In addition, we know that during the last three years the overseas markets in which C has been carrying out building contracts have suffered a serious economic recession.

The Eastlandia government is likely to reduce the level of spending on the infrastructure of the country and this will reduce the number of building contracts available. This could well result in the postponement of civil engineering projects within Eastlandia. Given that Eastlandia might represent 40% of C's order book, the effect of a recession could prove hugely problematic for C. The problem is further aggravated by the economic circumstances prevailing in C's overseas markets and this will probably lead to a fall in profitability. Whilst it is obvious that C is very well established as a quality contractor within Eastlandia, is should aim to develop new markets in order to reduce the risks of recession in any one country.

It may be difficult for C as a foreign contractor to compete in countries where preference is given to local organisations. C could avoid such potential situations by entering into strategic alliances thereby ensuring a presence in the market place. However C would need to be mindful of the potential problems inherent in such strategic alliances.

Currently, C provides subcontract services to an Eastlandian development company. It is quite possible that this company could get into financial difficulty and the spin-off effects of this would be serious for C. It is known that another company has already gone into receivership and so it is essential that the Board of Directors of C take measures in order to safeguard its position should the development company experience financial difficulties. C should, in future, seek to ensure the financial well-being of all organisations with which it becomes associated. The reasons for the delay in progress payments should be ascertained immediately. Perhaps the development company is already experiencing difficulties and, if this proves to be the case, then assistance should be offered in order to prevent any further activities relating to the contract from taking place if the position is thought to be irretrievable.

The contract work in Eastlandia represents 10% of the total business of C's turnover and thus constitutes a significant part of the total business. It is possible that any problems in Eastlandia could cause problems of a worldwide nature for C. This is another reason why C should take measures to ensure that it is not associated with problem companies as this could not only create financial difficulties for C but could also damage the image of C on a world-wide basis.

The current estimate is that the contract will be completed three months late which renders it likely that C will be liable for penalties in respect of the contract. C's management should attempt to ascertain the causes of any delay and put in place an action plan aimed at ensuring the contract completion occurs at the earliest possible date. C should inform other parties involved in the contract of the likelihood of the three months' delay in completion of the contract. It is quite possible that a fall in the share price of C will occur when the increased possibility of the occurrence of losses on the Eastlandia contract becomes public knowledge.

Work of a remedial nature has already been necessitated by the use of sub-standard materials. Acceptable materials should be procured otherwise additional cost will be incurred and C's profit will be reduced and its reputation damaged. Any loss of confidence in C by the government could have a significant effect on the level of orders received; this is particularly the case in Eastlandia where the government funds most civil engineering contracts. There exists also the possibility that faulty workmanship could be a cause of accidents and C might be associated with poor quality in the same vein as other companies within Eastlandia. C should institute a system of quality control with regard to raw materials and completed work. This should help to avoid the need to repair the roads soon after completion.

The financial performance of companies operating within Eastlandia will also be affected by the relative weakness of the Eastlandian currency. In addition since C is a sub-contractor to an Eastlandian development company, this would cause significant difficulties in the event that the development company met with severe difficulties. The expected fall in the value of Eastlands will have an impact on C's profitability. It was envisaged that the rate of exchange would be 7.26 to the £ in the current year whereas in fact it is now standing at 7.74 to the £. This represents a decrease of 6.6% in the current year. The situation worsens if we look one year ahead when it was originally expected that the exchange rate would be 7.54 Eastlands to the £, whereas in fact the forward rate is now being quoted at 8.56 to the £. This represents a decrease of 13.5% next year. The management of C should adopt a hedging technique in order to minimise the effects of the devaluation of the Eastlands currency.

Since Eastlandia is facing an economic downturn, C's management should seek alternative markets which may offer better long-term opportunities. The critical strategic decision facing C's management is the need to assess to what extent the organisation should commit itself to working within Eastlandia. In order to ensure long-term survival, C's management might decide to obtain more business in other countries even if profitability is reduced in the short-term.

(c) The **sources of external information** should provide details of intended government spending on infrastructure products. They should also provide indicators of the general economic climate. Data could be obtained from a variety of sources including the publications of trade associations and professional bodies. In addition the banks publish reports that contain information about the prevailing economic conditions in different countries. Such reports may provide the management of C with particularly useful information such as the likely level of investment in capital projects in different countries. Local and national government statistics may also include relevant information.

Particular areas that should be monitored are:

- The monetary policies to be adopted by the government particularly in respect of interest rates since these will have an effect upon the number of civil engineering projects that will be undertaken especially with regard to C's non-government customers. It is probable that government statistics are published and that it will be possible to forecast the level of economic activity within Eastlandia. Of particular importance would be the budgeted spending by the government on proposed capital projects.
- The building plans passed would enable C's management to make an assessment of their success in gaining contracts, relative to their competitors. It is possible that this information could be used to make future estimates of the number of contracts that might be obtained. Such information may be contained in economic surveys that are produced for both trade and economic journals.

- Prior to any decision being made which involves expansion into a foreign country the management of C should carefully assess the political stability of the country concerned. The political risk which companies involved in overseas businesses encounter vary from excessive bureaucracy to the extreme case of expropriation of assets within the country. Whilst it is acknowledged that political risk is very difficult to assess, management should obtain information so that an assessment of political risk is contained within any decision-making process.
- It is important that C monitors the activities of its competitors both in Eastlandia and other parts of the world. This will indicate their success and provide an indication of the overall demand for the type of work in which they specialise.

The **internal sources of information** that could be used are the historical records of clients which provide valuable details of matters such as payment history and facts that may be specific to particular clients. Analyses of customer account profitability would be particularly useful. Previous trends in terms of the size of orders and sales volumes would be particularly useful internal information.

An analysis of competitor activities in foreign countries including an analysis of turnover and profitability would prove useful. It would also be worthwhile to investigate the experiences of suppliers overseas as it might provide an insight into the particular problems that are faced in foreign territories.

C's management could also undertake an evaluation of the success rate of their previous tenders and, in doing so, might identify areas where the processes and procedures they follow could be improved.

There is an ongoing need to study customer and industry trends and this will provide information regarding market trends and the extent of the competition facing C. This is particularly the case with regard to Eastlandia, which is currently one of the major sources of business of C.

C should also monitor supplier quality in order to protect its own image within the market place.

(d) One of the advantages that accrues to C as a result of forming a strategic alliance with the Eastlandian civil engineering contractor is the fact that it will have knowledge and experience of the prevailing local conditions as well as the benefits of past knowledge and experience. The strategic alliance affords the opportunity for C to obtain benefits more quickly than would otherwise have been the case. It is quite possible that the benefits from the strategic alliance will be obtained at a lower cost than if either party to the alliance had to obtain knowledge and experience without help from the other party.

It is vital that C chooses its partner very carefully. High on the list of desirable attributes of a potential partner is the reputation for good quality. The management of the prospective partner should have a thorough understanding of the customs and culture of Eastlandia. The prospective partner should have knowledge of prevailing legislation regarding civil engineering activities. In view of the fact that many contracts will be initiated by agencies of the government, a good relationship with the Eastlandian government would be most useful.

The acquisition of local knowledge may help C to avoid or at least reduce the risks of default by a civil engineering developer. Since the failure of such a developer could precipitate major financial loss for C, any means of avoiding the occurrence of such losses would be worthwhile. On the other hand the local company would benefit from the quality of advice and the technology provided by C. In this respect the established reputation of C as a quality contractor would be very beneficial to any local developer.

C's expertise with regard to health and safety issues might also benefit local developers given the current incidence of accidents as a result of poor quality construction within Eastlandia.

C's management must be creative in their search for a strategic partner and attempt to find one with a complementary skill-set. The arrangements of the alliance need to be detailed carefully. In particular, C's management need to consider the financing arrangements, how decision-making will be managed within the alliance, and what procedures will be followed in the event of the local company experiencing financial difficulties. All these issues need to be agreed before the strategic alliance is finalised.

7 S GROUP AND AE DIVISION

(a) S will need information of good quality from both internal and external sources. This information will be both financial and non-financial in content.

Internal financial information

Obvious sources will be the audited financial history of the various divisions and subsidiaries as well as the current financial reports and budgets. The financial history and current data are the sources for the multi-period financial projections that would be required for strategic management's purposes.

Internal non-financial information will be obtained from the following sources:

- ***Marketing management*** will provide forecasts of future product developments and also market research.
- ***Sales management*** will provide essential information about customer tastes and behaviour. Human resources management will provide essential input on the skills and competences needed by S Group.

External information

This will be provided by competitor organisations from brochures, advertising Internet site information and from external agencies. Government agencies can also provide information about manufacturing activity, demographic statistics and similar.

Trading partners are a useful source of data for the products or services that they provide and their insights into business operations.

Banks and financial institutions are useful commentators on economic trends and activity, which is essential in formulation of strategy for a multinational organisation. Lastly, trade associations and research organisations may well collect valuable data for strategic purposes.

Using the information

The usefulness and integrity of the information is a function of the systems that are installed for the purposes of facilitating strategic management.

Most organisations of size have a commercial intelligence department that conducts research on a continuous basis so that top management is regularly informed of critical issues. The staffing of such a department is composed of persons with a high degree of academic excellence underpinned by commercial experience in the business sector concerned.

The finance function of a multinational organisation is staffed by people of considerable skill and experience obtained with high profile employers nationally or internationally. They are capable of setting up reliable systems for evaluation and appraisal in order to facilitate strategic planning.

The staff members employed in the other support functions such as marketing and HRM are generally skilled people whose opinions are respected and with a significant track record to support the esteem in which they are held.

Directors may also involve high profile consultancies on a short-term basis to provide essential input into the strategic management process.

(b) **Evaluation of AE division**

Reliance on a single measure such as ROCE can be ill advised and simplistic. ROCE as an accounting measure has a number of well-known drawbacks:

- It is a short-term measure.
- It is capable of manipulation or distortion by the misuse of accounting convention.
- It is a relative measure and must be used selectively if at all.
- It is not a good indicator of long-term survival as it is based on a view of the balance sheet at a particular moment in time.

In the case of AE division there are a number of complex issues regarding the controllability of the division. The reliance on the head office formula produces the following result.

	Last year	*Previous year*	*Change*
Net profit before interest and tax	25	200	–175
Average capital employed	2,020	2,000	+20
ROCE	1.24%	10%	-87.6%

Prima facie this is a poor result. However the following factors are relevant:

The head office costs are outside the control of the manager of AE division.

The transfer price of group components is also outside his control. In the most recent year the price of components has risen from K$26,667 to K$37,500. This may be a change in cost structure but is more likely to be an attempt to manipulate the transfer price for tax reasons. It is clear that comparison of the 'raw data' is not equitable because the most significant variation in performance is caused by the transfer price of the components.

It would seem perverse to condemn the division as a poor performer on such a subjective exercise. The position might be different if AE was evaluated on the basis of 'controllable profit' which would assume that the transfer price of components was capped at the level of the previous year. On this basis divisional results could be re-computed.

Figures in K$m	*Last year*	*Previous year*
Sales	800	750
Components at base year price*	427	400
Assembly	100	75
Gross profit	273	275
Average capital employed	2,020	2,000
ROCE	13.5%	13.75

*Based on K$m 400/15,000 = £26,667 each

On this basis the change in ROCE is hardly significant.

However, there are a number of plus points for AE division as illustrated in the following table:

	Last year	*Previous year*	*Change*
Sales volume	800	750	+6.67%
Budget shortfall in sales	–11.1%	–16.67%	+5.56%
	Last year	*Previous year*	*Change*
A negative point is the increase in assembly cost	K$6.25	K$5	+25%

Recommendation

The directors of S should reappraise the results of AE division after consideration of the following:

- The change in the basis of transfers pricing in the most recent year; there appears to be inconsistency in the basis of evaluation.
- Suitable non-financial performance indicators should be devised in order to evaluate both the division and the manager. These should involve a review of the business environment of AE division.
- Additional financial indicators could be used to supplement the ROCE measure. These could include residual income or other cash flow based measures.

(c) The factors that will require consideration by the Board of S would be as follows:

Quality of research. Any take-over involves a detailed examination of the background of the target company. The credibility of its financial record is a critical issue as many organisations are purchased with very little done in the form of investigative work. A due diligence exercise is both costly and risky in that it seeks to provide reassurance on such issues as values of assets, quality of earnings and modus operandi of the target company.

Business environment. Any successful take-over requires knowledge of the business environment, which involves identifying competitors key customers markets and distribution channels. The difficulties are compounded by a non-domestic environment, which will have its own local customs practices and risks.

Valuing the target company. The 'price tag' of take-over targets can be arrived by a variety of methods. One of the commonest is on the basis of future earnings.

An error or misjudgement in ascertaining earnings is compounded by the multiple chosen for valuation.

Economic viability. The project could be evaluated on whether it adds value to the group. Typical measures would be a positive NPV or an evaluation based on Internal Rate of Return (IRR) using the Group's cost of capital. Other measures could be the use of payback or (despite its drawbacks) ROCE.

Strategic fit. The acquisition should complement the Group's existing activities. The acquisition appears to be a defensive ploy in that it targets a competitor who once acquired will be neutralised as a threat and provide an opportunity for expansion.

Local legal and fiscal issues. The take-over should not present any burdens in terms of disadvantageous tax treatment or problems with local laws. For example, some overseas countries insist on shareholdings held by nationals as a condition of domicile (e.g. Malaysia).

Cultural issues. Any take-over in an overseas environment involves changes in attitudes and work practices. These can be quite critical to effective operation.

Funding implications. The acquisition will be funded by loan capital. This will send up the level of gearing and will also affect the credit rating of S. Loan capital carries its own risks. While equity is not diluted, loan stockholders have powerful rights to protect themselves from loss so they can act swiftly if a loan covenant is breached by invoking an administrative receivership arrangement.

(d) The drawbacks of single measure such as ROCE has been mentioned. Newer approaches focus on the ability of a division to add value to an enterprise. The concept of shareholder value is based on the idea that a business is worth the discounted value of future cash flows. Therefore any acquisition should be evaluated on its ability to add value to the enterprise. Adding value can be regarded as the increased value of the enterprise as a result of the acquisition that has been made.

Conversely a division can be evaluated to see if it can bear an economic cost of operation. EVA (Economic Value Added) is a measure developed by Stern Stewart and Co for divisional evaluation in order to find the economic profit of a segment. The formula is:

Operating profit after tax – (Invested capital × WACC)

Conceptually this is similar to Residual Income.

Assuming that the acquisition is made for £100m:

Earnings before tax	£40m
Invested capital	£100m
WACC 10%	£10m
Economic profit	£30m

Difficulties that are obvious include the problems of accounting convention and the subjectivity of the WACC.

Rappaport uses another measure called Shareholder Value Analysis. Shareholder value is defined as Entity Value – Value of Debt. Entity value is defined as the present value of free cash flows before interest but after tax and after adding back non-cash items such as depreciation. The internal measure used for divisional evaluation is to try to measure the increase in shareholder value that has been engineered through the new project or acquisition.

The equation used is: Value of strategy = Post strategy value – Pre strategy value.

Rappaport tries to measure the increase in value of an entity that results from a strategy and he identifies seven key value drivers that affect cash flow generation.

Six of the seven drivers suggested by Rappaport would be relevant in the evaluation of AE division:

- sales growth rate
- operating profit margin
- cash tax rate
- fixed capital investment need
- planning horizon
- cost of capital.

The directors of S could also apply some of the concepts associated with the concept of the **balanced scorecard** that examines both financial and non-financial indicators of performance. There are many non-financial indicators, which have much greater strategic significance than the short-term financial measures derived from accountancy.

Typical non-financial measures are:

- Customer perspective
  - Improvements in customer relations
  - Increase in customer base
  - Improvements in market share
- Quality perspective
  - Reduction in complains and quality breakdowns
  - Less scarp and spoilage
  - Zero defects in output
- Product innovation perspective
  - New processes and developments to save money
  - Creation of patents and intellectual property.

8 FNJ AND WT MERGER

(a) The business environment of FNJ is extremely volatile subject to very rapid change. The production and sales of compact discs (CDs) has been subject to dramatic change with the advent of Internet technology and there will be a major effect upon its chain of retail outlets. Illegal copying of CDs is also widespread and constitutes a very real threat to the music industry.

In contrast WT's business environment relates to motion picture production and retail stores. Whilst the motion pictures business is profitable, its costs have risen considerably during recent years. FNJ's retail music stores have achieved a gradual increase in profit over the last four years. There is a clear need for FNJ and WT to improve their profitability and improve shareholder value in trading conditions which have been difficult during recent years. After the merger has taken place management intend to undertake a reduction in headcount in order to improve the operating results of the combined entity.

Two of the main issues that require consideration are technology and technological development. It is clear that the FNJ and WT are subject to the effects of the speed of technological change. Of particular note is the digital downloading of music from the Internet to the customer's own personal computer which will have major impact on the entire music retail industry.

The merged group aims to achieve a high market share of the total worldwide music sales. Together with the reduction in operating costs as a result of the shedding of jobs, levels of profitability and shareholder value should improve. Shareholder value may well increase as a result of the successful development of distribution of music to customers via the Internet. The merged group will, however, have to change the marketing mix that was hitherto employed by FNJ. Although the merged group intends to effect further savings as a result of the non-renewal of contracts for some of the recording artists who are not achieving high sales, it needs to give consideration to the change in the power of the supplier in the new scenario.

The Internet may provide artists with a direct route to the market without the need for a large distributor. Thus FW needs to achieve a high market share and be a large player in the market in order to achieve economies of scale and give itself a better opportunity to the maintain relationships with artists.

(b) (i) The average annual sales of CD's over the last five years amounted to $100 million. Last years sales amounted to $90 million and the previous year was $95 million. Thus sales during the three previous years amounted to $315 million in aggregate, thereby giving an average of $105 million in respect of each of the three years. Last years sales are 14.28% below the average level in each of the first three years: ($90m – $105m)/$105m = 14.28%.

Projected increase in contribution per annum for CD and Internet sales based on forecasts provided by CJ

Last years sales amounted to $90 million. CJ projects that next years sales will increase by 20%, thus sales would be $90 million × 1.20 = $108 million.

The number of CDs sold last year was $90million/$20 = $4,500 million.

It is anticipated that the trend for CD sales is expected to continue and therefore the expected level of CD sales during next year is ($90/$95) × 4,500m = 4,263m.

The contribution earned from the sales of each CD next year is expected to remain at $16 therefore the total contribution from CDs next year should be $16 × 4.263m = $68.21m.

The sales revenue from CDs next year should therefore be $20 × 4.263m = $85.26m, which means that Internet sales are expected to be ($108m – $85.26m) = $22.74m.

The average variable cost of the Internet sales should be 25% below that of a CD. Therefore the average variable cost of each Internet sale should amount to 75% × $4 = $3. Thus average variable costs of Internet sales are expected to be 15% of the resultant sales revenue. (Since the current level of average variable costs of CDs is 20% of sales revenue, and it is forecast that this will reduce by 25% for Internet sales, then average variable costs will be 20% × 75% = 15% of the total revenue from Internet sales.)

Thus the expected contribution from Internet sales is expected to be 85% × $22.74m = $19.33m.

The total contribution expected next year from CD and Internet sales is therefore:

	$million
CD sales	68.21
Internet sales	19.33
Total	87.54

This represents an increase in the overall contribution as follows:

	$million
Projected contribution next year	87.54
Contribution last year ($16 × 4.5m)	19.33
Increase in contribution	87.54

Since no change is expected in the contribution earned per CD, it is clear that the increase in contribution is due to the advent of Internet sales. Thus the projected contribution to sales ratios are 80% and 85% for CD and Internet sales respectively.

Motion pictures

Revenue has increased from $1million to $2million, therefore the average increase in revenue has been 26% each year during each of the last three years. However, over the same period of time total costs have increased from $700 million to $1,900 million, which represents an average annual increase of 39.5%. Profit has declined from a level of $300 million to just $100 million. It is imperative that FW reviews its increasing cost base and assesses the future market demand for this business.

Retail music stores

There is no doubt that in the future music will be supplied via the Internet and that this will have a major impact upon the business. The threat to the popularity of buying from music stores has not really shown itself. Revenues have increased on an annual average basis by 1.2%. Total costs have risen by 0.02%. However there is a marked increase over the last to years from $131 million to $136 million. During this period costs rose by 3.8% whereas revenue only rose by 1.4%.

(ii) **Contribution volume variance (CVV)**

The average variable cost of a CD is $4, which represents one-third of total costs. The budgeted contribution per CD over the last two years was as follows:

	Last year	*Two years ago*
	$	$
Budgeted sales revenue per CD	22	20
Budgeted variable costs per CD	(1/3 × $15) = 5	(1/3 × $10.5) = 3.5
Budgeted contribution per CD	17	16.5
Shortfall on sales for each year:		
Actual sales	$ 90m/$20 = 4.5000m	$95m/$20 = 4.75m
Budget sales	$100m/$22 = 4.5455m	$100m/$20 = 5.00m
Shortfall	0.0455m	0.25m

	Last year	*Two years ago*
	$	$
Contribution per CD (see above)	$17	$16.5
CVV	(0.7735m)	(4.125m)

There has been a reduction in the adverse CVV over the last two years. However, the adverse sales price variance of $9 million (4.5million CDs were sold at $2 below the budgeted selling price per unit). This indicates that the sales budget was unrealistic especially as there was no change whatsoever in the average selling actually achieved.

(iii) **Recommendations**

FW must seize the opportunity to improve its music sales via the Internet. There is no alternative to pursuing Internet sales, as this is quite clearly the future direction of retail music sales. In doing this it can avail itself of the increased rate of contribution to be gained from sales via the Internet.

FW will need to attempt to find a buyer for its retail music stores since their value will inevitably decline as Internet sales increase. However, it is known that the resale value of FNJ's music stores is reducing because of the increasing popularity of alternative methods of shopping. The management of FJ should give consideration to finding an alternative use for the music stores. Perhaps they could be used by FW to house newly established businesses, selling products which complement the Internet sales.

There is a strong likelihood that the full development of the Internet will take a relatively long time and it is highly probable that CD players will remain on the market for several years.

FW must consider its investment in the motion pictures business. In order to remain in the industry FW must reduce its costs. FW will need to make an assessment as to the likely level of future demand for this type of business. Consideration needs to be given as to whether the popularity of movies as an alternative to home entertainment will remain. An assessment should also be made as to the likely impact of the Internet upon the popularity of the impact of the Internet will cause a decline in the popularity of successful movies.

(c) It is a widely held view that the object of business is to increase the wealth of its owners, who in commercial organisations are the shareholders. The increase in wealth is measured by dividends and capital growth. In order to measure the increase in wealth the economic value of strategic investments must be estimated by discounting future cash flows.

An assessment of the increase in shareholder value requires that the following three factors be taken into account:

(i) the rate of return earned by investments

(ii) the cost of funds associated with the investments, and

(iii) the amount the shareholders have invested in the business.

It can clearly be seen that the nature of the business is changing, but FW is expected to remain a viable business. The market has viewed the merger favourably and this is evidenced by the fact that the share price of FNJ rose by 11% after the merger was announced. Hence the market believes that increased shareholder wealth will result as a direct consequence of the merger. There is no indication at this stage that a request will be made that the existing shareholders provide any additional funds. However it is probable that more funds will be required in order to develop the Internet sales. On the face of it this appears to be a genuine merger as opposed to one company being acquired by another and subsequently reducing the combined headcount in order to effect a reduction in fixed costs. As a result the operational gearing of the company will improve which should precipitate an improvement in shareholder value.

In essence shareholder value analysis is concerned with long-term improvements. The merger is predicated upon the need to increase market share and position FW at the leading edge of technological developments in order to increase profitability. However, the shareholders should be aware of the difficulties faced by the management of FW. Notwithstanding the problem of what to do with the retail music stores, there are the numerous problems associated with running the combined businesses. Whilst synergies can and inevitably will arise, these are very often cancelled out by the costs incurred and problems involved in integrating the different businesses.

The management of FW face a difficult time since not only are they running a newly merged organisation but also must deal with a fundamental change in the way business is done. There are many potential pitfalls to be avoided in order to preserve let alone increase shareholder value. Nevertheless, due to the significant differences in the approaches to business within the music and entertainments industry, there does not appear to be much merit in the option of remaining separate entities.

9 Y-LAND FE

(a) Michael Porter in his book *The Competitive Advantage of Nations* tries to isolate the national attributes that further competitive advantage in an industry. It considers why some nations have successful international firms whilst others do not, how these firms maintain high levels of performance in world markets, and what impact this has on competitive strategy for an organisation and on government policy.

Porter's study argues that for a country's industry to be successful it needs to have the attributes and relationships illustrated by his 'Diamond' of national competitive advantage.

The four major elements of the theory are:

(i) favourable factor conditions

(ii) demand conditions

(iii) related and supporting industries

(iv) firm strategy, structure and rivalry.

The directors of the Y Corporation could undertake an analysis of these four elements to help determine whether the Far Eastern development should be undertaken.

Looking at each of these in turn:

Favourable factor conditions

Factors to consider include the availability and suitability of:

(i) Physical resources (the availability of appropriate land and the suitability of the weather would be relevant factors here).

(ii) Capital (availability seems to be good due to willingness of the host government to take a share; the cost of capital will need to be assessed in the light of rates available elsewhere).

(iii) Human resources (the directors would need to be happy that the quantity and quality of labour required is available; training needs will have to be assessed).

(iv) Infrastructure (does the site have the appropriate communications, transport and other infrastructure attributes or will they have to be developed. The partnership with the government is presumably an attempt to ensure that the appropriate infrastructure exists).

(v) The local legal and regulatory structure (health and safety, cultural, financial – in the form of possible subsidies) are all aspects of the local environment that need to be considered.

Demand conditions

Whilst high demand in the USA has enabled the Y Corporation to gain considerable experience in delivering entertainment, there has been less success in Europe. There must be a strong local (national) demand for the company's services whilst a too compliant domestic market can lead to management complacency, stagnation and lack of innovation. So the directors need to ask:

(i) Do the customer groups in the Far East exhibit characteristics that are similar to those existing in the home country and therefore predisposed to generating high demand?

(ii) Will the customers in the Far East demand the same or different services compared to the home market?

(iii) Will increasing demand lead to the need for continual development and innovation in all of the Y Corporation's markets?

Related and supporting industries

The success of an industry can be due to its suppliers and related industries. So, in this case, the directors must consider whether the appropriate service-related industries exist in the Far East as they do in the home and European markets.

Firm strategy, structure and rivalry

Organisational goals can be determined by ownership structure so the directors need to explore how the joint venture is structured and ensure that the attitudes of each partner are complementary. In addition the directors would need to establish the level of local competition it its market sector and the government's attitude to new entrants to the market. Hopefully the host government could provide information and reassurances on these issues.

The Diamond theory is based on a sample of countries surveyed by Porter. It relates to helping an organisation select countries for development of production rather than services. However it does emphasise the need to understand the characteristics of the market and this is crucial to the Y Corporation, particularly following its problems in Europe.

(b) (i) **Initial workings**

(W1) Calculate the **expected number of visitors in year 3**, the first year of operation.

Optimistic	8m × 0.25	=	2.0
Most likely	3m × 0.50	=	1.5
Pessimistic	2m × 0.25	=	0.5
			4.0

(W2) Then calculate visitors in subsequent years.

Visitors in millions

	Change factor	*Adults*	*Children and concessions*	*Total*
Year 3		1.60	2.40	4.00
Year 4	+50%	2.40	3.60	6.00
Year 5	–5%	2.28	3.42	5.70
Year 6	–5%	2.17	3.25	5.42
Year 7	–	2.17	3.25	5.42
Year 8	–	2.17	3.25	5.42
Year 9	–	2.17	3.25	5.42
Year 10	–	2.17	3.25	5.42

(W3) From the visitor numbers, **labour costs per visitor** can be established.

In year 3 labour costs per visitor are:

\$9.72m / 4m = \$2.43

Labour costs per visitor in the second year of operation (year 4 of the project) are:

(\$21.14m – \$9.72m) / 6m = \$1.90

(W4) Finally **contribution per visitor** can be calculated.

Contribution	*Adults*		*Children and concessions*	
Year 3	\$	\$	\$	\$
Revenue per visitor		50.00		30.00
Less:				
Labour costs	2.43		2.43	
Other costs	2.00		2.00	
		4.43		4.43
		45.57		25.57
Plus additional contribution		110.00		110.00
Total contribution		155.57		135.57

Contribution	*Adults*		*Children and concessions*	
Years 4 – 10	\$	\$	\$	\$
Revenue per visitor		50.00		30.00
Less:				
Labour costs	1.90		1.90	
Other costs	2.00		2.00	
		3.90		3.90
		46.10		26.10
Plus additional contribution		110.00		110.00
Total contribution		156.10		136.10

The discounted cash flow calculation

	Adults	*Children and concessions*	*Total*	$m
Year 3				
Numbers	1.6m	2.4m		
Contribution per person	$155.57	$135.57		
Total contribution	$248.91m	$325.37m	574.28	
Less fixed costs			100.00	
Net cash flow			474.28	
15% cost of capital at year 3			0.658	
				312.07
Year 4				
Numbers	2.4m	3.6m		
Contribution per person	$156.10	$136.10		
Total contribution	$374.64	$489.96	864.60	
Less fixed costs			100.00	
Net cash flow			764.60	
15% cost of capital at year 4			0.572	
				437.35
Year 5				
Numbers	2.28m	3.42m		
Contribution per person	$156.10	$136.10		
Total contribution	$355.91m	$465.46	821.37	
Less fixed costs			100.00	
Net cash flow			721.37	
15% cost of capital at year 5			0.497	
				358.52

Years 6 – 10				
Numbers	2.17m	3.25m		
Contribution per person	$156.10	$136.10		
Total contribution	$338.74	$442.32m	781.06	
Less fixed costs			100.00	
Net cash flow			681.06	
15% cost of capital at years 6 – 10			1.667	
				1135.33
Total Cash Inflow				2243.27
Less capital costs ($2,200m / 2 = $1100m × 1.626 (CPV 15% for 2 years)				1788.60
NPV				454.67

The return on investment per the formula applied by the Y Corporation is:

$454.67m / $2200.00m = 20.7%

(ii) **Commentary on the DCF**

Attendance figures

The directors would be advised to perform a sensitivity analysis on those factors, such as attendance figures, that are most subject to change. The 4m expected number of visitors in the first year of operation used in the calculation above does not actually occur in the table of probable visitor numbers supplied. Taking the most pessimistic view of attendance gives a total over the eight years of 2m + 3m + 2.84m + 13.54m = 21.39m. This is about half the number of visitors used above and it does have a 25% chance of happening therefore presents a considerable risk.

Return on investment

The calculation above shows a return of investment of just under the 22% required by the directors. However it might be more relevant to relate the NPV to the present values of the capital cost. This would give a 'better' result of 25.4% ($454.67 / $1788.6m).

Revenue and cost assumptions

The key question is how reliable are these? Examples of potential variations include: will the learning curve effects occur? How strong is the brand image of the Y Corporation in the Far East? Is the estimate of marketing decay accurate? Is it too pessimistic or optimistic? Do the set up costs include the inevitable promotion costs, etc?

Non-financial grounds

The DCF purely addresses the finances but the directors need to consider wider aspects. Questions such as how does this venture fit with the overall company strategy, what will be its impact on company processes, how will the customers react, what will happen to overall growth etc need to be addressed. A balanced scorecard approach to analysis and measurement could be adopted.

In a recommendation to the directors it would be appropriate to highlight areas where information does not appear to be available and which must be sought and assessed:

1 How appropriate is the park's local infrastructure (transport, etc)?

2 How will the park have to develop over its life?

3 Will funds be available to make the almost inevitable changes over time?

4 What is the state of the local competition (present and future)?

5 What lessons have been learnt from the European expansion and are they relevant to the Far East (e.g. climate)?

6 What would be the impact on Y's reputation should the venture be less successful than anticipated?

7 Are the directors fully committed to this long-term strategic venture?

8 Are they prepared to take the inevitable risks?

(c) The term 'shareholder value' reflects the view that when a person invests his or her money in a company, they do so in the expectation that their wealth will increase. It is assumed that the overall strategic aim of the company is to generate long-term economic value.

Changes in shareholder value can be measured crudely by looking at earnings per share. Future shareholder value is concerned with the economic value of an investment and, by discounting forecast cash flows by an appropriate cost of capital, one can work on the basic assumption that cash flows provide dividends and therefore lead to expected changes in share price. The Y Corporation can use this approach, and we have seen that, assuming the assumptions are correct, this Far Eastern project will almost yield the target 22% return.

However, whilst shareholder value analysis (SVA) purports to be only concerned with increasing shareholder wealth, the directors must look beyond the purely financial to decide what will impact ultimately on the company's value and share price. For example, the project would have a significant impact on the local community and this cannot be ignored. Investing in that community would no doubt add to costs in the short term (and therefore decrease shareholder wealth), but in the long term the directors of a service venture which relies on customer satisfaction, positive image and perceptions must take into account these broader issues.

Therefore the directors need to consider a range of stakeholders other than just shareholders. As well as the local community the directors need to consider employees – the performance of employees impacts directly on customer satisfaction and hence income. So the directors need to know how wealth is generated and what impacts on each factor.

Shareholder value added can be calculated by taking the difference between the return on investment and the cost of capital multiplied the investment made by shareholders. This is a simple approach that can often need refining to, for example, take account of the level of marketing research that is essential to the Y Corporation. The directors, need to realise that the calculation of SVA:

(i) is more difficult in periods of uncertainty (such as starting a major project)

(ii) uses accounting data not intended for this purpose and therefore open to manipulation

(iii) does not take account of intangible assets (such as the qualities of employees)

(iv) involves making predictions over, in this case, 10 years – for example can the cost of capital be accurately forecast over that length of time?

(v) is regarded as highly subjective

(vi) is a short-term approach that may not be appropriate when taking long-term decisions about their portfolio development.

10 ICS

Key answer tips

You need to have a framework for answering Part (a). The framework used here to discuss the advantages of corporate objectives are the five elements of formal planning: having a plan, communication of intentions, employee motivation, co-ordination of efforts and control.

The difficulty with answering Part (b) might be to avoid repetition of the same points. Try to make sure that your answer covers a sufficient number of different aspects and points.

To answer Part (c), it might be advisable to do the calculations required by the question, and use the information provided by your calculations, together with any other information in the question, to develop the rest of your answer.

(a) Setting corporate objectives can help a company in various ways.

- Corporate objectives provide a framework within which **plans can be made** and **decisions can be taken**. Managers can formulate plans and make decisions on the basis of whether they will contribute towards the achievement of those objectives.
- In a larger organisation, formally announced objectives provide a method of **communicating** the intentions of senior management to others in the organisation, so that everyone knows what the organisation is trying to achieve.
- Honestly stated objectives can also act as an **incentive to staff**. Employees often like to have the reassurance that the organisation they work for has worthwhile objective and that they can help to contribute towards achieving them.
- In a large organisation, formally announced objectives provide a basis on which different departments and groups can **co-ordinate** their activities. It is more likely that different parts of the organisation will all 'pull in the same direction'.
- Corporate objectives, formally announced, provide a benchmark by which management can **monitor and assess actual performance** and shareholders can assess the performance of management. Rewards for top executives often include a bonus for achieving results in line with or in excess of company targets.

Setting corporate objectives can, however, be obstructive and prevent the satisfaction of shareholder demands. It is assumed that shareholders seek to maximise their wealth, or to maximise returns on their investment consistent with the risks undertaken by the company. In the IT industry, the market is changing continuously and the industry is dynamic. Already in the case of ICS, its initial business of providing computer software to local firms has grown rapidly, but the rate of growth has now declined. Similarly, the diversification into emergency computer data retrieval services has provided some growth, which is now declining. For the company to continue to grow, or possibly even to survive, it will possibly have to continue diversifying. Its decisions about what to do, as in the case of the contract under review, might have to be opportunistic. In other words, the company might need to take opportunities as they arise, without regard to formally established objectives. If the company's objectives are too restrictive, the company might forgo opportunities to develop because they are inconsistent with objectives that might no longer be appropriate for the company.

The company should therefore be advised that corporate objectives can be beneficial, but should not be allowed to become restrictive in a volatile business environment. Objectives should therefore be reviewed regularly and often, and amended as changing situations demand.

(b) Although managers can sometimes make excellent decisions on a hunch or 'by instinct', in the long run their decision-making will be more rational and soundly based when they are properly informed. The **quality of management decisions** is always likely to be better when managers are well-informed about the different options available, and the likely outcome of pursuing each different course of action.

When the future is uncertain, management information helps to **reduce the uncertainty and analyse the risks involved**.

When the business environment is changing rapidly, organisations must adapt to survive and grow. Information systems can help managers to recognise the nature of the changes that are happening, and their potential significance. They can then formulate new strategies to adapt to the changing circumstances.

However, the **type of information required** by management differs between a rapidly changing business environment and a stable environment. In a stable environment, most information needs can be obtained from within the organisation and derived from historical results. The past is a useful guide to the future. In a rapidly changing environment, in contrast, information has to be more forward-looking, taking account of risk and uncertainty. Information sources are also likely to be sourced more from outside the organisation than from within.

The environmental data needed by management could relate, for example, to the actions of competitors, to changing technology or to changes in consumer tastes and habits.

The functions of management include the requirement to formulate and implement plans and to monitor and control actual performance. Planning and control systems, at an operational and a strategic level, depend on information. Feedback and feedforward systems of control are based on the provision of information for management to make their control decisions.

The best information systems are well-planned and structured. Given the developments that have occurred in information systems, ICS might well benefit from extensive integrated databases and executive information systems.

On the other hand, in a continually changing environment, it is also likely that much data and information reporting will become obsolete and unnecessary. Information is only worth having if the benefits from its use exceed the cost of collecting and storing it. It is therefore advisable for ICS to carry out regular reviews of their information systems, and remove unwanted data and eliminate unwanted routine reports.

In summary, managers need information to do their job properly. In a rapidly changing business environment, there will be a greater need for external environmental information. There will also be a continuing need for internally generated information, such as performance reports and statutory reports and statements. However, even if the nature of the information required changes rapidly as circumstances change, management information is essential.

(c)

	20X5	*20X6*	*20X7*
Retail	$000	$000	$000
Sales	4,290	3,575	3,150
Variable costs	3,003	2,502	2,205
Contribution	1,287	1,073	945
Fixed costs	1,070	890	790
Profit before interest and tax	217	183	155

	20X5	*20X6*	*20X7*
Industrial	$000	$000	$000
Sales	1,716	1,950	2,079
Variable costs	1,373	1,560	1,663
Contribution	343	390	416
Fixed costs	470	590	800
Loss before interest and tax	(127)	(200)	(384)

	20X5	*20X6*	*20X7*
Other	$000	$000	$000
Sales	594	975	1,071
Variable costs	505	829	910
Contribution	89	146	161
Fixed costs	190	270	310
Loss before interest and tax	(101)	(124)	(149)

	20X5	*20X6*	*20X7*
Total	$000	$000	$000
Sales	6,600	6,500	6,300
Variable costs	4,881	4,891	4,778
Contribution	1,719	1,609	1,522
Fixed costs	1,730	1,750	1,900
Loss before interest and tax	(11)	(141)	(378)

The information in this analysis indicates the following:

- The company has been making a loss for the past three years, and the loss has been increasing each year.
- The retail sector is profitable, but profits have been declining and a substantial fall in sales turnover would, at first sight, appear to be the main cause.
- The industrial and other sectors have been growing in terms of sales turnover but, in each case, the growth in fixed costs has exceeded the growth in contribution.

- The situation cannot be rectified by closing down the loss-making industrial and other sectors, because each of these sectors makes a contribution towards fixed overheads.

We are also aware that ICS has a cash flow problem, although the information set out here does not provide an analysis of the cash position, nor of operational cash flows each year.

The information here would seem to suggest that Z is not aware of the financial position of the company and the severe difficulties it is in. On its own, the information is also insufficient to assist Z in making decisions about what needs to be done.

In the short-term, it is recommended that a basic management accounting system should be introduced. This should include:

- a system for preparing a budgeted income statement, cash flow budget and budgeted balance sheet
- a system for regular reviews of cash flow
- a budgetary control system, in which actual results are compared regularly with the budget, and variances reported.

The company also needs to establish what needs to be done to turn the company round and back into profitability. Management information will probably be needed about:

- costs, with a view to identifying unnecessary sending and cutting costs
- revenues and the nature of sales demand
- whether additional sales are being achieved by offering products at a loss.

A simple management accounting system based on budgets and control reports with variances can be set up on a spreadsheet, and advanced IT knowledge is therefore not required.

(d) The variable cost/sales ratio for the industrial sector was 80% in 20X5. For the contract, it is expected to fall to 77.5% of 80%, i.e. to 62% of sales from the contract.

Year 1 analysis	£
Additional sales revenue (40% of £2,079,000)	831,600
Variable costs (62% of sales)	515,592
Additional contribution (32% of sales)	316,008
Additional fixed costs (20% of £800,000)	(160,000)
Hire of equipment	(100,000)
Net increase in profit in first year	56,008

The analysis suggests that the contract would increase profitability in its first year by about £56,000, regardless of whether or not it is then extended for a further five years. On this basis, ICS should bid for the contract.

However, there are important reservations with this advice.

- The profitability of the contract depends on variable costs being just 62% of the additional sales turnover. If the contribution/sales ratio were to be the same as for other sales to the industrial sector, total variable costs would be higher by about £150,000 (18% of £831,600) and the contract would make a substantial loss.

- Similarly, it has been assumed that although sales will increase by 40%, the increase in stepped fixed costs will be restricted to 20% of 20X5 fixed cost levels.
- In view of the loss-making history of the industrial sector, it is questionable whether the cost estimates – or indeed the revenue estimates – can be relied on.

Before bidding for the contract, Z should review the cost and revenue estimates, and re-assess their reliability.

11 THE WORLDAIR ALLIANCE

Key answer tips

Break the question down into all the separate requirements and answer each using a different heading. This ensures you answer each section properly. If you combine all requirements into one general answer it can be hard for the marker to see where you have met each requirement. There can also be a tendency for candidates to ignore certain parts of the requirement and only provide a general answer.

In Part (a) you have to discuss how being a member of an alliance impacts upon the setting of aims and objectives. The specific requirement is to outline the benefits and disadvantages of the Worldair Alliance in determining its aims and objectives. There is no need to discuss the broad benefits and disadvantages of being a member of the group. This would be the case if 'determining' was replaced with 'achieving' in the requirement.

In Part (b) you are required to assess the action the management team should make with regard to the bad publicity; outline the consequences of not taking action; and consider the availability and quality of data in the decision-making process. You are not required to conclude whether or not the Alliance should remove the 5% (20 per aircraft) seats. At present there is not enough information. Do ensure a range of actions are considered.

In Part (c) you are required to undertake a contribution analysis for each of the three companies in the Worldair Alliance. This analysis is for 'next year' and requires the use of the current year figures adapted for expected changes, most of which result from the recent bad publicity. You are also required to explain the value of such analysis.

In Part (d) you are required to discuss the attitudes of the different members of the Alliance towards a policy to address the bad publicity issue. Your discussion should outline different opinions they may have and why they have them. You also need to suggest how to reconcile such differences.

(a) **Effects of being a member of an alliance in determining aims and objectives**

Benefits

The benefits for PC of being in an alliance when determining its aims and objectives are as follows:

(i) *Shared information*

The competitors can share information between them to support each other's objective setting. Such benchmarking information about competitors can often be hard to obtain. PC might, for instance, find that AB is operating with a much lower number of administrative staff. This therefore allows them to be able to set realistic objectives for improvement in this area.

(ii) *Shared objectives*

Objectives for PC will naturally fall out of the consequences of being a part of the group because many of the group's operations will be interlinked with AB and US. This may make objective setting easier since it will have to follow the group as a whole.

For example, reduction in cost of 5% might be expected through economies of scale. This then becomes the objective for the company for the next year.

Disadvantages

The disadvantages of being a member of the alliance when determining objectives are as follows:

(i) *Agreeing consistent objectives*

The three airlines must agree consistent policies and direction in order to facilitate co-ordination and creation of a consistent image. The agreed aims are likely to be a compromise for all parties. The solution may therefore not be the one which is best for PC.

Being the smallest member of the group, PC may also find that they have less power in the relationship than the other parties, and that the competitor's objectives become imposed upon them.

(ii) *Time and effort*

Since objective setting may take longer if it needs to be negotiated with other parties, this may delay the process. This in itself costs money. It could also delay implementation of new ideas which could delay the benefits.

(iii) *Reliant on other parties*

PC might become reliant on the other parties for their success, and their own image will become reflective of the service provided by other parties. Some objectives, such as brand reputation and customer satisfaction, may therefore be linked to other parties and be dependent on them. A characteristic of a good objective, however, is that it is directly controllable by the person to whom it is being set. Finding directly controllable objectives may be difficult.

(iv) *Limitations on future strategy*

Being a member of the alliance may restrict PC's ability to follow its own desired strategic path in the future. It may, for instance, be restricted in expanding in the USA because of the conflict of interest with US. There has already been disagreement on the direction in relation to the bad publicity.

Examination tip:

Clearly separate points using headings. This clearly distinguishes each point you are making. This helps you to avoid waffling and helps the marker to see each distinct point.

(b) **Threat from bad publicity**

There has recently been bad publicity due to the lack of passenger space when travelling in economy-class seats on long-haul flights.

Consequences of not taking action

The possible consequences of not taking this action are as follows:

(i) *Possible reduction in passenger numbers*

Senior managers of the Alliance already predict that the expected 5% increase in passenger numbers will not occur in economy-class long-haul flights due to the bad publicity. If no action is taken the problem could get worse and passenger numbers could reduce in the long term, especially if competitors are proactive on this issue.

(ii) *Legal action*

If passenger discomfort from the cramped conditions were to cause medical problems (e.g. the recent publicity over deep vein thrombosis), the airlines could potentially face legal claims if they are not seen to be taking suitable action.

(iii) *Bad reputation*

The reputation of the Alliance members could worsen if they are seen to do nothing about the issue, especially if competitors respond more proactively. In the long term this could reduce passenger numbers for the Alliance companies.

Actions which the management team should take

The management team have a number of options to consider.

(i) *Undertake more research into the issue*

As a minimum the Alliance should be seen to be proactively researching the issue to find out to what extent the issue is a problem. For instance, are there any serious medical issues which could result from the cramped conditions?

It might also be important to find out how much extra space would be required to overcome any problems identified. This would enable revised seat spacings to be calculated and estimates of the financial effects to be made accurately.

This will also enable the Alliance to proactively influence the possible legislation which may result.

(ii) *Research alternative options*

There may be other alternatives beside reducing the number of seats such as changing seat layouts, seat types or encouraging people to do exercises periodically during flights. These options may be more economical and allay any concerns.

It may also be a way of demonstrating proactivity and hence enhancing image without significant investment.

(iii) *Legal advice/insurance*

The degree of liability for potential medical problems could be investigated to ascertain responsibility.

They should make sure any insurance which they have in place covers any legal action which could result.

(iv) *Show that they care – public relations*

It is important that the Alliance are seen to care about their customers. Being seen to research the issue or to be taking action by changing seat layouts will help to enhance the companies' reputations. A public relations programme should be put in place to ensure maximum benefit is gained from actions taken.

Availability and quality of data

There currently appears to be little confirmed data available on the issue. For instance, exactly how much extra space is required to overcome the problem? It is important that the Alliance does not rush into a response before more information is obtained. Simply removing 20 seats per flight may not give enough space to improve the problem.

(c) **Contribution analysis**

	PC $m	*AB* $m	*US* $m	*Total* $m
Turnover				
Economy				
– Long haul	(1,200 × 75% × 70%)	(2,540 × 50% × 80%)	(3,300 × 80% × 60%)	
(see W2)	630.0	1,016.0	1,584.0	3,230.0
– Short haul	(1,200 × 75% × 30% × 104%[W1]) 280.8	(2,540 × 50% × 20% × 104% [W1]) 264.2	(3,300 × 80% × 40% × 104% [W1]) 1,098.2	1,643.2
Other classes	(1,200 × 25% × 105%) 315.0	(2,540 × 50% × 105%) 1,333.5	(3,300 × 20% × 105%) 693.0	2,341.5
Gross contribution				
Economy (25% /10% /17.5%)	227.7	128.0	469.4	825.1
Other (70% / 85% / 80%)	220.5	1,133.5	554.4	1,908.4
Total	**428.3**	**1,261.5**	**1,023.8**	**2,733.5**
Other costs				
Refit costs	(30.0)	(50.0)	(80.0)	(160)
R&D and publicity	(70 × 1,200/7,040) (11.9)	(70 × 2,540/7,040) (25.3)	(70 × 3,300/7,040) (32.8)	(70)
Net contribution	**406.3**	**1,186.2**	**911.0**	**2,503.5**

(W1) **Effect of short-haul economy class travel**

Weighted average reduction in growth forecast =

(0.3 × 10%) + (0.4 × 20%) + (0.3 × 30%) = 20%

Growth forecast is 5% increase. This is therefore reduced by 20% to 4%.

(W2) **Reduction in seating capacity by 5%**

The reduction in seating capacity of 5% of economy class seats in long haul does not need to be taken account of in these figures since the airlines currently operate at 95% capacity, meaning that in this year the 5% reduction will not affect passenger numbers.

This does however mean that they will not be able to cope with increased demand in the future without increasing the number of flights operated and hence aircraft required.

Value of the analysis for strategic decision making

Strategic decisions must always be taken in light of the best available financial information about the consequences of decisions that are made. This analysis provides useful information about the immediate financial consequences of the new policy and can therefore support the decision-making process.

It is also useful since the split between gross and net contribution allows a simple comparison between the short-term effects (net contribution) and long-term effects (gross contribution). While there is a significant short-term reduction in contribution, the longer-term reduction is much smaller and more reflective of the long-term position.

This analysis also shows the impact of the change on the different companies. This helps to ensure that the strategy is appropriate for all members of the Alliance.

(d) **Different attitudes to policy**

One problem commonly found for companies who are members of an alliance is that they may be required to agree policies on issues on which the different parties have very different views. Each company will have its own culture, with different values and beliefs. Each will also be in a different position and affected by the issue in different ways.

In the case of the policy to create more space for economy-class passengers, PC and US favour swift implementation of the policy while AB favour waiting to see whether the bad publicity actually results in reduced passenger numbers before taking any action.

These different attitudes are probably reflective of the varying importance of economy class to the different airlines. PC and US get 75% and 80% of turnover and around half of their contribution from economy class passengers, while AB get only 50% turnover and just 10% of contribution from these passengers. A reduction in economy class passengers will therefore have a greater negative effect on PC and US than AB.

AB may view the fixed investment in refit, R&D and publicity as a poor investment since it is a large fixed cost for a part of their business which only produces a small return.

The amount of total fixed costs apportioned to each party may also be unfairly biased towards AB since the apportionment method used is based on the total turnover of all classes of traveller. AB will pay 33% of these costs, a total of $75.3m, a large portion given its focus on other classes of travel.

AB is also the least profitable of the companies and these profits are reducing. AB may therefore be averse to major investments given their position or simply not have the funds for investment.

Resolving the differences

The differences could be resolved in a number of ways.

(i) *Contract*

Some form of decision-making process was likely to be set down in the Alliance contract and agreed by all parties. The issue could simply be resolved by reference to this agreed approach.

If, for instance, all parties have to agree before a decision is made, then the Alliance should wait before implementing change. Alternatively a majority may be required in an equally weighted vote in which case the change should go ahead.

(ii) *Arbitration*

An arbiter could be used to make the final decision. Each party would present their view and the arbiter decides what action is taken. The arbiter could be the Alliance's management team if they were seen to be independent. Alternatively an independent arbiter could be employed.

(iii) *Compromising*

A compromise could be reached in which all parties would be kept happy without any one party's view representing the final solution. Before making the final decision they could perhaps agree to wait for a period shorter than AB would ideally like but which all parties could agree upon.

12 SYNFIB AND THETFIB

(a) A **mission statement** is directed primarily towards the employees of an organisation, and should help the company towards achieving its objectives. It might provide a statement of the company's culture, and also state the aims of the company and the business areas within which the company will operate. An alternative view is that a mission statement should include a statement of the business areas in which the company will operate and in addition, its reason for existence and the stakeholder groups who will be served by the company.

The mission statement of C is 'to provide its customers with the highest quality product at a reasonable price'.

This can be criticised as a mission statement for a number of reasons.

- It does not state the business areas in which the company intends to operate. Presumably, the company means synthetic fibre products, but the statement does not make this clear.
- It does not give a reason for the company's existence. In particular, the statement fails to give any indication why the company will be better than its competitors in what it does.
- It appears to focus on customer requirements only, and has nothing to say about other stakeholder groups, particularly employees and shareholders. It does not actually define who its customers are or who it wants its customers to be.
- It is dull. Short mission statements should be inspiring.
- The terms 'highest quality' and 'reasonable price' are unclear in their meaning. It is not clear what is meant by 'quality', nor what 'reasonable' is in terms of price. Assuming that it will be expensive to achieve the highest quality, how high might a reasonable price be?

Objectives might be phrased in general terms, as in the case of C, but to be of much value they should be more specific. It has been suggested that **objectives should be 'SMART'**, i.e. **specific, measurable, achievable, relevant and time-bound**. From the information provided, it seems that the objectives of C fail to meet these criteria.

- The stated aim is to 'satisfy the demands' of shareholders. Although there is reference to maximising shareholder wealth, and to setting limits to acceptable risk, there is no clear statement of what these objectives mean. They must be stated more specifically and put within a time frame. For example, an objective might be to increase profits and dividends over the next five years at the rate of at least x% each year. The risk limits would also have to be specified.
- The aim of reducing pollution to a minimum is also inadequate, because it fails to state what 'minimum' means or the time frame within which the objective should be met.
- The objective of maintaining secure employment is also vague and meaningless, except perhaps to indicate that the company will be reluctant to make members of its work force redundant, and this might be an unrealistic target. Again, a more specific objective is required.

- The objective of selling a high quality product to satisfy customer requirements has a link to the mission statement, but is also vague and so meaningless. Actual achievements cannot be monitored against such a vague objective.

Both the mission statement and the objectives should therefore be re-formulated along the guidelines suggested above.

(b) (i) **Optimum production quantity and profitability of Thetfib: Home**

Transfer price $40

Monthly quantity (million litres)	*200*	*400*	*600*
Sales price per litre	$70	$60	$50
	$m	$m	$m
Sales	14,000	24,000	30,000
Variable costs in Home ($15 per litre)	(3,000)	(6,000)	(9,000)
Transfer costs ($40 per litre)	(8,000)	(16,000)	(24,000)
Contribution	3,000	2,000	(3,000)
Fixed costs (emission control)	(2,000)		
Pre-tax profit	1,000		
Tax at 35%	(350)		
Profit after tax	650		

Note: Profitability is calculated only for the contribution-maximising output volume.

Transfer price $12

Monthly quantity (million litres)	*200*	*400*	*600*
Sales price per litre	$70	$60	$50
	$m	$m	$m
Sales	14,000	24,000	30,000
Variable costs in Home ($15 per litre)	(3,000)	(6,000)	(9,000)
Transfer costs ($12 per litre)	(2,400)	(4,800)	(7,200)
Contribution	8,600	13,200	13,800
Fixed costs (emission control)			(2,000)
Pre-tax profit			11,800
Tax at 35%			(4,130)
Profit after tax			7,670

By changing the transfer price from $40 to $12, the divisional manager M would decide to increase output from 200 million litres to 600 million litres each month, and the total profit for the division from the product would increase $7,020 million each month.

(ii) **Optimum production quantity and profitability of Thetfib: Foreign Transfer price $12**

Monthly quantity (million litres)	*200*	*400*	*600*
Sales price per litre	$70	$60	$50
	$m	$m	$m
Sales	14,000	24,000	30,000
Variable costs in Foreign ($15 per litre)	(4,400)	(8,800)	(13,200)
Transfer costs ($12 per litre)	(2,400)	(4,800)	(7,200)
Contribution	7,200	10,400	9,600
Fixed costs (emission control)		(600)	
Pre-tax profit		9,800	
Tax at 20%		1,960	
Profit after tax		7,840	

In this case, the manager of Foreign would choose to process 400 million litres each month. The profit for the division would be higher each month by $170 million than the profit that could be earned in Home at the same transfer price. However, output would be restricted to below the maximum level of demand.

(c) The figures show that the company will maximise its monthly profit by manufacturing 125 million litres of Synfib in Home and 400 million litres of Thetfib in Foreign. However, these output decisions are reached only if the transfer price is set at the marginal cost of the polymer, $12 per litre. When the transfer price allows an element for profit for the polymer production plant, and is set at $0, the decision by the producers of the profit centre managers for Synfib and Thetfib would be to make just 100 million litres of Synfib and just 200 million litres of Thetfib. This would not maximise the profit for the company as a whole.

The organisational objective might be expressed in general terms as maximising shareholder wealth. More specifically, this might be seen as a requirement to maximise profitability in the short-run (subject to constraints relating to product quality, job security, risk limitation, and so on). If this is the case, a management accounting system will be unsatisfactory if it is restricted to reporting divisional profitability within the framework of a profit centre arrangement and a transfer price of $40.

The problem exists for the company because additional units can only be sold by reducing the sales price for Synfib and Thetfib, whereas the transfer price would be a fixed unit cost, regardless of transfer quantity.

The introduction of transfer pricing would therefore have implications for the type and quality of information provided by the management accounting system.

In order to help the company to achieve its objectives, whilst still allowing the profit centre managers autonomy to make their own output decisions, calls for the provision of suitable information for decision-making. Each profit centre manager should be provided with information about the costs of production in each centre, and about sales demand for the end products at different selling prices. On the basis of this information, the managers should be encouraged to negotiate transfer prices. Using the information, the managers might be able to identify opportunities for increasing profits for the benefit of both profit centres concerned, for example, they might agree on a lower transfer price for transfer quantities above a certain amount each month.

It is essential that management at headquarters should be kept fully informed, to allow them to monitor company and divisional performance, and the efficiency of the system as a whole.

If the decision is to switch production of Thetfib from Home to Foreign, there could be implications for reporting performance in a foreign currency and translating results into the domestic currency of C. There could be foreign currency exposures, which should also be reported. The management accounting system would also need to incorporate data for computing tax liabilities on profits in Foreign, and (if any) withholding taxes on the transfer of dividends.

Management accounting systems inevitably focus primarily on financial figures rather than on non-financial considerations. It is perhaps worth noting that, if the company decides to produce Thetfib in Foreign rather than in Home, there could be job loss implications in Home. This would seem to run counter to the objective of providing secure employment.

(d) The directors of C should **begin by establishing the organisational objectives** the company is trying to achieve. In order to achieve these objectives, **key performance indicators** need to be established, and actual performance measured and monitored for each of those indicators. Tom Peters argued that 'what gets measured gets done'. By implication, unless something is measured, it does not necessarily get done.

The primary organisational objective is likely to be maximising shareholder wealth. This will probably be monitored in terms of growth in divisional profits, both in the short term and the longer term. It might be decided that key performance indicators might relate, for each division, to sales revenue growth, cost efficiency or effectiveness in achieving budgets. In the longer term, there should be performance indicators for innovation, since the company will need to continue innovating to succeed in a competitive environment.

The company will probably have some objectives for product quality. For each division, there should be quality targets, and performance can be monitored in each division in terms of those targets. Similarly, targets can be set for each division for pollution reduction (although it is significant that if Thetfib is manufactured in Foreign pollution will not be minimised, despite the company's stated objective).

Within a divisionalised structure, **the divisional managers need to agree with the performance measures** against which their performance will be judged. Having agreed the nature of the measures to use, specific targets can be set, for example annually within the budget. This process of discussion and agreement might take some time: it is important that performance measures and targets should not be imposed.

For each measure of performance, the company must **establish a system for monitoring actual results.** Profitability is perhaps fairly straightforward. In addition, however, measures might be required for factors such as quality, pollution emissions, customer satisfaction, and so on.

Once a system of performance measurement has been agreed and implemented, it should be **kept under review regularly**, to ensure that the system is helping the company to achieve its objectives. Any weaknesses in the system can be removed, for example by introducing different measures of performance or different methods of measuring actual results.

13 MW AND FS

Key answer tips

Sections (a) and (b) are relatively straightforward. Students, however, should relate to the case.

Part (c) requires students to note the Examiner's comments that there are only 10 marks available for the narrative part and 17 marks for the calculations.

(a) (i) **Production of a SWOT analysis for MW**

When developing a strategic plan it is useful to undertake a SWOT analysis. At the current time MW is seeking to enhance its shareholder value, its main objective. Therefore the SWOT analysis can be used to identify how the business can build on its strengths and take corrective action for its weaknesses. This in turn will increase both profitability and market share for MW.

Strengths

- Secure financial base.
- Well established in the North.
- Increased share price and profitability.

Weaknesses

- Prior experience in takeovers is limited.
- Lack of experience in managing the takeover process itself.
- Not maximising use of capital resources.
- Not much opportunity for further organic growth in the North.
- The company cultures will be different, so will require integration.

Opportunities

- Takeover will mean improvements in both competitiveness and market share.
- An increase in gearing will mean that the company will make increased use of debt, in turn resulting in lower costs, as debt is cheaper than equity.
- Takeover of FS will mean expansion into the South.

Threats

- Staff morale may fall when stores are sold after the takeover takes place.
- The bid cost may rise if competitors are also interested in purchasing FS.
- If MW does not do the takeover, it risks stagnation in its own market.
- The family shareholding will be diluted if the takeover goes ahead.
- Another competitor could purchase FS, meaning that MW would see a reduction in its competitiveness as well as losing market share.

(ii) **Explanation of how the SWOT analysis will assist MW in achieving its organisational objectives**

The SWOT analysis for MW has highlighted the fact that the northern market is reaching saturation. This means that for MW to increase shareholder value it must increase both the market growth rate and its market share, so consideration should be given to the possibility of a takeover. However, care must be taken by MW to ensure that the weaknesses identified in the SWOT analysis are addressed. Therefore consideration should be given to how the takeover process will be managed, given MW's lack of experience in this area. Also, it must consider that its bid may be unsuccessful, resulting in the loss of expenses incurred prior to the decision being made.

(b) Rappaport's seven drivers can be applied to MW, as follows:

- **Increase in the planning period** – In order for MW to develop a longer income stream it needs to be able to develop growth over a longer period. The past approach of organic growth will prove ineffective due to the size of the market, so a takeover appears logical.
- **Decrease in fixed capital investment rate** – The purchase of fixed assets results in a negative effect on short-term cashflows. However taking a longer term view will highlight that the short-term expense will represent an increase in shareholder value in the longer term, as investment will need to be made during the takeover.
- **Increasing sales growth** – Higher sales will mean that the cash flows increase resulting in an increase in shareholder value. Currently MW is doing this – for example an 8% increase in sales over the last financial year. However, long-term the company will have to perform a takeover in order to continue to increase its market share.
- **Increase in operating profit margin** – Similar to the above, MW's net profits have increased over the last year, so proving that it has the ability to convert higher sales into higher profits. It has also shown that it can be more efficient by demonstrating that as sales rise it can reduce the proportion of fixed overheads.
- **Decrease in cost of capital** – The takeover will mean a change in capital structure, meaning that MW will have more debt than at the current time. The cost of capital being lower will mean that future cash flows will be enhanced and so shareholder value increased. This will be the case providing that the level of debt does not become too high, as this would mean that shareholders would discount their returns by a higher rate to represent the higher risk.
- **Decrease in the cash income tax rate** – By the use of a more efficient capital structure MW will find that it will pay less tax; this is because the extra level of debt will benefit by being tax efficient.
- **Decrease in working capital** – The nature of MW's business means that high levels of inventory are required. There is a delicate balance between having too much inventory and not enough, meaning shelves are left bare. So the higher the inventory turnover rate the better as it keeps the shelves full but also minimises the cost of working capital.

According to Rappaport, business value equals 'The present value of future free cash flow from operations plus the value of marketable securities'. This means the cash that the business generates that becomes available for distribution in the form of dividends. This formula shows that market capitalisation will increase as shareholders buy the shares to take part in the capital and dividend growth, so forcing the share price up. Marketable securities are investments held by the company, which can be realised with little or no effect on current operations. Finally, when you then take away the value of debt from the business value this leaves shareholder value.

Therefore the shareholder value of any business can be increased by enhancing business value, reducing debt value or a mixture of both.

(c) **A report highlighting the benefits and risks of the acquisition of FS**

To: The Chairman of MW

From: Management Accountant

Date: 25 May 2004

Subject: The benefits and risks of acquiring FS

This report was requested in order to discuss the benefits and risks of the acquisition of FS. Bearing in mind that the prime objective of MW is to enhance shareholder value, this objective has been considered carefully during the writing of this report. Early sections of this report will make use of calculations made on the data set provided for both MW and FS this information is provided in an appendix.

Analysis of the data provided using appropriate calculations

It is immediately apparent from the calculations that the FS stores do not reach the level of absolute profitability enjoyed by MW. They do, however, have better gross profit to turnover levels. This means that MW is more efficient in terms of its overhead costs. If the takeover goes ahead shareholder value will be enhanced providing MW is able to achieve overall the same ratio of gross profit to turnover that FS currently achieves. Also, in order to increase shareholder value the net profit to turnover ratio of MW will need to be achieved within the new company, by carrying out efficiency improvements within FS. Inventory turnover is a good example of where MW currently has greater efficiency than FS, as FS holds inventory for 75% longer on average, meaning there is a potential to reduce costs by putting MW's policies in place.

Looking at the sales, gross profit and net profits per customer, it is apparent that FS uses premium pricing in comparison with MW. For example, if a comparison is made between the sales of northwest MW and the southwest FS stores the following calculation can be made:

$$\text{Volume of customers} = \frac{\$10\text{ million}}{\$6\text{ million}} \times 0.15\text{ million} = \frac{\textbf{0.25 million customers}}{\text{(MW's pricing policies)}}$$

This compares to 0.3 million customers of MW in the northwest, so reinforcing the fact that the higher sales and profits are a result of premium pricing.

In FS stores the gross profit to turnover is higher than in MW stores, whilst the profit per square metre of FS stores in the southwest is comparable to the northeast MW stores, but lower in the southeast. Also net profit per square metre is lower for the FS stores. This demonstrates that the increased gross profit to turnover ratio of FS is achieved by premium pricing and not efficient use of space. This means that this is another area where MW could add shareholder value, by increased efficiency in the use of floor space in FS stores.

It is also apparent from the calculations that the staff of MW generate more turnover per employee than those of FS. This again supports the fact that, if MW's efficiency can be implemented in FS stores, this will result in increased shareholder value. This lower level of turnover per employee could be caused by the fact that FS staff get paid less than MW employees doing the same job, meaning that staff morale could be low. I feel that this should also be looked at within the different geographical areas of MW, as at the present time there is a difference in salaries between those working in the northwest and the northeast.

An analysis of the potential impact of the takeover on shareholder value

The effect of the takeover on both sets of shareholders will be that the emphasis needs to be on MW increasing its profit to sales ratio, at the same time as replicating its efficiency within the FS stores. Providing both of these are carried out then shareholder wealth should increase.

The P/E ratio for both companies is 20, however when looking at the trends it becomes apparent that MW's has increased 100% in the last two years whilst FS's has fallen 33% in the same period. Also the share price for FS is sluggish in comparison to the movements on the MW share price. When looking at these two factors together they show that the market has more confidence in MW than FS.

A statement regarding strategic issues, which I feel, should be addressed by the board prior to the bid

Prior to making the bid the board must consider a number of issues. Competitors need to be considered as to what action they might take if the bid is made, for example a counter bid may be made and a contingency plan should be put in place by the board of MW to ensure a plan is in place if this occurs. The board should also consider at what level the bid should be set; the price should be high enough to ensure FS's shareholders agree to the takeover whilst not so high that it has a negative effect on MW's own shareholders. If competitors do put in a counter bid then consideration needs to be given as to how high the company is willing to bid, before it becomes detrimental to the existing shareholders of MW.

From a strategic viewpoint the takeover of FS appears to be in line with the objective to increase shareholder wealth, providing that MW ensures the proper advice is sought as to how to manage the takeover appropriately. It appears that the traditional organic growth that MW has utilised in the past will not be an appropriate growth strategy for the future. So the takeover strategy is the only other alternative available if the company wants to continue to grow in the long term. MW should take care not to incur damage to its own share price and consideration should be given to the fact that MW's shareholders will see a dilution of control.

Appendix

The P/E ratio for MW is therefore $\frac{\$3}{\$0.15} = \mathbf{20}$

The earnings per share for MW is: $\frac{\$4.5\text{ billion}}{\$3}$ = 1,500 million shares. $\frac{\$225\text{ million}}{1{,}500\text{ million}} = \$0.15$

The P/E ratio for FS is therefore $\frac{\$2}{\$0.10} = \mathbf{20}$

The earnings per share for FS is: $\frac{\$4\text{ billion}}{\$2}$ = 2,000m shares

$\frac{\$200\text{ million}}{2{,}000\text{ million}} = \$0.10$ per share

The inventory turnover rate for MW is 2 days and 3.5 days for FS (from information derived from scenario).

Calculations based on data provided in the scenario

	MW				FS			
	Northeast		*Northwest*		*Southeast*		*Southwest*	
Gross profit (excluding wages)	**$5 million**		**$6 million**		**$3.2 million**		**$4.0 million**	
Gross profit / Turnover	$5 million / $8 million	**62.5%**	$6 million / $10 million	**60%**	$3.2 million / $5 million	**64%**	$4 million / $6 million	**67%**
Net profit / Turnover	$1.4 million / $8 million	**17.5%**	$2 million / $10 million	**20%**	$0.5 million / $5 million	**10%**	$0.8 million / $6 million	**13.3%**
Gross profit / Sq metre	$5 million / 6,000	**$833**	$6 million / $6000	**$1,000**	$3.2 million / 4,800	**$667**	$4 million / 4800	**$833**
Net profit / Sq metre	$1.4 million / 6,000	**$233**	$2 million / $6000	**$333**	$0.5 million / 4,800	**$104**	$4 million / 4800	**$167**
Sales / Customer visit	$8 million / 0.2 million	**$40**	$10 million / $0.3 million	**$33.33**	$5 million / 0.1 million	**$50**	$6 million / $0.15million	**$40**
Gross profit / Customer visit	$5 million / 0.2 million	**$25**	$6 million / $0.3 million	**$20**	$3.2 million / 0.1 million	**$32**	$4million / $0.15 million	**$27**
Net profit / Customer visit	$1.4 million / 0.2 million	**$7**	$2 million / $0.3 million	**$6.67**	$0.5 million / 0.1 million	**$5**	$0.8 million / $0.15 million	**$5·3**
Turnover / Staff	$8 million / 56	**$143k**	$10 million / 69	**$145k**	$5 million / 51	**$98k**	$6 million / 56	**$107k**
Salaries per manager and supervisor	$1 million / 12	**$83.3k**	$1 million / 15	**$66.7k**	$0.6 million / 12	**$50k**	$0.7 million / 14	**$50k**
Other staff costs per staff member	$0.7 million / 44	**$16k**	$1 million / 54	**$18.5k**	$0.6 million / 12	**$15k**	$0.7 million / 42	**$16.7k**

14 ACEP (PILOT PAPER)

(a) ACEP plc (ACEP)

Workings

Calculation of annual net profit

Probability	*Volume*	*Weighted volume*
0.4	10,000	4,000
0.5	12,000	6,000
0.1	14,000	1,400
Expected volume		11,400

	£
Retail price per copy	2.00
Less margin to retailer	0.50
Net retail	1.50
Variable costs	0.45
Contribution per copy	1.05
Expected monthly contribution	11,970
Advertising revenue	18,000
Total	29,970
Less monthly promotion cost	12,000
Less fixed costs	16,000
Monthly net income	1,970
Annual net income	23,640
Net income for 50 stores	1,182,000

However, if sales volumes are considered separately:

Sales volume	*10,000*	*12,000*	*14,000*
	£	£	£
Contribution per copy	1.05	1.05	1.05
Expected monthly contribution	10,500	12,600	14,700
Add advertising revenue	17,000	18,000	18,000
Total	27,500	30,600	32,700
Less monthly promotion costs	12,000	12,000	12,000
Less monthly fixed costs	16,000	16,000	16,000
Monthly net income	500	2,600	4,700
Annual net income	–6,000	31,200	56,400
Net income for 50 stores	–300,000	1,560,000	2,820,000

It should be noted that the figures on which these calculations have been based have been provided by the equipment vendor and may be optimistic. *(The calculations apply probabilities to the volumes rather than the final net income figure.)*

As can be seen from this calculation there is, in fact, a 40% chance of only 10,000 units of sale a month with a potential loss of £300,000. It is only with the sales volumes above 10,000, which have a collective probability of 60%, that the venture will show a profit. In the light of the losses already being made in the music division this would seem to represent an unacceptable risk to the company and the shareholders.

Bearing in mind the problems that the industry is experiencing with the illegal downloading of music via the Internet, the company would need to be sure that its target market is likely to take up the opportunity of legally downloading music in retail outlets. As the 13 to 30 age group become even more computer literate, and as the pressure mounts on the recorded music industry to reach an arrangement with the companies that produce file-sharing software, it is unlikely that this venture will be profitable in the longer term.

(b) Portfolio analysis is probably one of the best-known and most widely applied techniques of strategy analysis that has been developed. The two most commonly quoted models are the GE/McKinsey portfolio analysis matrix and the BCG matrix (or Boston box).

The matrix examines the position of a business unit or division in terms of the two primary sources of profitability – industry attractiveness and competitive position. In the case of the GE/McKinsey matrix the two parameters of industry attractiveness and competitive position are composites whereas for the BCG matrix they are single variables, simply using annual real rate of market growth and relative market share, respectively.

The fundamental idea is to represent the businesses of a diversified company within a simple graphic framework that can be used to assist in four areas of strategy formulation:

1 **Formulating business unit strategy**

On the basis of the same two criteria – industry attractiveness and competitive position – portfolio analysis yields simple and straightforward decision rules for strategic behaviour for the company. For instance, depending on the position in the McKinsey matrix, the recommendation will be to grow, hold or harvest. Similarly classification within the Boston Box will result in SBUs being labelled as 'Stars', 'Cash Cows', 'Question marks' or 'Dogs' with recommendations to invest for growth, milk, invest for growth or dispose, and dispose respectively.

2 **Resource allocation**

This facilitates the comparison of its investment attractiveness against that of other business units within the firm and will offer guidance on the attractiveness of further investment.

3 **Setting performance targets**

The classification within the matrix may assist in the estimation of reasonable expectations of profit performance for the particular business.

4 **Analysing portfolio balance**

It is useful to have a single diagrammatic representation of all of the different businesses within the company to assess the overall balance, cohesiveness and performance potential of the portfolio. Several dimensions can be used when assessing company performance such as cash flow, continuity and risk. For a diversified company, seeking independence from the capital markets, the balance of cash flow will be important as businesses in their growth phases, which are net absorbers of cash, can be balanced with, and supported by, cash generative divisions. With this in mind companies will often try to maintain a portfolio of businesses which are at different stages of their life cycle so that, as older ones mature and, eventually die, they are replaced by younger, growing businesses.

The concept of the BCG matrix was developed by the Boston Consulting Group at the same time as the consultancy was promoting the learning curve as a means of determining aggressive pricing for market domination. This, in part, leads to the major criticisms of portfolio models:

- The assumption that each business is independent and that any complementary features they may have is ignored.
- It is not always the case that market share and growth rate are necessarily determinants of profitability.
- The ranking of the business units against the two variables of market growth rate and market share will depend heavily on how the market is defined.

- The normative strategies offered in some versions of the matrices should only be considered as a guide. Over-dependence on these prescriptions might prevent insightful analysis and "out of the box" thinking. For instance, a number of companies make a good return from investing in businesses at the end of their life cycle and becoming a supplier of last resort. As others leave the market the last supplier enjoys increasing market share.

In terms of the classification of the businesses in which ACEP operates, both publishing and radio occupy a strong position regarding market share. Publishing represents market leadership in its target market and radio is one of three equally placed market leaders. Both operate in a mature market in which little real growth can be expected. ACEP's other interests, television and music, are a different matter. Both are relatively small in terms of their contribution to the company's profits and in terms of market presence. We may assume that the growth rate for television production is relatively low, while that for music is actually declining due to the factors explained in the case. A straightforward application of the decision 'rules' arising from either product portfolio matrix would suggest that the portfolio is not balanced and that there is a need for a new vehicle for growth. Further it would suggest that possibly television production and, definitely, music should be divested since neither have a significant market share.

However, while it is difficult to justify continuing to support the music division, there can be a strong case for retaining and trying to grow the television production SBU. The cross marketing opportunities between television, magazines and radio could be exploited to the full.

(c) (i) As an initial step, an analysis of the business environment concentrating on political, economic, societal and technological factors should be conducted. Likely areas of concern under each might be:

Political

Legislation concerning foreign ownership of media, language content of media, moral issues on content of media, sourcing of materials and working practices. Protectionism in any form and level of bureaucracy.

Economic

Taxation, minimum rates of pay, exchange rates and company law. Strength of advertising market, production costs and prevailing rates of pay. Cost of magazine quality paper.

Social

Issues of taste and culture, particularly the portability of youth and English culture, working practices, reading habits, attitude to music and other forms of leisure as well as other considerations of lifestyle. The position of magazines in the life cycle. Age profile and size of target market. Management working practices and organisational culture.

Technological

Print process, availability of ISDN and other media transfer.

This initial analysis might lead to the following conclusions about risk:

- the company might not understand the foreign country's business culture
- the company may not know how to deal effectively with the nationals
- the company might underestimate foreign regulations and incur unexpected costs

- the foreign country may change its commercial, media or employment laws
- the company may not have suitable managers to deal with an international situation
- the established players may react to keep ACEP out of the market.

(ii) The company has two possible avenues for entering the European market, by acquisition or via a joint venture.

Both opportunities are reasonably attractive in purely financial terms. The acquisition at £10 million yielding a contribution each year of £3 million and increased fixed costs of £1 million. The joint venture involves ACEP in an investment of twice as much at £20 million but will bring an annual contribution of £4 million and increased fixed costs of £1 million. Additionally since advertising revenue depends in part on the economy, ACEP will be spreading part of its business risk.

The main considerations for the decision are non-financial. Aside from the risks described above a number of other factors should be considered.

Generally joint ventures can offer significant advantages in surmounting import quotas, tariffs, nationalist political interests and cultural roadblocks to the product. Economic, competitive, and political realities of nationalism often require a domestic partner so as to gain access to the foreign national market. Local knowledge of the accepted ways of doing business and necessary contacts together with ACEP's acknowledged expertise may well make a winning combination. The formation of a joint venture will reduce competition - had ACEP entered the market in any other way, its potential partner would have been a competitor.

Additionally ACEP could use the joint venture to gain better market knowledge should it subsequently decide to enter the market by acquisition. There is likely to be less resistance to a joint venture than to an acquisition. Against these potential advantages must be set the possibilities of cross cultural management conflicts and how such conflicts would be resolved. There is a considerable difference between the management cultures across European countries. To compound these differences the potential partner is privately owned and this may well mean there is quite an entrenched culture within the firm.

A decision should be made at an early stage as the likely duration of the joint venture and the intended end game. Is the intention to learn the market and methods and, with that experience, buy out the partner and make acquisitions? Additionally some thought should be given to the intentions of the potential partner; is it entering this venture with an intention of learning from ACEP, so that it may launch into the home market?

However with an acquisition there can be no disagreements on strategy, structure and control, and relative freedom to act. Against that must be recognised that publishing is a service business and human capital is of vital importance. If key members of staff leave post-acquisition there will be a greatly reduced chance of success.

The question states that 'a potential target has been identified'; no mention is made of the attitude of the present owners to the prospect. If they are willing vendors and are prepared to remain with the company to facilitate the transition this will significantly increase the chances of success. Although the company has a good reputation for post-acquisition rationalisation in the publishing industry this is not something it has done in geographically and culturally different markets. If this were to be a hostile takeover, that rationalisation task would be made much harder. The issue of management culture is as important for this option as it is for the joint venture. Regardless of the quality of the due diligence done prior to the purchase, it is very few acquisitions that do not result in some surprises once ownership is established.

There have been many cases where cross-border acquisitions have failed and the joint venture would appear to be the route with the least risk.

(d) **Internal Memorandum to the Board of Directors**

From: Financial Controller

Recommendations to purchase CD downloading equipment, move into Europe and/or dispose of the television and music divisions. My recommendations are based on the workings contained in Appendix 1.

The opportunity to install CD downloading equipment in the retail outlets should be rejected. While, according to the equipment supplier, there is a 60% probability that the venture will be profitable, there is a 40% probability of a loss of £300,000. It must also be borne in mind that the calculations are based on figures that have been supplied by the equipment vendor and may well be biased to provide an attractive picture of the project. As the stable of bands which ACEP controls are of specialist interest, the demand figures cannot be certain and should be treated with some scepticism. Additionally, acceptance of this project would require retention of the music division and the current losses of £14 million.

The prospect of an agreement being reached between the software manufacturers and the major record labels is quite possible and downloading from the Internet to home computers becoming acceptable practice should not be ignored.

Additionally, the prospect of a computer-literate market ignoring the legality of the situation and continuing to download to its PCs makes the demand forecasts, similarly, less reliable.

However, in the event that this type of business does become viable it would attract the attention of the larger record labels which, with a superior knowledge of the music business, and a significantly stronger back catalogue of music, would be likely to be interested in entering the market and would compete strongly.

The five institutional shareholders, who wield considerable power – since the rest of the shares are widely held – cannot be ignored. The music division has not performed well since acquisition and could be argued to be outside the competence of the company where senior management has, primarily, a background and expertise in publishing. As the company is responsible for some of the top magazine titles in both the lifestyle and teenage markets this expertise is considerable. Since the music division is trying to serve a market for specialist bands it is unlikely that there is much cross marketing between this division and the other three divisions of the company. The recorded music industry is going through a period of increasing consolidation, with increasingly larger players at one end of the market. However, a number of small bands are starting to distribute their music via the Internet. The smaller producer is likely to be squeezed out of the business in the foreseeable future.

While it is not known how much capital employed is represented in the Music division boosting the PBIT for the past year by £14 million would have a significant effect on the results of the company. Whether the sale price of £10 million suggested by the shareholders is realistic or not is not known, but the division should be sold, preferably as a going concern, to one of the larger record labels.

However, in terms of PBIT/sales the television division is attractive and in the last year has shown a better margin than publishing. For this reason, and the opportunities for cross-marketing with the radio and publishing divisions, the television unit should be retained.

The move into mainland Europe should be undertaken. With the board's proven expertise in consumer magazine publishing and its leadership position in both teenage and lifestyle magazines it should develop this expertise abroad. There is talk of a 'global teenager' and lifestyle marketing translates across the developed world. Of the two options for entering the market the acquisition would involve capital expenditure of £10 million with a forecast to increase PBIT by £2 million in the first year before ACEP's talent for rationalisation is applied. This, however, might not prove to be that easy to achieve in a foreign market where differences in culture and management style might affect the ability to bring about change. Additionally the risk of key, local, staff leaving cannot be ignored.

However, the joint venture at £20 million capital expenditure is projected to increase PBIT, in the first year, of £3 million. On a crude payback calculation this is not as attractive as the acquisition option, but it carries a significantly lower risk. As long as the management of the two companies can co-operate effectively, then the prospect of ACEP bringing its expertise to bear in terms of rationalisation may well bring about a greater increase in PBIT in subsequent years. ACEP should approach this as an exercise in testing the market with a view to developing sufficient knowledge to more fully enter the market in subsequent years.

The presentation to the institutional investors should make the following points:

- Recognising that there is little synergy between the music division and the rest of the business, the music division should be sold as a going concern at the earliest opportunity.
- This should increase PBIT by £14 million in terms of this year's results and, should the estimates of sales proceeds be correct, provide £10 million for other growth opportunities. It must be noted, however, that there may well be offsetting costs of disposal.
- This will allow management to concentrate on the core business of information and entertainment for the 13 to 30 age range market, seeking to maximize opportunities for cross marketing across the media, that is publishing, radio broadcasting and television.
- This is expected to consolidate the underlying gains in PBIT which occurred during 1999 and 2000 in these divisions. The adverse results for 2001 and 2002 in those divisions would appear to have been brought about by the depressed advertising market which is dependent upon the general state of the economy.
- To reduce the dependency on the UK economy and its impact upon advertising revenue, the company intends to enter an additional European magazine market via a joint venture. Capitalising on local knowledge, via the joint venture partners, and ACEP's skills in rationalisation and magazine launch are expected, initially, to add £3 million per year to PBIT.

It is recognised that there are no further opportunities for expansion in the radio broadcast industry since the company has the maximum number of licences. Since growth by acquisition in publishing within the UK is not possible, overseas expansion and/or organic growth are the only options open to ACEP. The company will continue to launch new titles within the UK where lifestyle surveys suggest that this is feasible, but is taking the exploratory step of expanding into mainland Europe.

Appendix 1

Workings

£ millions	*2002*	*2001*	*2000*	*1999*
Sales				
Publishing	425	500	523	419
Radio	350	375	380	320
Television	65	75	80	70
Music	20	30	40	44
Total	860	980	1,023	853
Variable costs				
Publishing	208	225	235	189
Radio	91	94	95	80
Television	12	19	20	18
Music	4	6	8	9
Total	315	344	358	296
Fixed costs				
Publishing	161	160	162	155
Radio	150	150	148	128
Television	40	40	40	35
Music	30	30	32	32
Total	381	380	382	350
PBIT				
Publishing	56	115	126	75
Radio	109	131	137	112
Television	13	16	20	17
Music	–14	–6	0	3
Total	164	256	283	207
Capital employed	900	900	870	805
ROCE (PBIT/CE) %	18.22	28.44	32.53	25.71
PBIT/Sales				
Publishing	0.13	0.23	0.24	0.18
Radio	0.31	0.35	0.36	0.35
Television	0.20	0.21	0.25	0.24
Music	–0.70	–0.20	0.00	0.07
Total	0.19	0.26	0.28	0.24

15 PIPECO (MAY 05 EXAM)

Examiner's Comments

Common errors that occurred in May 05 exam

(a)
- Incorrect application of NPV, using incorrect discount factor, or incorrect methods of calculation.
- No profitability calculations.
- No non-financial analysis of the strategic options.
- No recommendations provided, or recommendations which did not fit with strategic analysis carried out.

(b)
- Lack of depth to answers.
- Little mention of each country's competitive environment.
- Lack of application to the scenario.

(c) (i)
- Lack of knowledge of relationship marketing.
- Lack of application to the scenario when presenting the advantages of relationship marketing.

(ii)
- Lack of knowledge of relationship marketing.
- Lack of application to the scenario when presenting change management activities relating to both relationship marketing and the acquisition.

(a) **Recommendations**

The main issues to consider in choosing between the different options are as follows:

Expected impact on shareholder wealth

- The impact on shareholder wealth is given by the NPV of each option.
- Under option 1, an investment in Country A should increase shareholder wealth by $195,000 (W1) and an investment in Country B, $199,000 (W1). This would suggest that Country B is best under option 1, although the difference is marginal.
- With option 2 the expected increase in shareholder wealth would be $213,000 (W2), suggesting that option 2 is better than option 1.

Expected profitability

- The parent group is under pressure to improve profitability, particularly over the next five years.
- Within option 1, Country B is preferred to Country A, as it will boost profit by the most over the next five years (W4).
- Based on weighted average outcomes, option 2 would generate more profit than option 1 (W4) making option 2 preferable.

Risk

- While option 2 has the highest expected NPV, there are three possible identified outcomes with this project. There is a 50% chance of barely breaking even, a 30% chance of making $837,000 and a 20% of losing $208,000 (W3). Overall there is only a 30% chance of performing better than option 1.

- A similar analysis applies to profitability. On average option 2 makes the greater profit but there is only a 30% chance of option 2 actually making a higher profit than option 1 in year 2 or thereafter (W4).
- This makes option 2 more risky to shareholders than option 1, unless the forecasts for option 1 already incorporate a similar analysis.
- One way of incorporating this may be to use a higher discount rate for option 2 but with the figures calculated shareholders may prefer option 1 as it makes nearly as much on average and is less risky.
- One could also argue that option 2 is more risky as it involves different technologies than used currently. This would make the management of Pipeco more dependent on the existing team at the target company until the learning curve has been experienced.
- There would also be the risks associated with acquiring another company and the integration issues that follow. Management are already considering changing the marketing approach under option 2.
- A counter argument could be that the product under option 2 is likely to be higher margin and differentiated. This would normally result in a higher margin of safety compared to break-even.

Staffing issues

- Option 1 would involve relocating some existing staff to other countries and keeping the remainder on only until existing contracts finish. The attractiveness of this option to staff would depend on which country was chosen and how far away it is from Pipeco's domestic country.
- Option 2 involves buying another company. Given that it is based in the same country as Pipeco, any staff relocation will be easier. However, there will probably be fewer staff retained as the target company will already have experienced staff and the construction techniques are different.
- On balance staff would probably prefer option 1.

Cash flow and capital rationing

- As stated above, positive expected NPVs indicate that both options are worthwhile. The natures of the projects suggest that they are independent so both could be undertaken should funds permit. If the capital rationing is 'soft' – i.e. due to budgetary constraints – then the parent company should consider releasing more funds.
- If the capital rationing is 'hard,' i.e. due to problems raising capital – then under option 1 Country A becomes more attractive than B as it uses $500,000 less cash initially, which could be freed up for investment in other group companies. The NPVs of such investments would have to be calculated to see if the switch from B to A is worthwhile.
- The capital rationing also adds to option 2's attractiveness, as it only requires an initial investment of $1,450,000 – less than either investment under option 1.
- A major problem with option 2 is that further cash of $425,000 is required at the end of the first year, seriously limiting the potential dividends at that time.
- If there are ongoing liquidity problems, then option 2 is preferred as it has a shorter payback period (again based on expected values) (W5).

Other strategic issues

- Option 1 appears to generate cash flows over a longer period than option 2, suggesting that option 1 will make the firm's long-term future more secure. However, this is probably due to differences in planning horizons as one would expect the firm's existing product to have a finite life in new countries, just as has happened in its home country once infrastructure has been developed. Option 2 would give a more secure long term future.
- Success under option 2 is based more on the reputation and core competences of the target company, whereas under option 1 Pipeco would still benefit from its existing goodwill and expertise.
- Option 2 would also involve a change in competitive strategy - Pipeco's existing competitive advantage seems to be based on cost but a strategy of differentiation would be needed under option 2. This would require a major change in culture and performance appraisal methods to be successful.

Summary

The option of doing nothing is not acceptable, as it will result in lower dividends and few future prospects.

Within option 1 there is little to choose between the two countries without further information. They have very similar NPVs and paybacks. Country A requires less investment but Country B has better profitability.

Financial analysis indicates that option 2 is better than option 1, having a higher NPV, higher profit and shorter payback, all based on weighted average outcomes. However, it is also the more risky option and less likely to appeal to staff. The resolution of these factors would depend on the risk: return preferences of the parent group and its shareholders.

Workings

(W1) **Option 1: NPV approach**

Country A

Time	*Narrative*	*Cash flow* $000	*Discount factor* *@10%*	*Present value* $000
0	Investment	(1,500)	1	(1,500)
1 – 5	Contribution (42 × 5)	210	3.791	796
6 – 10	Contribution (64 × 5)	320	6.145 – 3.791	753
11 – 15	Contribution (20 × 5)	100	7.606 – 6.145	146
	NPV			**195**

Country B

Time	*Narrative*	*Cash flow* $000	*Discount factor* *@10%*	*Present value* $000
0	Investment	(2,000)	1	(2,000)
1 – 8	Contribution (63 ×5)	315	5.335	1,681
9 – 14	Contribution (51 × 5)	255	7.367 – 5.335	518
	NPV			**199**

(W2) **Option 2: NPV approach based on expected values**

Time	*Narrative*	*Cash flow* $000	*Discount factor @10%*	*Present value* $000
0	Investment	(1,450)	1	(1,450)
1	Investment	(425)	0.909	(386)
1 – 10	Contribution*	333.5	6.145	2,049
	NPV			**213**

* Expected contribution = 300 × 0.5 + 435 × 0.3 + 265 × 0.2 = 333.5 pa

(W3) **Option 2: NPV approach based on possible outcomes**

Annual contribution $000	*Probability*	*Calculation*	*NPV* $000
300	0.5	– 1,450 – 386 + 300 × 6.145	8
435	0.3	– 1,450 – 386 + 435 × 6.145	837
265	0.2	– 1,450 – 386 + 265 × 6.145	(208)

(W4) **Profitability for the first five years**

	Option 1		**Option 2**	
	Country A $000	*Country B* $000	*Year 1* $000	*Year 2* $000
Contribution	210	315	333.5	333.5
Depreciation (straight line over 10 years)	(150)	(200)	(145)	(187.5)
Annual profit	**60**	**115**	**188.5**	**146**

Note: With option 2, we are told that the initial investment is in plant and equipment as well as containing the purchase price of a company. The depreciation in the first year would be $1,450,000 / 10 = $145,000. In subsequent years the depreciation would be $1,875,000 / 10.

If possible cash flows are used for option 2 rather than weighted average flows, then there is a 70% of a lower profit than under option 1 for country B:

Probability	0.5	0.3	0.2
Annual contribution	300	435	265
Fixed costs	(187.5)	(187.5)	(187.5)
Profit	112.5	247.5	77.5

(W5) **Payback periods**

Option 1	Country A	6.4 years
	Country B	6.3 years
Option 2		5.6 years

Tutorial note: There are a number of ways of trying to reflect the capital rationing in the calculations:

- Calculate the NPV per $ invested at time zero: This is the standard approach of key factor analysis, though strictly only applies if options are independent and divisible. Option 2 in particular is unlikely to be divisible.
- Calculate the NPV / PV of invested funds: This is a variation of the first approach and would be more useful for option 2 where the investment is spread over two periods.
- Calculate PV of inflows / PV of outflows: Another type of profitability index.

(b) **In deciding between the two countries under option 1, the following additional information would need to be gathered:**

Proximity

- A closer country would make relocating existing staff easier.

Government policies

- Would the government concerned practise any form of protectionism, e.g. favouring domestic firms for contracts?
- What are the stated policies of the government regarding growth in infrastructure?
- At what level within government are decisions regarding contractors made?
- What are the governments' policies on taxation? A country with higher tax is more likely to see funds reinvested in infrastructure.

Economic strength

- A country with a stronger economy is more likely to see high investment in infrastructure.

Nature of clients

- Other than government departments, who will be the main clients and how much power will they exercise?

Competition

- How many competitors already operate in the countries concerned?
- What are the relative strengths and weaknesses of these competitors?
- Do they already have well-established links with government departments, for example?
- Are other international firms planning on entering these markets?
- Would any existing firms be suitable partners for a joint venture?

Other issues

- Is the country a member of the EU yet or planning to become one?
- What is the local legislation regarding staffing, health and safety and pollution?

(c) (i) Relationship marketing has been defined as the technique of maintaining and exploiting the firm's existing customer base as a means of developing new business opportunities, rather than just focusing on new customers.

Relationship marketing focuses on building customer loyalty by developing strong relationships with existing customers. Some firms are guilty of chasing new customers while neglecting existing ones. Customers should not be treated as strangers every time they return for repeat business.

Payne suggested a six-market model, where the firm should widen its view of marketing to include customer markets, supplier markets, recruitment markets, referral markets, internal markets and influence markets.

Relationship marketing would benefit the company as follows:

- Lower risk of losing existing customers to competitors – the strong relationships developed effectively act as switching costs.
- An increased spend per customer as customers stay customers for longer.
- A greater chance of architects recommending the firm to other potential customers due to increased satisfaction.
- Better information about customer needs facilitating more effective product development.
- More attention to customers would increase the perceived value of the product in the minds of customers
- A reduction in the power of customers, particularly larger retail outlets, as they would be less inclined to switch suppliers.
- Better motivation for sales staff that will see the long-term consequences of their actions.

(ii) There are two aspects of change associated with option 2 to be considered:

1 Implementing relationship marketing

2 Managing the acquisition

If both are implemented simultaneously, then the demands on management are greater, so it is even more important to manage the changes quickly and efficiently.

The main issues to be considered are as follows:

Management issues

- With any acquisition it is important to assess the senior management of both firms with a view to deciding who stays and who becomes a 'synergistic saving'.
- Given the large differences between the two companies, the existing owner should be kept on for an agreed period to facilitate the transfer of expertise and goodwill. An 'earn-out' arrangement for the purchase would help here.
- A driver of successful change is having an united, committed senior management team. Many firms find that it is helpful to appoint a change agent or champion of change from this group to take responsibility for managing the overall process.

Organisational issues

- Management need to decide whether the two marketing departments should be merged or kept separate. Having one department will make integration and staff training easier but two departments may be more efficient reflecting the two very different markets the group will be operating in.

- Either way, the management of Pipeco will need to examine the existing marketing department of the target company to analyse its existing KPIs, culture, management style and marketing approach.
- Given that the target company is small, there is a possibility that it does not have an existing marketing department in which case the decision becomes whether to create one with a new culture and methods from the start or change Pipeco's existing department.

Staffing issues

- With any acquisition there is the danger of staff losses from the acquired firm due to uncertainty. Staff from both firms will fear for their jobs, so it is vital that the management of Pipeco communicate their plans and vision to employees to prevent key workers leaving.
- Marketing employees of either firm who have had any prior experience of relationship marketing need to be identified and retained.
- A training programme needs to be developed to train staff in the concepts and best practice of relationship marketing. An external training firm will be best unless the target company already has expertise in this area. Note that this should be extended beyond just the marketing employees.
- Existing production employees of Pipeco who are best suited to retraining in the new processes need to be identified, retained and a training programme developed for them.

Objectives and target setting

- A key aspect of change management is to ensure that a clear vision is developed and communicated to all staff as quickly as possible.
- All methods of communication should be used to ensure that unhelpful rumours and misinformation are eliminated. These can include regular emails and staff meetings.
- A new system of targets and rewards needs to be introduced in the acquired firm as soon as possible, particularly to facilitate strong financial control.
- There is an opportunity here to give great publicity to employees who successfully embrace new procedures, whether marketing or production. This will help reduce resistance to the changes.
- The KPIs for marketing will probably need to be changed to include customer retention and total spend per customer, assuming that theses are not present already.

16 S COMPANY (NOV 05 EXAM)

(a) **Threats**

Key answer tips

PEST and Porter's five forces models are useful ways of identifying threats, though you did not have to structure your answer around them. Also, as well as the direct threats to S, you need to think why passenger and freight transportation are needed and look at the threats from those directions.

S faces the following threats from changing market conditions:

Threats to the islands' agriculture industry will affect the amount of freight S carries. Such threats could include:

- Flowers and vegetables being grown more cheaply in developing countries and brought to mainland markets using on improved distribution infrastructure. (For example, this has been a major problem for flower growers in the Channel Islands as supply has switched to Africa from where flowers are flown to UK markets using refrigerated aircraft.)
- Consumer tastes changing in favour of more exotic vegetables not grown on the islands.
- Increased pressure on island farmers from mainland supermarkets.

Likewise **threats to the islands' tourist industry** will affect the demand for S's passenger places. Such threats could include:

- other destinations becoming more fashionable
- other destinations becoming more affordable due to cheaper air fares
- global warming affecting local weather conditions.

Other threats to the local economy, such a recession on the mainland would also impact the demand for S's services.

Increased competition from other airlines serving the islands would be a threat both to S's airline revenues and to its shipping. The erosion of the price premium for flying will make travel by ship less and less attractive. The threat from other airlines is a major problem as:

- customers have better information on the internet allowing them to shop around more for flights
- it is difficult to create switching costs, tying customers in, other than by the use of loyalty schemes
- the airline industry has very high fixed costs so pressure to drop prices is intense.

There may also be a **potential threat of increased competition for sea freight and passengers.** Other ship operators may be attracted to enter the local market, especially if the tourist industry continues to grow. S has little experience of dealing with such rivalry.

Increases in oil prices due to political uncertainty in the Middle East have affected fuel prices and profits to date and future volatility is likely to increase.

Price rises and / or increased competition for mooring rights would adversely affect profit and even the viability of shipping. S Company is very reliant on securing mooring rights both on the islands and the mainland.

Emerging stakeholder groups may be able to exercise considerable power over S. M, for example, will have significant power in five years' time to demand price cuts and tighter control measures if S is to keep the contract.

Other **political threats** include changing laws and governments. These could include tighter safety regulations with a corresponding increase in S's costs.

Together these result in considerable uncertainty in the decision-making environment and the need to spend to reduce it – for example on scenario planning systems. It also highlights the problems with the availability and quality of information gained.

(b) **Pricing calculation using discounted cash flows**

Key answer tips

There are a number of areas where you might interpret the numbers differently so it is vital that you state your assumptions.

£000s	*0*	*1*	*2*	*3*	*4*	*5*	*6*	*7*
Contribution from additional freight			2,000					
Contribution from extra ship passengers (W)				1,123	1,123	1,123	1,123	1,123
Contribution from extra air passengers (W)				156	156	156	156	156
Buy / sell new ship			(7,000)					4,000
Building works			(1,000)					
Scrap existing ship			250					
Net cash flow	0	0	(5,750)	1,279	1,279	1,279	1,279	5,279
Discount factor @ 20%	1	0.833	0.684	0.579	0.482	0.402	0.335	0.279
Present value	0	0	(3,933)	741	616	514	428	1,473
NPV =	**–161**							

Equivalent annual cost = NPV / annuity discount factor years 3 to 7= –161 / (3.605–1.528) = 77,500 pa.

The minimum payment required from M is thus £77,500 per annum.

Assumptions

All of the extra M customers are transported by S, either by sea or air. (***Note:*** You could easily assume that we are only bidding for the sea passengers.)

The extra capacity of 450 sea passengers can be carried in addition to the existing 200 on the new ship, so no profit is lost from existing activities.

The £12 per passenger cost is assumed to be per trip, so each passenger generates £24 cost overall to shipping costs.

Air fares are the same as for sea and no incremental costs have been included for the extra air passengers.

Taxation has been ignored to arrive at a pre-tax minimum price. This is reasonable provided all cash flows are taxed in the same way – effectively we have assumed that all capital expenditure qualifies for 100% FYAs. In reality the timing difference between the tax flows for capital and revenue items would affect the answer.

Workings

Total number of guests at the resort = 500 × 52/2 = 13,000 pa.

Of these, 90% (11,700 p.a.) will travel by sea and 10% (1,300) by air.

The annual contribution from the extra passengers on the ship will be 11,700 × (120 – 24) = £1,123,200.

The annual revenue from extra air passengers = 1,300 × 120 = £156,000.

Key answer tips

The calculations could have been made easier by setting t=0 as being in two years' time. The annuities would then have been at times 1–5. The approach used above is easier to visualise, however.

(c) **Control measures**

Key answer tips

The question requirement is ambiguous – is a 'control measure' a performance indicator or a control device /system? This answer covers both but has concentrated on the former interpretation.

During the bid process S will be seeking to monitor and control its existing activities and to impress M. Critical success factors will thus include passenger satisfaction, safety, reliability, maximising the contribution per passenger and managing the assets (ships and aircraft). If the bid is accepted, then these issues are still critical. The main difference is that the areas will need to be monitored for new as well as existing passengers to ensure that the contract is retained. Additional measures would relate to the construction of the new building works, but that is beyond the scope of this question.

To monitor these CSFs, S could implement the following control measures:

CSF	*Financial measures*	*Non-financial measures*
Passenger satisfaction		• Results of satisfaction surveys • # complaints received
Passenger safety	• Amount spent per passenger on safety equipment	• # reported accidents • # reported illness on board • % of staff fully trained in safety procedures
Reliability	• Refunds given due to delays/cancellation	• % crossings / flights made on time • % of trips cancelled/delayed due to bad weather • % of trips cancelled/delayed due to mechanical problems
Maximising contribution per passenger	• Average passenger spend on drinks, food and gifts • Profit margins by product line	• Inventory holding periods on different product lines to identify slow sellers
Managing the assets	• Cost per mile • Cost per passenger • Service costs v budget	• % capacity filled • Time lost due to repairs / servicing during the tourist season

In terms of control systems, S should ensure that its routine reporting and internal audit functions are operating effectively. These could include periodic reporting on performance indicators, variance analysis, analytical review, control account reconciliations and the use of feed-forward forccasts.

(d) **Future directions for growth**

Key answer tips

The question asks how S could develop its business. This is ambiguous as it could refer to the directions for growth (e.g. tourism) and/or the method of growth (e.g. organic growth). The answer given here 'plays it safe' by covering both angles. An obvious framework to use here would be Ansoff's Matrix but the question requirement does eliminate market penetration and market development by asking you not to look at transportation.

S could develop its business in the long term by extending its operations in the following ways:

Direction for growth	**Method of growth**
Product development	
Offering cruises for tourists – as well as transporting passengers to the islands, S could offer short trips around the islands. Depending on the local marine environment this could incorporate whale watching during winter months.	This option is best facilitated by organic growth. S could purchase a smaller boat to enable access to quiet coves, etc. The main risk will be due to competition from existing operators.
If M's plans for a holiday complex turn out to be successful, then S could consider imitating their approach on another island. As well as generating profits in its own right, the plan would also lead to greater demand for transportation services.	This option is likely to be more risky so a joint venture would give S access to the expertise required and would share the risks involved.
Even without building new holiday complexes, S could move into offering holiday packages on the islands, including transportation and accommodation.	Rather than buying up properties on the islands, S could act as a travel agent, working with existing hotel and B&B owners. The main costs will relate to marketing but these could be reduced via Internet selling.
S could move into catering to get an even bigger share of tourist spending.	A move into catering is best done through buying some restaurants on the island.
Diversification – vertical integration	
S could expand its aircraft repair business by offering servicing and repairs to the other airlines flying to the islands.	This could be done with little further investment into existing facilities.
S could try to gain control of the local airport / airstrip on the island. This would allow some cost savings but would give S more control over the access given and costs charged to its competitors.	This would probably involve S buying the airport.

17 CCC CAR MANUFACTURER (MAY 06 EXAM)

Key answer tips

Section (a) asks for a Porter's five forces analysis of the environment in which CCC operates. Your answer should thus focus on the specialist car industry rather than the car industry in general. A lengthy explanation of the model was not required.

In part (b) it is vital that you assess SSS not CCC. Given that 12 marks are available for calculation you should assume 1 mark per ratio and thus aim to calculate at least eight ratios. Key ratios (i.e. where industry comparisons are available) must be explained and discussed.

In part (c) ensure you assess the options you suggest, and conclude.

(a) **Porter's five forces analysis**

Porter's Five Forces Model analyses the profit potential in an industry by examining the competitive forces involved. The collective force will determine the overall industry profitability and a firm's ability to deal with the forces better than competitors will determine individual profitability.

Porter's five forces model can be applied to the specialist sports car industry as follows:

Competitive rivalry between existing firms

There are only six specialist sports car manufacturers in Europe who appear to have carved out separate niches for themselves through product differentiation. Major car manufacturers are not considered to be rivals as they do not offer the same level of individual bespoke work as firms like CCC. (***Note:*** This is probably unrealistic as major manufacturers own brands such as Ferrari and Aston Martin that would probably be considered as competitors.)

Overall competitive rivalry is a low/medium threat.

Threat of entry of new firms

New entrants can compete away profits so barriers to entry need to be considered. Within the specialist sports car industry the main barriers are:

- brand name and reputation
- expertise (note: high salaries make poaching of key staff more expensive)
- capital requirements – e.g. design, sales promotion and marketing.

Overall these are high enough to make the threat of entry low.

Threat of substitute products – high

The availability of substitutes puts a ceiling on the price firms can charge for their products. Substitutes for luxury sports cars include many other 'expensive toys' such as yachts, helicopters and powerboats. However, the types of customers who might consider such vehicles can probably afford the substitutes as well, so overall this threat is considered to be low.

Power of suppliers

Powerful suppliers can force up prices, eroding manufacturers' margins. Supplier power is linked to the size and number of suppliers and the availability of alternative sources of supply.

Where suppliers provide products that are easy to source elsewhere, such as tyres, then supplier power is low. If, on the other hand, a manufacturer is dependent on a supplier with a strong brand name that supplies a major component, such as an engine, then supplier power is higher. This is the case with CCC and SSS, discussed in more detail below.

Power of customers / buyers

Powerful customers can force suppliers to cut prices, eroding margins. Buyer power is linked to the size and number of buyers and the availability of alternatives. Customers for specialist sports cars can easily switch to alternative suppliers and are in a position to negotiate prices down, owing to the bespoke one-off nature of the work.

Overall, customer power is high.

Summary

Overall competitive forces appear to be strengthening, as shown by a decline in CCC's profit margins from 20% in 2002 to 7.5% in 2005. It is vital that CCC examines how to deal with key forces, such as supplier power, more effectively to halt this trend.

(b) The financial position of SSS can be assessed by reference to the key areas of profitability, liquidity and finance. Supporting calculations are shown in working (W1).

Profitability

SSS's pre-tax margin is 7.7%, much higher than the industry average of 4.3%. This could be due to greater cost efficiencies but is more likely owing to SSS being able to exercise greater supplier power and charge higher prices.

Similarly pre-tax ROCE is 17.9%, significantly higher than the industry average of 11.2%. Again this could be due to greater efficiency and asset utilisation but would support the argument that SSS is able to charge higher prices than is typical for its work.

Revenue per employee is 2.4× the industry average and pre-tax profit 4.3×. In some industries this could be explained by greater automation reducing the headcount, but SSS's processes are very labour intensive so the most likely cause is (again) high prices.

The gross margin of 43.1% appears high but comparative figures are needed to draw any firm conclusions.

Liquidity

The current ratio is greater than one, so appears reasonable. However, the quick ratio is less than one, indicating that SSS may have liquidity problems. Again comparative figures are needed for further analysis.

SSS holds 61 days of inventory, which could indicate that it holds high inventory levels of specialist parts that are used to replace standard engine components. The engines received from CCC are unlikely to be classified as inventory so would not affect this figure.

Receivables days are 22 days compared to an industry average of 65, indicating that SSS exercises considerable power over its customers to get such attractive terms. It is not known what terms CCC receives.

Payables days are 64 compared to an industry average of 28, indicating that SSS exercises considerable power over its suppliers as well. There may be the danger here that SSS is too aggressive with suppliers, resulting in poor goodwill.

Overall SSS's working capital management seems very impressive.

Finance

Dividend cover

SS has a dividend cover of 2.05× indicating that the dividend is low risk. However, given the unquoted owner-manager nature of SSS, this is not a major issue.

Summary

Overall SSS appears to be very efficient and successful, exercising considerable influence over both customers and suppliers. The only possible casues for concern are the low quick ratio and aggressive credit policy towards suppliers.

Workings

(W1)

Ratio	*Calculation*	*SSS*	*Industry average*
Profitability			
Gross profit margin	(2,455 – 1,398)/2,455	43.1%	–
Pre-tax profit margin	190/2,455	7.7%	4.3%
Asset turnover	2,455/(960 + 100)	2.32×	–
Pre-tax ROCE	190/(960 + 100)	17.9%	11.2%
Revenue per employee	2,455/8	€306,875	€128,500
Pre-tax profit per employee	190/8 128.5 × 4.3%	€23,750	€5,526
Working capital			
Current ratio	(232 + 146 + 32)/244	1.68	–
Quick ratio	(146 + 32)/244	0.73	–
Inventory days	365 × 232/1,398	61 days	–
Receivables days	365 × 146/2,455	22 days	65
Payables days	365 × 244/1,398	64 days	28
Finance			
Dividend cover	133/65	2.05×	–

(c) The power of SSS can be overcome by a mixture of the following:

More aggressive bargaining

It is likely that CCC is a major client for SSS and could thus exert more customer power to force SSS to drop prices. However, this approach does not appear to have succeeded to date and a more aggressive stance could undermine CCC's relationship with SSS, resulting in even worse terms. At present CCC's customers place a high value on SSS's input, so CCC would not want to risk a situation where SSS refused to supply them.

Seek alternative sources of supply

CCC could investigate finding an alternative supplier with a reputation as good as (or better than) SSS. Key concerns here would be:

- whether customers view the new supplier as being as good as SSS, and
- the time and costs involved in switching to a new supplier.

Bring tuning services in-house

CCC could bring tuning in-house by recruiting mechanics / engineers with the appropriate skill base. Given the high salaries CCC pays to staff, this should be feasible. This could involve headhunting key staff from SSS if necessary, though there should be many possible 'targets' from the arena of professional motorsport.

As with seeking alternative suppliers, the issue would be whether customers would perceive the quality of cars to fall without SSS's involvement.

In the UK when TVR decided to reduce its reliance on Rover for engines in its sports cars, it set up works teams to compete in motorsport to raise the company profile.

Acquire SSS

Backwards vertical integration by buying SSS would reduce supplier power without the risk of eroding customers' perceived value. It would give the benefit that CCC could prevent SSS from doing work for CCC's competitors.

The main concerns here would be:

- whether the existing owner would be willing to sell, particularly given the strong position SSS currently enjoys. Offering a mixture of cash and an equity stake in CCC could make the offer more attractive
- financing a possible acquisition as SSS is likely to be worth around €1 million (W2), though again offering shares would make this easier.

Workings

(W2) **Valuation of SSS**

- Net asset value = 100 + 960 = €1.06 million
- Earning based value = P/E × earnings = 7.5 × 133 = €1.00 million

Note: Given that SSS is not quoted, this figure should be reduced by between a ¼ and a ⅓, giving a value of €0.7 million, say, though a premium will need to be offered to convince the existing owner to sell.

18 AAA AND BBB (NOV 06 EXAM)

Key answer tips

This is a very accessible excellent question asking you to analyse a business using balanced scorecards and benchmarking perspectives. Key to success here is to discuss the figures and ratios calculated and to try to draw out possible implications ('make the numbers talk').

(a) The appraisal of AAA last year can be assessed using the balanced scorecard as follows. Note that supporting calculations are given in working (W1).

Financial perspective

From a financial perspective AAA's performance was disappointing compared to budget.

- The closing share price at J$334.50 was 16.4% lower than the budgeted figure of J$400, indicating that market expectations of future profitability are lower than expected.
- This is partly due to last year's earning per share figure of J$46.00 being 8% lower than the J$50.00 budgeted. This would reduce investors' forecasts of future profitability.

- Pre-tax profit at J$652m was 7.5% lower than expected, due partly to sales units being 2% down on budget but mainly to a drop in margins – gross margin at 66% was two points down on budget and pre-tax profit margin at 36% was five points down on budget.
- This, together with capital employed being higher than expected, resulted in a ROCE of 23%, down eight points on the budget figure of 31%. This would have been particularly disappointing to external analysts.

Customer perspective

Despite a drop in the average selling price from the J$809 budgeted to J$763, sales were still down 2% in volume terms. This is mainly due to poor customer satisfaction:

- Returns from customers were higher at 28 per thousand compared to the budgeted figure of 20. However, this figure does not reveal why customers were unhappy.
- Warranty claims were also higher at 56 per thousand compared to the budgeted figure of 30. This clearly suggests a problem with poor quality.

Innovation and learning perspective

On a positive note, AAA developed twelve new product lines, two more than the budgeted ten, reflecting management intent to take the business forward.

However, of these, only one line was successfully launched compared to the four budgeted. This equates to an 8.3% success rate, compared with the target of 40%, indicating a major problem in translating new ideas into successful products. Further analysis is required to determine why – e.g. perhaps AAA needs to commission more in-depth market research before launching new lines.

Internal business perspective

The possibility of problems in quality is further reinforced by the fact that the percentage of finished goods requiring reworking is higher at 2.3%, compared to a target of 1.3%. While this does not prove that sub-standard televisions are reaching customers, it may indicate other underlying problems that are not always picked up by quality assurance staff.

The percentage of purchases rejected is also higher than budget at 4.25% compared to a target of 3%. While this could indicate more scrupulous testing, it is more likely that there are problems with existing suppliers that could be having a knock-on effect on the manufacturing process. This is more worrying as only samples of purchases are tested.

A positive element is that AAA managed to achieve 98% of budgeted sales with 11.4% fewer employees than budgeted. This could explain some of the quality issues if staff had to work overtime to make up for fewer resources.

Another favourable element of this section of the balanced scorecard is that the number of days lost to disputes was 22% lower than expected at 2,500 days. This could indicate higher employee motivation and satisfaction, giving AAA a platform upon which to build higher quality.

Summary

The main issue facing AAA is how to improve quality to turn around a disappointing year.

(W1) **Balanced scorecard**

Financial perspective

Goal/CSF	*KPI*	*Actual Performance*	*Budget*
Shareholder wealth	Share price (closing)	J$334.50	J$400
	EPS	J$46.00	J$50.00
Profitability	Pre-tax ROCE	652/2835 = 23%	790/2550 = 31%
	Pre-tax profit	J$652m	J$790m
	Gross margin	1177/1793 = 66%	1320/1941 = 68%
	Pre-tax margin	652/1793 = 36%	790/1941 = 41%
Liquidity	Holding period of inventories	50.4/616 × 365 = 30 days	29.8/621 × 365 = 18 days

Customer perspective

Goal/CSF	*KPI*	*Actual Performance*	*Budget*
Customer satisfaction	Sales (units)	2.35 million	2.40 million
	Returns	28 per 1000	20 per 1000
	Warranty claims	56 per 1000	30 per 1000
	Average sales price	J$763	J$809

Learning and innovation perspective

Goal/CSF	*KPI*	*Actual Performance*	*Budget*
Product innovation	New lines developed	12	10
	New lines successfully launched	1	4
	% of new lines successfully launched	8.3%	40%

Internal business perspective

Goal/CSF	*KPI*	*Actual Performance*	*Budget*
Employee motivation	Days lost due to strikes	2,500	3,200
Production efficiency	Average cost per unit	J$262	J$259
	Sales units / employee	2.35m/2259 = 1040	2.4m/2550 = 941
Quality	% finished units reworked	54/2350 = 2.3%	30/2400 = 1.3%
	% purchases rejected	4.25%	3.00%

(b) REPORT

To: Directors, AAA

From: Management Accountant

Subject: Benchmarking

Introduction

At the request of the directors, I have benchmarked AAA's performance against that of BBB, a major competitor.

Benchmarking analysis

Details of benchmarking ratios and associated calculations are given in the appendix below. The main issues of note are as follows:

Profitability

AAA managed to achieve higher selling prices than BBB (J$763 verses J$718), which would indicate higher perceived quality, particularly given the lack of trade restrictions between the two countries.

AAA's average cost per unit was 17% higher at J$262. This could be due to higher quality or could indicate areas where AAA should seek to improve.

The combination resulted in AAA generating a higher margin per unit of J$501. However the percentage gross margin was lower at 66% compared to 69% and the pre-tax profit margin was lower at 36% compared to 40%.

An area of greater concern relates to the ROCE. AAA achieved a ROCE of 23% compared to BBB's 35%, indicating that AAA should analyse its asset base and then consider how to become more efficient at using it. For example, it may be that BBB relies more on automation that AAA or utilises more modern manufacturing technologies.

Quality

BBB experiences only 25 warranty claims per thousand units sold compared to AAA's 56. Along with the recent balanced scorecard exercise, this would suggest that there are problems with quality control that need addressing.

Working capital

AAA holds 30 days of inventories compared to BBB's 14, suggesting inefficient inventory-holding policies and/or a lack of information regarding planned customer sales. While the difference is not excessive, AAA should re-examine its working capital policy in this respect.

Staffing

Even though AAA has fewer staff than budgeted, it still generates less sales units per employee than BBB. This could indicate the need for greater efficiency or further automation.

Conclusion

AAA appears to be able to command higher prices than competitors but needs to examine how to improve production quality and efficiency.

Appendix: Benchmarking ratios

	AAA	*BBB*
Gross margin	66%	(1400 – 435)/1400 = 69%
Pre-tax margin	36%	557/1400 = 40%
ROCE	23%	557/1589 = 35%
Holding period of inventories	30 days	17/435 × 365 = 14 days
Warranty claims per 1000 units sold	56	19,800/780 = 25
Number of units sold per employee	1040	780,000/740 = 1054
Average selling price (J$)	763	(1400m ÷ 2.50)/780k = 718
Average cost per unit (J$)	262	(435m ÷ 2.50)/780k = 223
Average margin per unit (J$)	501	718 – 223 = 495

(c) **Knowledge management**

Knowledge management is the management of the information, knowledge and experience available to an organisation – its creation, capture, storage, availability and utilisation – in order that organisational activities build on what is already known and extend it further.

Knowledge management is a relatively new approach to business in which an organisation consciously and comprehensively gathers, organises, shares and analyses its knowledge to further its aims.

The introduction of knowledge management could benefit AAA as follows:

An intranet could allow knowledge sharing to link different parts of the organisation:

- If quality assurance (QA) were aware of which components had failed purchasing checks, then they could pay more attention to those components when testing finished goods, in case other substandard components had been missed.
- Likewise if QA are aware of the specific areas where televisions had to be reworked under warranty claims, then they could examine those areas in more detail.
- Production managers need to be aware of areas that cause problems with quality assurance and reworking in order to consider how to improve production to prevent the errors occurring in the first place.
- Disclosure of benchmarking results would motivate all employees to work harder to close the gaps highlighted.
- Details of customer returns and warranty claims would allow managers to identify whether certain customer contracts are more at risk due to excessive problems. They could then prioritise those customers' orders to ensure quality is improved.
- In general terms an intranet would allow more targets to be set (e.g. on quality issues) with staff being able to see at a glance the latest actual performance figures. This should improve target setting and control.

An extranet would improve communication and knowledge sharing with customers and suppliers:

- Suppliers could become aware of problem components sooner and take steps to improve their own quality control procedures.
- Customers could place orders online allowing better scheduling so AAA can reduce inventory levels and save on costs.

Improved communication via emails and newsletters should also improve staff motivation, with the knock-on result of improved quality.

If AAA plans to improve the use of technology in production (e.g. MRP I, MRP II, ERP or OPT), then improvements in knowledge management are key.

Section 4

ANSWERS TO SECTION B-TYPE QUESTIONS

BUSINESS STRATEGY

19 N

Key answer tips

Your answer should differentiate between strategic management and operational management and discuss the changes necessary within N to introduce a strategic management. There is no need for an explanation of the strategic management process.

(a) Strategic management has a number of important differences from operational management, including the following:

Scope

Strategic management takes a broad approach and relates the whole undertaking to its external environment. It takes into consideration the interests of all the organisation's stakeholders and covers the whole company i.e. every function.

Operational management is concerned with specialised activities carried out at departmental level. It is primarily concerned with internal allocation of resources and will have a narrow scope i.e. relating to each operating department in N.

Time horizon

Strategic management is based on predicting future events that will affect the organisation. N is a small family-controlled company so the strategic time horizon will be about ten years.

Operational management is concerned with the day-to-day running of the business. It will mainly deal with solving operational problems, organising resources each day and week and implementing procedures. The time horizon used will be short-term i.e. the days and weeks ahead.

Timing

Strategic management is carried out on an ad hoc basis, adapting to an ever-changing situation.

Operational management tends to be done on a routine and repetitive basis with many tasks being done on a daily, weekly or monthly basis.

Responsibility

Strategic management is the responsibility of top management i.e. N's Board of Directors. It is of a complex nature and needs considerable expertise to do it well.

Operational management is the responsibility of low level management, e.g, departmental supervisors, and is relatively simple.

Driving force

Strategic management is driven by the external environment and the need to change e.g. to keep up to date with technological change.

Operational management is resource driven, its main task being to use scarce economic resources efficiently and effectively.

(b) To successfully introduce strategic management N will need to make the following cultural and organisational changes:

Objectives

N's management needs to set some clear long-term objectives, setting out where the company wants to be in a number of years' time. From these definitive performances, targets can be set, such as an annual growth rate. At present, N probably relies on short-term targets which do not contribute to long-term growth.

Perspective

The management perspective of N must become much broader and look at the external environment, e.g. the reasons why the company's performance in recent years has declined must be found. Market research must be undertaken and information about the external environment obtained. Currently, N's managers know very little about the business's environment and their outlook is too narrow.

Leadership style/structure

No information is given on N's current management leadership style but, from the company's deteriorating performance and lack of strategic management, changes should begin at the top. N's top management should retain control over the company as a whole and introduce a degree of decentralisation by dividing the company into Strategic Business Units, involving lower level management. This will motivate lower level managers and introduce a degree of flexibility in the company's structure.

Innovation

N will need to introduce an innovative culture which is forward looking and sees change as a challenge. This will involve managers looking at the way things are done and questioning whether it could be done differently. It will also mean looking for new opportunities such as new markets and new products. The company appears to be set in its ways, which will mean this change will be difficult to introduce.

Communication

At present N is probably organised as a functional structure with mainly vertical communication channels. N's communication systems will need to be changed so there is more horizontal communication with managers and staff co-operating and communicating as team members. This will involve creating task culture and developing a strong value chain within the company.

Good communication links should also be established between the company and its external stakeholders e.g. suppliers and customers.

20 MISSION STATEMENT

Key answer tips

A good answer will discuss the reasons for producing a mission statement and give an explanation of how the performance of a not-for-profit organisation can be assessed. You are not required to provide a detailed description of a mission statement, to discuss performance measurement of business in general or to give a detailed explanation of performance measures.

(a) Mintzberg defines a mission statement as a statement which describes an organisation's basic role in society. An organisation's mission statement is the overall statement that covers all the organisation's objectives.

A mission has no tangible form and needs to be communicated to the organisation's stakeholders. A mission statement serves the purpose of formally defining the organisation's mission and giving it tangibility. The mission statement is an important document used in the strategic planning process. The reasons why its publication is important include the following:

- A mission statement gives the organisation's mission a tangible existence that stakeholders can see and relate to i.e. it states what business the organisation is in.
- It communicates details of the organisation's mission to those people who are interested in it and need to know it e.g. managers, employees, shareholders of a limited company and customers.
- A mission statement explains why the organisation exists and what its standards and values are. This can give direction to stakeholders, especially managers and employees.
- A mission statement can act as a focal point for strategy formulation and can motivate managers to achieve higher standards of performance.
- It can be used to co-ordinate policy. When lower level objectives are in conflict, reference to the mission statement should enable the primary objective to be established.
- Mission statements can be used as a basis from which benchmarks and other performance evaluation criteria can be derived.

(b) When assessing the performance of a not-for-profit organisation three important issues must be taken into account. These are:

- There is no profit motive objective so many traditional financial performance indicators cannot be applied e.g. the ROCE.
- No particular stakeholder group dominates not-for-profit organisations, as do shareholders of a limited company.
- It may be difficult to find other, similar organisations that can be used as benchmarks for assessing the performance of the undertaking.

Despite these difficulties it is important that not-for-profit organisations such as registered charities and government departments maintain control by continuously monitoring their performance.

The performance of such undertakings can be assessed by:

- Setting performance standards

  These will be of a non-financial nature and will be based on efficiency and effectiveness. For a not-for-profit undertaking these will be related to the reasons for existence, but are more likely to be of a social nature. A good example of this is the National Health Service, for which:

  – patient recovery rates

  – patient waiting lists, and

  – efficient utilisation of resources

  all feature as major performance measures.

  Performance standards should be realistic and be agreed by the various stakeholder groups who have an interest in the results.

- A mechanism of feedback and reporting on performance

  Parameters should be set for identifying variances, investigating those considered material and setting up a reporting system.

21 SPK

(a) **Approaches to strategy formulation**

There are many different approaches to strategy formulation, including the following:

- the rational approach
- the emergent approach
- logical incrementalism.

The rational approach

Here strategy is pre-planned with a series of clear stages:

1 Establish the goals of the organisation (often expressed through mission and objectives).

2 Perform a corporate appraisal of the organisation, including a review of internal factors as part of a position audit and external environmental factors.

3 Evaluate the different options and choose a suitable strategy.

4 Implement the strategy.

5 Set up control mechanisms that lead to an ongoing review of the organisation's position.

This deliberate, formal rational strategic process represents the traditional prescribed view of strategy development.

The emergent approach

The rational view started to be challenged during the late 1970s. Observers noticed organisations diluted the rational model by, for instance, omitting key stages.

A more emergent view of strategy development became recognised as an alternative. This approach recognises the need for constant strategic adjustments and adaptation in order to survive in a dynamic, rapidly changing external environment. Academics such as Minzberg (1990) and Porter (1985) led the debate that proposed an alternative 'way', with Mintzberg classifying strategies as intended, deliberate, realised, unrealised and emergent.

Logical incrementalism

Logical incrementalism sees the role of management as one of moving the organisation forward in small incremental steps, rather than relying on grand visions and rigid strategic plans. Lindblom first used the term in a negative way but others writers, such as Quinn, have argued that it is appropriate for some firms. Such an approach will usually rely on the following:

- A network of communication, both formal and informal, results in senior staff being well aware of the issues facing the firm.
- Managers build support for new ideas in a political way that avoids opposition and conflict.
- Commitment and consensus grow gradually for the new plan.

Application to SPK

In the case of SPK a rational approach to strategy would not be appropriate for the following reasons:

- It would be seen as too rigid, formalised and probably counter productive.
- SPK partners and managers operate in an autonomous way 'sensing' business opportunities and trading on reputation and knowledge.
- Partners would not wish to compromise this autonomy by switching to a more formalised system of operating.

The emergent approach is generally suited to a fast moving area of private sector. Although it seems that SPK strategic approaches are shaped and arise based on experience there is no evidence from the question that SPK operates in a fast moving environment.

Logical incrementalism would give the best fit for SPK for a number of reasons:

- Partners are strong willed and work independently of one another. Unveiling a new strategy could lead to damaging and unwanted internal conflicts
- The SPK way is consistent with strategy development through political means in a logical, incremental way.

(b) **Public sector organisations and strategy development**

There are many ways in which strategic planning for public sector organisations differs from that for profit-focused firms.

Objectives

Unlike privately owned businesses, the public sector's main purpose is for social rather than financial reasons. This is made more complicated by the fact that organisations such as hospitals, schools and local government have social objectives that can be multiple and contradictory. (For example, improving the quality of patient care in a hospital while reducing waiting lists.)

Stakeholders

Rather than existing for owners or shareholders, public sector organisations exist to serve a wider range of stakeholders. It follows that strategic processes need to be explicit, deliberate and involve or consider stakeholders.

By contrast SPK's objectives are straightforward (profitability and reputation maintenance) and the clearly dominant stakeholders are the senior partners.

The role of central Government is often significant and the logical methodical approach makes it easier to build in their requirements.

Funding

As they are funded from public funds, public sector organisations owe a duty of stewardship to society demonstrated through a process of public accountability. They must be able to justify that they have acted in a logical, thoughtful way. The rational approach is better suited to demonstrating such a process.

Scrutiny

Public sector organisations come under much external scrutiny. Public interest in behaviour, and the careful public monitoring by politicians and the media means it must be seen to deliver strategy fairly and properly, and the rational planning process provides such a mechanism whereby strategy is clear and political opinions made explicit.

Summary

In summary, strategy formulation in public sector organisations is shaped by wider stakeholder involvement, limited resources and central political priorities. The rational model can most easily accommodate these features.

Performance measurement

The main issues with public sector performance measurement are:

- A lack of direct competition means no comparison of performance is easily made.
- The lack of a profit motive can lead to suggestions that they are not interested in cost reduction or that services provided have little incentive to be improved upon.
- The need to demonstrate value for money in the use of available resources.
- Many of the key objectives are non-financial and difficult to quantify (e.g. quality of patient care).

One often used framework for setting objectives and subsequently assessing performance is the 'three Es': Economy, Efficiency and Effectiveness.

Economy

Economy relates to resource acquisition or inputs. Metrics could relate to:

- purchase costs
- quality of inputs
- the extent to which the organisation was able to obtain inputs (e.g. whether schools were able to recruit enough teachers).

Efficiency

Efficiency is the process stage whereby the resources are used to produce outputs. Typical indicators here could include:

- cost per patient treated
- productivity measures such as the number of operations carried out per consultant in hospitals or average class sizes in schools
- % of beds empty.

Effectiveness

Finally, effectiveness looks back on original objectives and considers success at meeting these aspirations. These could include:

- mortality rates
- average waiting times for surgery
- % of children achieving key stage targets in schools.

Indicators of performance need to be used in conjunction with intra organisational comparisons (for example similar sites or departments within the same body), or historical patterns and trends can be developed.

Within the UK there has been a growing trend towards the use of multi performance indicators and ratios and the publication of these in the form of 'league tables', giving a form of inter-organisational benchmarking. This is a controversial area with some critics arguing that the league tables over-simplify the situation and misrepresent performance.

Such comparisons allow people to identify 'good practice' and areas for improvement.

22 CTC TELECOMMUNICATIONS (NOV 06 EXAM)

Key answer tips

This is a standard question on objectives and strategic planning. The key is to apply as much as possible to the specific circumstances of CTC.

(a) The objectives of CTC will have to change for the reasons discussed below.

Shareholder wealth

Before privatisation CTC's main stakeholder was the government of C with the main objective of providing the best service the nation could afford. Income was set by the government to cover resources, so CTC was not expected to do more than breakeven financially.

Now the key stakeholders are shareholders and CTC's primary focus should be to maximise shareholder wealth and be profitable. Objectives will need to be set to support this over-riding objective.

Competition

Before privatisation CTC had the luxury of being a monopolist with the government setting service and price levels. Now the market in C has been opened up to allow foreign competition.

This will force CTC into ensuring that it does offer a quality service with value for money or customers will switch to the competition. Objectives will need to be set by reference to market conditions and the actions of competitors.

Customer preferences

Before privatisation CTC had to deliver the best service the country could afford. Now, service levels are determined by what customers are willing to pay for. Some may be prepared to pay higher amounts for additional services, so CTC will need to develop a range of new services and tariffs to meet demand and set corresponding objectives.

CTC's whole approach needs to become more market-driven rather than doing the best it could with the allocated resources.

Efficiency

Many state monopolies are inefficient. Given imminent competition and more demanding customers, CTC will need to become much more efficient. Firms that have already made such a transition have usually found that radical changes are needed to improve cost control and change the culture of the organisation. Objectives will need to be set regarding cost and efficiency levels.

Resources

Prior to privatisation the level of resources was determined by the government. After privatisation the directors need to attract investors and other financiers and will set resources levels. As a consequence the directors need to consider the key issues for such investors – e.g. risk, growth prospects and so on – and set corporate objectives accordingly.

(b) Suitable strategic objectives for CTC could include the following:

(1) **Market share**

e.g. 'CTC aims to retain 60% of its domestic market over the next five years.'

This is a suitable objective, as market share must be defended from new entrants to ensure that CTC can benefit from economies of scale to be competitive.

(2) **Market development**

e.g. 'CTC aims to develop other markets so 25% of its revenue is derived from outside C within five years.'

This is a suitable objective, as CTC must look to other markets to ensure future growth and to reduce its risk exposure. These are necessary to increase shareholder value in the long run.

(c) The directors should adopt the rational planning model as a basic framework for future strategic planning. This involves the following steps:

(1) **Strategic analysis**

Strategic analysis essentially involves three aspects:

- CTC should perform external analysis to identify opportunities and threats. In particular, it should assess the risk of new entrants into the industry and perform detailed competitor analysis on potential rivals.
- CTC should also perform internal analysis to determine its own strengths and weaknesses. Weaknesses will need to be rectified in order to be competitive and CTC will need to develop core competences upon which to build strategy.
- The third aspect of strategic analysis involves identifying stakeholders and assessing their expectations and power. This should allow CTC to formulate a mission statement and to set strategic objectives for potential strategies.

(2) **Strategic choice**

Strategic choice also involves three aspects:

- How to compete – CTC will need to decide whether to compete against new rivals as a cost leader, relying on economies of scale, or as a differentiator offering a higher quality product. The latter seems less likely so a detailed strategy focusing on costs needs to be formulated.
- Where to compete – as well as its domestic market, CTC needs to consider expansion into new markets. This stage will involve identifying the most attractive markets and deciding whether they are worth investing in.
- Choosing the method of expansion – once suitable foreign markets have been identified CTC will need to decide whether to expand via organic growth, acquisition or via a joint arrangement.

(3) **Strategy implementation**

Strategy implementation involves the following:

- translating long-term strategic objectives into detailed tactical and operational targets
- setting detailed budgets and performance appraisal to control the business.
- ongoing assessment as to whether the plans are on track and, if not, what action needs to be taken to rectify the situation.

With all of this CTC should ensure that planning is not a formal once-a-year exercise but an ongoing process where there is the flexibility to allow strategies to emerge in response to a changing market. This effectively blurs the distinction between steps 2 and 3 above as they happen simultaneously.

THE COMPETITIVE ENVIRONMENT

23 WATER SUPPLY

Key answer tips

Your answer should demonstrate that you appreciate the importance of considering external influences when determining the objectives and designing the strategy for an organisation. Your answer should consider the expectations of the various stakeholders including any regulatory authority. Although not essential, your answer *could* be presented as a report.

Every organisation must consider the external influences when they are formulating their objectives and designing their strategies. The environment exerts three basic forms of influence on the organisation. It **offers threats and opportunities**; it **provides their resources**; and it **contains interest or 'pressure groups'** that have some kind of direct interest in their organisational activities.

The advice given to the board of directors when formulating the organisational objectives and strategies would be based on a range of influences including customers, competitors, investors, legal, political, economic, social, technological development and cultural.

The first and most important consideration is that the water is safe to use. As a supplier of water, the company will be responsible for the health and safety of the community and this places a significant level of responsibility on it. Customers will expect to receive a high quality service and the board must be confident that the quality of the water supplied is acceptable. A breakdown in the water supply would cause major disruptions to ordinary households and industrial users so it important for management to take steps to ensure that the company can cope with most difficulties that are likely to arise.

The level of quality and the expectations of the consumer will need to be taken into account when determining the amount of investment that is planned. If significant amounts of capital are required to improve the service, some degree of compromise may have to be reached if an acceptable strategy is to be devised. Because some customers may also be shareholders there will be conflicting views regarding the performance of the company.

Competitors are not a major influence because, as a supplier of water, the company will have some element of monopoly power. However, the company's performance will be compared with similar water suppliers and these comparisons will have an influence on the decisions taken at board level.

Shareholders will expect a return on their investment and so their expectations will influence the formulation of both objectives and strategy. It may be possible to adjust the pricing policy to meet the expectations of both the existing and potential shareholders but the level of return expected from their investment will affect the decisions taken by the company's strategic planning team.

When the water supply was privatised, the government established a regulatory body which has a major influence on the decisions taken by the management of water companies. The regulator is able to set pricing and service criteria, and it is essential that the company performs satisfactorily because an unfavourable report from the regulator might prove to be costly to deal with.

The **political, economic and social environment** will also influence the company's objectives and strategy formulation. Issues such as pollution, pricing policy and quality will be discussed within the community and the company must be aware of any concerns raised when formulating their future policies.

While social issues have to be considered to identify the changing needs of consumers, technological changes need to be forecast to identify how those needs might be met in the future. It could mean the installation of extensive testing and quality control procedures, which would increase the costs of the company and consequently reduce the profit available to the shareholders. New technology is constantly being developed in treating and supplying water of sufficiently high quality for customer use and decisions on whether, when and how much to invest will have a major influence on management decisions. It is essential, however, that the health aspects of the product are always paramount in establishing the objectives and devising the strategy to be adopted by the company.

The **organisational culture** is a particularly important factor to be considered when the strategy is being developed and decisions taken regarding both the short- and long-term future of the company. Culture is a set of behavioural attitudes and values that we as members of a society learn, accept and pass on to others. It holds groups of people together. The working environment for the water industry has changed dramatically, with new forces disrupting the smooth predictable progress of earlier years when it was publicly owned. Because the supply of water is a sensitive and emotional issue, the organisational culture needs to reflect this in its provision of a reliable service to the public. The task facing the board is to place the supply of clean water high in the company objectives and to cope with and drive the cultural change within the organisation.

Strategic planners are being challenged by the changes in their business environments. Social, cultural, technological and legal factors are all ingredients in the mix of environmental problems they face. The company's strategic planning team must be sensitive to the wishes and expectations of all their stakeholders, and should bear in mind the conflicts of interest between them and resolve them in a satisfactory manner.

24 DON MAC

Key answer tips

Part (a) requires you to justify PEST analysis as a tool to use to evaluate an overseas environment. Part (b) asks for a discussion of the issues arising from applying the framework. There are also other issues, particularly relating to the specific industry environment, not covered by PEST analysis which you need to suggest. In Part (a) you do not need to say why a PEST analysis might not be suitable. In Part (b) you do not need to describe Porter's Five Forces, the typical model also used alongside PEST analysis to examine the environment. ***Note:*** The answer given here is longer than you could be expected to provide in an examination.

(a) **Using a PEST analysis to assist the environmental analysis**

PEST analysis examines the broad environment in which the organisation is operating. PEST is a mnemonic which stands for Political/legal, Economic, Social and Technological factors. These are simply four key areas in which to consider how current and future changes affect the business. Strategies can then be developed which address any potential opportunities and threats identified.

In entering a new overseas market, an environmental analysis is important to help the organisation understand the factors specific to that market so that the specific opportunities and threats posed can be assessed and appropriate action taken.

It is a useful tool for the following reasons:

1 *It ensures completeness*

The majority of issues relevant to an organisation will be covered under one of the four areas of PEST analysis. By reviewing all four areas, Don Mac can be sure that it has done a full and complete analysis of the broad environment.

2 *All four elements are relevant to examining new markets*

Political/legal

Each new country entered will have different political systems and laws. Don Mac will need to understand these differences to ensure that they operate within the law in Borderland. They will also want to ensure that there is political stability within the country which will ensure long-term viability of the new operations.

Economic

Economies are different in different parts of the world. Understanding the local economy in Borderland and how it is expected to develop enables Don Mac to assess the potential within that market as well as any economic issues which they need to consider.

Social

Each country will have its own cultural differences, and Don Mac can change how they operate depending on Borderland's culture. Don Mac has already shown its willingness to change for each country's different tastes and will want to do so in Borderland too.

Technological

Each country has a different level of technological expertise and experience. Don Mac might need to change processes to accommodate local systems, or implement training programmes for staff unfamiliar with their technology.

3 *It is a well-known tool which is easy to understand and use*

PEST analysis is a very simple tool that does not require detailed understanding. This means that it is easy to use by the team and simple for Directors to analyse and understand.

(b) **Main issues arising from applying the framework**

Various issues which Don Mac will need to consider include:

Political/legal factors

(i) *Government grants*

Some countries may have grants available for investment in the country. Considering the requirements to gain such grants may enable Don Mac to make use of these.

(ii) *Political stability*

Given Don Mac's worldwide penetration (over 120 countries) it is likely that Borderland is in a developing region which may be more politically unstable than many countries in which they currently operate. This may affect the long-term potential in the market.

(iii) *Regulation on overseas companies*

There may be regulation on how overseas companies can operate in the market. In China, for instance, it is common for joint ventures with local companies to be a prerequisite for western companies entering the market.

(iv) *Employment legislation*

Each country will have different employment legislation e.g. health and safety, minimum wages, employment rights. Don Mac may have to change internal processes from the US model to stay within this legislation within Borderland. Being a good employer is also one of Don Mac's specific strategies.

(v) *Tax legislation*

Tax laws will impact the profits available for distribution to the group. High tax levels may discourage Don Mac from entering the market.

(vi) *Tariffs and other barriers to trade*

Tariffs may be imposed on imports into Borderland. This may put Don Mac at a significant disadvantage compared with local competitors if they aim to import a significant number of items (unlikely on food items, more likely on clothing, fittings etc).

Economic factors

Things to consider include:

(i) *Economic prosperity*

The more prosperous the nation the more money people will have to invest in 'fast-food'. Examining the current and likely future prosperity enables the organisation to understand the potential of this market and the likely future investment required.

(ii) *Interest rates*

This affects the cost of borrowing within Borderland. If high it may mean overseas funding is necessary. A big differential between interest rates in Borderland and the US is also likely to cause instability in the exchange rate (see below).

Interest rates also affect the availability of money for the people of the country. Low interest rates mean more disposable income to spend increasing the potential for Don Mac.

(iii) *Exchange rates*

Don Mac will be affected by exchange rates for items they export to Borderland (clothing, fittings). An unfavourable movement in exchange rates could make exporting to Borderland expensive and reduce profitability. It can also affect the value of profits when converted back to US dollars.

(iv) *Position in economic cycle*

Different countries are often at different positions in the economic cycle of growth and recession. The current position of Borderland will affect the current prosperity of the nation and the potential for business development for Don Mac.

(v) *Inflation rates*

High inflation rates create instability in the economy which can affect future growth prospects. They also mean that prices for supplies and prices charged will regularly change and this difficulty would need to be considered and processes implemented to account for this.

Social factors

Things to consider include:

(i) *Brand reputation/anti-Americanism*

As a global brand, the reputation of Don Mac might be expected to have reached Borderland. If not, more marketing will be required. If it has, the reputation will need to be understood and the marketing campaign set up accordingly.

This is particularly relevant given the anti-Americanism which is prevalent currently in some countries. Don Mac may have a significant hurdle to climb to convince people to eat there if this is the case in Borderland.

(ii) *Cultural differences*

Each country has its own values, beliefs, attitudes and norms of behaviours which means that people of that country may like different foods, architecture, music and so on, in comparison with US restaurants. By adapting to local needs Don Mac can ensure it wins local custom and improve its reputation.

Different cultures also need to be considered when employing people, especially given the importance to Don Mac of employee relations. People might have different religious needs to be met or may dislike being given autonomy so the management style needs changing.

(iii) *Language problems*

Different local languages can create problems, firstly in communication with staff. Secondly, product names need to be considered to ensure they are acceptable in the local language. General Motor's Nova suggested that 'it won't go' in Spanish, for example.

Technological factors

Don Mac may need to train people in the use of their technologies if the local population are unfamiliar with them e.g. accounting systems or tills. In addition, technology might have to be adapted to work in local environments, such as different electrical systems.

Tutorial notes:

Note that there are far fewer factors to consider under technological factors. Do not assume the same mark allocation for each section in a model like this; instead tailor your answer to the points you have generated ensuring you have enough points in total covering all four PEST areas. Here a total of about 10 should be your target.

Other information required on Borderland

Other information which would be useful to find on Borderland might include:

Supplier information

The availability of materials, particularly food which being perishable would need to be sourced from Borderland, is important. They should look at local prices, quality of local produce, number of alternative suppliers, reliability of supply, and the supplier power in the market – it may for instance be a government monopoly who would have significant power and hence control over prices.

Competitor information

The extent of competition in Borderland is important to consider since it will affect the strategy adopted. If, for example, there are already many competitors providing very similar products to Don Mac's, then an aggressive marketing campaign and low prices initially might be a suitable strategy to build market share.

Information that might be collected on competitors might include:

(i) number of competitors

(ii) prices

(iii) market share of existing competitors

(iv) reputation/brand awareness

(v) products sold.

Threat of new entrants

The likelihood of other competitors, King Burger for instance, entering Borderland needs to be considered, since this will affect the profitability of the local market and the strategy adopted will need to be different.

If Don Mac is the first overseas company to enter the market but if other entrants are expected soon, it may adopt a market penetration policy – keeping prices low, advertising heavily and opening up many outlets to build barriers to entry and deter new entrants.

25 FIVE FORCES

Tutorial note:

This question offers a fairly straightforward structure for an answer. There are five forces to discuss, and for each you need to suggest performance indicators, with reasons, and give a rational opinion about whether you agree or disagree with the MD's views in each case.

Porter's Five Forces Model provides a structure for analysing the competitiveness within an industry. The strength of competitive forces affects the ability of a company to achieve profits, and will affect strategic decisions such as whether to enter a new market, withdraw from an existing market or invest further.

The managing director has asked for suitable performance indicators. These could be either quantitative or qualitative. In the recommendations below, a preference is shown for quantitative indicators, because these are likely to be more objective.

Threat of entry

The threat from the possibility of entrants coming into the market as new competitors is difficult to measure. However, we can consider both how attractive the market might be to new entrants, and the barriers to entry that will deter them.

The attractiveness of a new market to a potential new entrant is its profitability. If a firm can see an opportunity for a satisfactory return, it will be tempted to enter a market. Profitability in a market can be measured by accounting ratios, such as return on capital employed. Monitoring changes in such a measure could act as a warning sign that the industry is becoming more or less attractive.

A second influence on the threat of new entry is the existence of strong barriers to entry. Porter identified a number of different barriers acting as a deterrent to new entrants. These include economies of scale and brand image. In a consumer industry, such as cosmetics, both could be important. Suitable performance measures to monitor could therefore be:

- Cost per unit of output, and changes in cost per unit. Maintaining low costs, or even reducing costs, would perhaps indicate that a new entrant would struggle to compete.
- Consumer views on brand image. Market research surveys should be carried out regularly to monitor consumer views of the company's brands.

The managing director could be correct in his view that the threat of new entrants is low. If economies of scale are significant, it seems likely that a small group of companies can dominate the market. However, a new entrant is likely to exploit either a special niche in the overall market, or a new channel of distribution. If the opportunity for profit exists, someone will try to exploit it. Developments in market niches or channels of distribution should therefore be monitored.

Power of buyers

In a consumer market, the consumer is king. The company should therefore put substantial amounts of resources into marketing. In terms of strategic planning and the Five Forces Model, the power of buyers relates to the ability of buyers to influence pricing and profitability due to the strength of their influence on the market. According to Porter, buyers are particularly powerful when rival products are undifferentiated: to some extent this is the case in the cosmetics industry, although rival companies try to create distinctive products. Buyer power is also greater when the amount of purchases is a significant proportion of buyers' total spending, which is not the case with cosmetics. Thirdly, buyer power is strong when the quantities purchased by any buyer are a large proportion of total sales by the company, which is not the case with E.

Therefore, although buyers are important in a consumer market, it is questionable whether buyer power is as significant a competitive force as the managing director suggests.

Measures for monitoring buyer power could include:

- from market research, consumer spending on cosmetics as a percentage of total spending. If this proportion increases, buyer power could become stronger
- the percentage of sales by the company that are purchased by the top 10 or 20 customers. When a company has significant customers, buyer power will be strong
- through market research, consumer attitudes to the company's product should also be monitored.

Power of suppliers

Supplier power exists when suppliers are in a position to raise prices or reduce their product quality without the company having much influence over their decisions. This can occur when suppliers are large companies relative to the buyer. With E, the opposite appears to be the case, and the managing director's views are probably correct.

However, even if the power of suppliers is not seen as a threat currently, the management at E might have to review this assertion in the future. As E is a global company, the chosen suppliers' prices might be forced down as they become dependent on the contracts placed with them. Pressure groups could highlight this as bully-boy tactics and there could be a public backlash. As also there might be with regard to health risks, allergic reactions and the exploitation of cheap labour in developing countries. Another risk is that suppliers may cut quality to achieve price targets.

Performance measures for monitoring supplier power should focus on the extent to which the company relies on suppliers in general, and on individual suppliers in particular. Suggested measures are:

- material purchase costs as a percentage of total costs
- the percentage of total material purchases from the top, say, six or seven suppliers
- price increases from purchasers in relation to price increases by the company to its own customers.

Substitute products

The managing director is correct to suggest that the cosmetics industry is well-established, with a wide range of competing products, and that there is no obvious substitute for cosmetics as a generic product. However, a substitute product can be defined as any product that the company does not make. Within the cosmetics markets, there are presumably some products that E does not make, such as cosmetics with homeopathic ingredients or environmental-friendly ingredients. New products can emerge to create a new niche in the market, and the threat should not be ignored.

It is probably difficult to identify quantitative performance measures for monitoring this threat although, through market research, information can be obtained regularly on:

- the number of new products introduced
- developments in consumer habits and preferences.

In addition, the company can monitor its own innovations, checking the number of new product launches it makes. A company that is not innovative is more likely to be exposed to the threat of new substitute products than a company that continually introduces new products to meet customer demands.

There is always the danger that a threat might not be realised until it is too late to arrest its entry to the market. Monitoring spends on R&D and innovation throughout the industry might help E to avoid any nasty surprises.

Rivalry among competitors

The managing director is almost certainly correct in his views on the threat from rival competitors. Porter suggests that rivalry among competitors will be highest when there are many competing firms in the market, a large proportion of costs are fixed costs, exit barriers are high and there is relatively little product differentiation. To a large extent, these conditions exist in the cosmetics industry.

Performance measures for monitoring competitive rivalry, and the threat from competitors, might include:

- Market share statistics, and whether the company's share of the market is rising or falling.
- Information about innovation. The number of new products introduced by competitors, compared to the number of new products launched by the company over the same time period.
- Comparative spending on advertising, measured perhaps in the number or length of advertising campaigns.
- Price discounting statistics, and the nature of discounts offered by competitors to their customers.
- Market research information into consumer attitudes to the products of rival companies.
- Profitability of rival companies, compared to the company's own profitability, measured as much as possible from the published accounts of competitors.

Conclusion

The performance measures required by the managing director are intended to monitor the competitive forces in the cosmetics market. To provide useful information, it is essential that:

- management should understand the purpose and potential significance of each measure
- measurements should be taken regularly and monitored over time.

26 UNCERTAINTY AND THE FIVE FORCES MODEL

Key answer tips

Your answer should demonstrate that you know what the Five Forces Model is, but you need to develop arguments as to whether or not the model can be used when there is uncertainty in the business environment. The Five Forces Model should be seen as a method of developing strategy within a rational planning model, and the existence of uncertainty in the environment might suggest that a theme to consider in your answer is whether a formal rational model for strategic planning is applicable in conditions of rapid change.

Uncertainty in the business environment is caused primarily by the rapidity of change, much of it unforeseen and unpredictable. For example, the development of the Internet has transformed business opportunities for many companies within a relatively short period of time but, at the same time, many organisations at the forefront of the 'dot.com' expansion have not survived. Similarly, the world economic recession that started in 2001 was not foreseen by many forecasters and companies were caught by surprise, often without a clear strategy for moving forward in difficult economic conditions.

When change is unexpected and rapid, the usefulness of long-term planning systems can be brought into question, because the plans that have been formulated might quickly become irrelevant. Even worse, if a company tries to adhere to its long-term plans when conditions have changed, it might lose much of its competitive edge.

The Five Forces Model was developed by Michael Porter as a technique for devising strategic plans. The model can be used to analyse the strength of the competitive forces within an industry. When competitive forces are strong, profitability will be restricted. Porter suggests that there are five competitive forces within an industry: the threat of new entrants, buyer power, supplier power, the threat of substitutes and rivalry between competitors. In any industry at any time, each of these forces could have differing strength and influence.

Within a rational planning framework, an analysis of competitive forces can be used to reach strategic decisions about whether to enter or withdraw from a market, or whether to invest further in a market. In addition, an understanding of competitive forces can help management to formulate competitive strategies for the company.

The model can also be used to **assess the strength of each of the competitive forces**. For example, Porter suggested that the threat of new entrants into a market is reduced by barriers to entry. Barriers to entry include economies of scale (whereby a firm needs to build up a large volume of operations to achieve competitive unit costs), the strength of branding of existing products and access to distribution channels. Rivalry between competitors is stronger when there is a large number of competitors in the market, the products they sell are not differentiated from those of competitors, the costs of leaving the market are high so that even loss-making competitors are reluctant to give up and there is only slow growth in market demand. By assessing the factors that contribute to competitive forces, it might be possible to reach a view on how powerful each of those forces has become.

However, the model provides an assessment of the current situation, and **is not predictive**. It is not used to make judgements about how competitive forces might alter in the future due to unforeseen developments. For example, the development of satellite, digital and Internet technology has forced a radical reassessment of competitive forces in the markets for information provision, such as publishing and entertainment services. When the environment is changing, strategies based on a static Five Forces Model analysis will cease to be viable.

Growing uncertainty in the business environment has led to a much greater focus on risk management. An **understanding of risk** is a key to business survival and prosperity, but is not a factor in the Five Forces Model. It can therefore be argued that Porter's model is incomplete, and on its own is insufficient for carrying out a strategy appraisal. Risk analysis can be carried out with techniques such as risk modelling and simulation modelling.

In summary, the Five Forces Model has value, but also some limitations. It can be used to develop an understanding of the current situation, and the strength of competitive forces in the industry, and the reasons for the strength (or weakness) of each of the five forces. As the business environment changes, an understanding of the 'current' situation can also provide some guide to how the situation might develop and so also some guide as to how the company should perhaps react to the new developments.

On the other hand, other techniques for strategic analysis are needed, in particular methods of risk analysis. It is also doubtful whether a rational strategic planning model is appropriate. It might be more appropriate for the company to be more 'opportunistic' in its approach to strategy formulation.

27 2XA (MAY 05 EXAM)

Examiner's Comments

Common errors that occurred in May 05 exam.

Part a

- Answering part (b) in this part of the question, instead of focusing on explaining industry analysis.

Part b

- Misinterpretation of the question, with few candidates focusing upon the information content of the models.

- Internal analysis models used such as SWOT, BCG and internal value chain. Although these have some relevance, they are not most appropriate to external/industry analysis.

Part c

- Generic lists of information sources with little reference to the scenario.

(a) **Industry analysis**

The term 'industry analysis' is a fairly general one that can incorporate a number of different models, depending on what the question asks for.

1 A PEST analysis could be carried out to determine whether and why the industry is growing. It will identify key drivers of change and growth and hence opportunities and threats.

2 A Porter's five forces analysis looks at the threat to the firm's profit margins using the following five headings:

- Competitive rivalry
- Power of customers
- Power of suppliers
- Threat from new entrants
- Threat from substitute products.

Such an analysis would help 2XA understand the overall profit potential of the industry and how best the firm may compete within the industry.

(b) **2XA**

A PEST analysis for 2XA could include the following issues:

Political factors

- EU enlargement would present further opportunities and threats – it is likely that the new firms competing with 2XA are from other EU countries.
- Government policies on fuel tax could affect the long term demand for specialist cars and light aircraft, in turn affecting the demand for 2XA's products. 2XA has derived demand so the management should do an analysis of their customers' industries as well as their own.

Economic factors

- Specialist cars are a luxury product so the demand for them will be linked to the strength of the economy.
- The strength of the Euro, if 2XA is within the Eurozone, and its domestic currency if not, will affect 2XA's competitiveness against companies from outside the EU.

Technological factors

- Technological advances for military and large aircraft are likely to have an impact on the manufacture of light aircraft.

A Porter's five forces analysis for 2XA could include the following information:

Competitive rivalry

- 2XA's strong relationships with customers reduce the ability of competitors to steal customers.

- 2XA only operates in one country, so may lack the economies of scale of international competitors – a key issue here would be to examine the nature of 2XA's competitive advantage – are they trying to compete on cost or have they differentiated their product in any way?

Power of customers

- Customers are all small companies, suggesting that none have significant power individually. This could be investigated further to determine what proportion of the customer's total cost is made up of 2XA's components, whether substitutes exist and so on.

Power of suppliers

- 2XA would need to analyse suppliers to see if it is over-reliant on any.

Threat from new entrants

- Strong relationships with customers should create significant barriers to entry for new firms hoping to target 2XA's customers. However, recent events suggest that the barrier is not significant enough.

(c) **Sources of information**

Possible sources of information include the following:

- The published accounts of competitors and customers could indicate changes in the industry, growth profiles and provide useful information for benchmarking.
- Government departments could be contacted to determine government policy, both locally and nationally – for example, to see attitudes towards encouraging foreign firms to invest.
- There are likely to be many government publications regarding the state of the economy, average earnings, growth estimates and so on. Many of these would indicate the demand for customers' products, in turn indicating 2XA's future demand.
- There are likely to be industry publications for both cars and aircraft. These could be a useful source for information regarding technological advances.
- National and local press could be scanned for information on competitors – for example, job losses.
- Industry trade associations, standard setters and benchmarking groups can provide valuable information on competitors' activities.
- Industry regulators can indicate areas of concern – for example, possible changes in legislation.
- Watchdog groups could indicate areas of concern in the industry, allowing 2XA to avoid potential problems.
- Specialist market research agencies will provide detailed industry analysis for a fee.
- Suppliers of machinery would be willing to share information on technological advances with 2XA.

28 D4D (MAY 05 EXAM)

Examiner's Comments

Common errors that occurred in May 05 exam.

Part (a)

This question was answered reasonably well. Most candidates demonstrated a sound knowledge of Porter's diamond, but few candidates provided comprehensive answers which included the role of government and the nature of clustering of firms within countries.

Part (b)

- Poor application to the scenario.
- Only identifying the aims of D4D and not those of the inward investing company.
- Focusing upon how to attract inward investment (see part (c) answer).

Part (c)

- Lack of depth and focus upon D4D.

(a) **International competitive advantage**

A popular model for discussing the link between competitive advantage and geographical location is Porter's diamond. Porter claimed that countries do not have an overall competitive advantage per se but that specific industries can exploit their location to gain a competitive advantage internationally. Porter identified four areas to consider:

Factor conditions

These include basic and advanced factors of production. Basic factors are unsustainable as they are easily copied (e.g. unskilled labour) whilst advanced factors can convey the advantage, as they are less easy to emulate (e.g. scientific expertise).

They include human, physical, knowledge, capital and infrastructure e.g. Linguistic ability of the Swiss has provided advantage in the banking industry.

D4D's weather may give firms an advantage in growing certain crops. Similarly the young, educated workforce is likely to convey an advantage in high-tech industries.

Demand conditions

Sophisticated home demand can lead to the company developing significant advantages in the global market place. Fussy consumers set high standards for products whilst past experience of the product's progress through the life cycle in the home market can provide valuable input to new strategic initiatives. e.g. Japanese customers have high expectations of their electrical products which forces producers to provide a technically superior product for the global market place. They are so used to dealing with sophisticated customers that, when they come across unsophisticated markets, they excel way beyond the competition.

Related and supporting industries

An advantage can be conveyed by the availability of superior supplier industries e.g. Italy has a substantial leatherwear industry which is supported by leather working plants and top fashion and design companies.

Strategy, structure and rivalry

Different nations have different approaches to business in terms of structure and the intensity of rivalry that can take place. If a company is used to dealing with strong competition then it will have experience of rivals' attacks and so will be better able to fight them off.

Domestic rivalry can keep the organisations 'lean and mean' so that when they go out into the global market place they can compete more successfully with the less capable foreign competition e.g. Nokia and Finland's approach to the regulation of telecoms.

(b) **Aims**

The government of D4D will have the following aims:

- To attract as many foreign firms as possible to invest in D4D
- Protecting domestic firms from excessive competition – clearly there is a possible conflict between these first two aims
- To ensure that the foreign firms concerned are reputable and will invest in infrastructure such as education
- To maximise tax revenues
- To ensure compliance with relevant legislation re health and safety, pollution, etc
- Increased employment
- Reinvestment of profits by foreign firms to create growth and more jobs
- To develop clusters of similar firms, based on the Porter's diamond analysis. This will encourage competitive advantage and will attract yet more firms.

Companies seeking to invest in D4D will have the following aims:

- To maximise profit
- To minimise global tax liabilities
- Compliance with legislation
- To invest in countries with stable governments, a strong economy, good infrastructure and a skilled and well educated workforce
- To make the investment an attractive place for overseas posting of existing staff
- To reduce distribution costs by being near to other markets
- To develop strong relationships with government departments
- To get financial assistance, e.g. tax breaks, development grants and soft loans, from the government.

In most respects the aims of the D4D government are consistent with the aims of foreign firms seeking to invest in D4D:

- Both want to see profits, growth and jobs created
- Both want a country with a well educated workforce and strong infrastructure
- Both want political stability and an environment that encourages investment.

However, there are areas of possible conflict:

- Tax – the government will want to maximise tax revenue but companies will seek to minimise their liabilities through careful planning. They may also expect tax breaks as an incentive to invest in D4D (see below).
- Remittances – companies may want to take funds out of the country but the government will want to see them reinvested. This could affect dividend policy, for example.
- Competition – once established, a firm may not want to see competitors encouraged to invest in D4D.
- Employment – the government will be keen to see jobs go to locals but the firms may prefer to use staff from their domestic country.
- Finance – the company may want more 'sweeteners' than the government is happy to give.

(c) The government of D4D should focus on the following areas to make the country more attractive to outside investors:

Factor conditions

Porter suggested that the root of sustainable competitive success is 'advanced factors' so the government of D4D should focus on these.

- Government policy could be aimed at improving D4D's communications and transport infrastructure.
- Similarly, training and development policies could be focused on key industries to assist in enhancing the skills and knowledge required to achieve world-class excellence.
- Financial assistance could be offered to the unemployed to undergo retraining in certain key areas, and firms in certain industries could be incentivised to take on the unemployed.
- Additional government policies could be aimed at encouraging firms to invest more in R&D, such as tax incentives.
- Tax breaks and other assistance such as cheap loans should be offered to foreign firms seeking to invest in D4D.
- The government may make it easier for firms to raise capital by developing a strong capital market.

Demand conditions

- A second potential set of government policies might be to encourage consumers to be more demanding of product performance through increased spending on education and training and through consumer protection and product safety legislation.
- Similarly, government policies could be introduced to encourage best practice in:
  - product design and development
  - supplier and manufacturer partnership relations to deliver quality to consumers
  - marketing and selling overseas.

Firm strategy, structure and rivalry

- One potential government policy is to encourage, rather than discourage, competition at home. This can be achieved through less government intervention such as quotes to discourage foreign competition. It can be argued that increased rivalry among firms within an industry forces superior practice and, therefore, strengthens the industry.

Related and supporting industries

- The government could also acquire consultancy advice from experts within existing world-class industries overseas.
- Similarly, the government could set up development agencies in the key industries.

29 FIVE FORCES MODEL (NOV 05 EXAM)

Key answer tips

Surprisingly at this level, this question is essentially bookwork. The main problem for students in the exam was whether they felt they knew the topics in sufficient depth to pass.

(a) **Competition**

Over the last three decades, business has focused on one fundamental idea – the pursuit of sustainable competitive advantage. While the idea of competition is not new, Michael Porter in particular has expanded the concept from competing with rivals to incorporating the struggle for power between the firm and five competitive forces.

Porter argued that each of these forces can reduce overall industry profitability and the individual firm's share of that profit – their 'profit potential' – because they can influence prices, costs and the level of investment required. One of the forces is competitive rivalry – suppliers and customers are also included.

Customers / Buyers

Porter argued that buyers can reduce profits in an industry by exerting their market power, usually through demanding higher quality and/or lower costs. In principle this is no different from profits being competed away by other rivals.

For example, the UK grocery business has been concentrated into the hands of a small number of large powerful retailers, resulting in dramatically reduced profitability in agricultural markets.

The power used by buyers can also have the secondary effect of increasing competitive rivalry by forcing down prices, bargaining for higher quality or improved services and by playing competitors against each other. All three of these are at the expense of industry profitability.

Not everyone agrees with Porter – some would argue that the idea of satisfying customer needs should not be abandoned in favour of a view that sees customers either as direct competitors or as means to the firm's end. Customers are not objects whose reason for being is to be fought over by competitors seeking 'sustainable competitive advantage'.

Suppliers

In a similar way Porter argued that suppliers can exert bargaining power over companies within an industry by threatening to raise their prices and threatening to reduce the quality of their goods and services.

The effect of this power is to squeeze profitability out of an industry unable to recover cost increases by raising its own prices.

This can be seen in the PC business, where software and processor suppliers make great profits, but PC manufacture remains relatively less attractive.

(b) **Transfer prices**

There are four specific criteria that a good transfer pricing policy should meet:

- it should provide motivation for divisional managers
- it should allow divisional autonomy and independence to be maintained
- it should allow divisional performance to be assessed objectively
- it should ensure that divisional managers make decisions that are in the best interests of the divisions and also of the company as a whole.

This final feature is usually referred to as goal congruence and is perhaps the most important of the four.

Given this, the following issues should be considered when setting transfer prices within a large, complex organisation.

Relative buyer/supplier power

Porter's views on buyer and supplier power are particularly relevant for transfer pricing.

High buyer power can occur if, for example, the receiving division has a choice of alternative supplies but the supplying division has no external market for its product. In such a case, the negotiated transfer price is likely to be very low with the following consequences:

- The profit of the receiving division is overstated and that of the supplying division understated. Both profit figures fail to reflect the true performance of the divisions.
- The supplying divisional manager may become demotivated as they will be less likely to hit their targets.
- The supplying division may elect not to supply the receiving division and instead seek more outside sales or even halt production. This might force the receiving division to outsource with the consequence of an overall higher cost for the group or compromised quality if outsourced items are inferior.

High supplier power could occur if the supplier produces a high quality product that is unmatched in the market place. It could thus sell these in the outside marketplace, whereas the receiving division would struggle to find alternative supply. High supplier power would result in a very high transfer price with the following results:

- The profit of the supplying division is overstated and that of the receiving division understated. Again, both profit figures fail to reflect the true performance of the divisions.
- The receiving divisional manager may become demotivated as they will be less likely to hit their targets.
- The receiving division may elect to outsource with the consequence of an overall higher cost for the group or compromised quality if outsourced items are inferior.

The degree of decentralisation

Buyers and sellers should be completely free to deal outside the company. If this autonomy is restricted, then the bargaining power of the two parties will be affected and the objectives of transfer pricing compromised.

Negotiation

Prices of all transfers in and out of a profit centre should be determined by negotiation between buyers and sellers. Head office interference with the transfer price could compromise the objectives set out above.

Information

Negotiators should have access to full data on alternative sources and markets and to public and private information about market prices to try to balance the power between them.

Negotiators should also be fully informed on the significance of the transaction in relation to the profitability of the company as a whole. This is an attempt to guarantee goal congruence but could compromise negotiations if managers feel under pressure to arrive at the 'right answer' for the firm as a whole.

Market prices

Most negotiated transfer prices rely on the existence of market prices to act as a reference point. Howver, there are a number of problems with using market prices:

- There may be no intermediate market price. The product or service might not be readily available on the open market (an example might be a partly completed car being transferred from one division to another).
- The market price might not be independent. This would occur if the transferring division were in the position of a monopolist both within the company and in the outside market.
- Difficulty in agreeing a source of market prices. Debates will occur over the size, quality, timing and location of internal transfers compared with a range of published prices.
- The need to adjust prices for different volumes. Prices quoted may well not relate to the levels of transfers that are likely to take place; in the same way, the extent of reductions due to saved selling costs will be difficult to estimate.
- Published prices may be fictitious. This is a variation on the previous problem but is typified by those products for which it is customary for a seller to publish a price then the buyer to negotiate a lower figure.

30 FFF COMMUNICATIONS (NOV 06 EXAM)

Key answer tips

This is an in-depth question on competitor analysis. The main problem is that many students will feel that they cannot generate enough (different!) ideas to ensure a pass.

(a) Competitor analysis can be defined as 'the systematic review of all available information (marketing, production, financial, etc) on the activities of competitors in order to gain a competitive advantage'.

The advantages of adopting a formal approach to competitor analysis are as follows:

Understanding relative competitive advantage

A detailed analysis of the value chains of existing competitors will allow FFF to assess the basis of competitive strategy used by itself and its competitors. This will enable FFF to assess whether its existing competitive strategy is sustainable and which aspects of the value chain need addressing to improve it.

Identifying potential new competitors

As well as analysing existing competitors, competitor analysis will help FFF identify potential new entrants to the industry and act accordingly – for example, by reviewing how barriers to entry can be strengthened.

Understanding competitors' current and potential strategies

By analysing competitors' past and current strategies, it may be possible for FFF to anticipate likely future moves and plan in advance, rather than having to react to competitor actions. This should reduce future levels of risk and uncertainty.

Understanding how competitors may react to FFF's actions

FFF will want to know which strategies to avoid because a particular competitor's response may be very aggressive.

Developing future strategies

Competitor analysis should allow FFF to decide with whom it should 'pick a fight' in the industry and in what way. This should increase the chances of success of such strategies.

Influencing competitors' future actions

By understanding how competitors assess whether particular market segments are worth targeting, FFF may be able be able to deter them from entering its markets – for example, by lowering prices.

Forecasting

An understanding of competitor behaviour will improve the accuracy of FFF's forecasts.

(b) The key stages of a formal competitor analysis process are as follows:

Step 1: Identify competitors

The first step is to identify which competitors should be analysed.

Clearly all significant existing competitors need to be analysed, but even here the definition of a 'competitor' can be wide ranging.

Kotler identifies four types of competitors:

- *Brand competitors* include firms most like FFF with a similar product portfolio, of comparable size and targeting the same customers.
- *Industry competitors* offer similar products but in different segments – for example, firms who just make mobile phones or who just target oil company customers.
- *Form competitors* aim to satisfy the same customer needs but with different types of products – what Porter would refer to as 'substitutes'. For FFF this could include providers of land-line phones, for example.
- *Generic competitors* compete for the same income or budget as FFF. Thus armaments manufacturers could be seen as competing with thermal imaging products for government military budgets.

Forecasting potential new entrants is more difficult and could include the following:

- firms that are not in the industry but could overcome barriers relatively cheaply.
- firms that could gain obvious synergy if they entered the industry
- customers or suppliers who may wish to vertically integrate into the industry.

Step 2: Analyse competitors

Porter suggests that, once selected, competitors should be analysed with respect to the following headings:

Objectives/ goals

It is vital to understand what drives competitors' behaviour. Knowledge of goals will allow FFF to understand whether competitors are satisfied with their current position and how likely they are to change that position. It will also enable FFF to predict likely responses to FFF's strategies.

For example, a competitor focused on short-term financial targets may not be willing to spend much to defend an attack.

Objectives can be determined from historical behaviour, investor communications and the chairman's statement in published accounts

Assumptions

This section looks at the assumptions a competitor makes about itself and its industry, even if these assumptions are unrealistic and outdated.

For example, a competitor may still see itself as the market leader despite problems over quality and falling sales. If it further believes that it still has high customer loyalty, then a speculative price cut by FFF to win customers may be met with little response. Identifying such blind spots can expose major opportunities for FFF.

Assumptions are more difficult to identify, but may include trying to understand the value systems of senior executives and main advisors.

Strategy

Analysis of strategy involves looking at where and how competitors are competing. Often what firms disclose in press statements is more revealing of how a competitor understands their strategy than looking at what they do.

Capabilities

This section looks at competitors' strengths and weaknesses and whether they have the competences and resources required for success in the industry. This can involve detailed analysis of financial statements (e.g. ratio analysis), scrutinising press reports and trade publications, discussions with ex-employees and discussions with customers.

Step 3: Develop competitor response profiles

The analysis of step 2 should allow FFF to create competitor response profiles that identify the strategic changes the particular competitor might initiate and also how they might respond to FFF's initiatives.

Competitors' goals, assumptions and strategies will indicate the nature, probability, strength and timing of a response but their strengths and weaknesses will indicate their ability to respond effectively.

Kotler suggests four typical response profiles:

- *Laid back* competitors are unlikely to respond to any initiatives.
- *Selective* competitors react to attack in selected markets only.
- *Tiger* competitors always respond aggressively.
- *Stochastic* competitors exhibit no predictable pattern of behaviour.

REGULATION IN MAJOR MARKETS

31 DF

Key answer tips

This question requires a discussion of the issues that need to be addressed by the management of an organisation considering establishing an overseas manufacturing and distribution base. The opportunities and threats faced by the organisation should be discussed. Organisational management issues include different operating conditions and working practices, culture, language and the need for training. Financing issues include exchange risk and restrictions on borrowing and remittances. As is often the case, it is useful to distinguish between long-term and short-term finance issues. Government regulatory issues should include an assessment of political risk.

Organisational issues

The decision to set up overseas will affect DF in three possible ways:

1 **Existing organisation structure**

The manufacturing activities will be scaled down, as certain activities will be carried out overseas. This may involve some reduction in headcount with the attendant problems of staff unrest. The exporting activities of the company will either be phased out or dramatically reduced. This will involve losses of staff of managerial grade along with support staff. DF must consider its future options carefully. If the opportunity arises to export in a market that is geographically less remote, a core of competence must be retained.

2 **Setting up overseas**

The overseas subsidiary would be run as a **Strategic Business Unit** within the framework of the Group. This would mean that local management would be encouraged to run the new business with considerable autonomy and very little in the way of direct input from Head Office. Initially it may be advisable to have a core of top management who are existing employees who would move to the country concerned. Most overseas subsidiaries are run by expatriates with good local support staff who can then be part of the plan of succession if the venture is successful. Local management will be free to develop their business plans over a set-planning horizon of say three years.

3 **Retention of Head Office functions**

Certain functions may be retained by Head office. Treasury management is an essential function that will be retained in order to deal with the issues of funding both in the long and short term and in the circulation of surplus funds and foreign exchange management. Internal Audit is likely to be another area where Head Office is likely to maintain an entrée for supervisory control.

Strategic management at Head Office and the local Chief Executive Officer will agree a range of performance indicators and targets for evaluation purposes.

Finance issues

Finance issues – long term

Setting up overseas will involve an injection of long term and short-term funds. The long-term funds would be in the form of both equity and loan capital. Equity capital may be a useful instrument in giving a minority interest to local management as a strategic incentive to compensate them for the risks of starting a risky new venture overseas. Equity capital may also provide a means of obtaining funds from local entrepreneurs who may wish to obtain a minority stake in a prestigious venture.

Loan capital is useful in that it can (subject to any local restrictions) be repatriated to the UK when the venture is successful.

Finance issues – short term

The new venture will need significant working capital in order to establish it successfully. This may involve setting up a line of credit with the local arm of the company's UK banker or obtaining an introduction to an overseas bank of quality and stability to provide the necessary funds. An alternative is to fund the SBU by a loan on current account so that it is put in funds with a local bank and can commence operations without any cash constraints.

Potential government issues

Potential government regulatory requirements

Setting up overseas will involve a number of issues such as:

Compulsory participation by host government

Some countries compel overseas companies to offer an equity stake either to a government agency or to a local citizen (e.g. Malaysian nationals are a legal requirement in any overseas organisation). This may involve some negotiations with the host government concerned.

Taxation issues

This is an obvious area of concern. The SBU will be subject to local taxes and the interaction between local taxes and UK corporate taxes must be evaluated. There may be restrictions on pricing policies, which may inhibit any strategy for trading with other countries from an overseas base.

Foreign Exchange restriction

Many host countries impose controls on dividends and on the ability for overseas corporations to repatriate funds by way of dividends.

Customs duty and tariffs

The impact of customs duty and any protective tariffs may also inhibit profitable operations. Some countries have very high indirect taxes and this can affect the freedom to price goods competitively.

32 CLOTHING COMPANY

Key answer tips

Part (a): you should take care to ensure that you use the circumstances outlined in the scenario when applying models such as PEST.

Part (b): your answer should demonstrate an appreciation of the importance that management identify and understand the issues that are important to workers and appraise the cultural influences, which may affect the local workforce.

(a) Before entering negotiations to build an overseas factory, the company should consider the environmental issues, which can be categorised into the following headings:

- demographic
- technological
- economic
- social and cultural
- regulatory
- political
- business.

Demographic environment

The trends in sizes of segments of the national population should be investigated both in the UK and abroad. Clothing products can be particularly associated with certain age groups or socio-economic groups (e.g. bold fashion clothes for teenagers and pinstripe suits for professionals), so it must be confirmed that products are to be offered to populations with the appropriate breakdowns.

It is also important that the company can recruit employees of the right skills mix at an affordable price. The strategy appears to be to seek low-wage labour, so a pool of such potential employees must be available. Developing countries may be more appropriate therefore than other EU countries with their high social costs.

Technological environment

Clothing has historically been a low-tech, high-labour industry, a fact underlined by the desire to seek low-wage labour, so relevant technological factors are more likely to be the infrastructure in which the company operates rather than the operations of the company itself.

The existence of good telecommunications and transport networks will be important so that head office managers can keep in touch with the new site managers, and so that raw materials can be delivered to and finished goods from the new site.

Economic environment

Levels of inflation, interest rates, gross national products and exchange rates will be investigated to assess the stability of the country in which the investment is made. Some countries offer comparative advantage in particular areas, e.g. high skills or low wages.

Social and cultural environment

The head office management will already be familiar with the social and cultural values that exist in the UK in relation to clothing in particular and business in general. Some market research may be necessary to investigate the values in prospective overseas markets, for example to ensure that the styles and fabrics of proposed clothes will be acceptable to the overseas customers, and that working hours and ethics can be agreed.

Regulatory environment

Are exchange controls in force between any overseas country and the UK? The ultimate objective of any overseas investment is presumably to remit funds generated by successful operations to the UK for distribution to the shareholders. If funds are blocked from being remitted to the UK, that country may be judged inappropriate.

Also, what burdens are placed on businesses operating abroad? If taxes or environmental controls or social costs are unacceptably high, again perhaps a different country would be a better choice.

Political environment

Stable free-market countries with a long democratic tradition are the safest countries in which to invest; the company would not want to join the list of companies whose overseas assets have been expropriated without compensation by foreign governments in the past. Political risks can be insured against, but the premiums are expensive and it is safer to avoid such risks altogether.

Business environment

The customers in the foreign country must have enough disposable income in their pockets and purses to buy the new clothes that they wish. There is little point in locating a manufacturing/selling plant in a country where the population spends all its income each week on feeding the family members, with no money left over for discretionary purchases of fashion clothes.

The current phase of the UK economy will be well known to UK managers, continuing to emerge slowly from recession. Some market research may be necessary to determine the cyclical prospects of an overseas economy.

(b) The UK company is proposing to establish a manufacturing unit overseas and staff it with local labour. The effectiveness of the local labour will be governed by many influences which should be investigated before the decision is finally taken to set up in a particular country. The investigation can be started inexpensively by speaking to representatives of the foreign country's embassy or trade mission in the UK; more detailed information could be obtained by procuring the services of a specialist consultant. The four categories of influences are dealt with in turn:

Local education and training

If the country is selected to be a low-wage economy, it is possible that employees cannot be found who already have the necessary skills to do the job. Therefore local people must be trained; who pays for the training costs may be a source of disagreement. The company would wish to pay a low wage to employees during their training period, and pay a higher wage to fully trained staff who can add value more efficiently. Such a scheme may simply be unacceptable in some cultures where older people cannot be seen to have lower status than younger people, and men are unhappy to have lower status than women. What seems objectively fair in the UK may have to be adjusted before it can be applied overseas.

Technology

In some cultures there is a deep mistrust of machines, owing to the belief that machines displace people from jobs, so sensitive education and training may be required before technology can be installed in the midst of the community. The alternative would be to site the manufacturing unit at some distance from where families live, providing transport to and from the unit, so that noise and pollution are kept away from homes.

Working hours

In the UK people are generally good timekeepers and will be at their workplace at 8.30 in the morning if this is their start time. Other cultures have a much more relaxed attitude to timekeeping and a manager's call for promptness will be met with incomprehension. If people work on their own or are paid a piece rate, perhaps this is not a problem. If production is organised on a line system and some people are absent, then there will be a real problem which will have to be resolved sensitively. Perhaps offering free transport to the factory will attract everyone to turn up for the bus on time.

Another contentious area might be time off for religious observance during the day and on special festivals. Such matters have to be planned for before they become a problem; close liaison between employer and employee representatives will bring benefits in this area.

Domestic amenities

In some cultures the employer is expected to provide housing for employees and perhaps also their families. If this housing is close to the factory (as is likely), this will lessen the timekeeping problem described above, but the cost of providing housing must be budgeted for.

Other amenities may also be traditionally provided for employees, for example food, leisure activities, free samples of the company's goods, etc. An employer who meets the usual responsibilities of local workplaces will be accepted more positively in the local community.

In conclusion, an employer must research the cultural norms of workers in overseas countries before establishing a manufacturing site there, so that possible areas of conflict can be identified and solved before they become real problems. If men in the foreign country are not used to taking orders from women then it would be insensitive to send out an all-female management team from the UK to run the factory. If a laid-back attitude to timekeeping is the norm, then one should not sack workers who arrive ten minutes late on their first day at work.

Most of these problems can be avoided by research before establishing the site and by establishing works committees once the site is up and running. However, one final word of caution can be given concerning works committees; the participative style popular in the UK where workers treat each other as equals might have no place in a different culture. Such a style might be seen as weakness on the part of management and could lead to disciplinary problems in the future.

33 SOCIAL RESPONSIBILITY

(a) (i) About 20 or so years ago, the idea that profitability was overwhelmingly the principal objective of a business would have been uncontroversial. Today's climate is different: increased public awareness of the social impact of large organisations has broadened the range of objectives which businesses must aim to achieve. New factors to be considered include pollution control, conservation of natural resources and avoidance of environmental damage.

In the short term, the measures described in the question would reduce profits; all of them involve increased profits or revenue forgone. And reduced profits imply reduced shareholders' wealth in the form of dividends and capital growth.

However, this analysis, though relatively straightforward in the short term, may not be so clear-cut in the long term. Many commentators argue that the reputation and image of corporations will suffer if they do not respond to heightened awareness of social responsibility amongst consumers. Given that many companies are already taking steps along this path, and making good public relations out of their efforts, there is pressure on other companies to follow suit. Failure to do so may lead to long-term decline.

(ii) A conflict between company objectives implies a picture of managers pulling in opposite directions, some trying to meet criteria of social responsibility, others hell-bent on maximising profit. Given that all of the managers in a company are drawing on the same pool of resources this is a recipe for disaster.

However, this does not mean that companies are doomed to fail if they pursue more than one objective. The ideal is to agree on a balance between conflicting objectives, and to settle on a strategy which satisfies both sets of objectives, to the extent that they can be reconciled.

(b) Part of the difficulty in pursing aspirations towards social responsibility lies in the relative novelty of the concept. Managers brought up in a culture of profit maximisation may find it hard to appreciate the importance of other objectives, and to adapt their behaviour accordingly. To 'operationalise' social responsibility involves, as a first step, making managers aware of the need for it. This may be achieved by:

- appropriate training
- dissemination of targets and measures related to social objectives
- formal incorporation of social objectives into the decision-making process
- collaboration with other organisations to launch a common approach
- appointment of external consultants to assess existing performance in this area and to recommend improvements
- monitoring achievement by logging and publishing of performance indicators
- appointment of committee to review and implement social and ethical policies.

(c) An organisation's stakeholders include:

- owners/shareholders
- employees
- business contacts, such as customers and suppliers
- the general public
- the government.

Owners/shareholders will be interested primarily in profitability, but the analysis in Part(a) above suggests that long-term profitability may depend at least in part on the adoption of social objectives.

Employees obviously have a very direct interest in at least some social objectives: for example, the question mentions a policy of paying wages above national minimum levels.

Business contacts have a less direct interest in this issue. However, as a minimum, creditors will be impressed with an ethical policy of paying debts on time, and customers who themselves have social and ethical interests may exert pressure on their suppliers to conform as well.

The general public, as already mentioned, have shown themselves increasingly aware of these issues, and prepared to back their principles with direct action (such as refusing to invest in companies whose objectives they disapprove of).

The government must meet international obligations as well as satisfying the demands of their own electorate. Both factors mean that they will take an interest in the social and ethical policies of organisations.

34 DROSSWAITE PLC

Key answer tips

Our answer to Part (a) is longer than you could manage in the time available. If you include three or four well-explained examples under each heading, that will suffice. Part (b)(ii) should be straightforward. In Part (b)(ii) be aware that not all of the arguments you may have learned about are relevant in this case, so don't just write down everything you know.

(a) According to the analysis of Braithwaite and Drahos 'actors' means anyone with an interest in regulation, 'mechanisms' are tools that actors use to achieve their goals, and 'principles' are the ideas that are used to justify the supremacy of the actors' values, goals and desires.

Actors

The full range of 'actors' who may have an influence on the way an organisation conducts its business are as follows:

- organisations of states, such as the WTO or the EU
- individual states
- organisations formed by businesses with common agendas, such as Chambers of Commerce.
- corporations
- Non-Governmental Organisations (NGOs)
- mass publics: large audiences of citizens who have a common concern about an issue
- knowledge-based (epistemic) communities who share a common discourse based on shared knowledge. CIMA is an example.

The last three groups may be collectively termed 'civil society' and they may include, among others, trade unions, charities, co-operatives, environmental groups, consumer organisations, and the media.

Mechanisms

Mechanisms are the tools that might be used to get the regulatory outcome that you desire. According to Braithwaite and Drahos these can be summarised as follows:

- Capacity-building: This means helping other actors get the technical competence to satisfy standards, where they wish to meet them but lack the capacity to do so.
- Economic coercion: the threat, fear or use of economic sanctions.

- Military coercion: the threat, fear or use of military force. This is not an option available to businesses, or at least hopefully not, but business objectives might be achieved through the actions of governments.
- Modelling: basing your own rules on rules that have demonstrably worked for others – though your version may have many local changes.
- Non-reciprocal coordination: this occurs when movement toward common rules happens without all parties believing they have a common interest in that movement. One party believes the new rule is in their interest, but this belief is not reciprocated. This underlies the legal battles between Microsoft and Netscape and Sun: the world standardised on Microsoft's versions of technologies invented by the other companies.
- Reciprocal adjustment: parties agree to adjust the rules they follow without coercion, for example all parties agree to drive on the left side of the road to avoid crashes.
- Rewards are offered to those who comply with a regulation, for example government contracts may only be offered to suppliers who are ISO 9001 certified.

Principles

Principles very often conflict with each other. For example, mere 'rule compliance' conflicts with 'world's best practice': the former might lie behind a cost-minimisation strategy while the latter would underlie a total quality strategy.

Here are the principles identified by Brathwaite and Drahos.

- Continuous improvement: The idea that you should do better every year than the previous year in terms of a regulatory objective such as protecting the environment, even if legal requirements were exceeded in the previous year.
- Harmonisation: As already mentioned, the idea that everyone should set the same rules.
- Liberalisation-deregulation: The idea that the number, stringency or enforcement of rules should be reduced.
- Lowest-cost location: Economic activity should be located wherever and under whatever regulatory rules it can be transacted most cheaply. For example, it could be argued that NAFTA was a piece of regulation that enabled US firms to relocate their activities to Mexico, where much lower wage rates could be paid.
- Most Favoured Nation: This is the principle that any regulatory benefit accorded to importers or exporters from one nation should be accorded to importers or exporters from other nations.
- Mutual recognition: The argument here is that different levels of government and different governments should recognise one another's rules and allow economic activity to be performed under one another's rules, even if the rules are different.
- National sovereignty: This is the principle that the nation-state should be supreme over any other source of power in matters affecting its citizens or territory. For example, following a BSE scare a country may ban imports of another country's beef in defiance of a ruling by a body to which both countries belong.
- National treatment: The principle that a state should regulate foreign corporations according to the same rules as national corporations.

- Reciprocity: Unlike the most favoured nation idea, the argument is that if one nation grants a regulatory benefit to importers or exporters from a second nation, the second nation should grant the same regulatory benefit to the first nation, regardless of the regulatory benefits it accords third nations. The EU works like this, as we have seen.
- Rule compliance: The idea is that companies should go as far as the rules require (e.g. in reducing pollution) but no further.
- Strategic trade: Designing the content and stringency of regulation so as to advantage national exporters or importers over foreign exporters or importers.
- Transparency: This proposes that 'any person should be able to observe regulatory deliberation or easily discover the outcomes (and their justifications) of the deliberation'. For example, it might be argued that consumers should be able to find out how food standards are set and if the standards for hygiene, say, are lower than they might expect, what the justification for that is.
- World's best practice: The principle that economic activity should be conducted under rules that substantially exceed the requirements set by present practice or regulation.

(b) (i) Country analysis attempts to answer questions such as the following:

- How has the economic condition of Kenya changed over the last 10 years as measured by macroeconomic indicators – including GDP, inflation, trade balance, exchange rates, etc?
- How many mobile phones were sold in China last year; who were the top competitors in this market; and what were their respective market shares?
- How stable is the government in Nigeria from the perspective of a prospective American investor?

Although we are not told what activities Drosswaite plc is involved in, many of the activities involved in production, marketing and servicing need to be tailored to the particular requirements of the country of operation. Strategic planners therefore need a wealth of information about the countries in which they intend to do business:

- economic conditions and latest indicators: domestic data (GDP, inflation, interest rates, unemployment, etc.); forecasts for commodities prices and estimates for manufactured goods, exchange rates and so on
- industry reviews: status reports on the condition of an industry in a particular country
- distribution, sales and marketing information, e.g. how consumer markets are segmented, current sales trends, demographic data (population, life expectancy, languages, literacy rates, etc)
- infrastructure e.g. the quality of the road infrastructure
- banking and financial markets e.g. the credibility of the central banks, and the availability of sources of finance
- local business regulations
- human resources: what skills are available?
- political structure and developments

- legislative differences, tax rules
- the degree of interdependence between the national economy and global economies and susceptibility to changes in the global economy.

Up-to-date and accurate information may be quite hard to collect for developing countries. It is likely that Drosswaite will need to use the specialist services of organisations such as LexisNexis and the Economist Intelligence Unit in the first instance.

(ii) Many barriers to free trade may exist because governments try to protect home industries against foreign competition. Protectionist measures include tariffs or customs duties, import quotas, government subsidies to its own local businesses and government deterrents (non-tariff barriers) such as complicated and time-consuming import regulations and documentation, strict safety standards for imported goods and so on.

The main arguments that may be put forward in this case to support protectionism include the following:

- **Keeping money in the country**. The theory is that an excess of exports over imports will preserve and increase the wealth of the country. The major flaw in the argument is that a country that exports much and imports little is depriving its population of goods and services, thereby reducing the domestic standard of living.
- **Strategic industries**. Many governments impose trade restrictions because they wish to pursue objectives other than output maximisation. Examples would be the desire to maintain output of the armament and agricultural industries for strategic purposes.
- **The infant industry hypothesis**. Arguably a newly developing industry in the home country requires some kind of protection so that it can develop to the point where it can compete. Similarly, a young economy may wish to diversify its activities so that, for example, it can reduce its dependence on a limited number of primary products whose price is likely to fluctuate quite dramatically. The major problem arising from this argument is the determination of exactly when the infant industry or economy has achieved sufficient maturity to be able to compete satisfactorily. It is natural for such industries to suggest constantly that this stage has not yet been reached.

35 MTM GROUP (NOV 05 EXAM)

(a) **Expected values**

The limitations of the use of expected values are discussed below:

Probabilities

The probabilities of the different outcomes are very hard to predict with much certainty. In some cases there may be objective probabilities based on past experience of similar scenarios. In others the probabilities are much more subjective.

With MTM it is likely that the reduction in profit of 20% is based on past experience of similar legislation in other countries but the 40% chance of such a ban is speculation at best.

Possible outcomes

The expected value may not correspond to any possible outcome.

If the Government implements a ban, then profits will fall in SAC by 20%. If they don't, then profits will not change. The 8% drop is not a possible outcome and so, it can be argued, should not be used as a basis for decision making.

One-off event

Expected values can be useful when the same decision has to be made many times or when the firm has a number of independent projects with a portfolio effect. In such circumstances the expected value can be equated with the long run or overall average outcome and is thus more useful.

It is less useful when the situation relates to a 'one-off' scenario as we have with MTM. One decision in one country is being considered.

Risk

The average calculated gives no indication of the possible results, either in terms of their spread or skewness. It thus fails to convey information about the risk of those outcomes and is seriously limited unless risk is incorporated another way.

Using an 8% drop in profits is not the same as recognising that there is a 40% chance of the viability of MTM's operations in SAC being compromised!

Using the technique

It is important that the full implications of each outcome are included in any estimates. With MTM the marketing manager has incorporated a 20% drop in profit rather than the possible knock-on implication of closing SAC operations.

(b) To take into account the possible new legislation, MTM should consider the use of scenario planning where a few possible outcomes are explored rather than focusing on just one average outcome.

This could involve the following stages:

1 Develop scenarios to study the possibilities for the external environment and identify key trends and uncertainties

MTM planners have identified two scenarios – either there will be a ban or there won't. They should also consider different times for a ban to be introduced and could also consider the possibility of a partial ban.

2 Build an analysis and strategic option against each scenario

Rather than working with an 8% drop in profit, MTM needs to clarify its strategies assuming the ban does not occur and then consider the impact of the ban as a separate analysis. Will it compromise the viability of the operation in SAC? Why? Does MTM have production facilities in SAC or just distribution? Could MTM relocate production? Could MTM put pressure on the government for a partial ban to 'limit the damage'? MTM should construct forecasts and budgets for each scenario to consider the impact.

3 Look for the main strengths of the business and link to the scenarios

Some strategies make sense whatever the outcome, usually because they capitalise on or develop key strengths of the firm. For example, MTM has a global brand name and could seek to strengthen it in SAC by increasing its advertising spend in the short term. If the ban is agreed, then MTM has still increased awareness among its target group. If the ban does not materialise, then MTM should still benefit from a boost in sales.

4 Consider probability of occurrence

5 Identify new resources and competencies that may be required

The seriousness of a ban could prompt MTM to recruit experts in political lobbying.

6 Modify the strategic options

The new plan may be to increase pressure on the government.

7 Constant monitoring of reality to see which scenario is unfolding

8 Redeploy scenarios and unveil strategic options as appropriate

(c) MTM could influence the government of SAC by the following methods:

Lobbying

Specifically, the act of lobbying government can be defined as to include:

- attempting to influence the making or amending of legislation and regulations
- attempting to influence the making or changing of government policies or programmes
- attempting to influence government decisions in the awarding of grants, contracts, contributions, or any similar benefits
- attempting to influence government appointments to boards, commissions and any other public office.

In some countries, particularly the USA, there are powerful lobbying organisations that can be employed to present your argument in the most effective manner.

Political donations

Firms can influence governments by providing funds as there is always the possibility of withdrawing those funds if the government acts against the interests of the firm.

Appoint politicians as (usually non-executive) directors.

Some firms have decided that the best way to influence government is from the inside. Having politicians on the payroll can be effective, though in some countries members' interests must be declared and conflicts of interest highlighted.

Executives running for public office

This is another way of influencing political decisions from the inside.

Publicity

Some firms seek to influence governments by publicly expressed support for a candidate or party and publicly expressed views on issues. This is particularly effective if the firm controls a section of the media and can seek to change public opinion to help influence government.

Others

Some firms have been accused of attempting to bribe officials to get their way. Others have threatened to close factories, with the resulting job losses, if governments do not do as they say. Obviously these would not be recommended as they are unethical!

Out of the above, political donations and appointing leading politicians to the board are most likely to be effective in SAC and may even be the norm for large business.

STAKEHOLDERS

36 DIGWELL EXPLORATIONS

Key answer tips

In Part (a) you are required to discuss the ethical issues posed by the new mining operations within Eastborough. A brief discussion of what ethics are a useful precursor to the specific issues: defining key terms from the requirement is often a good way to start an answer and is one of the easiest ways to get marks in the exam. A discussion of stakeholder conflicts is also required. There are many possible combinations of conflict so it is useful to pick the main conflicts and discuss these. In Part (b) you are required to outline a framework for analysing stakeholders. Mendelow's matrix is the model most people will use. This needs to be explained in relation to the scenario and the likely response Digwell will take to different groups based on their position in the matrix. In Part (a) you are not required to discuss in detail any broad ethical issues which are not related to the mining issue from the scenario. In Part (b) you do not need to discuss the business objectives or mission in detail – two topics often linked to stakeholder analysis.

(a) **Ethics**

Ethics are a code of moral principles that people follow with respect to what is right or wrong. General examples might include staying within the law, not engaging in bribery or theft or endangering other people.

Also a part of ethics is social responsibility; the duty towards the wider community or society in general which includes environmental issues, public safety, employment and exploitation of third world workers.

In this case ethical issues which the government should have considered when granting permission for mining include:

1 *Employment in the local area*

The government has a duty toward people to provide them with jobs. In Eastborough there is significant unemployment so it is particularly important to the government to generate jobs in the area. The effect of the mining on employment levels should therefore be considered.

2 *The local economy*

The government has an obligation to the people of Eastborough to improve the wealth of the people there. This largely depends on a successful economy. The local economy of Eastborough has been performing badly despite various initiatives based around tourism. The effect of mining on the local economy generally must be considered (i.e. jobs create income which is then spent in local shops, demand for property increases and prices rise for all in the area).

3 *Environmental concerns*

Eastborough has a beautiful coastline with rare birds nesting there. The government has a debt towards society generally to preserve areas of natural beauty for all to appreciate and enjoy, and a moral obligation towards other species on the planet to protect them from extinction.

The effects of the mining operations on the rare birds, the beauty of the coastline and any pollution caused in the locality should therefore have been considered by the government.

4 *Rights of local individuals*

Individuals have the right for their quality of life to remain high. While employment and an improved economy may improve the quality of life of many, there may also be negative effects for some local people such as increased noise and traffic congestion. These broader effects on villagers is likely to have been considered.

5 *Right to free operation of business*

Many capitalist countries believe in free trade and removing barriers to trade. This may be seen as a right of the business, and it may be considered as part of the decision to allow Digwell to open the mining operation.

Conflicts between stakeholder groups

Stakeholders are people who are affected or interested in some way by the mining operations.

In this case stakeholders include:

- national government
- local government
- local people
- wildlife protection groups
- environmental groups
- directors of Digwell
- employees of Digwell
- shareholders of Digwell.

The conflicts which may exist include the following:

1 *National vs local government*

Local government will be interested in Eastborough and its interests. National government have to balance those needs with the needs of all people of the country. There may be a conflict over the amount of funding available to support local initiatives such as to help start up the mining operations.

2 *Unemployed vs people based near mining operations/working people*

Unemployed people of the area will notice a direct benefit from the mining operations through increased jobs and are likely to support it. Other local residents may simply view the operations as disrupting their existing life (noise/congestion) and oppose the idea.

3 *Shareholders/directors of Digwell vs environmental/wildlife protection groups*

Both shareholders and Directors of Digwell wish to make profits from Digwell's operations. The mining operations will enable them to make full use of an asset they own (tin reserves) and hence increase profit. They will wish it to go ahead, and may have very little interest in the broader impact. Environmental groups aim to protect the environment and are likely to oppose any part of the mining operation which will effect the environment irrespective of profitability.

(b) **Stakeholder mapping**

A useful model that can be used to examine stakeholders and how an organisation should deal with them is Mendelow's Matrix.

Mendelow said that there are two key aspects of understanding stakeholders:

1 *Power*

This is the degree to which the stakeholder group can exert influence over Digwell, its operations and likely profitability. The local government, for instance, have the power to grant or refuse planning applications and hence have a lot of power in the tin mining issue.

A local individual who feels strongly against the mining operations may have little power because whatever they do they are unlikely to be able to influence the decision. A large local group of people, on the other hand, have more power since they may be able to influence the local authority who must ensure the best interests of local people are met.

The greater the power a group has the more their views will be considered when decisions are being made. Digwell, for instance, will have ensured that all local government concerns are met in order to get permission to undertake mining.

2 *Interest*

The level of interest which the stakeholder has in the company (or in this case the mining operations) is also important to the company. If a party is not interested then the company will not need to concern itself with communicating with them or adapting to meet their needs.

In this case for instance Central Government is likely to have little interest in the local issue even though they have significant power. As long as the issue is not seen to affect national issues they are likely to remain unconcerned.

The matrix

Stakeholders can be placed into Mendelow's matrix according to their interest and power. Depending on where they fall, a different response will be necessary from Digwell.

POWER \ INTEREST	Low	High
Low	**Minimal effort** General public outside Eastborough	**Keep informed** Local people Environmental groups Wildlife protection groups Digwell employees
High	**Keep happy** Central Government Digwell shareholders Large customers of Digwell	**Key player – keep close** Local Government Digwell directors

The responses required are as follows:

Key player – keep close

Key players must be kept close to the company in all major issues relating to the mining operations. For example, close relationships should be built with the local government so that they are continually kept informed of new plans. This ensures the plans are acceptable and within regulation. Any new requirements are also quickly understood and can be dealt with promptly.

Keep happy

For example, the Central Government should be kept happy by ensuring that the issue does not affect their main concern, national issues as a whole. So long as this is the case they are unlikely to get involved in this local issue and exert their considerable power.

Keep informed

For example, Digwell employees will be very interested in the effect of the new operations on jobs. It may, for instance, create job security for them, or mean they have to relocate. It is therefore very important to ensure they understand the impact on them and expectations of them. Without formal notification, information will spread via rumour which may be inaccurate and cause undue concern.

Minimal effort

It is important to clarify which groups have little power or interest to avoid unnecessary effort being made. An example here is the general public outside Eastborough. They are likely to have little interest or power and so no effort needs to be made to keep them happy and there is little benefit from keeping them informed.

37 SHAREHOLDER VALUE ANALYSIS

Key answer tips

In Part (a) you need to discuss the term shareholder value and the difficulties encountered in its assessment – noting that the analysis is based on discounted cash flows. You should discuss the fact that the focus should be long-term, EPS is unreliable and Rappaport suggests a 10-year horizon for calculation of NPV from cash flows. In Part (b) you could use the 'Balanced Scorecard' technique as a basis for your answer.

REPORT

To: Finance director

From: Management accountant

Date:

Re: **Shareholder value in our reporting system**

(a) The term 'shareholder value' reflects the view that when a person invests his money in a company he does so in the expectation that his wealth will increase or, to paraphrase Robert Kaplan, 'the overall goal of the corporation is to generate long-term economic value'. There are various crude ways in which this can be measured. The well-known indicator of earnings per share attempts to measure this. The market value of the company is another method. EPS is fallible and market values are transient. Finance directors want to evolve a method of measurement that is neither crude nor transient but which facilitates strategic direction to improving long-run gains for shareholders. Writers such as Rappaport have suggested a 10-year horizon for calculation of NPV from cash flows. This also is highly subjective. Companies such as Apple Brown and Root have experimented with the identification of various value drivers, many of which are non-financial but are expressed in terms of financial surrogates. The essence of the exercise is to identify those matters that influence competitive advantage and thus affect the chances of longevity and ultimately an increase in shareholder economic value.

(b) The traditional basis of reporting divisional performance has been angled towards financial measures that are short-termist such as ROI or residual income (RI) or even controllable profit. The more modern orientation towards maximisation of shareholder value demands a process of re-education. The balanced scorecard approach originally written up in the Harvard Business Review has now been widely accepted in both the US and the UK. The technique is to focus on four perspectives that influence competitive advantage. This is set out in the chart below:

Financial perspective	*Internal business perspective*
ROI Cash flow Project NPV	New business Repeat business
Customer perspective	*Innovation and learning perspective*
Satisfaction	% revenue from new business Revenue per employee

Reports structured around this concept are more forward looking and concerned with continuous improvement associated with techniques such as re-engineering. The technique focuses on a variety of indicators. Traditional financial indicators are not overlooked. They are complemented by non-financial indicators which have considerable strategic significance. No single measure will provide a focus on the key variable that ensures long-term survival and growth, namely sustained competitive advantage. In the past, the fixation on financial data meant that the unmeasurable (in financial terms) was downgraded to a soft variable; interesting but difficult or impossible to measure. What were once regarded as 'soft' variables (unmeasurable) have now become hard variables. The identification of critical success factors and the mechanisms for measurement will focus efforts on improving those features of business activity and bring about greater economic value.

The **design of the scorecard** will vary according to the entity assessed. Some years ago (before its takeover by RBS) the National Westminster Bank discovered that it needed one scorecard for retail banking and another for group results. However, the most striking aspect of the literature has been the recognition of non-financial issues and their impact on financial plans and investment appraisal processes.

The scorecard also **changes the way in which reports go to the board** and the way in which information is communicated to stakeholders. A stakeholder in a bank does not want just a recital of dry financial statistics. The information that is needed should inform him on the crucial issues of competitive advantage, product innovation and customer satisfaction. The common thread is the customer; if we lose customers we lose our business. Hence the importance of the customer perspective.

The **development of the appropriate indicators** to satisfy the four perspectives will take time and effort. The pioneer in this field, Rockware, developed their scorecard over a year-long project which involved customers, management and their principal shareholder. They acknowledge benefits in efficiency, profitability and customer satisfaction.

The balanced scorecard approach encourages managers to think about the strategic consequences of their actions. A decision to cut advertising could boost ROI but lose long-term benefits in market share. A decision to reduce headcount could destroy morale and quality standards even if profits rise in the short run.

In conclusion, although the immediate consequence might be an administrative burden to cope with, experience reports that the trade off should be cohesive and effective for management at group and divisional level.

38 SCHOOL

(a) For a commercial company, customer groups can be identified and categorised quite easily. In a public sector organisation such as a school, a wide range of stakeholders can be regarded as 'customers', in the sense that directly or indirectly they receive a product or a service from the school.

Pupils

The current pupils of the school are customers, because they are the direct recipients of the services the school offers – teaching. They are affected by the amount and quality of the teaching they receive and by the range of topics that are taught. The aim of most or all pupils is presumably to achieve certain qualifications before leaving, and possibly to go on to further education.

Parents

The parents of the pupils are customers indirectly. They are responsible for their children and are likely to have as much, or quite probably more, concern than the pupils themselves for the quality of the teaching and the examination results their children obtain. If the standards of education at the school appear to fall below the levels expected, it is the parents rather than the children who will complain and bring pressure to bear.

Although the school has a maximum annual intake, it still needs to attract pupils to fill the places. Parents of children are therefore potential customers of the school, and need to be 'targeted' to persuade them to choose the school as the preferred option for their child.

Universities and other institutions of further education

Universities and other institutions of further education have to attract students when they leave school. A school should therefore think of these institutions as customers, in the sense that they should be interested in taking on the school's pupils when they reach leaving age. Universities therefore have an interest in the abilities of the children at school leaving age, and what the school has successfully taught them.

Employers

Similarly, employers have an interest in those children who leave school to take up a job. They will have a concern about the quality of the teaching provided and the standards the children have reached, particularly in English and mathematics.

Local authorities and central government

Local authority organisations provide funds to the school and have a direct interest in how the funds are used. Central government also provides funds, and in addition sets targets for educational standards. Government has an interest in whether a school succeeds in bringing a sufficient number of its pupils to the required national standards.

The general public

The general public has an indirect interest in all schools, and standards of education in the community. Many people see themselves as the providers of funds for state education, through taxation, and (like health services) education is an area where public opinion is very strong.

Although all the customer groups have the same broad concerns, namely the standard of education provided by the school, each group could have different points of view. The head teacher of a school should keep in touch with the views of each group. The opinions of current pupils can be sought regularly, by arranging discussions with groups of older children at the school. The views of current parents can be canvassed through parent-teacher associations, and by inviting parent representatives to sit on the board or committee of school governors.

The opinions of government can be obtained partly through any representatives on the school's board, but also through official communication channels with local and central government departments.

The views of universities and other colleges can be monitored through meetings and forums between head teachers and the universities. The head teacher should also maintain contacts with the local community generally, including employers, through attendances at local events. Inviting former pupils back to reunions at the school can also provide a useful sounding board of opinion. Head teachers can also compare their findings with those of colleagues, through attending head teachers' conferences.

Communication between the school and the various 'customer' groups needs to be continuous, rather than occasional.

(b) The **BCG matrix** analyses the products or services provided by a firm according to the relative market growth for the product and the market share that the firm has for the product. Products can then be categorised according to a combination of market growth and market share as stars, cash cows, problem children and dogs.

Applying the same type of analysis to a school, it would be possible to identify categories of pupils. The school could then analyse its teaching services to each of these categories. (In effect, each category of pupil could be regarded as a 'product' of the school.)

- **Relative market share analysis** would be measured in terms of what proportion of that category of children does the school teach, in comparison with other schools in the area. For example, a school might teach a high proportion of children in the local area with special learning difficulties. Similarly, a school might be regarded as a 'specialist' in certain topics, such as engineering or science.
- **Relative market growth** would relate to the numbers of students in each category locally, and how the total numbers in each group are increasing (or falling) relative to others.

As the question indicates, **pupils could be categorised** by socio-economic group or ethnic background. Children of different ethnic backgrounds, for example, might require particular services to be provided by the school, such as different arrangements for morning assembly. It might also be possible to use different categories, such as grouping children according to intellectual ability, although the BCG matrix might not lend itself readily to this. (For example, how can children of different abilities be grouped according to relative market growth?)

BCG matrix analysis provides a method for analysis and strategic decision-making. In the case of the school, analysing pupils by category, and assessing the 'relative market share' and 'relative market growth' for each category, is simply a starting point for planning.

A school has only limited resources and, unlike a company, it cannot choose to abandon pupils in the low-growth, low-market share quadrant (the 'dogs') or to ignore children in the low-market share high-relative growth quadrant (the 'problem children' or 'question marks'). The application of BCG matrix analysis must therefore be different.

The matrix could help the school to make decisions about where most of its resources should be directed, with most effort going into dealing with categories of pupils for which the school attracts a fairly high market share.

For example, the school might choose to categorise its pupils by socio-economic background. An assumption might be made that the expectations of children and their parents are higher for those from richer backgrounds and lower for poorer groupings. If the school establishes that it is attracting a relatively large proportion of children from wealthier backgrounds, and that the numbers of these children in the area appear to be rising relatively quickly, the school can address its strategies for how to provide teaching services to these children. Their expectations will be relatively high for examination results and moving on to university, and these children might also demand teaching in a wider range of discretionary subjects or teaching to a higher level (e.g. mathematics A level as well as mathematics GCSE).

If the school is attracting more children who are perceived to have a high potential, the interests of other 'customer groups' will change. For example, parents will probably demand more say in the way the school is run, but might also contribute more money through parent association activities. Money from parents' activities can be used to buy equipment, such as new computer equipment, that might otherwise be unobtainable.

As stated earlier the BCG matrix was devised for analysing product profitability and making strategic decisions about investing or disinvesting in products, and ensuring that the company has a sufficient number of 'cash cows'. The same analysis cannot be applied to a school. It is entirely appropriate for a school to look at the make-up of its students and to consider how the demands of different children should be met. It is also appropriate to recognise that children from different backgrounds might have different requirements and expectations.

However, the greatest concern about BCG matrix analysis would be that it will encourage the school to limit the amount of teaching and support it provides for categories of children where its market share is relatively low. Children in these groups might therefore be deprived of the levels of support they need, because they are a burden on the school's resources. If this were to be the case, the school would probably be failing to fulfil its responsibilities for teaching in the community.

In summary, it would seem that the school should analyse its students and assess their requirements, but that using the BCG matrix methodology to do this is perhaps inappropriate.

39 DOCTORS WITH WINGS (PILOT PAPER)

(a) Stakeholders can be defined as people and organisations who have a say in what the organisation is to do, what resources the organisation can have and what is to be achieved. They are affected by, and feel they have a right to benefit from, or be pleased by, what the organisation does.

Beneficiaries can be considered as both intended beneficiaries and collateral beneficiaries who will benefit indirectly from the success of the organisation or the service it provides.

The process of stakeholder analysis would best be served by a brainstorming process using a focus group drawn from within the company. Stakeholders should be categorised as internal or external to the organisation. It should be remembered that stakeholder groups are not mutually exclusive and there will be overlap between them.

The stages of the process should be:

- Identify stakeholders.
- Identify their interests, values and concerns.

- Identify sources of stakeholder power.
- Identify what claims they can make on the organisation.
- Rank the most important stakeholders from the organisation's perspective in terms of their ability to influence the organisation.
- Map the relationship between the stakeholder groups.
- Identify the resulting strategic challenges.

When looking to determine the stakeholder values, these could be considered in terms of what they want the organisation to do for them, what the organisation actually does for them, and how well they judge the organisation's efforts. The organisation should also consider how it is informed of stakeholder perception of its performance. It is important to consider why the stakeholders choose to come to this particular organisation – do they have a choice? Some organisations talk of holding particular values, but do not actually live them in practice. It is important to distinguish between the desired, spoken and lived values. For instance, a public transport service may well have a desired value of no delays for passengers. The spoken values, espoused in terms of targets set, will relate to a lesser performance level. The lived values may well be at an even lower level.

Having determined the stakeholders' value systems there should be an assessment of the power they can exercise on the organisation. Power can arise by virtue of:

- possession of expertise
- control of or access to resources
- control of or access to information
- preparedness to fight
- charisma or referent power
- networks.

All stakeholders will have an element of power in their dealings with an organisation to a greater or lesser extent. The power that a stakeholder can bring to bear in dealing with the organisation should be carefully considered since this can affect the way an organisation chooses to deal with that particular stakeholder or stakeholder group. The greater their power the more influential they become.

The importance of stakeholders at any point in time will depend upon their interest in the strategic initiatives being planned at the time. If the initiative ties in with their values and concerns then they must be considered important in the next stage of analysis. Alternatively where a stakeholder may have limited, or little interest in the successful completion of an initiative, they will need to be convinced of the importance for the organisation as a whole.

Once stakeholders have been classified in terms of their importance and influence they can be ranked in terms of the way the organisation must deal with them, if strategies are to be successfully implemented.

The organisation will need to develop excellent working relationships with those stakeholders who have both high degrees of influence and high importance. They are potential partners in the planning and implementation of any initiatives.

Those stakeholders who have high degrees of influence, and can affect the initiative's outcomes, but are of limited importance at this point in time, are a source of risk requiring careful monitoring and management. They must be consulted and kept informed.

Stakeholders who are highly important, but of low power to influence, should be kept informed, but can do little to affect the outcome of the strategic initiative.

Stakeholders of both low influence and low importance will require limited monitoring and evaluation but are, at this time, of low priority.

Having conducted this type of stakeholder analysis 'Doctors with Wings' will benefit from a clearer idea of the way forward in implementing any strategy it proposes. Strategic initiatives will invariably involve change management and without the support of the stakeholders are unlikely to succeed. By developing a better knowledge of stakeholders, their power and their value system, it will be far easier for the organisation to make decisions on how it should deal with the different groups as it introduces any new strategy.

More informed decisions are needed when the organisation comes to answer the following questions:

- Should it deal with stakeholders directly or indirectly?
- Should it take the offensive or deal defensively with resistance?
- Should it accommodate, negotiate, manipulate or resist stakeholder claims?
- Should it operate with a combination of these approaches or select a single course of action?

(b) The list of stakeholders includes:

Government funding agencies

Government agencies would expect to see value for money and the good name of the host country promoted. It is unlikely that a government would want to be associated with the funding of a charity which played an active part in a medical emergency arising from a conflict in which that government had an active, or vested, interest. Depending on the proportion of funding they provide their power could be quite considerable. They also have network power in that they can influence other foreign governments and supranational funding agencies such as UNESCO to assist the charity or, if not impressed, to damage its interests.

Corporate donors

These have similar interests to government agencies in that they would want to see transparent and cost effective operations, gaining reputational capital by association. It is unlikely that they would want to be seen to be supporting one side in areas of conflict if they had interests in the region. Their power would again depend on the size of the donation they made to the organisation. It should be remembered that the donation might not be purely financial in that they might offer transport and other facilities in the affected area and would gain additional reputational capital from so doing.

Medical companies that donate

Aside from philanthropic interests, medical companies would want to improve their reputational capital by being seen to do the right thing. Power would again depend on the size of the contribution to the costs of the organisation but, additionally, in particular medical emergencies they may well provide power in terms of pharmaceutical expertise to the doctors.

Public donors

The interest of public donors is philanthropic – they would wish to have a satisfied feeling from having done the right thing. Power is not limited to resource manipulation in the size of the donation made, but would also involve their ability to raise the profile of the charity where word of mouth marketing is important.

Doctors and nurses donating time after qualifying for the first time

The interest of the donors is both philanthropic from a desire to put something back, but also to gain good quality post-qualification experience. There will also be an element of self-esteem in taking an interest in the charity. Their power is high being based on their expertise and preparedness to do the work.

Doctors and nurses returning from medical emergency

The interest is again philanthropic, and there is also a desire to increase reputational capital. Their power is high both in terms of expertise and charisma or referent power.

Teaching hospitals facilitating doctors donating time

The interest is primarily based on reputational capital in that those they have trained are seen to be "doing the right thing". Their power is relatively high in terms of referent power.

Staff working at 'Doctors with Wings'

The interest is primarily to do with self-esteem and, bearing in mind the likely salary, somewhat philanthropic. Their power is primarily resource-based in that they provide their services and time for relatively low rewards.

Other similar charities

Other charities will be interested in the performance of 'Doctors with Wings' from the perspective of both competition for resource from donors, but also quite possibly as collaborators when some emergencies reach the proportions that, unfortunately, attract a lot of interest.

Beneficiaries and victims of medical emergencies

The interests of the beneficiaries will be purely self-serving in that they will want prompt and effective treatment and relief. Their power is virtually non-existent.

40 5E INTRANET UPGRADE (MAY 06 EXAM)

Key answer tips

Part (a) requires in-depth knowledge of IT/IS issues that were beyond most students.

In part (b) ensure you use the stakeholders referred to in the scenario and, for each, explain their position in the matrix.

(a) To upgrade the Intranet as planned, 5E would need the following hardware and software:

Hardware

- A powerful intranet server to host the knowledgebase, manage traffic and facilitate access.

- A separate webserver to host the website. Keeping this separate from the rest of 5E's activities is advised for security reasons.
- A high speed broadband connection to allow many customers to access the Intranet quickly. It would also be advisable to set up a Virtual Private Network (VPN) for the firm's many offices.
- The system to ensure that only authorised users can access the data may involve the purchase of hardware such as challenge-response smart cards to generate passcodes.

Software

- ISP software to manage email traffic and host the website.
- Password software (e.g. encryption, public/private keys, digital signatures, etc) to ensure only authorised users can access data.
- Software to run the intranet – preferably the same as that used by X to ensure a straightforward handover.
- If web design is to be performed in-house then a web design package, such as Macromedia Dreamweaver, will be required.
- It may be felt that the level of e-security will need to be upgraded so suitable software (e.g. anti-virus, adware, spyware, firewalls, etc) for data and system security will be required.
- If documents are to be sent / received, then the simplest way would be to use FTP software.
- If it is planned to allow clients to interrogate and process data, then the processing should be server based (e.g SQL) rather than PC-based (e.g. MSAccess) to allow greater speed and volume.

(b) Mendelow designed his power-interest matrix to analyse stakeholder conflict:

Stakeholder Mapping: The Power Interest Matrix

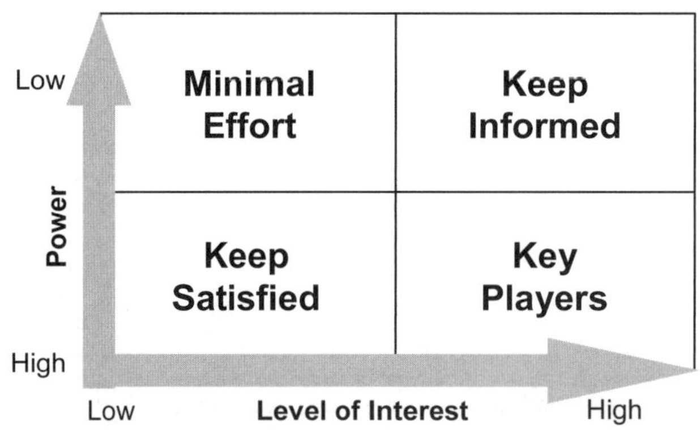

Within the context of the Intranet upgrade the key stakeholders are as follows:

5E partners

- Partners have a high interest in the project. If it is successful, then it will allow 5E to offer clients a wider range of services, thus enhancing the firm's competitive advantage and reducing the likelihood of clients switching to competitors. Problems on the other hand (e.g. client confidentiality compromised) could result in a loss of goodwill.

- The partners also have high power as they ultimately control the firm and could terminate the project if they wished.
- Partners thus fall into the 'key players' quadrant.

X

- X has a high interest in the decision as it currently manages the Intranet and will lose 5E's business and the fees involved, which may be significant.
- X cannot prevent 5E from switching to in-house provision, though it could make the transition very awkward and could even charge for helping data migration.
- Overall X will thus fall into the 'key players' quadrant.

Clients

- The interest of clients will vary and will be higher if they have approved cases for inclusion and if they make extensive use of the knowledgebase.
- Clients have the power to veto the use of cases involving them. Other clients can influence the firm by expressing their intention to move if such a system is not implemented, though the extent of this power will depend on whether or not they are considered to be major clients.
- Overall clients will thus fall into the 'keep informed' quadrant.

Ms Y

- Ms Y has a high interest in the project as she has proposed it and, presumably, will be held responsible for the ultimate success or failure of the project.
- Ms Y has medium power as she will exercise operational control over the project, subject to partner approval and intervention.
- Overall Ms Y will thus fall into the 'key players' quadrant.

Existing ISP

- The existing ISP has a low interest in the decision. While it will lose 5E's business, it is unlikely that fees are significant.
- The ISP has very low power to prevent 5E from switching to in-house provision.
- Overall the ISP will thus fall into the 'minimal effort' quadrant.

41 EEE FLAVOURINGS (NOV 06 EXAM)

Key answer tips

This is a relatively straightforward question on stakeholder analysis. Mendelow's power-interest matrix is the obvious model to use for part (b) and has the advantage of generating action plans for part (c).

(a) The advantages of EEE conducting a stakeholder analysis are as follows:

- EEE will be able to select investments that are more likely to satisfy the expectations of key stakeholders. For example, institutional shareholders will want to see shareholder value increased, so EEE should assess projects on the basis of their NPV.

- EEE will be able to incorporate the opinions of powerful stakeholders when designing projects.
- Identifying and winning over powerful stakeholders will make raising and using resources easier. For example, if the trade union agrees with the project, then staffing changes will be easier to implement.
- Anticipating stakeholder responses will allow proactive management and avoid conflicts. EEE will be able to identify potential objectors to investments and could then adjust how projects are done to reduce resistance. For example, by identifying the fact that some residents will complain about the smell, EEE could spend extra to reduce leakages.
- EEE will be able to identify the level of involvement each group requires – for example, which groups need to be included in detailed discussions and which simply need to be kept informed.

(b) The principal stakeholders of EEE can be analysed using Mendelow's power interest matrix as follows:

Trade union representative – high interest, high power

The trade union representative will have high interest as the decision could reduce the risk of job losses in the future. This person will also be very interested in their role as a local council member as the project will affect the local community in terms of jobs and also pollution.

They will also exercise considerable power as they could call for industrial action and council intervention if unhappy.

Overall one would expect that they will be for the project due to the job implications, although they may feel some conflict of interest as they will not want to see pollution in the community they represent.

Affluent local residents – high interest, low power

More affluent residents are more concerned with the leakages and associated smell than the local economy.

They probably have low power to influence the company's decisions, although their wealth may give them powerful friends.

Affluent residents will be against the investment because of the smell.

Other local residents – high interest, low power

Other local residents will be more interested in the future fortunes of the company due to it being a major local employer.

These residents also have low power to influence the company's decisions.

Most of these residents will be for the project due to the impact on the local economy. Some may object on environmental grounds.

Institutional shareholders – high interest, low power

Institutional investors will take high interest in all of their main investments, especially focusing on share price and future prospects.

With a collective shareholding of 20%, however, they have little power to influence decisions.

Overall they will be positive about the investment as it improves future prospects.

Customers – low interest, high power

As long as supplies are of suitable quality at reasonable prices, then it is unlikely that customers will take much interest in events. However, should adverse publicity arise over leakages, then they could take more interest as they would not want their images compromised.

Major customers will be able to exert some power by threatening to switch suppliers.

Customers will probably be pro the investment as it will increase supply and may reduce prices.

(c) In the light of the above analysis, EEE should take the following action:

The trade union representative should be invited to participate in discussions and decision making to represent the views of both workers and local government. This could be facilitated by setting up a project team to manage the project and appointing them as a member of that team.

Local residents and institutional shareholders need to be kept informed. This should ensure that their interest does not result in them trying to gain power. For example, a report detailing the impact on future jobs and profitability should be communicated to shareholders and in local papers. A full environmental report should also be commissioned so edited highlights can be released to local residents reassuring them of their concerns.

Customers need to be kept satisfied. A brief communication stressing how the investment will lead to greater supply in the future should prevent them taking more interest in the project should they hear any adverse publicity concerning pollution.

CUSTOMERS AND SUPPLIERS

42 VIRTUAL ORGANISATIONS

(a) **Virtual networked organisations; key strategic issues as potential strategic strengths or weaknesses**

There have been many critics of virtual companies because of their perceived inherent strategic weaknesses. Charles Handy, for example, once described them as a 'bag of contracts'. Others have claimed that virtual organisations do not possess any core competences.

The best examples of virtual organisations are dot.com companies. Many Internet companies have gone bust, fuelling the criticisms described above. Even companies held out as success stories have had a very mixed performance. Amazon, for example, describes itself as: 'the premier international retailer of books, music, and movies' and claims to deliver an 'online store, reliable shipping and delivery, and renowned customer service'. However, even Amazon failed to make a net profit until recently.

Advocates of virtual companies highlight their strengths as including the following:

- flexibility
- focus
- high growth potential, and
- asset efficiency.

Virtual organisations are highly dependent on the relationships that have been developed within and outside the organisation so the ability and skills needed to foster and develop these relationships are key to whether the firm has corresponding strengths or weaknesses.

Suppliers

When looking at relationships with suppliers, the following are often key issues that may result in strengths or weaknesses:

- What happens when 'things go wrong'? How reliable are suppliers? What back-up procedures exist?
- Is the organisation over-reliant on a few suppliers or have they multi-sourced?
- What systems are in place to manage suppliers?
- What expertise exists in managing suppliers?

Customers

Having a good relationship with customers and satisfying customer needs must be viewed as threshold competences – failure to deliver will spell disaster for the firm. When looking at relationships with customers, the following are often key issues that may result in strengths or weaknesses:

- Does the organisation feel 'real' to customers to give them confidence to buy?
- How secure are its buying processes – for example, are customers' personal information and credit card details kept private?
- What record does the firm have over delivery – what percentage of orders are delivered within the advertised timescales? This obviously ties into the relationship with the delivery firm used.
- Does the quality of packaging materials used reinforce the 'reality' of the organisation?
- How does the firm deal with complaints, errors and customer queries? Many firms have been criticised by watchdog groups for outsourcing customer care to call centres, others for not having enough staff to respond to problems.

Other

Other key issues can include the following:

- Learning and innovation often arise from the experience of doing things in-house.
- Virtual organisations can have isolated areas of expertise and knowledge without being able to integrate them, resulting in a lack of capacity for innovation.

An organisation that fails to resolve these issues of internal relationships will show a strategic weakness.

(b) **Environmental analysis in an organisation that is highly networked**

Environmental analysis has been described as 'external auditing' or 'scanning' and relates to the collection of information on the environment within which an organisation operates.

Benefits

The benefits of environmental analysis for highly networked organisations are predominantly the same as for any organisation:

- Generates information to help formulate strategy and to drive change.
- Identifies opportunities to exploit and threats to defend against

- Helps the firm choose and develop its competitive advantage
- Allows the firm to be responsive to market developments – for example, the actions of competitors.
- Identifies changing customer's demands and helps the firm to respond appropriately.

Areas of specific concern for networked firms include:

- Understanding the environments of suppliers to be able to anticipate potential problems and how best to manage them.

Difficulties

The main areas of difficulty are as follows:

- Increased difficulty obtaining information about (often chaotic) business environments in virtual organisations than in traditionally structured organisations.
- Information gathering is usually more effective when the whole organisation is coordinated to do it. In virtual organisations it can often fall to just a few departments or individuals.
- The organisation may become cut off from useful information that will now be obtained by sub-contractors and suppliers rather than internal departments. (Note: organising suppliers' forums may help here)
- There will be less scope for employees from different areas to communicate ideas through general discussion and 'chats'.

Together these can result in a failure to obtain up-to-date relevant information for decision-making.

43 V

Key answer tips

Part (a) requires an explanation of the effect refunds will have on shareholder value. Part (b) requires a discussion of how customer account profitability analysis could be used to provide information which would provide the basis of commission payments to sales staff. Your answer should include an appreciation of the fact that sales staff are vital to the success of the company.

(a) V currently sells a superior quality floor covering and is charging a premium price for its product. This means that the company has identified a demand for a superior product that is hardwearing and can withstand the rigours of industrial use. Hence the fact that it will be used more in industrial as opposed to domestic environments. The problem that has been identified is that there is a much higher than expected demand for refunds, as unsold inventories floor coverings are being returned by retailers.

An analysis of the inventories returned has clearly shown that they have been returned from retail outlets that primarily supply domestic purchasers as opposed to industrial purchasers. This indicates that the sales staff have been selling to outlets that are less likely to sell the floor coverings that are intended for use within an industrial setting.

As a direct consequence of the remuneration system that is operation within the organisation the sales staff will have benefited from the commission that they have received. In fact the system is encouraging sales to be made to retail outlets that are unable to sell the firm's products to the end users. Thus, not only is commission being paid on goods that have been returned, but also distribution costs are being incurred unnecessarily thereby further exacerbating the situation. Moreover the continued frequency of returns could well impact adversely upon the company's reputation and this could cause a decline in future levels of sales and profitability. This in turn would impact adversely upon future shareholder value. It is therefore of paramount importance that the management reviews the basis upon which sales staff are remunerated.

If management analyses the current problems and successfully formulates a strategy that will reduce the level of costs and wastage, then profitability and thus shareholder value will improve.

(b) Currently, sales staff are paid a basic salary and commission that is determined in proportion to sales turnover. In order to address the problems that are currently being experienced the Sales Director is considering the appropriateness of alternative remuneration methods.

Customer Account Profitability (CAP) would identify the profitability of the company's customers. This would be a much better basis on which to base any commission paid to sales staff, as it would encourage them to sell the products to those outlets that generate the most profit for the organisation and buy regularly from it.

Currently, only total sales revenue is used in order to calculate commission payable upon sales. However, if CAP were used, all of the costs incurred in production and distribution of the products would be taken into account. Notably, the costs of servicing each customer or groups of customers would become visible and this would result in a different pattern of behaviour by sales staff. By focusing on the attainment of profit as opposed to sales revenue, it should encourage the sales staff to sell those products to the outlets that provide the best outcome for the organisation.

However, it is highly improbable that the sales staff would be prepared to accept the change in the basis upon which their commission is determined. Currently some sales staff earn very high levels of commission and therefore M should expect opposition to any proposals that would be perceived to reduce their overall remuneration package.

A problem attached to the use of CAP lies in the fact that many of the costs of servicing the customer are outside the control of the sales staff. This could precipitate problems since the basis of the sales commission will not be easy for the sales staff to determine. It is established practice for the sales staff to keep a record of the sales that they make on a daily or weekly basis. It will require considerable persuasion on the part of M for the sales staff to abandon this as the basis of their commission.

The deficiencies of the present system are clearly visible and thus M has made a suggestion that repeat purchases are used as the basis of payments in excess of basic salary to sales staff. This would help align the fortunes of sales staff with those of the organisation and mean that the sales staff would focus their sales effort on the shops that are selling the floor coverings. This is likely to lead to a reduction in the level returns experienced by V and would appear to be a solution to the current problem. Repeat purchases are an indication of customer satisfaction and thus it is imperative that every effort is made to encourage loyalty among retailers and end users alike. If regular customers become significant in determining the level of commission paid, it is possible that this would reduce the number of new customers that are obtained.

Under this scheme it is possible that sales staff might only target existing customers and thus it might be expedient to give a large financial incentive to sales staff who sell to a new customer who subsequently purchases the product regularly.

Such a change is likely to be unacceptable to the sales staff. However, it is vitally important that any new method of determining sales commission is clearly understood by them. If it is not both understood and accepted by the sales staff, the consequences could be serious for the firm.

Therefore it may be prudent for M to discuss the problem of returns with the sales management and suggest that some of the costs incurred, as a direct consequence of the returns, should be borne by the sales staff. Not only would they lose their commission paid upon the recording of the original sale, but also some of the additional costs could be deducted from their commission in the event that goods were returned. This would precipitate a change in the behaviour of sales staff and alleviate the problems currently experienced by the organisation.

It is probable that this also would be unacceptable to the sales staff. It will be difficult to define the conditions under which financial penalties could be levied against commissions earned by sales staff. However, this is a matter that would clearly have to be resolved and agreed after the longer-term consequences of the current problems are explained to all sales staff. It is essential that M presents the issues clearly and that the changes in the remuneration package of sales staff are accepted. If the organisation is to be successful, it is important that sales staff are content, as they have a vital role to play in achieving the success of the organisation.

44 BXA (MAY 05 EXAM)

Examiner's Comments

Common errors that occurred in May 05 exam

Part (a)

- Poor structure, with lack of definition between the three managerial levels.
- Poor application to the scenario and use of IT as an outsourcing example.

Part (b)

- Poor application to the scenario i.e. providing only a generic list of supplier characteristics.

(a) The advantages and disadvantages of outsourcing the IT function are as follows:

Advantages	**Disadvantages**
Strategic level	
• The supplier will have economies of scale reducing BXA's cost base. This is particularly important given recent consolidation in the industry. • The supplier will have expertise and core competences in excess of BXA's, improving BXA's use of IT in the market place. • Together these should improve BXA's competitive advantage. • This should also reduce BXA's risk exposure. • The supplier will have greater RnD competences and spend in the field of IT improving BXA's innovation. • There may be greater flexibility to respond to future industry advances.	• Control of a vital part of BXA's business has been passed to a supplier, possible resulting in control problems. • It may not be cheaper to outsource, as the supplier will incorporate a profit element in their pricing. • BXA may become over-reliant on the supplier.

Managerial level • Management can focus on other areas of the business where they have expertise. • Existing bugs and incompatibilities will be eliminated quickly. • Problems integrating the two firms' IT systems will be avoided.	• Problems implementing the changeover could seriously compromise BXA's competitiveness if the process is not controlled effectively. • Managing the merger and the IT changes simultaneously could prove very time-consuming for management.
Tactical level • Better information due to the possibility of networking systems, quicker systems and standardisation.	• Monitoring and controlling the quality of the service provided will be difficult. • Staff losses in IT need to be handled carefully to avoid loss of morale. • There will be extra training needed to educate staff in the new processes and systems.

(b) BXA should look for a supplier with the following characteristics:

- Financial strength – BXA needs to ensure that the supplier is profitable and shows the ability for sustained growth. Credit reports should be sought and its financial statements analysed.
- Good reputation – BXA should see the supplier's existing client base and seek references where possible.
- Quality badges – has the supplier been awarded quality marks such as the ISO 9000 series?
- Strong technical support department.
- Strong innovation – particularly to deal with the challenges of the merger and the rapid changes in the industry.
- Size – BXA does not want to outgrow its supplier's capacity. One of the benefits of outsourcing is to gain from the supplier's economies of scale.

(c) The following factors should be included in a service level agreement:

- A detailed explanation of exactly what service the supplier is offering to provide.
- The targets / benchmarks to be used and the consequences of failing to meet them.
- Specific targets / expected performance for handling the merger issues.
- Expected response time to technical queries.
- The expected time to recover the operations in the event of a disaster such as a systems crash, terrorist attack, etc.
- The procedure for dealing with complaints.
- The information and reporting procedures to be adopted.
- The procedures for cancelling the contract.

45 EXTRANET (NOV 05 EXAM)

Key answer tips

Make sure you analyse S's perspective, not C's. The question would be much more straightforward if you had to examine the benefits to C.

(a) **Sole supplier relationship**

The advantages and disadvantages to S of the sole supplier relationship described are as follows:

Advantages

Growth – The main advantage to S is the immediate 200% increase in volume. This should result in higher profitability and shareholder value.

Low risk attached to earnings – the contract is for five years, giving stable earnings during that period.

Economies of scale – manufacturing systems usually afford economies of scale in areas such as materials purchasing, improved scheduling and specialisation. These should reduce S's cost base giving it higher margins both for the C contract and other existing sales.

Enhanced reputation – being an approved supplier for C may lead to other business opportunities.

Disadvantages

Risk of penalties – S will incur cost penalties if it fails to deliver on time. What is not clear is whether this only applies to production schedules disclosed, say, a week ahead, or whether C could request extra parts at short notice. This will be a particular problem if C's production increases significantly, whether because of special promotions or extra demand for new number plates. Whatever the reason, S will probably have to hold some stock to act as a buffer, with the resulting holding costs.

Systems and control – S will need to increase the scale of operations in production, probably resulting in considerable investment. Alongside this there will be the need for new control systems as S cannot afford for quality to be compromised.

Human resources – S will have to recruit and train additional staff. This will take time and money and there is a danger of quality being compromised if it is not carried out effectively.

Capacity constraints – S may not have the capacity to deal with large orders from C without displacing and losing sales to other customers.

Over-reliance on C – while C is also tied in for five years, C will gain significant power when the contract is up for renewal. Losing such a major contract could compromise S's future viability. There is also the problem that S's prospects become over dependent on C's – if C's cars under-perform in the competitive car market, then S will suffer too.

Working capital – the terms of payment by C and the enforcement of those terms are vital. If C delays payment or routinely takes too long to pay, then S's working capital position will be significantly affected.

Conclusion

Most firms would jump at the chance to treble turnover with one contract and s should seriously consider accepting the contract. However, S should ensure that the penalty clauses are not unfair, that acceptable payment terms are agreed and should also ensure that it pursues other customers over the next five years to reduce reliance on C.

(b) **Allowing S to access C's extranet**

Key answer tips

Make sure you evaluate the benefits as well as describing them.

The main benefits to S of access C's extranet are as follows:

Planning

The main advantage to S is that it will be able to plan production better to match the requirements of C. For example, if C's volume is expected to increase in a particular month, then S can plan to arrange extra staff or overtime working to meet demand. The detail of information available on the extranet is vital to enabling S to do this without incurring penalties.

Working capital

S's ability to anticipate C's inventory needs and plan accordingly will also reduce delays in ordering and delivery. C appears to want to implement a JIT policy – the extranet may allow S to do the same. This should increase S's inventory turnover, reduce inventory holding costs and speed up cash collection.

Together this will give a significant benefit to S's working capital management. This particularly important given the huge growth the sole supplier agreement has brought to S.

Customer relationship management (CRM)

The ability of C to record details of support calls and problem resolution on the extranet will improve communication, collaboration and discussion between S and C. Ideally, this will reduce the likelihood of C moving to another supplier.

Other less significant benefits include:

Improved information

S will obtain access to C's buying preferences and tender specifications, enabling it to be more successful in meeting C's needs. Any changes by C will be highlighted on the extranet giving S quicker response times.

Critical information will not get lost in the mail or buried in an email in-box, and busy employees will not miss or forget key events.

S will also be able to access information not available to competitors, giving it an advantage in a changing industry.

Flexibility

By using the extranet, S can operate when and where it is most convenient. This self-serve approach frees S from unnecessary meetings and phone calls, and it cuts down on the costs associated with in-person information exchanges. For example, the extranet may allow S to process orders outside of regular business hours.

Administration savings

Once S's staff have learned how to use the new extranet, they will spend less time in the repetitive tasks involved in receiving and processing an order, thus reducing costs. The extranet should also lead to fewer errors in processing orders.

IT AND COMPETITIVE POSITION

46 SERVICE SECTOR STRATEGY

Key answer tips

The question very clearly requires you to use a service company for your examples. Although you may not work for such an organisation, you surely deal with one (your bank for example) so it should not have been too hard to think of illustrations. If you found it difficult to think of points to make you could have used a framework such as Earl to stimulate ideas. You should have been able to explain the information intensity matrix from textbook knowledge but it is also important to **apply** it to a service business.

(a) **The need for an IT strategy in a service business**

Many service businesses are highly information intensive. Frequently the final 'product' (a set of accounts, an insurance policy, a legal agreement) consists entirely of information. But on the other hand it could be argued that such businesses have very simple IT needs: most work can be done using basic office software, and at most IT has a support rôle.

The implication in the question is that 'live' human contact and communication is so essential to service businesses such as accounting firms that IT may not be a crucial consideration.

This view is mistaken. Even if IT is primarily a support service, an international firm will nevertheless need to provide desktop and/or laptop computers and associated software for almost all staff, and so it will have a considerable investment in IT. That investment should be properly managed and guided by an IT strategy.

An IT strategy is also desirable for a number of other reasons.

Few if any staff in such a business act autonomously. Members of staff in different specialisms will need to communicate with each other – for instance staff who are expert in standards compliance will need to be able to talk to staff who specialise in corporate taxation. At the very least the company will need e-mail links to their colleagues; they may well benefit from collaborative groupware.

It is important that such a business sets up and adheres to common work standards and this may entail the development of common templates, standard audit programmes and the like. These will be much easier to maintain on a computer-based system.

Likewise the firm's corporate identity and its image with clients may be more easily maintained by using standard formats for all of its publications and communications.

Customers are likely to expect such an organisation to have a fairly sophisticated Customer Relationship Management system such that, if a customer calls the firm and gives basic details such as an account number, the person they are dealing with will have all the relevant information at their fingertips or else, or in addition, the call will be automatically diverted to the appropriate person. This kind of service is now the norm rather than the exception from almost all large organisations.

In such a business a good deal of work is done away from the office on the client's premises, yet staff will still need to be in contact with the main office so that they can access knowledge databases, expert systems, and so on.

New information and communications technology offer the opportunity to provide existing services in an alternative form and also to invent entirely new services. For instance the firm may be able to offer a user-friendly, easily searchable version of its own knowledge base on matters such as accounting standards and tax legislation as an extra information service to clients.

The senior management of the firm are likely to use IT for planning and control purposes and may need an extensive EIS for purposes as varied as planning staff allocation on particular jobs, assessing the need for new recruits, judging performance, planning new investment, and so on.

Accountancy firms typically need to be able to audit their clients' computer systems and this may require IT skills and capabilities such as specialist knowledge of the workings of various accounting packages, extraction of data from one system and input into another for testing purposes. This implies considerable and ongoing investment in IT systems and appropriately qualified staff.

Many accountancy firms provide management consultancy services to their clients, and this will almost always require advice on how clients' systems can be improved.

Each of these points indicates that IT is of very considerable importance to a service business such as an accountancy firm, and that it merits close attention from senior management.

(b) **The relevance of the information intensity matrix**

Porter and Millar's information intensity matrix considers the role of IT and suggests how it can be exploited for competitive advantage. The matrix evaluates the information intensity of the value chain (how product value is transformed through activities and linkages in the value chain) against that of the product (what the buyer needs to know to obtain the product and to use it to obtain the desired result).

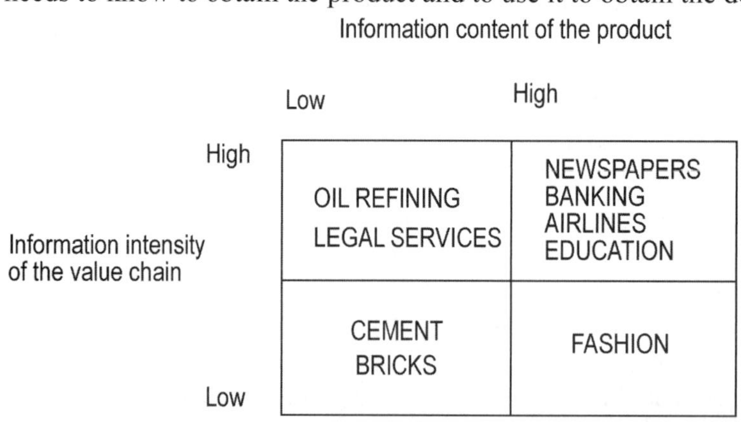

When assessing the degree of information in the product itself, oil, for example, has a low information content and banking has a high information content. The degree of information in the value chain also varies. It is low in the case of a cement manufacturer who makes a simple product in bulk, but high in the case of a complex, sophisticated process such as oil refining.

If the information content of the product is high, information can be used in the product, for instance Internet sites for newspapers. When the information in the value chain is high, it implies that sophisticated information systems are required to manage the linkages optimally.

As noted above, for a service sector business such as an accounting firm the main product can be considered to be pure information and so it is appropriate to place an accounting firm in the top half of the grid. It will either be in the **High:Low** section (for standard services like straightforward tax returns or formulaic products following standard wording, like audit reports) or in the **High:High** section (for *ad hoc* reports on recommended improvements to accounting systems and procedures, the implications for a client of new employment legislation, and so on).

The information intensity matrix can thus be regarded as highly relevant to an accounting firm, and in several respects.

47 KN COMPANY

Key answer tips

This question appears to focus on the 'standard' comparison of centralised and distributed systems. When thinking about the latter source of information, consider the topics previously studied such as data mining and data warehousing because they may also help to provide relevant points in the answer.

Regarding the format of Part (a), note that you need to explain the relative merits. So, it is probably not worth explaining the advantages and disadvantages of centralised and decentralised systems in four different sections of the answer. Providing two sections noting the advantages of centralisation (for example) and mentioning the disadvantages of decentralisation at the same time, will help to explain the relative merits.

In Part (b), the scenario is moving from a decentralised system to a centralised system. You need to think of where the data is going in this situation – that is from many locations into one. The problems involved in this transfer then start to become apparent when information from each location is merged. Issues such as age and duplication can be explained in the answer.

(a) **Individual departments v central database**

The KN company has followed part of the IT development path described by Nolan. The company has already passed through the initiation, contagion and control steps and now appears to be on the way towards integration, administration and strategic development.

Until the integration step is reached, each department will tend to have developed its own applications; data will not be shared between departments to any extent and the separate systems in each department may not even be capable of communication with each other. Integration implies that the separate systems will link together and that data can be shared. Administration implies that the database stage has been reached and that the data must be administered and guarded carefully as it is of such importance to the organisation.

On another level the planned changes can be looked on as a change from a decentralised to a centralised system and there are well known characteristics of each of these types of IT organisation.

Advantages of individual IT systems

Individual IT systems imply a decentralised data processing environment and this is likely to have the following advantages:

(i) IT development is likely to match exactly each department's specific requirements. The IT applications will be tailor-made for each processing application and are likely to have evolved into efficient systems.

(ii) Each department has its own IT personnel who are dedicated to serving just that department. Therefore, any problems or system changes required are likely to be dealt with promptly by staff who understand the department's processing needs well. Systems development appears to be responsive to user needs.

(iii) Processing power (hardware capabilities) will have evolved with the departments and their software. Response times are likely to be acceptable to users.

(iv) As processing is carried on locally, each department can decide on its own processing priorities.

(v) Ownership of the data, for example what data is held and under what circumstances it can be changed, will be well understood and its design will reflect each department's requirements.

(vi) Because data is held and processed locally, there is likely to be local pride in its accuracy and integrity. Users feel responsible for their data and this will tend to increase its accuracy.

(vii) Separate systems will be resilient to processing failure. Hardware breakdowns, software errors, computer viruses and unauthorised access will normally be confined within each department. Data held in other departments will be unaffected.

Disadvantages of individual IT systems

(i) Duplication of effort can occur. For example, two departments may each independently develop software which performs the same processing tasks.

(ii) The same information may be held in more than one department. This increases the processing needed and data which should be the same can begin to diverge and become inconsistent.

(iii) Information will be difficult to share between departments. It might be held in different formats on incompatible systems. It is almost certain that different departments will need to be able to access and use data held in other departments. For example, if the company wants to run a large marketing campaign it will need to access all customer records. If it wants to raise and post invoices it will have to have access to the sales ledger, nominal ledger and stock files.

(iv) Processing will be restricted and limited simply because of the technical difficulties of using data drawn from different systems. Processing should be driven by business needs not inhibited by system constraints.

(v) There is likely to be a wide variety of processing and security standards; some departments will have high standards, others low. As the importance of IT grows it will be important to ensure that standards are maintained at a high level. If processing is centralised into a database system, it will be easier to impose uniform standards. There is a chance that, because there are many separate IT departments each with its team of experts, the average level of skill will be lower than if IT is centralised. Then, the company may be able to enjoy economies of scale which will allow fewer but more highly skilled staff to be employed. For example, organisations which have a large database system are likely to employ a database administrator who will monitor the contents of access to and development of the database.

(vi) Security of processing and data can be more difficult in individual or distributed systems. Many people have access to the data, programs and hardware. For example, backups of data should be taken regularly. However, it may be difficult to ensure that all departments are diligent in this; centralising the data and most of the processing in one place under the control of dedicated experts will make it easier to ensure that regular backups are taken.

(b) **Problems with amalgamation**

The following problems are likely to be encountered when the company attempts to amalgamate the company's data into one central database:

(i) Security. All the company's data will be held in one place. It is vital that the company designs and enforces stringent security measures to protect the important resource which will have increasing strategic importance. The security measures should include physical access controls, user access controls (for example passwords), back-up procedures, disaster action plans, anti-virus software.

(ii) A feeling in user departments of a lack of control and degradation of IT service. If user departments have been satisfied with their individual arrangements they may resent control and custody of the data being removed to a central department.

(iii) The design of the database must therefore be carried out very thoroughly. Ideally, no department should find that a facility that it had found useful becomes unavailable when the central database is established.

(iv) If all data is held on a central computer (such as a network file server) and distributed to departments as they need it, there could be problems with the volumes of data that have to be held and transmitted. It is essential that users perceive no degradation in the speed of responses.

(v) There will be a problem of amalgamating data which has been developed at different times and under different methodologies. This problem is obvious where the data is very different (for example, receivables ledger and stock ledger) but will also be a problem where the data appears to be the same: names and addresses could have different formats and space designated for each field.

(vi) Duplication of data could arise. For example, two departments could hold information about the same customer and the customer could appear twice in the final database.

48 DATA COLLECTION

Key answer tips

In Part (a) a common problem was lack of knowledge of exactly what intelligent agents are. A significant minority of candidates provided a description of some form of James Bond as a human intelligent agent! Weaker answers merely provided very general comments about intelligent agents (for example, having a 'drill down facility') rather than in-depth knowledge of the specific features of intelligent agents.

The danger in Part (b) is focusing on too few points to obtain a pass standard. Common errors included spending too much time on the use of information (for example, forecasting road repairs, new roads, positioning of traffic lights, timing of road repairs and so on at the expense of other relevant areas) and providing very little information on the weaknesses of the information being accumulated such as not being able to identify the driver of a vehicle or the purpose of a journey.

(a) **Data mining** has many different definitions but almost all of them involve using advanced analytical techniques to discover useful relationships in large databases. Data mining therefore is the analysis of data to unearth unsuspected or unknown relationships, patterns and associations. These relationships help provide a more detailed understanding of the data and provide rules for predicting future trends arising from that data.

An **Intelligent Agent** (IA) is a software program that has a specific task to perform such as finding or analysing data in a database. One of its characteristics is that the program reports back to the operator when its task is complete or when it needs additional information in order to complete the task. IA programs can be found in a company's intranet or databases, as well as on the Internet.

IAs have the following **benefits** within the context of data mining:

(i) They can review large amounts of data relatively quickly and because of the sheer amount available they will find relationships that a person would probably miss.

(ii) They can be left running permanently so they can review data as it is added to the database so unusual relationships are spotted as they occur rather than having to wait until the data is specifically reviewed at a later time.

(iii) They save the time of knowledge workers who can perform other tasks whilst the database is being reviewed.

(iv) They can identify unusual relationships or trends that might otherwise be hidden. Examples might be unusual sequences of trends, correlations between one type of information and another, and patterns in data that can lead to predictions about the future.

However IAs do have **limitations**:

(i) They can be expensive to set up and program for relatively small databases (although some general IAs can be purchased off the shelf rather than having to be written in house).

(ii) An IA is only as good as the data itself and therefore if controls over the data being entered into the database are poor leading to, say, inaccurate or incomplete data, then the results provided by the IA will also be poor.

(iii) They need careful programming to result in appropriate and valid search results. For example, a relationship may well be found between two sets of data but they may not be related at all but both affected by a common influence that does not appear in the database.

(b) Collecting information on **vehicle movements** under the circumstances described can have several strategic benefits but in each case care must be taken when analysing the results.

Producing a **database of road usage** can assist traffic management planning. Busy periods can be identified, as can the usage trends over periods of time. By using the information new roads can be planned, traffic could be limited at certain times by traffic lights etc, peak and slack times identified so that differential tolls could be established to discourage or encourage road use, or times identified when repairs could be completed to minimise disruption.

However the information may be inaccurate as it may not discriminate between different types of vehicles (10 lorries will take up more road space than 10 small cars), there may be other factors which are not included in the database that affect road usage (e.g. the weather), and the use of scanners may in themselves affect road usage (e.g. discourage some drivers who do not want to be observed and their movements recorded).

As more data is collected future road usage could be predicted so that road improvements can be planned. However the forecasts could be inaccurate because they might not take into account changes in the mix of vehicles on the road, other forms of transport may become available or unavailable (e.g. trains) or external factors might affect road usage (e.g. the price of fuel, government policy on fuel emissions etc).

By using scanners the police could track the movements of criminals or suspects in real time. However the data collected would only identify the car involved, not the driver. Issues of human rights and privacy could arise in certain circumstances.

If the scanners are placed near meeting halls or concert halls attendance could be monitored but the data does not identify how many people are in each vehicle or who they are, so the results could be very misleading.

THE INTERNET AND ELECTRONIC COMMERCE

49 WEBSITE

Key answer tips

There are two areas of knowledge to be combined for this answer. Hopefully, you have used an Internet site and are aware of its features. Similarly, you will have opened a paper-based catalogue and may have ordered goods on the telephone from that catalogue. In that case, you can compare the two different media and show how the website can provide a more user-friendly presentation than the catalogue.

The second area of knowledge is explaining the advantages and disadvantages of the two media. Again, if you have used both Internet and catalogue then you can start this section. However, it may be wise to provide a plan, to help ensure that your answer is complete.

Finally, there is some information in the scenario that can be used within the answer. You should be able to note the weaknesses in the competitors' websites, and so be able to show how the important company objectives (including good customer care) can be continued even using the Internet.

(a) **Advantages and disadvantages of SK Products providing information on a website**

The main advantages of a website over a paper-based catalogue are:

- **It is far easier to update**. Changes can be made quickly to the HTML and JavaScript code (or to an underlying database) that would be used to create the site. Very often a minor change can have a dramatic effect, e.g. the substitution of images for text.

- **It is much cheaper over the longer term**. With SK Products having many customers and providing a catalogue three times a year it makes economic sense to create and maintain a website. For example, incurring three lots of printing, postage and stationery costs each year can be avoided.

- **A website can be more dynamic than a paper-based catalogue**. For example, it can use text, pictures, graphs, cartoons, diagrams and moving images as well as sound to more fully illustrate the various products. This would be particularly apt for the complicated electrical assemblies where added value can be achieved by showing how they work, i.e. their place within the final assembly can be illustrated by schematic diagrams. Additional ways could be found of attracting customers by providing further information or installation instructions on receipt of an e-mail address from an enquirer or potential customer.

- **The availability of the website worldwide means it can potentially reach an audience of millions of people**. Awareness of both the company and its products can increase considerably. Again prompts for e-mail addresses can be included in the site, so that SK Products can build up an electronic mailing list, e.g. so that special offers could be sent out. In addition, the site could contain free downloads not only in respect of the product range, but also software for 'screensavers' for example which could contain an advertising message in the same way that Guinness did. This would make it a much more dynamic site to visit and would generate a lot of interest.

The main disadvantages are:

- **The set up costs and the time** it takes to develop the site. To create a truly multi-media site that is dynamic and interesting needs some careful preparation and planning. The creation of the site can take a lot of time if done properly. It may also need to involve some extra security requirements including additional equipment and software.
- **Keeping the site up-to-date** is like any other software maintenance task, i.e. it can be a chore unless it is properly documented and supported by appropriate resources and a planned upgrade path is followed. The site can lead to further developments building on the same Internet protocols and both intranet (for employees) and extranet (for customers and suppliers) could be created. Obviously these additional facilities would cost and a big danger at the moment is that development plans are unclear, which can lead to projects becoming more expensive than they should be.
- **Websites are becoming standard features for organisations and in order to attract visitors it is no longer sufficient to have a static site**. The number of Internet users is growing as fast as expectations and this means that new sites have to be better than before. This creates a strain on the resources a firm is likely to use to support the site, i.e. there is a popular misconception that once a site has been created then that is the end of the involvement. In fact, it is more likely just the beginning of the process particularly with e-business just around the corner.
- **Out-of-date websites and/or pages are another disadvantage**. In effect, they are telling the whole world that the organisation is 'not up to speed'. It is symptomatic of inefficient management and ultimately will do more harm than not having a website at all.

(b) **Information SK Products can provide on its website to help customers**

- The website can provide installation instructions. This is particularly apt for the range of products sold. With over 100,000 items, electrical engineers will quite often need help with installation. The big attraction is that if installers have portable computers they can either log on or download the instructions so that information is available in situ. This will reduce training requirements as the instructions can be provided in words and pictures with on-line help and a frequently asked questions (FAQ) section.
- The website is a ready source of reference for specification details, tolerances, industry and legal standards etc. So instead of having to refer to several books and/or catalogues, one source of comprehensive information is all that the engineers need to know. This information could be made country-specific and could possibly attract a subscription premium because of the potential savings.

- Additional users for products can be developed by showing for example electrical equipment with other uses, e.g. water pumps as garden features. The various uses of products can be illustrated in 'safe' conditions so that people can see the applications (rather than trying products on a 'trial and error' basis) and decide if they are appropriate. This can generate a lot of ideas for product development.
- Information about product sizes, distribution quantities, colours, delivery and suitable applications can all be provided. So the customers can see at the touch of a button everything they need to know about the product ranges. Performance statistics can also be shown so that expected replacement periods can be calculated which can be important when it is not easy to replace components because of where they are installed. The site will facilitate future linkages such as intranets and extranets, which provide additional facilities and information for full electronic trading. The information can therefore be extended to include for example stockholding and ordering details when such features become available.

50 DLN

Key answer tips

Apparently very few candidates attempted this question when it was set, which is scarcely surprising considering it uses the term 'electronic trading room' which is most unusual in this context. What is actually described is a mixture between a business exchange (such as is common in certain industries like the aerospace industry) and an auction site like eBay.

(a) **Effects upon DLN**

Given that GKR is DLN's main customer, and other customers are likely to follow suit in the near future, DLN has little option but to adapt to the new way of doing business.

It is not clear from the information given that DLN even has Internet access at present. Its EDI links mean that it must have communications links of some kind, but older EDI systems used their own non-Internet protocols. In the unlikely event that DLN does not have Internet access, or only limited Internet access, it will need to invest in suitable hardware and software and in training for as many staff as will be required to use the new system.

It will be necessary to monitor customers' trading rooms constantly so that DLN is aware of any new contracts posted and can start considering whether to make a bid. (See Part (b).) The trading room monitoring system will be dependent on having a broadband (always-on) connection, since some customers may be operating in different time zones, and ideally DLN will need to duplicate its facilities and provide backup systems to make sure that it does not lose the opportunity to place its bid due to a hardware or software failure or a power cut.

It seems likely that DLN previously gained much of its business through repeat orders as a tried and trusted supplier. In future it will have to be much more aware of competition, since contracts are awarded to the lowest bidder, apparently irrespective of other matters such as previous good relations, quality of parts supplied, speed of deliveries and so on.

Information about competing suppliers' prices cannot be obtained directly from the trading room since bids are effectively sealed, and apparently remain so even after contracts are awarded. Nevertheless DLN will probably still be able to obtain information from their competitors' marketing materials (websites, catalogues, advertisements in the trade press and so on). If the company does not undertake such activity already this may mean a significant amount of extra work.

In the event that DLN's current prices are uncompetitive it will either have to accept lower profit margins or find ways of cutting its costs.

DLN's existing on-line ordering systems may become redundant in a relatively short time if all of its main customers decide to use systems like the one set up by GKR. The existing systems probably represent a fairly considerable investment and there may have to be a large write off.

The new way of doing business may also involve a return to manual data entry into accounting systems (with associated problems of human error and so on), whereas EDI by definition involves electronic exchange of data without human intervention. However it may be possible to persuade companies like GKR who set up such systems to provide data on the website in a suitably compatible format, or to pass the order via the normal EDI system once a contract has been won.

There may be implications for production scheduling and stockholdings, although this depends on the timescales involved and the systems in use. If customers expect next day delivery after they award a contract, inventories may well have to increase considerably so that such orders can be fulfilled immediately. More probably customers will make some allowance for lead time, but planning of production will be much less certain than before. Staff may be idle at times when they would once have been working steadily to fulfil known orders, but working large amounts of overtime on other occasions if an order is won unexpectedly.

(b) **Placing bids on an appropriate timescale**

As mentioned briefly in Part (a) it will be necessary to monitor customers' trading rooms constantly so that DLN is aware of any new contracts posted and can start considering whether to make a bid.

It would probably be wise to use some kind of intelligent agent software fully devoted to spidering the sites in question and advising the relevant DLN staff (probably by an e-mail message containing a link to the appropriate page on the trading room site, as soon as new contracts appear). This would be far more effective and less time consuming than relying upon individuals to monitor sites manually.

Once new contracts was identified there would need to be some means of channelling the details to the appropriate staff member: again ideally this would be done automatically, based on keywords in the contract description. It might be possible to persuade customers to use special codes for different types of orders, although if each customer used a different system this could quickly become very complex, and orders for entirely new types of product might be missed entirely.

Once a contract was identified as being one that DLN would like to bid for, managers would first need to check that it could be fulfilled in the required timescale, either from stock or by using available production capacity and time. Previously this was most likely an automatic process, part of the EDI on-line ordering process, so the necessary systems should already be in place and able to be adapted.

All being well a decision would have to be made about what price to bid. Initially this would be very difficult, and it is likely that the company would simply consult its existing price list and quote the price given there.

In time and after some trial and error with pricing it ought to be possible to build up historical data along the following lines:

Date	Customer	Goods required	Our bid (£)	Successful? (Y/N)

This would provide some guidance as to whether a bid of the same amount was likely to be acceptable to this customer or whether a lower price should be quoted.

The managers would also need some guidance as to the minimum amount they could bid. The company might set a floor limit on the margins to be achieved.

So far as such information can be obtained, the manager should also have access to lists of likely competitor prices, as indicated in Part (a). The database containing this information would need to be updated constantly (again intelligent agent software might be used, at least so long as the competitor had a website and published its prices). There would also need to be some way of monitoring the market to identify new suppliers. This information may be available from trade associations or professional bodies.

Finally, it is assumed that the customer operating the trading room will have set up appropriate security measures to ensure that bids placed could not be read by others and were submitted via SSL and strong encryption. In a situation like this, however the risk of industrial espionage is very high and all possible measures should be taken internally to ensure the security of DLN's bidding data.

51 SDW (PILOT PAPER)

Requirement (a)

Establishing the website

Before Mr M tries to establish an Internet strategy, he should look at his overall business strategy. In doing this he should find answers to a number of questions, such as:

- Is he only going to continue to operate between three domestic cities?
- How far does he want to expand both internally (in the home market as indicated) and beyond (internationally)?
- Does he have the capacity to take on more bookings should they arise?
- Is he aiming at a different market sector?
- Does he have a business plan?

Checking this strategy is essential because the IT strategy must be seen to support the overall strategy of the company and not drive it. In the case of the SDW Company, this does not appear to be an issue; the owner wishes to develop an e-commerce facility on the Internet site. However, care must be taken to ensure that the site does not cause unnecessary disruption to other systems within the company.

Having determined his business strategy, he needs to look at his IT strategy. Would an Internet site for bookings be part of his overall IT strategy or simply an add-on? Piecemeal implementation could affect other areas of his business systems.

The SDW Company already has an Internet site, so development of any new site must take this into account along with the overall requirements of the business. Expert advice needs to be obtained as to whether or not to amend this site or design a new one. Experts in web design may have to be employed if this expertise is not available in-house.

Additional care will be required in implementing the IT, for example in ensuring that no incompatible systems are introduced. The IT systems being used in the new Internet site must be able to connect to the existing call centre systems. Similarly, the initial focus of the site must be on selling seats on the company's trains; other services may be offered later, but establishing the core business first is essential.

Deciding on e-commerce may have an impact on other parts of the business. For example, setting an objective of a given percentage of business through the Internet will decrease percentages of business in other areas. Within the SDW Company, there will (hopefully) be a fall in the use of the call centre. This change must be anticipated and planned for. Staff in the call centre must be kept informed concerning the setting up of the Internet site, and then assurances given regarding job prospects and training, either within the call centre or other areas of the company. Where reductions in staffing are required, it is better to obtain these naturally rather than by compulsory redundancies.

Mr M should also attempt to obtain information on competitors' sites (and more broadly, sites relevant to the travel industry), to assess particularly their design and ease of use. This would be relatively easy to do – he could even visit the sites himself. This would not tell him how successful the sites were, although some companies boast about the use of their sites in published information. Some travel operators even offer discounted fares for booking this way. He should be careful that any claims are verifiable, and not just another way of attracting publicity. It may be possible to commission some survey information to obtain potential customers' views on booking through a website.

Given the need for security and the current lack of in-house knowledge, setting up an e-commerce system will require specialist assistance, either by recruitment or outsourcing the writing and monitoring of the site.

The services to be offered through e-commerce must also be determined. Decisions regarding services will have a direct impact on the writing of the website, as the authors will need to ensure that the required services can be made available. As already noted, the initial focus must be on travel bookings. Additional services and products may be made available after this core business activity has been satisfied.

Whichever method of writing the website is chosen, budgets must be set for this activity and agreed at Board level. If necessary, a cost benefit analysis will be required, partly to justify the cost of writing the site and partly to show the potential benefits from using the web site rather than a call centre.

Implementation issues

The charges (if any) for providing services to customers must also be determined. If ecommerce is to be encouraged, then some discount or other benefit can be expected to attract customers to this service. Given that this method of booking results in lower costs than when booking via a call centre, then the SDW Company can pass on these cost savings to its customers.

Prior to the e-commerce service being made available, it will have to be advertised. The Board will need to decide where to advertise and how much the advertising budget will be. Possibilities will include mail-shots to existing customers, perhaps by e-mail, and advertising on the websites of other organisations.

One of the aims of the provision of e-commerce is to try and remain competitive. A review of competitors' and other on-line sites is advisable to help determine the content and structure of the SDW Company site. This review may also help to identify other areas where competitors currently have an advantage so that the Board can address this.

Requirement (b)

Features of Internet sites focusing on cost reduction

The site must, of course, be very easy to use. SDW should specify simple instructions on a site that is easy to understand and quick to load. The omission of detailed graphics and providing an 'uncluttered' site will also decrease programming costs.

Incentives to book on-line such as obtaining loyalty benefits, cheaper prices or being able to book earlier (which may not be available on off-line bookings) could be offered.

Although this may not save costs on the Internet, it will provide overall cost savings by decreasing reliance on the call centre, thus limiting the number of staff employed.

Removing reliance on other more expensive selling media, such as the call centre, removes not only salary costs but also accommodation, pension, equipment and similar costs. Focusing on one booking medium becomes easier to support as only one cost structure is required.

Providing appropriate support to customers within the website which does not involve additional human contact. For example, provision of FAQs, a good help system and advice on each stage of the booking process. Customers are encouraged to resolve their own problems, which limits intervention from expensive staff.

Provision of other information on the website to attract customers to it, for example details of company performance or similar information already available within the organisation. Placing the information on the website is relatively inexpensive given that the information is already required in-house. Setting up web-specific information would be more expensive.

Innovative uses of Internet technology, for example suggesting destinations on a limited budget rather than customers specifying where they want to go. Providing these ideas as unique selling points will attract more customers to the website, again limiting reliance on other media.

52 JURANIA (NOV 05 EXAM)

(a) Competitive advantage

Key answer tips

This requirement looks at the link between competitive advantage and location. Porter's diamond is a tool designed to explore such a link.

Michael Porter, in his book *The Competitive Advantage of Nations*, tried to isolate the national attributes that further competitive advantage in an industry. He argued that, for a country's industry to be successful, it needs to have the attributes and relationships shown in the diagram below.

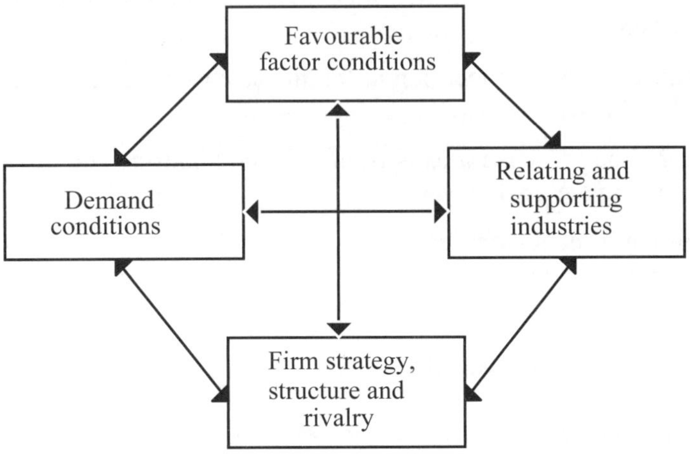

These can be applied to 222 as follows:

Favourable factor conditions

Industries can benefit from local factors such as physical resources, weather, capital, human resources, knowledge and infrastructure.

222 has clearly benefited from the local availability of suitably qualified staff, due partly to the excellent reputation of Jurania's university.

222 wishes to expand into other African countries so its factors need to be compared with those countries rather than globally. While it is doubtful whether the university at Jurania is producing better IT graduates than universities in the USA, for example, they will not demand such high wages either. There is more of a case, however, that 222 may have an advantage over firms from other African countries, with the possible exception of South Africa, provided 222 is not competing with any global foreign firms operating in those markets.

Overall, therefore, this should give 222 a competitive advantage in its chosen markets.

Demand conditions

There must be a strong home market demand for the product or service. This determines how industries perceive and respond to buyer needs and creates the pressure to innovate.

222 has benefited from the economic growth in Jurania and neighbouring countries in creating demand. Included within this demand are many top 100 companies who, presumably, put pressure on 222 to deliver better solutions than competitors. However, it is more doubtful that these firms will be as demanding as global customers encountered by global competitors.

As with factor conditions, it is likely that 222 has an advantage over indigenous local competitors but not against global players.

Relating and supporting industries

The success of an industry can be due to its suppliers and related industries.

222 has benefited from being close to several IT hardware and software companies and the country's largest ISP. However, there is little indication that any of these suppliers are world class and would have contributed to 222's competitive advantage.

Firm strategy, structure and rivalry

Porter found that domestic competition was vital as a spur to innovation and also enhanced global competitive advantage.

There is no indication that competition in Jurania has been intense so 222 will not have benefited in this way.

In conclusion, 222 has a basis for expansion into neighbouring countries but should be wary of becoming a global player.

(b) **Risks of proposed internet strategy**

Key answer tips

Make sure you identify and evaluate risks.

Using the services of a local specialist web designer

The main risks here are:

- The local specialist may not produce a site as well designed as that from a major firm with more experience and expertise.
- The local specialist may go bust and not be able to service future changes to the site.

As long as the local specialist can demonstrate a proven track record and evidence of financial stability, these risks should not deter 222. The advantages of having a local expert to deal with issues when they arise should outweigh the risks.

Having a sophisticated website with case studies

The risks here include:

- The site may be too complicated for users.
- The case studies may disclose secrets to competitors, thus eroding competitive advantage.
- Previous customers may refuse to allow their details to be posted, reducing the effectiveness of the idea.

The first risk is not significant as 222 sells to organisations that in most cases will have more sophisticated buyers with some knowledge of the technology involved. The others can be managed by careful disclosure on the website.

222 to host the website

The main risks of 222 hosting its own website and buying a powerful web server are:

- 222 may not have the expertise that suppliers have, particularly to deal with problems. This could result in greater website downtime and lost business.
- There will also be the extra operating gearing risk due to investment in hardware, more expensive software licences, etc.
- There is also the risk of obsolescence regarding the server.

The first of these is the most significant risk and is unnecessary. All of them can be eliminated by using an external host. Competition to host is intense as firms could be based anywhere in the world and the cost of external hosting is low.

Fibre-optic broadband

Fibre-optic broadband is growing in popularity around the world so would appear to be a low risk option. However, there are risks associated with the choice of supplier:

- The supplier is a new company so may not have the experience required to develop a problem-free network.
- The supplier may not have the financial strength to ensure its medium-term future, so may not be around to service any problems as they arise.

These risks are significant so it may be more prudent for 222 to use a more established firm.

STRATEGIC OPTIONS

53 GAP ANALYSIS

Key answer tips

Part (a) asks for an evaluation of gap analysis as part of its position within the rational model. It is therefore important to explain the role that gap analysis plays and why it is useful. You must also criticise the rational model approach. Beware of discussing the disadvantages of gap analysis since this would repeat many of the points in Part (b). Part (b) is more practical and probably the more difficult part, especially since the mark allocation is higher here. You are required to say why gap analysis has become used less often and outline why it is still particularly useful in public sector organisations. You are specifically asked to give examples so good marks would be gained for doing this.

(a) **Role of gap analysis in the rational model**

The rational planning approach provides a step-by-step model to consciously and formally plan and implement a business's strategy. It provides a clear, justifiable strategy based on the information available about the company's current position, environment and competencies ensuring a well thought through and effective strategy is followed.

The rational planning approach consists of a number of distinct stages:

(i) **Strategic analysis**: defining the direction (mission and objectives), analysing the environment, doing an internal analysis of the firm and summarising this in a corporate appraisal.

(ii) **Strategic choice**: selecting strategic options and choosing options the firm is going to follow.

(iii) **Strategic implementation**: putting the strategies into practice including polices and strategies for marketing, finance, R&D, structure and so on.

(iv) **Strategy evaluation and control**: evaluating the success of the strategy by measuring actual performance against objectives and taking control action by amending future strategies and objectives.

Gap analysis fulfils a vital role in the strategic analysis and choice stage of the rational model.

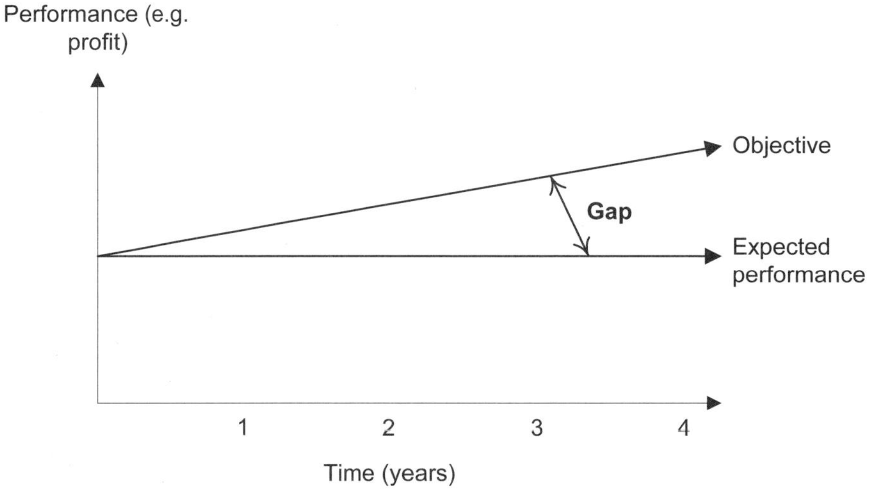

Based on the strategic analysis, gap analysis starts by estimating the expected performance over time if the company were to continue with its current approach and strategy. During the analysis stage, objectives will have been set outlining what the business aims to achieve in the future. During gap analysis these objectives are estimated over time. A comparison between objectives and current position can then be taken.

Usefulness of gap analysis as part of the corporate appraisal

This is a useful part of the corporate appraisal process since it:

- brings together the objective setting, environmental analysis and position appraisal into a model where a direct comparison can be made
- takes the current position and estimates what this means for the future – something that may not have been undertaken in previous analysis
- forces the general analysis to be converted into expectations based on clear measures of performance (e.g. profit, market share, numbers of customers, etc) which enables a more suitable comparison. It can also be useful in the review and control stage when comparing actual results.

Usefulness of gap analysis as part of strategic choice

Gap analysis is useful to help decide upon the extent of change required by the business. The bigger the gap found between the expected performance and objectives, the bigger the change required and the more strategies which will be needed.

It is also useful when evaluating strategies. An assessment of the extent to which each will close the gap can be made to evaluate whether they are suitable.

Criticisms of a rational planning approach

The criticisms of a rational approach to planning include:

(i) *Time taken*

The approach can involve significant investment of time from staff to undertake the analysis, thus using this valuable resource. It may also delay decisions being taken since they first need to be agreed as part of the planning process. Opportunities may therefore be missed.

(ii) *Cost*

The analysis will use people's time (as discussed above), involve investment in collecting information (e.g. market research) and could involve employing external parties to assist in the process (e.g. strategy consultants). The process can therefore be expensive.

(iii) *Inflexibility*

Once the plans are set down, the organisation is constrained by them. This means that it is hard for new opportunities to be taken at short notice or for changes to be made when there is environmental uncertainty.

(iv) *Reliant on information obtained*

If the information obtained and/or analysis undertaken is incorrect the new strategy will be poor. For instance, in gap analysis, the prediction of future performance might be difficult due to uncertainties in the environment.

(b) **Reasons why gap analysis might have declined in popularity in the private sector**

Gap analysis might have declined in popularity for the following reasons:

(i) *Uncertain environment*

The business environment has become a highly dynamic and fast changing place. Globalisation has heightened what was already significant competition in the marketplace. With increased competition comes a need to change more often and respond to changes. This has meant that a gap analysis which focuses on the effects of strategies on the business in the long term has become a less useful tool.

(ii) *Inaccurate forecasts*

The uncertain environment can also make it hard to make accurate forecasts. Since gap analysis relies on this the analysis becomes less useful.

(iii) *Defensiveness during the recent world recession*

During recessionary times companies become more conservative in their expectations. This means they are less likely to set significant growth targets and more likely to focus on maintaining existing operations. This may cause the gap to naturally reduce and gap analysis to become less useful.

(iv) *Short-termist approach*

Many companies in the UK and US have been accused of taking a short-termist approach to their businesses mostly because of the focus of investors on short-term financial performance. In this environment the benefit obtained from looking at long-term strategies reduces.

(v) *Time consuming to undertake*

Forecasting future results can be a time-consuming process to do accurately, and may take longer in the current uncertain marketplace.

Gap analysis in the public sector

Gap analysis could be particularly helpful in the public sector for the following reasons:

(i) *Stable environment*

Public sector companies work in a more stable environment than the private sector. They do not usually have competition so do not have to respond to competitors' changes as private sector companies do. They are also largely based within national borders so are less effected by globalisation.

The NHS for example operates within the UK with only minor competition from the private sector. There is little benefit for overseas competitors to enter the UK market since they are unlikely to secure public funding and hence find it difficult to compete against the free service offered by the NHS.

(ii) *Long-term budgeting (four years)*

Public sector organisations usually have a long-term budget. The MoD for example agrees budgets every two years for a four-year period. This means that they can plan for the long term with relative certainty about their income levels in that period. Gap analysis is a useful tool to support such long-term planning.

(iii) *Considering demographic factors*

Long-term changes in demographics can be predicted accurately and hence make gap analysis a useful tool. Requirement for schools in an area can be predicted using birth rates and compared against current position if no changes are made.

(iv) *Demonstrating a need for more funding*

Following on from point (iii) it is a useful tool to demonstrate the need for additional funding – an important part of ensuring the continued success of any public sector organisation.

(v) *Can be used across a wide range of measures*

Since they do not have a profit motive, public sector organisations usually use a range of performance measures, often set by government and based around the three areas of economy, efficiency and effectiveness. Gap analysis can be used for any of these measures.

54 PA POSITION AUDIT

How a position audit should be carried out

A position audit should focus the attention of senior management on the organisation's current situation, by examining 'where are we now?'. Understanding the organisation's current position can then provide a starting point for developing strategies for moving forward. The focus of the audit is primarily, although not entirely, on strengths and weaknesses.

The PA company is calling for a position audit because it recognises that the company could be facing serious difficulties. The services provided by PA appear to be going through the **classic 'product life cycle'** of establishing itself, followed by a period of growth, a longer period of stability and maturity and, more recently, the start of a decline. Unless measures are taken, it is quite likely that the decline will continue. If this is seen to be the case, the position audit is the first step in a major planning review.

The initiative for the audit has come from the managing director and, as an initial step, the **terms of reference** for the work should be agreed and set out in writing. The terms of reference should state that the audit will carry out a review of the resources of the company, both tangible and intangible assets, including staff and management, and its finances, services and markets, operating systems, internal organisation, current results and returns to shareholders. It is essential that the audit should review everything that could have a significant influence on the organisation's performance.

A **timescale** should be agreed for the audit to be carried out. In view of the urgency of the matter, the aim should be to complete the work within as short a time as is reasonably possible, without affecting the quality of the review. Although the audit could be carried out by an individual consultant, it is more likely that a small **audit team** should be appointed. The team members might all be external consultants, but there would also be benefits in appointing some of the company's staff. If so, it will be necessary to arrange cover for their normal work for the period in which the audit is being carried out.

The **audit team should be multi-disciplinary**, and should collectively have experience in all key areas, such as the company's markets, finance and accounting, human resources and IT systems. Since the company's customers are public sector organisations, a team member should also have thorough knowledge of the complexities of 'public-private' contracts, including the legal issues.

The audit team should be allowed **full access to all the information it requires**, and **should be able to interview anyone** within the organisation. It is probable that questions asked by members of the team will be searching, which means that there is some risk of meeting resistance and non-co-operation. It is therefore essential that:

- the managing director should have the full backing from the rest of the board for carrying out the position audit
- the audit team should therefore have the unqualified support of the board, and
- the company's staff are properly informed about the audit and its purpose, and are asked to co-operate in full with the investigations.

The issues that need to be addressed

It has been suggested that the issues to be addressed in a position audit can be remembered more easily by noting that all the issues begin with the letter M.

Men (or manpower)

The human resources of an organisation can be either a strength or a weakness, but they are a key resource. A position audit should look at the composition and numbers of the workforce, and their training and experience. The rate of labour turnover might be significant. The work carried out by the 'front line' service providers – providing meals and cleaning services – brings many staff into contact with elderly people, and their ability to provide an efficient and friendly service could be a critical factor for the company.

Money

The 'money' aspect of the position audit will look at the financial position, and the profitability and cash flows of the company. The analysis should look back over a period of several years, and seek to trace the decline that has occurred. The current position of the company should also be considered, both in terms of profitability and liquidity (cash flows). The ability of the company to pay its creditors in full and on time could be a critical issue in the short term. The analysis should also look at returns to shareholders, in the form of dividend payments. It might be necessary to establish shareholder attitudes to the returns they are currently receiving, and their expectations for the future.

Management

The skills of the management team are an important attribute in a company. Unfortunately, the PA company has suffered some decline in recent years, and serious questions might have to be asked about the effectiveness of the management team. There should be members of the team independent of the senior management who are able to bring an independent and critical mind to bear on this aspect of the position analysis. It is also essential that in the event that members of the management team are criticised, the audit team retains the full support of the board as a whole. This part of the work will probably be the most 'politically sensitive'.

Make-up

Make-up refers to the organisation's structure and culture. The audit team should look at how the organisation structure developed, and whether that structure is appropriate. The culture of an organisation is more difficult to define and analyse, but will include factors such as the willingness and ability of staff to act on their own initiative, and the general state of morale.

Machinery

'Machinery' refers to the tangible assets of the company. The major assets of the company might include land and buildings, but the significant operational assets will be the transport vehicles used by the company for making deliveries and the nature of its cleaning equipment.

Methods

The audit team will also look at the procedures and systems used by the company for performing its various tasks. These include the methods by which staff are allocated to particular tasks, and the processes by which meals, cleaning services and laundry services are provided. The efficiency and effectiveness of the methods used should be questioned. Key issues are whether the services are provided to the standard required by the customers, and whether they are provided in an efficient way and at an appropriate cost.

Markets

The audit team should analyse the markets in which the company operates. This has changed in the past, with the privatisation of public services, and might still be changing in ways that the company has not properly analysed. The markets of the company cover both the public authorities with which the company contracts, and the individuals who receive the services. The analysis should look at who the customers are, and whether they have changed over the recent years. It should also consider whether there are segments of the market that the company has failed to reach in the past, but which might be a suitable target for future development. The markets might also be affected by competition, such as a new competitor who is successfully winning business. Possible changes in government policy could also have an impact on the markets in the future, so any current policy announcements should be checked.

Another aspect of the markets analysis should be the company's own marketing efforts. An analysis of marketing will consider who does the selling to customers, who is responsible for customer liaison, whether the company uses advertising and, if so, how effective its advertisements appear to have been. The success of the marketing efforts should be assessed. In view of the recent decline in sales, this will probably be another key aspect of the audit.

Materials

This part of the audit will mainly consider the relationship between the company and its suppliers. There are likely to be major suppliers for both meals and cleaning materials, and the audit should look at whether deliveries are both reliable and at a suitable price. The company might also use contract labour from a supplier for some of its work: for example, it might sub-contract some cleaning services. If this is the case, the audit should assess the relationship with sub-contractors, and the amount, quality and cost of the services they provide.

Management information

This aspect of the audit will assess the amount and quality of the management information currently provided. The quality of the information relates to the relevance, accuracy and timeliness of information provision, and also to the question of who receives the information and in what form. The information should be analysed for what it lacks as well as what it contains. In particular, it will be important to know how much information is provided to management about revenues, costs and profits, and about environmental factors such as the company's markets, customers and competitors.

Summary

The position audit will be a wide-ranging review of the company and will be the starting point for a strategic re-assessment. Its importance cannot be under-estimated and the work should begin as soon as possible.

55 ENVIRONMENTAL UNCERTAINTY AND SCENARIO PLANNING

Key answer tips

(a) Students must consider how strategic thinking *might be affected* within organisations and *not* write everything they know about strategic thinking.

(b) Although the examiner does not explicitly make the point in the question, students are required to:

- (i) describe scenario planning
- (ii) assess the usefulness of scenario planning, and
- (iii) assess the potential difficulties of scenario planning.

(a) Johnson and Scholes summarise the rational approach to strategic planning as:

- strategic analysis – an analysis of the external and internal environments and the analysis of missions, goals and objectives
- strategic choice – the identification and evaluation of strategic options
- strategic implementation – the implementation of appropriate strategies and the monitor and control necessary to ensure that the organisation achieves the objectives set.

The above approach to strategic thinking may be viewed as only being helpful in a rational environment.

Given the level of uncertainty in the external environment has increased due to such factors as technological change, globalisation, competitive pressure, political risk and consumer diversity, the approach to strategic thinking has necessarily changed.

How environmental uncertainty might affect strategic thinking within organisations

One way in which strategic thinking may be affected is to question the conclusions that established models, such as Porter's Generic Strategies, make about strategy. For example, Porter suggests that if organisations decide to 'focus' they should either go for a 'cost leadership' or 'differentiation' strategy.

If we consider cost leadership as an internal efficiency strategy and differentiation as an external effectiveness strategy then, in today's world, where many turbulent forces disrupt the external environment to increase the level of uncertainty, strategic thinking within organisations is to implement both 'cost leadership' and 'differentiation' strategies.

A second way in which strategic thinking may be affected is in relation to the planning time horizons. Given the increased environmental uncertainty, the planning horizon has changed from five years to two or even one year. This reduced time scale will also have other consequences for strategic thinking, for example, the need to rely more heavily on emergent approaches to strategy formulation.

A third way in which strategic thinking may be affected is the need to be more risk averse. Given the reaction and power of pressure groups, for example, high-risk strategies will be avoided and incremental rather than transformational strategies will be more favourably looked upon. As a result, innovative strategies may be replaced by 'follow the leader' strategies.

A fourth way in which strategic thinking may be affected is the need to incorporate scenario planning with PEST analysis and Porter's Five Forces when forecasting the future. One approach to scenario planning is to consider 'extreme worlds' within the scenario.

The strategic objectives set by organisation may be the fifth way in which strategic thinking may be affected. When such objectives are set, more time and effort must be put into the process to ensure that they are achievable given the uncertain external environment.

Finally, some would argue that strategic planning should be abandoned in a world of high levels of uncertainty. This affect on strategic thinking is invalid, however, since 'organisations that fail to plan, plan to fail'.

(b) A number of large organisations have been using scenario plans for some time. For example, Shell scenario planned for the oil crisis in the 1970s and thus survived the crisis better than most.

Scenario planning

This approach requires organisations to develop future scenarios (strategic stories) for key environmental forces such as political, economic, social, technological, competitive, suppliers and buyers.

A number of future scenarios would be developed including, in some industries such as oil, 'extreme world' scenarios. This will enable management to avoid crisis as they will be in a position to implement appropriate plans having already considered the 'extreme world' future before it occurs.

Schoemaker suggested the following staged approach to scenario planning:

Stage 1 Identify key trends and uncertainties in the external environment and develop appropriate scenarios.

Stage 2 Formulate appropriate strategies to 'fit' each scenario.

Stage 3 Build core competences to take advantage of opportunities or minimise threats from the scenarios.

Stage 4 Implement appropriate strategic options over time as the key trends and uncertainties reveal themselves.

Assessment of the usefulness of scenario planning in strategy formulation

Under conditions of extreme uncertainty, scenario planning is useful because:

- Decision-makers are forced to consider potential volatile conditions and produce a plan for the continued operation of the business. This would have proved invaluable for some businesses during the 11 September tragedy.
- It focuses planners on the importance of external factors impacting on the organisation as well as internal factors.
- It will necessitate the involvement of many people within the organisation, including the strategic management accountant. This may have motivational benefits as well as strategic benefits.
- It forces the organisation to consider key threats from the PEST and competitive forces. The organisation may be able to influence some of the forces such as 'political' through lobbying, for example.

Assessment of the potential difficulties of scenario planning

- Strategic storytelling may be seen as unreal and unrealistic and, therefore, inappropriate as a 'technique'.
- It could be viewed as expensive in time and money if many people are involved.
- The scenarios may be 'wasted' if they are ignored, i.e. Stage 2 of the Schoemaker approach may not be implemented.
- Managerial conflict may arise because different managers may see the future in different ways.

56 NO-FRILLS AIRLINES (PILOT PAPER)

Requirement (a)

Key answer tip

While candidates could apply the industry life cycle and recognise that the traditional airline industry is entering a mature stage, or refer to the strategic groups that exist in the industry, Porter's Five Forces model needs to be used to determine industry attractiveness.

Porter made the observation that the essence of strategy formulation is not just coping with competition, but also requires that a company competes with both suppliers and customers for negotiating power.

Companies must understand the five forces on which the nature of competition depends and which determine the industry's potential for profit. Where there are weak forces there is the possibility for superior profits, but where the forces are strong, there is more likely to be perfect competition and poor profits.

The five forces are:

- the bargaining power of supplier groups
- the bargaining power of buyers

- the threat of new entrants
- the threat of substitution
- the degree of competitive rivalry within the industry.

Considering the air travel business as operated by the traditional airlines, the barriers to entry have been relatively high because of:

- high capital costs of aircraft
- regulation of routes and landing slots has restricted access
- government affection for, and ownership of, national flag carriers
- the restrictions on airport services.

The power of suppliers has been medium because:

- there are only two major aircraft suppliers: these are global suppliers. Regulation places limits on the second hand aircraft market. However, both suppliers are also volume dependent which reduces their power
- although major oil companies supply aviation fuel, the price is determined by OPEC, which effectively fixes the price of crude oil
- increasing outsourcing of non-core activities such as catering, baggage handling, and airport services
- however, labour power has been high; cabin and crew are traditionally well paid with many concessions.

The power of buyers has been increasing because:

- the buyers are becoming more knowledgeable and information more freely available
- the buyers no longer need to use intermediaries
- there is an increasing commodity mindset
- recent press has reduced the power of the brand

The threat of substitutes has increased because:

- high speed rail is a viable substitute across EU
- teleconferencing for the business market is cheaper and is a lower risk post-terrorist incidents.

Competitive rivalry within the industry has increased because:

- cost-conscious customers put pressure on premium fares
- high fixed cost component
- high exit barriers
- excess capacity partly offset by concentration through alliances and cross airline
- loyalty programmes.

The budget airlines by contrast have manipulated the five forces as follows. Barriers to entry to the market have been reduced by:

- using secondary airports that are largely remote from city centres, where landing slots are more freely available along with subsidies
- leasing aircraft rather than buying

- only flying point to point rather than adopting a hub and spoke model
- focusing on short haul.

Supplier power has been reduced by:

- leasing aircraft from intermediaries
- dispensing with many services such as catering and baggage handling
- negotiating different agreements with labour force.

Buyer power has been reduced by:

- focus on consumer segment of market
- recognising the service as a commodity and dispensing with intermediaries
- building a brand and reputation for cost effectiveness.

Also:

- the threat of substitutes has been reduced by competing on price
- competitive rivalry remains intense within the target market.

Requirement (b)

The source of competitive advantage for an organisation is an appropriate collection of strategic assets, capabilities and competencies – and an appropriate value chain to ensure that they are used together effectively to provide some distinctiveness in the eyes of the customers.

Assets will only be strategic if they are rare (or unique), valuable, difficult to acquire or copy, and with no freely available substitute resources.

Capabilities are based on behaviour within the firm and the perception that customers have when they deal with the organisation. On the basis of these perceptions they will decide whether they will continue to do business with the organisation. Capabilities will arise because of an underlying set of competencies present in an organisation.

Competencies are more general in that an organisation may have a superior ability in R&D or in control.

Having reconfigured their value chain, the budget airlines have resegmented the market for air travel appealing to a more cost-conscious group. Having recognised the potential of this market, the companies concerned have enjoyed first mover advantage over the traditional airlines who have continued to offer relatively high quality service to their travellers. When the budget airlines started, the traditional airlines adopted a wait and see policy, suspecting that the budget model would fail.

The source of competitive advantage that the budget airlines enjoyed was purely first mover advantage.

The business model operated by the budget airlines depends on their ability to compete on price and while volumes are maintained and there are no changes to the five forces model they have a reasonable chance of survival.

Theoretically, when a company competes on price it is essential that they maintain large volume sales. This makes the budget airlines susceptible to any environmental factor that can affect their passenger numbers. The threats of terrorism and economic downturn affecting discretionary disposable income are difficult to ignore as factors which can reduce volumes.

The companies concerned have manipulated the barriers to entry by choosing secondary airports which were under capacity and by negotiating favourable contracts with those airports. Additionally, they were able to secure subsidies from the local government who wished to promote business or tourism in the area. The passengers were left to make their own arrangements to travel from the airport, often at considerable cost and inconvenience. As other budget airlines have started to use those secondary airports the balance of power in negotiations is shifting towards the airports and costs may rise. As traveller volumes have increased, regional subsidies have shrunk since the objective of the local authority has been achieved.

As the budget airlines are charging lower prices and are dependent upon large volumes, their contribution to sales ratio is far lower. Any cost increases, such as increased lading fees, have a bigger impact on their profit figures. Similarly, the prospect of increased carbon taxes on the use of fuel and even fuel price increases themselves will have a significant effect on their cost structure.

The traditional airlines have reacted to the buyers' view of airline travel as a commodity and have become more price competitive, taking customers away from the budget airlines. Since they are using landing slots at airports which are more central to cities, the surrounding infrastructure is better and the impact of delays is less pronounced.

Although budget airlines have developed a business model that has been successful in the short term, by virtue of first mover advantage, it is unlikely that they will continue at these levels of success in the future. Sustainable competitive advantage is only rarely achieved by competing on price.

57 QUALISPECS

Key answer tips

You are required to undertake a corporate appraisal for Qualispecs and use this to suggest suitable strategies for the company. It is vital that you use the information given to you in the scenario for this question which is highly practical in nature. You do not need to perform a detailed analysis of the company using models such as PEST, Porter's Five Forces and so on. In Part (b) an alternative to Ansoff's matrix would be the use of a TOWS matrix which involves a process of conversion, matching and remedy. This involves converting Threats into Opportunities and Weaknesses into Strengths by building on the SWOT analysis. In practice, one would probably consider the strategies suggested by Ansoff's matrix and the techniques implied by the TOWS matrix in order to produce a strategy.

(a) **Corporate appraisal**

A corporate appraisal is an overview of an organisation's current position. It leads on from the internal and external analysis undertaken as part of the business planning process.

As the company works towards achieving its objectives, the corporate appraisal is a summary of the company's:

- strengths within the organisation relative to competitors
- weaknesses within the organisation relative to competitors
- opportunities available from the external environment
- threats from the external environment.

The company must develop a strategy which:

- capitalises on the strengths
- overcomes or mitigates the impact of weaknesses
- takes suitable opportunities
- overcomes or mitigates the threats.

In the case of Qualispecs:

Strengths

- Reputation for quality

  Quality is a major reason why people buy products, and continuing to build on this reputation will ensure customers continue to buy Qualispecs's products.

- Financially secure/large cash reserves

  Qualispecs does not need to rush into the implementation of new strategies. It can take its time to ensure strategies chosen are appropriate for the business and implemented effectively. They also have funds to invest in new ventures without having to raise external funds.

- Backing of a famous sports star

  This helps to improve the image of Qualispecs's products which in turn should result in higher sales, particularly amongst the younger market that might be influenced by the sports star.

- New Chief Executive

  The group has a new Chief Executive who has joined from a rival, Fastglass. Fastglass has been a successful and innovative company and the Chief Executive may be able to bring new ideas and provide a fresh approach.

- Established group with many stores

  The group has a good basic infrastructure including many stores and experienced staff. This allows them to implement new strategies quickly and easily.

Weaknesses

- Slower dispensing of spectacles

  Customer service is worse than competitors in this respect and may be a reason for the reducing customer loyalty.

- Less trendy products than competitors

  Some competitors have successfully sold designer frames. These are likely to be stylish and trendy compared to Qualispecs' traditional products. Qualispecs may need to update products more often with the latest designs.

- Smaller product range than competitors

  Some competitors have a wider product range than Qualispecs. This provides more choice which may attract customers and also gives competitors the opportunity to on-sell products, i.e. selling prescription sunglasses at the same time as standard spectacles.

- Older production methods causing higher costs

  This will either cause prices to be higher than competitors or margins to be less. In either case competitors have a distinct advantage.

- Varying performance around the group

  Little action is being taken to improve performance of poorly performing stores causing varying performance around the group. This indicates a weakness in internal control systems and perhaps also in development and training programmes.

- Little autonomy for shops

  Without autonomy there is little a shop manager can do to improve local operations. In London, for instance, pay may need to be higher to attract the right staff. With no local control over pay levels, shop managers may find it hard to employ good staff and hence improve their business.

  This lack of autonomy may also be demotivating to managers. Responsibility was one of the major factors outlined by Hertzberg in his motivation theory as a way to motivate staff.

- No incentive to improve for staff

  The use of group-based bonuses means that people cannot be rewarded for good individual performance. Individuals have little incentive to improve therefore.

Opportunities

Note: Opportunities should be in relation to the market as a whole. They therefore need to be available to all competitors in the market.

- To adopt new technologies to reduce costs (see earlier)
- To stock a wide range of up-to-date products (see earlier)
- Consumer spending will continue to increase

  Despite a slowdown in the economy, consumer spending is likely to increase suggesting an increasing market size in the future. There is therefore further opportunity for all competitors to increase sales.

- Targeting 18 to 30 year olds

  The 18- to 30-year-old age group offers a particular opportunity since its spending is likely to increase especially quickly. There is therefore an opportunity to understand this group's needs and to target its specifically.

- Develop a partnership with a high street shopping group

  Fastglass has already done this successfully and Qualispecs could follow suit. There are likely to be limited suitable partners so Qualispecs must act quickly before other firms make arrangements with the best partners.

Threats

- Intense competition/eroding customer loyalty

  Existing competitors are adopting new strategies with great success (e.g. Fastglass developed joint ventures). This has resulted in Qualispecs's customers moving to competitors, thus reducing profits. This is likely to be a continued threat to Qualispecs who needs to respond.

- Downturn in the economy

  In the long term, if the downturn continues it will affect all industries and consumer spending will be likely to fall as people become more defensive in their spending habits.

Key strategic challenges

In summary, the key strategic challenges are to:

- Improve the current lack of clear generic strategy ('stuck in the middle')

  Examining Michael Porter's generic strategies Qualispecs appears to have neither a cost leader differentiation nor a focus on any particular niche. While traditionally quality has been their focus, new innovations from competitors have eroded its position as the highest quality spectacle retailer. In the long run it will find it hard to compete effectively if it does not rectify this.

  Note: When asked to discuss current or future strategies Porter's Generic Strategies is always a good model to use. It is common in the exam to present failing companies (like Qualispecs) and you usually find such companies are 'stuck in the middle' and need to clarify their generic strategy in order to compete.

- Be more innovative in product and market development

  Competitors have successfully developed new strategies while Qualispecs has done very little. This has seen it lose business to competitors. To be successful in the future it needs to update their product range regularly and be more innovative in developing new strategies (e.g. joint ventures).

- Improve performance on a divisional basis by updating internal policies and procedures

  Current policies and procedures are demotivating staff and causing varying divisional performance.

(b) **Strategies to move the business forward**

Generic strategy

Given the key strength of Qualispecs as having a reputation for quality spectacles, and their current weakness in the cost of products produced, it would appear logical for Qualispecs to refocus activities on quality by producing very high quality spectacles (modern design, hard wearing, up-to-date features) with a high quality service (fast dispensing, knowledgeable staff).

Ansoff's Matrix

A useful model to develop business strategies is Ansoff's Matrix. Business strategies can be examined in all four boxes of this matrix for their suitability to the business compared to the corporate appraisal.

		PRODUCT	
		Current	*New*
MARKET	*Current*	Market penetration Consolidate Divest	Product development
	New	Market development	Diversification – Related – Unrelated

Current product/current market

Qualispecs would benefit from consolidating its current strengths and refocusing on quality. It should invest in new technology in order to reduce costs which will it to them be competitive. This also capitalises on its significant cash reserves.

It needs to improve its internal processes to ensure that staff are motivated through a good incentive scheme, quality training and by being given autonomy. This will capitalise on its skilled workforce and overcome the weakness in the way it is managed.

Current market/new products

Product development is a vital new strategy for Qualispecs to follow. Its competitors have been successful in doing this. One aspect of providing a high quality service is being able to offer a wide range of products to meet varying customer needs. Qualispecs may need to invest more in Research and Development and implement new product development programmes.

New market/current products

A joint venture strategy with a retailer who competes based on quality (e.g. Marks and Spencer) would both build on the reputation of Qualispecs and also introduce it to a new group of customers who will buy its products through association with the retail group. The retail group may also have outlets in other parts of the country (or even internationally) which would allow Qualispecs to expand its markets.

Diversification

There appears no need at present to diversify. The disadvantages of operating in new markets with new products (e.g. lack of experience and reputation) outweigh any possible advantages.

58 STATUTORY TRANSPORT AUTHORITY

Key answer tips

Your answer should explain the criteria for evaluating options, quantifying a social service and discuss funding for a transport service. You are not required to recommend an option or give a detailed evaluation of each proposal.

(a) When evaluating different options to find the best value for money, a statutory transport authority should consider:

Financial criteria

Financial objectives should be set, against which all three options can be evaluated. M is offering to provide a limited service with no authority funding whereas O requires a subsidy from the authority of £3,000 per week but provides a more flexible service and N requires variable funding.

Standard of service

This covers criteria such as frequency of service, timing of the services, facilities offered for disabled passengers and reliability.

Each of the three options plans a different standard of service. M is offering a limited, fast service. N plans a more flexible service with O offering the most flexible service of all. The practicality of each of the options proposed should be evaluated.

The area covered

M's and N's proposals only offer services between urban areas. O is catering for people living in rural areas who would not be served by M's and N's proposals.

Acceptability to the local population

Local people need to be consulted to establish their travelling needs. Meeting the needs of people will be a value for money factor because if it doesn't meet their requirements people will not use it.

(b) A statutory transport authority can quantify the value of a social service transport undertaking in many ways, including:

Financial measures

- Cost per passenger mile.
- Revenue per vehicle mile.
- Contribution per vehicle mile.
- Profit/loss per passenger mile.

Efficiency measures

- Capacity loadings of vehicles on each route.
- Punctuality rates for each service.
- Reliability ratio e.g. services cancelled and breakdown rates.

Other measures

- Reduction in other motor vehicle traffic.
- Number of passengers carried.
- Average length of journey.
- Analysis of use e.g. percentage of journeys made for leisure, travel to work and visits to hospital.
- Customer satisfaction.
- Impact on the quality of life of local people.

(c) Sources of funding for a rural transport facility, other than passenger fare revenues and public funds, include:

- Revenue could be earned by carrying advertisements on the inside and outside of vehicles and at vehicle stops. Companies could also pay to have vehicles painted in their corporate colours.
- Through tickets could be sold for longer journeys using other services. Commission could be charged for the sale of these through tickets.
- Tickets can be sold to include travel and entry to local tourist attractions. Again commission could be charged for the tourist attraction part of the price.
- Contract hire for school transport services and staff bus services for local employers in the area covered.
- Private vehicle hire on an ad hoc basis for local organisations.
- Running excursions during the tourist seasons.

Providing a back-up service for railway operators during engineering work and other emergencies.

59 DDD CHEMICALS

Key answer tips

This is a tricky question on identifying and responding to likely threats. The main problem lies in generating enough ideas to score well. In part (a) Porter's Five Forces Model has been used in part to provide at least some framework to help.

(a) DDD is exposed to the following threats due to the imminent expiry of patents:

Increased competitive rivalry

Without patent protection to stop them, existing rivals will be able to produce cheaper copies of DDD chemicals. This will reduce the price DDD can charge for its products and reduce margins.

(***Tutorial note:*** Some pharmaceutical firms have seen drug prices fall by 90% once patent protection is removed.)

Also, since the patents are attached to processes rather than specific chemicals, there is the threat that competitors will be able to use the processes to develop new chemicals before DDD.

Increased threat of entry

Existing patents also act as barriers deterring new entrants into DDD's markets. Without this barrier, there is a greater threat that new firms will enter the market, increasing competition and driving down prices and margins.

Increased power of customers

At present DDD exerts considerable power over customers as they have limited ability to switch suppliers. This is reflected by DDD's current high margins. Once patent protection is removed, competitors will be able to make similar chemicals, giving customers more choice.

The pharmaceutical companies will thus be able to exert more influence over DDD in areas such as price (as discussed above) and also credit terms, delivery terms and so on.

Increased power of suppliers

Any fall in volume will reduce DDD's power over suppliers and bulk discounts may be lost.

Staffing issues

The expected fall in profits will affect the value of share options, which in turn will affect employee motivation. Also the likely fall in volumes could require DDD to consider redundancies.

(b) Possible courses of action include the following:

Try to establish new patents for existing processes

By changing various aspects of existing processes, it may be possible to establish new patents for them, eliminating the threats outlined above. This option should be pursued first by discussions with patent experts to assess the likelihood of success.

Develop new processes / products as part of product portfolio management

Presumably part of DDD's long-term planning process is such that it anticipates patent expiry as a normal part of its business and has already developed new patent-protected processes and chemicals to replace the ones concerned. If not, then resources need to be allocated to such portfolio development.

Cut prices to retain customers

DDD could seek to retain customers by cutting prices and relying on its existing good relationships with them. Low prices may also act as a deterrent to new entrants.

Volume economies of scale may still enable DDD to produce the chemicals concerned at a lower cost than competitors, allowing it to make a reasonable margin even with lower prices. However, if larger manufacturers enter the market, then this advantage would quickly become eroded.

Long-term contracts

An alternative way of retaining customers could be to offer them lower prices in exchange for signing long-term contracts. Particularly where patents are not due to expire immediately, customers could be tempted by lower prices now and the guarantee of no price rises in the future.

This would also be a way of responding to current pressure from customers to reduce prices.

Buy major threats

If DDD can identify specific threats from competitors, then one option would be to buy them. This is unfeasible given DDD's small size.

(c) Summary

It is recommended that the directors adopt the following course of action:

(1) Try to establish new patents for existing processes to eliminate the threats.

(2) If option 1 fails, DDD should try to get customers to sign up to long-term contracts in exchange for price cuts. This will create switching costs for customers and act as a barrier preventing new firms from entering the market.

Alongside this DDD should be developing new processes as part of its long-term portfolio management.

PRODUCT PORTFOLIO EVALUATION

60 SPORTS CENTRE

Key answer tips

You were asked to recommend how the local authority could market its sports and services. It is only possible to do this if you know the market conditions that face the local authority. What you are really being asked to do is to produce a plan of how the local authority should go about acquiring the market information it needs. You should make sensible suggestions as to how it might respond to certain outcomes.

(a) The reduction of funding and the increased charges indicates that the sports centre is subject to some sort of financial reporting responsibility. It may not necessarily have to make a profit, but it does appear that some return is required.

This required return should underlie its research as it may have to analyse the return of each of the facilities offered and this may influence the decision as to whether some activities should be curtailed and others expanded.

The authority should undertake market research of the competing sports facilities to find out what facilities are offered, the prices at which they are offered, the quality of the facilities, and the typical customer profile of the people who use and pay for those facilities.

It should then compare the results of that research to its own experience. Thus, for example, if it finds that badminton everywhere is in decline then this could be a reason for looking more closely at whether it should continue to provide badminton. However, if it finds that its own badminton is in decline because badminton supplied by other centres has expanded significantly, then it should perhaps consider its own badminton provision to see whether it can compete, perhaps by better facilities, or some other inducements to make its own badminton appear more attractive.

The fact that it was built next to a supermarket development suggests that it is in a good area as regards customer access and also suggests that there would be a significant number of people visiting that area throughout the day. It may be that it could run a joint promotional campaign with the supermarket which could benefit both the supermarket and the sports centre. This is one example of how it might explore its own competitive advantage and part of its market research should have established the competitive advantage that other competing sports facilities might enjoy.

(b) The importance of the **product life cycle** is that not only does it highlight whether an area is growing or declining, but it also highlights the costs of maintaining the various facilities. There is no hard and fast rule which says that if an activity is at the maturity or decline stage that its costs of support will be increasing; it is up to the local authority to investigate each activity and, having identified in which phase of the life cycle it is located and whether the costs are increasing or decreasing, to then make a commercial judgement as to whether it can feasibly continue with that activity and possibly have to undertake significant reinvestment.

Looking at the particular activities, **martial arts** has little take-up but this is unlikely to require significant capital or absorb significant resources. The provision of gymnasium facilities and suitable matting is the only real capital requirement and the variable costs in the form of advertising and the instructor will be varied according to take-up. This may therefore be seen as a low risk operation.

Squash does have a significant capital cost both in terms of building new courts and also in the maintenance of such courts. It is however at a growth stage and the authority may well take the view that it is worth investing in the courts and other facilities to support this activity.

The **gymnasium facilities** are at the maturity stage but due to their low maintenance are probably something of a 'cash cow' and should probably be continued.

The **swimming pool** may present more of a problem. We are told that there are continual increases in maintenance costs and it may be that the pool will at some stage in the near future require a significant overhaul. Also, water purification costs are increasing and there may well be future directives which require even greater efforts in this area. Likewise Health and Safety requires the provision of lifeguards. The council may therefore have to take some fairly serious decisions in the near future about providing a significant capital injection into the swimming pool and in addition have to decide whether the fairly heavy fixed costs of this operation will be met by the current volumes and even more worryingly the lower volumes should the swimming facility move into the decline phase.

We are not told whether **badminton** has high costs but it clearly absorbs space that could perhaps be transferred to the squash facilities and the council may consider doing that. As said above, it would have to enquire into the reasons for the decline before taking any decision.

(c) The authority should consider the results of its market research in Part (a) and the expected revenues and costs of the various facilities offered and form a decision about whether they should be continued or discontinued.

It appears that the martial arts should be continued as should the squash and gymnasium facilities.

The swimming pool perhaps offers the greatest problems in view of the likely required investment and high fixed costs of operation set against a possible declining market. Similarly badminton needs careful consideration and, as indicated above, the causes for its decline needs to be investigated before any final decision can be taken.

61 GC CONGLOMERATE

Key answer tips

This question presents the market share and market growth position of the five strategic business units that comprise a conglomerate group. Additional information is provided regarding the level of profitability of each SBU. The application of the BCG Growth/Share matrix to analyse the performance of each SBU is required together with a discussion as to how strategic development could be pursued.

Market growth	High market share	Low market share
High	STAR Software development	PROBLEM CHILD Parcel carriage
Low	CASH COW Food manufacturer	DOG Brick and decorating

(a) The BCG matrix uses short emotive titles to illustrate how a portfolio of products/SBUs can be analysed for strategic planning purposes by using two important criteria of attractiveness. Market growth is shown on the vertical axis and market share by the horizontal axis. In this framework the '**Star**' is the software development company because it possesses the attributes of high market share and expected high market growth. The food manufacturer is a steady cash generator and is termed a '**Cash cow**'. It posses the attributes of high market share but low/declining market growth. The top right-hand quadrant describes the characteristics of the '**Problem child**' .The parcel carriage business has low market share and no prospects for growth. Lastly the two companies in the building and allied trades are identified as '**Dogs**' in that they have low market share and low market growth.

(b) The management of GC faces a problem that is typical of any conglomerate, which is to devise a strategy that provides value to the shareholders in the long term and thus enable the combined business to improve its chances of long-term survival. The strategy must focus on the following issues:

- Should we dispose of the companies in the building and allied trades ('Dogs')?
- How do we exploit the food manufacturer (Cash cow)?
- What resources need to be injected to develop the software business (Star)?
- How do we retain the position of the parcel business in an increasingly competitive market (Problem child)?

Divestment strategy

The declining profitability of the building brick SBU and the loss-making aspect of the painting and decorating business make them prime targets for divestment. Both companies serve a volatile business sector and require a degree of specialist management skill, which may not be available in a conglomerate. The Board could formulate plans to sell them off. The building brick company may fit into the portfolio of an organisation that is a supplier of material to the building and civil engineering sector. The painting and decorating company could fit into the portfolio of a company that provides support services like office cleaning and laundry. In the short run profits may be boosted by disposal surpluses and by elimination of trading losses. The cash generated by the sale could be used to finance the software development company as well as to support the parcel carriage service.

Improvement strategy

The food manufacturer activity is a steady cash generator but in the long term this cash generation could reduce. The Board could review their investment strategy. Will further investment in new technology improve their product range and prolong the ability to generate cash?

The development of new products could reverse the trend of declining market growth and improve the position of the business.

A profit improvement plan could examine the issue of reducing infrastructure costs and thus improve the profit in the medium term.

Promotion strategy-parcel carriage

The cash released by the disposal of the 'Dogs' could be invested in the parcel carriage business where the market place is becoming increasingly competitive. The increase in market entrants with a proven record in quality service provision (e.g. Fedex) and the possibility of the privatisation of public sector services makes investment a critical issue if the business is to survive. The fragmented nature of the market (the market leader holds 6% only) makes this business viable in the long term if an aggressive strategy of promotion is backed up by the necessary investment.

Investment strategy – software development

This SBU is likely to be the 'trump card' in the years to come but it will absorb considerable amounts of cash in product development in order to improve market share and generate value for the shareholders. The absence of a market leader is a good sign as well as the fact that the market share of 10% is higher than that of the nearest competitor. This SBU will therefore make a more pressing claim for the largest amount of any funds released by the divestment strategy outline above.

62 BCG

Key answer tips

Part (a) of the question requires you to explain how the BCG Growth Share Matrix could be used. In Part (b) you should demonstrate an appreciation that BCG can make an effective contribution to the strategic development of a mainly public-funded service since it will place the different services it provides into categories where they can be considered in a more effective manner. Also stress that rate of market growth and relative market share are important to all organisations.

(a) Most products, markets and even industries pass through clear stages of a life cycle. The position of a product can range from its introduction to the market, through a period of growth in sales and profits until its saturation, decline and eventual obsolescence. Ideally, a company needs a balanced range of products passing through different stages of the life cycle. The **BCG Growth Share matrix** is one of the methods used to analyse the balance of the product portfolio and illustrate the expected changes in the cash flow as products move through the various stages. The model is deliberately simplistic in that it focuses on cash flow and uses two variables, growth and share. As a generalisation, the **cash characteristics of the products** are defined by the quadrants into which they fall:

Rate of growth of market (%)		Relative market share (log scale): High	Relative market share (log scale): Low
	High	Cash in balance STAR	Cash user PROBLEM CHILD
	Low	Cash generator CASH COW	Cash in balance DOG

The matrix identifies four types of product or service – dogs, cash cows, problem children (question marks) and stars–and suggests appropriate strategies for each.

Cash cows are high share SBUs operating in a low growth industry and should be generating substantial cash inflows. The period of high growth in the market has ended, (the product life cycle is in the maturity or decline stage), and consequently the market is less attractive to new entrants and existing competitors. Cash cow products tend to generate more cash than is needed to sustain their market positions. These businesses should be a source of substantial amounts of cash that can be channelled to other areas.

A **star** product has a high relative market share in a high growth industry. This type of product may be in a later stage of its product life cycle. A star may be only cash neutral despite its strong position, as considerable expenditure will be required to defend its position against competitors. Failure to support a star may lead to the product losing its leading market share position, slipping eastwards in the matrix and becoming a problem child. A star, however, represents the best future prospects for an organisation. As the growth rate for a star slows, it will drop vertically in the matrix into the cash cow quadrant and its cash characteristics will change.

A **problem child or question mark** is a low market share product in a high growth industry. Substantial net cash input is required to maintain or increase market share in the face of strong competition. The planner must decide whether to market more intensively or get out of this market. The questions are whether this product can compete successfully with adequate support, and what that support will cost.

Dogs are low share SBUs in low growth markets. They are often cash users and can perpetually absorb cash, because of the investment required to maintain position. An organisation with such a product can attempt to appeal to a specialised market, delete the product or harvest profits by cutting back support services to a minimum.

Once the products are analysed using the model, a strategy for improving overall market share can be developed. Most organisations take cash from the cash cows to fund both development of future SBUs, and those problem children that have the potential to gain share to achieve star status.

(b) All organisations should carry out some form of corporate strategy activity. The need for involvement increases with the complexity of the organisation and the turbulence of its environment. Even government-funded organisations are subject to competition, and their managers should develop a strategy to cope with this, and also to convince the representatives of the government that the public funds are being used in a responsible manner. The Boston Matrix can be used as a strategic planning aid for individual business units if the current position of the business can be identified and the future rate of change forecast with reasonable accuracy. Identifying the generic strategic thrusts for the different stages of development can be helpful in selecting the most appropriate competitive strategy and management style. It also helps to match the strategy with a suitable level of financial risk.

Parcel post is a market in which both public-funded and private companies operate. In many instances, the two services compete directly with each other. The post office is mainly government funded and must not only provide a service that can compete directly with the privately-owned companies, but also meet the public service requirements.

The **Boston Matrix is a useful tool in portfolio analysis**. It shows the position of products or services in terms of market growth and relative market share and also incorporates the impact of the product life cycle. The rate of market growth is taken as a prime indicator of the level of attractiveness of the industry, because most organisations would prefer to be involved in a rapidly growing market rather than competing in a very mature or declining one. However, the parcel post market is a mature, well-established one and, unfortunately, the post office parcels service is constrained and unable to move into other markets. Its operations are controlled more rigidly and some of its aims and objectives are imposed on it.

The relative market share is also of interest to organisations in the industry as it is a guide to the competitive strength of the business in the particular market. This is of interest to an organisation that is funded by the government, because research has shown that companies with dominant market shares tend to produce higher financial returns. The relative market share is also an indicator of whether the organisation is meeting the needs of the users of the services offered.

Analysing the post office products and services and dividing them into the four categories of cash cows, stars, problem children and dogs helps to create a convenient method of making decisions – in particular, decisions regarding the amount of promotional expenditure that should be allocated, the likely cash flows that can be expected and the extent of the business and financial risk. In a mature market with relative stability that is forecast to continue for a reasonable period, organisations such as the post office can invest in automation and other ways of increasing fixed costs, while reducing variable costs by a larger amount. The appropriate management style is that of 'controller' because the business can be managed for profit. The emphasis of the management accounting analysis is placed on relative cost comparisons with competitors and on considering ways to improve the existing cost position of the organisation.

The strategies chosen for any business will change as the product or service develops through stages of the life cycle. Using a method of analysis such as the BCG matrix will assist in the formulation of the organisation's strategy, as it helps to place the different products or services into categories where they can be compared with competitors and considered more effectively.

63 3C PHARMACEUTICALS (MAY 06 EXAM)

Key answer tips

Part (a) asks for application of the product lifec ycle to 3C (many students completed a BCG analysis, which was not required!). It is vital that you comment on each product in terms of the overall portfolio and not just in isolation.

In part (b) it is again vital that your comments concerning each option are put in the context of the impact on the portfolio as a whole.

In part (c) ensure that you discuss each option, explain why there is an ethical issue and conclude.

(a) The product life cycle model classifies products into four main phases:

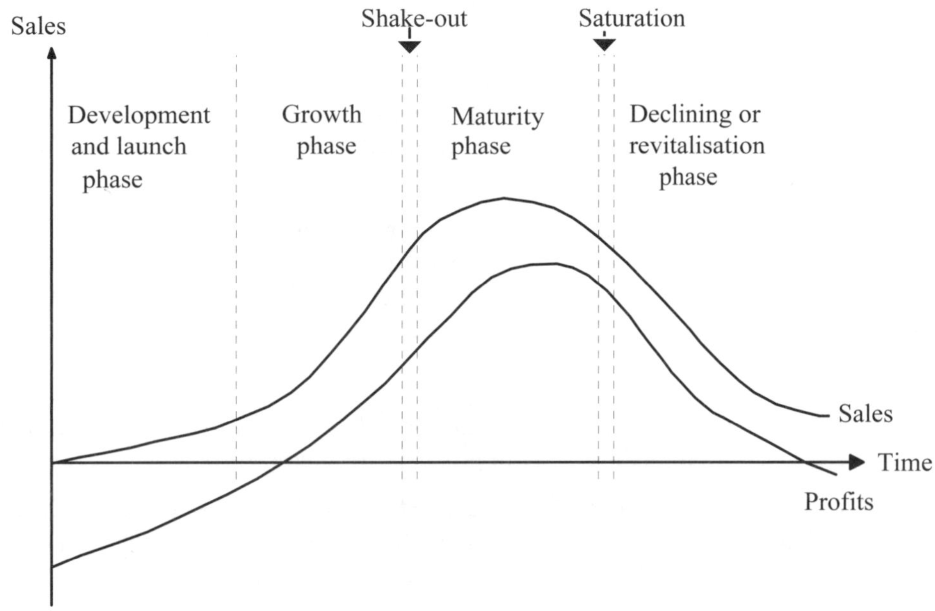

The model is normally used to assess the overall balance of the portfolio with respect to:

- growth – e.g. new products replacing those at the end of the life cycle
- cash flow – e.g. positive cash flows from some products can help finance those that are currently cash negative
- other resource requirements
- risk – e.g. having some stable low risk products to compensate for other high risk ones.

The model can be applied to 3C as follows:

3C has 240 drugs at various stages of development, either being tested or undergoing clinical trials. All of these fall into the 'development and launch' phase of the product life cycle. While being a significant drain on company resources, they are an essential part of the portfolio as they are needed to ensure the firm's future profitability by replacing older drugs that have come to the end of their life cycles.

- Epsilon is at the end of the 'growth' phase and is entering 'maturity', as high sales growth has come to an end. As such it should be a net cash generator to help finance other products in the portfolio that are currently cash negative. However, it will not contribute to future growth.

- Beta is at the latter stages of the 'development and launch' phase as significant growth in sales has yet to occur. As such it is unlikely to have reached breakeven sales and is still a drain on the firm's resources.
- Alpha is coming to the end of the 'maturity' phase and will be entering 'decline' in 12 months' time when patent protection expires and generic copies flood the market. At present it is likely to be cash positive, helping to finance product development but will neither contribute to cash flow nor future growth beyond the next year.

  Overall the portfolio is reasonably balanced in terms of future growth potential and cash flow. Beyond the next year it is vital that Beta becomes cash positive and further products move from development to launch.

(b) The three options will affect the portfolio as follows:

Alpha2

Alpha2 has already completed clinical trials so is ready to launch. This would effectively allow the patent protection for Alpha to be extended a further five years, thus preventing Alpha from entering the decline phase and lengthening the maturity phase.

This should prevent the portfolio from becoming unbalanced with respect to cash flow as the revised Alpha2 will generate cash to finance other products in the portfolio. It will also reduce the risk of the portfolio as sales for Alpha2 will be more certain than estimated returns for other products currently in development.

Beta

Investing in a marketing campaign for Beta would move it into the growth phase and improve the immediate growth prospects of the portfolio.

However, the presence of a close substitute in the market increases the risks attached to Beta and may result in lower growth than expected and even delay Beta breaking even as extra funds would be required to establish Beta ahead of its rival. In the short term Beta may place greater demands on the portfolio cash flow rather than helping it.

Gamma

If Gamma completes the final clinical trials successfully, then it will quickly move from development and launch into the growth stage. Even if prices are set at a high level, expected demand should result in very high growth, improving the overall growth balance of the portfolio. However, there is no guarantee that Gamma will be successful and, on balance, is the most risky option presented.

The impact on overall portfolio cash flow will depend, to some extent, on the price set. While a low price may still generate positive contribution and cash flow in the immediate future, when Gamma is viewed over its whole life cycle a loss and negative cash flow may result.

A higher price will enable 3C to finance many more other drugs that are still in the development phase.

Recommendation

On balance, investing in Alpha2 appears to offer the safest way to balance the portfolio in terms of cash flow whereas Gamma offers the highest growth and profit potential. The final decision will depend on the risk aversion of the directors.

(c) Social responsibility is the idea that an organisation should behave responsibly in the interests of the society in which it operates.

The social responsibility implications of the three options given are as follows:

Alpha2

Extending the patent in the way described would delay competitors from producing cheap generic copies. The ethical argument here is that, if 3C invests, then customers would not have access to cheaper pain killers so, in effect, 3C is increasing the pain of many sufferers.

However, there are many alternative pain killers on the market, including generic drugs, so the comparison is really between cheap pain relief and more expensive but better pain relief.

Beta

The ethical position with Beta is the other way round – one could argue that 3C has a moral duty to invest in Beta as this will increase the availability of drugs dealing with serious infection. However, if 3C does not invest in Beta, then there are equivalent drugs on the market for patients and hospitals are likely to prioritise such treatments anyway. What investment in Beta would achieve is a likely fall in the price of such drugs due to extra competition. It could be argued that this should allow health trusts' funds to go further, thus treating more patients.

Gamma

The situation with Gamma is very different. Millions of people around the world are infected with HIV/AIDS and, although progress is being made with anti-retroviral drugs, Gamma would be a major step forward in treatment.

A separate ethical issue is the price that 3C should charge for Gamma. Selling Gamma at the lowest price possible would ensure greater access to sufferers, particularly in poorer countries in Africa where the situation is at its worst. A high price would effectively exclude such people from treatment.

There is thus a major ethical conflict between the higher profits that 3C could earn for its shareholders verses increased treatment for people in the developing world. While it could be argued that 'the business of business is business' and that it is up to governments to make funds available to pay for drugs, the ethical argument here is compelling.

Conclusion

On ethical grounds further investment should be put into Gamma. In fact, the key ethical argument against investing in Alpha2 or Beta is that they preclude investment in Gamma. The pricing issue is more complex.

BENCHMARKING AND VALUE CHAIN ANALYSIS

64 COMPETITOR ANALYSIS AND COMPETITOR BENCHMARKING

Key answer tips

(a) Students must explain the terms 'competitor analysis' and 'competitor benchmarking' and then compare and contrast the two.

Students must also evaluate the importance of each process.

(b) A useful tip for answering this part of the question is to think of 'well known' public sector organisations such as colleges and hospitals.

(a) **Competitor analysis**

A competitor analysis is undertaken prior to engaging in competitor 'attacks' or competitor strategies. This analysis involves a systematic review of the competitor(s) to be attacked in relation to strengths and weaknesses. All available information is analysed in relation to the competitor's marketing, structure, systems, process, people and financial position.

Competitor benchmarking

Benchmarking is a diagnostic approach to performance improvement. The technique is holistic in that it considers all aspects of performance – financial and non-financial. Benchmarking can involve collaboration with a competitor or against an entity with a reputation for 'best practice'. The essence of benchmarking is to identify areas of poor performance and to develop a vision on how these can be improved by challenging the methods systems and procedures in all business processes.

The modus operandi of the benchmarking partner is then used to devise improvements that will generate added value.

The importance of competitor analysis

Competitor analysis is an important part of the strategic analytical process for the formulation of marketing strategies such as pricing and product development strategies.

Competitor analysis is therefore important for gaining and monitoring a competitive advantage, especially in markets where competition is intense such as fashion and entertainment.

A further reason why competitor analysis is important is that it forces the organisation to consider important questions such as:

- Who are our competitors?
- What are our competitor objectives?
- What are their strengths and weaknesses?
- How are they likely to react to our competitor strategies?

If customer switching costs are low, then competitor analysis is vital to assess the actions and reactions of competitors. Competitor price cuts, product modifications, new product launches, increased promotional activity and distribution channel strategies all need to be monitored and forecasted in an attempt to grow and maintain market share.

A number of important functions are served by undertaking a competitor analysis, namely:

- a better understanding of the firm's competitive position in the market place
- a clear picture of which core competences need to be strengthened
- a more accurate competitor intelligence database for the development of competitor strategies.

The importance of competitor benchmarking

The most important aspect of competitor benchmarking is that it provides a system whereby *relative* performance can be assessed. As Tom Peters put it in his book *Thriving on Chaos*: 'If the other guy's getting better, we had better get better faster, or we are getting worse'.

If senior management needs to know how well the organisation is truly performing in its key areas, it must implement a competitor benchmarking system.

If all employees are encouraged to be part of the competitor benchmarking system and recommend areas for improvement then the system is important for motivating staff which can result in the organisation improving its efficiency, effectiveness and economy. In this respect, unlike competitor analysis, strategies do not require outcomes from the process of benchmarking.

The process of competitor benchmarking is also important for improving a firm's products, service levels, quality and internal processes. Although some competitors may not be willing to participate in the benchmarking exercise, competitor information can be obtained on 'sensitive' factors through industry associations and/or mystery shopping.

A further important factor associated with competitor benchmarking is improved customer satisfaction, better quality and lower costs.

A number of important functions are served by undertaking a competitor benchmarking exercise, namely:

- a better understanding of relative performance levels
- an understanding of the steps to be undertaken to improve performance
- it identifies the performance level targets to be set for an organisation's KPIs.

(b) In answering this question, examples will be drawn from public sector colleges and hospitals.

How benchmarking might be successfully applied

Although competitor benchmarking may be inappropriate for certain public sector organisations, internal benchmarking, process benchmarking and external benchmarking may be applied to improve public sector performance in efficiency, effectiveness and economy.

Internal benchmarking might be successfully applied to compare the internal administrative processes within different hospitals. The administrative procedures performed in the hospital that adopts 'best practice' can then be transferred across all hospitals to improve administrative efficiency within the health service.

Similarly, internal benchmarking can be adopted across colleges to discover ways of improving the quality of service to students.

The choice of college to benchmark against, however, needs to be considered carefully. For example, a college that trains students only for catering services may prove an unsuitable comparator for colleges preparing students to be mechanics!

To successfully apply benchmarking in the public sector, it will be necessary to identify the processes and activities which are to be compared. Colleges and hospitals, for example, will have multiple social objectives and, therefore, it will be necessary to identify the measures which are the most appropriate given the multiple objectives.

Information would be obtained on the most important factors and the implications of underperforming in any of these areas must be clearly understood.

To successfully implement a benchmarking system in the public sector requires managers to believe that the system will result in improvements in efficiency, effectiveness and economy.

65 PAL

Key answer tips

In Part (a) you must outline suitable performance measures for the home insurance division of PAL, a banking group. Do use the three areas suggested by the survey to base these around. When benchmarking it is possible that organisations will be biased towards their own performance and this can creep in when measures used are subjective. For each measure you suggest you must advise on the extent of subjectivity and how to avoid this bias. You are only required to suggest performance measures for home insurance, not PAL as a whole. In Part (b) you must analyse the strategies followed by PAL. You must examine how benchmarking can support these strategies. Do use theory to support your answers. In our answer, the use of Porter's generic strategies is useful. In addition, strategies linked to Ansoff's matrix could be used as a basis for your answer.

(a) **Performance measures for benchmarking**

Benchmarking is the comparison of your own performance against that of another comparable party using key measures. In the case of PAL they are considering competitive benchmarking where PAL's results will be compared against those of competitors. Based on the comparison, lessons can be learnt about where PAL is doing well and where it is not doing so well, so that appropriate improvement can be made.

In addition to price, PAL has identified three areas that are critical to the success of the organisation and so it is important that performance measures used identify whether the home insurance division is being successful in these areas.

Delivery

Delivery for an insurance firm means the swift delivery of insurance certificates, documentation and quotations.

A good measure here might be the time between insurance policy being taken out/quotations requested to the day documents are received.

This information could be obtained by purchasing insurance from all competitors and requesting quotations from competitors and measuring their response times.

Subjectivity: This measure is objective. It can be measured precisely and so there is little opportunity for internal bias to creep in.

Technical content of literature

Measures could include:

(i) *Number of errors made per page in literature*

An expert might be used to review material produced by both the home insurance division and that of other home insurance companies for errors made. The number of errors made per page could then be calculated. High quality literature will have few errors.

Subjectivity: Although the measure itself should be objective, internal experts may well have had input into their own company's material. They may be familiar with it, and this familiarity could cause them to overlook their own mistakes or be more inclined to be thorough when reviewing competitors.

An independent company could therefore be employed to undertake the review to avoid such bias. Alternatively someone with no link to literature production could be used.

(ii) *Clarity of technical content*

One problem often found with technical information is that it is not presented in a clear, understandable way.

Subjectivity: It is hard for technical experts to rate the clarity of literature since they read material in light of the knowledge they have. The general public, particularly those who would be likely to purchase home insurance, could be independently selected and paid to rate the clarity of technical content of different company's material. While this is subjective, their opinion is a very useful indicator of performance.

Customer service and correspondence

Customer service for an insurance firm could include the quality of advice given, the speed of quotation, the friendliness of staff, and the clarity and speed of receiving correspondence.

Customers of both PAL and their competitors could be asked to rate the level of service they receive against a number of customer service measures. This could then be used to create an overall rating by applying a predefined scoring system.

Subjectivity: While the measure itself is subjective (it is based on customer opinion), each customer only comments on their own experience with their own supplier so there is little opportunity for bias. The information obtained would be useful.

(b) **Analysis of current strategies**

PAL have followed two key strategies to date:

1 *A cost leadership strategy within a reduced geographical area*

Up to now PAL has been keeping costs low by focusing on the mortgage market and providing few additional customer services. By comparing prices of loans with those of competitors they are able to sell loans at a low rate of interest and thus attract customers.

Using the terminology of Michael Porter, they have a cost focus strategy, focusing their cost leadership strategy in and around the capital city. This enables them to build a well known brand within this area for a low total cost. It also allows them to provide a comprehensive range of outlets in that area.

While this strategy has been successful, a cost leader is the lowest cost producer in the market as a whole. As a small producer it is hard to gain the economies of scale that a large national producer can. In the long term such a strategy would be likely to result in low profitability.

How benchmarking supports this

PAL have successfully used benchmarking data to ensure they have the lowest prices available.

Benchmarking can also provide cost information relative to competitors. One useful source of cost information is from financial accounts. Using this comparison, PAL will be able to learn where they are successfully keeping costs low and where competitors are operating at a lower cost than they are.

Benchmarking will also give them cost targets which can be used to drive cost reduction programmes.

2 *Additional services*

Using their current strategy, PAL have found that they lack competitiveness and need to introduce additional customer services. This indicates that customers expect a range of services from one supplier. Low cost is not their only focus.

Providing additional services has the following advantages:

- broader service giving customers a more complete service
- ability to on-sell products to existing customers and therefore capitalise on the customer base.

On the downside however:

- Overheads might be incurred setting up and developing these businesses which might reduce profitability and damage the company's cost leadership positioning.
- New expertise is required which they do not currently have. They may find it hard to compete against companies who have already progressed up the learning curve.
- The early stage of business and lack of experience may make it hard for PAL to match competitors' prices for these new services. This may make it hard to compete on the same low price basis as they do in the mortgage market.
- The company may lose its consistency of image by aiming to operate in a number of different markets and using different generic strategies (if they are a cost leader in the mortgage market and not in others).
- The new services may have different competitors who compete in different ways. Analysis and benchmarking against many competing businesses may therefore be time consuming and difficult. Also it may not be possible to compete on the same basis in different service areas. This will depend on the strengths of competitors in each market.

Benchmarking to support this

Benchmarking will enable:

- PAL to understand best practice for new services and set realistic targets
- price comparisons against new competitors to ensure competitive prices are being charged
- ongoing improvement to be achieved through comparing against the best competitor in each market and setting targets to match this.

66 SUPERMARKET

Key answer tips

In Part (a) you are required to discuss the main components of the value chain giving examples for a supermarket. Explanations should be four to five lines long. You also have to explain skills of the management accountant in analysing the value chain. This is a harder requirement where you should be looking for about three points. Ensure you explain why each will help with a value chain analysis – a common mistake in questions like this is to give the skill and not explain it in relation to the questions asked. Avoid over-elaboration of your value chain description and a detailed analysis of its use in a supermarket. There simply isn't enough time given that the value chain contains nine sections and there are only 17 marks for this and the accountant skills question. You do not need to draw a diagram of the value chain as, although not wrong, it is probably a waste of time.

In Part (b) you have to explain how the value chain could be used in supporting the development of generic strategies. Some texts call Porter's 'generic strategies' his 'competitive strategies' so ensure you learn this term. A brief description of these would be useful to support the answer. Examples are a useful way of elaborating on your description.

(a) A company receives inputs into the organisation and converts these into outputs. In doing so it adds value to the inputs so that it can sell the outputs for more than the sum of the input costs, hence creating a margin. By examining the activities between inputs and outputs (i.e. the value chain) the organisation can understand what is adding value to the customer and increase the margin and profits.

The value chain is split into two sections containing a number of activities. The first section contains the primary activities, which are those activities involved directly in the buying and selling of goods to customers. Each activity can be examined to understand how value can be added to the customer.

Primary activities

1 *Inbound logistics*

These are the activities required to receive and store products prior to them being put onto shelves. A supermarket will have central warehouses where they receive goods from suppliers. Orders will be made by different supermarkets around the country and goods distributed from the warehouse to the supermarkets prior to being put onto shelves.

2 *Operations*

Operations for a supermarket are the running and management of the retail outlets themselves. This will involve stacking shelves, serving customers, removing out-of-date products and operating tills. For Internet-based sales this is also the production and management of the Internet site.

3 *Outbound logistics*

These are activities required to get the product out to the customer. In stores this means enabling customers to get the products easily from the tills to their cars. It might mean having a good car park layout.

For Internet sales, supermarkets have people who pick orders for customers and fleets of delivery vans and drivers who take the product directly out to customers. Outbound logistics is very important for this new and growing area of supermarket business.

4 *Marketing and sales*

These are activities which inform buyers about products and services and induce them to visit their store and buy their products. This might include developing advertising campaigns, sales promotions (buy one get one free), promoting the website with links or moving higher on search engine lists.

5 *Service*

These are activities required to keep the product or service working effectively for the buyer after it is sold and delivered and to keep the customer happy after sales. For a supermarket this might mean no quibble refunds on products.

Support activities

The support activities are those involved in supporting the other areas of the business. They are necessary for the efficient running of the business.

1 *Procurement*

Procurement is the acquisition of inputs, or resources, for the firm. This includes managing supplier relationships and managing the purchasing mix of the firm (the right quantity of product, at the right time; the right quality, at the right price).

This can cut across all areas of the business so would mean purchasing goods for re-sale, assets, distribution contracts, advertising campaigns, IT equipment and so on.

2 *Human Resource Management*

This consists of all activities involved in recruiting, hiring, training, developing, compensating and laying off personnel.

Supermarkets are heavily labour-intensive businesses with large workforces, many of whom are relatively low skilled. Employment processes to employ and organise the workforce are particularly important.

3 *Technological development*

This pertains to the equipment, hardware, software, procedures and technical knowledge of the firm. Supermarkets are heavily reliant upon EPOS systems to speed customers through tills and to provide up-to-the-minute stock information. They also use automated purchasing using Electronic Data Interchange to speed up processing, automate internal processes and cut costs.

4 *Infrastructure*

This ties together the different parts of the organisation and consists of functions or departments such as legal, finance, planning, public affairs, government relations, quality assurance and general management. Supermarkets are huge organisations who will have all these departments and more.

Skills of a management accountant

A management accountant should be able to provide the following skills in the analysis of the value chain:

1 *Wide business expertise*

Management accountants deal with all parts of the organisation to support the business. They also have training to help understand different business functions so can bring this broad expertise to bear in doing the analysis.

2 *Financial skills*

These will be useful in terms of analysing the costs of each activity and being able to advise on the impact of cost reduction.

3 *Performance measurement*

A management accountant also measures performance using non-financial measures such as customer satisfaction and can analyse and advise on the performance of each activity.

4 *Investment appraisal*

The management accountant has investment appraisal skills to be able to review new investments from both a financial perspective (e.g. NPV calculation) and also a broader business perspective to advise whether value is truly being added to the customer.

(b) **Implementing generic strategies**

Michael Porter identified two basic types of generic strategy necessary to ensure the success of the business: cost leadership and differentiation.

Cost leadership

Cost leadership means being the lowest cost producer in the market. For similar products selling at the market price the cost leader will generate higher profits. They can alternatively sell at lower prices and generate market share.

Differentiation

A differentiation strategy calls for the development of a product or service that offers unique attributes that are valued by customers and that customers perceive to be better than or different from the products of the competition.

Ways in which differentiation can be achieved include:

(i) better quality product

(ii) better customer service

(iii) better brand image

(iv) different features from the competition

(v) better after-sales service.

Focus

Porter also noted that both cost leadership and differentiation strategies could be followed with narrow market focus. In this instance an organisation focuses effort and resources on a narrow, defined segment of a market. Competitive advantage is generated specifically for this niche.

Value chain and generic strategies

The value chain provides a useful way to examine whether the business is effectively following its chosen generic strategy across all the activities of the whole organisation.

If a company chooses to be a cost leader, for instance, it would examine each activity to look for ways to reduce costs to a minimum while maintaining the value to customers. This is known as reducing non-value adding activities.

For a supermarket within the 'operations' activity this might mean using relatively low-skilled staff paid at around the minimum wage, using low-cost shelving and lighting, and opening stores in cheaper locations.

Within the 'service' activity it might mean offering relatively little or no after sales service e.g. statutory refunds only perhaps and no customer service desk.

A company following a differentiation strategy of high quality will examine every activity of the organisation to ensure quality is ensured throughout. This might mean in 'procurement' buying high-quality supplies from trusted brands and in 'human resource management' giving staff significant training to ensure good customer service.

67 E5E (MAY 05 EXAM)

Examiner's Comments

Common errors that occurred in May 05 exam

Part (a)

- Lack of depth i.e. basic lists of notes, with little explanation.
- Lack of application to E5E.

Part (b)

This was generally well answered by most candidates. However, the biggest weakness was lack of application to E5E.

Part (c)

This question was generally well answered. Most candidates adequately identified the problems for staff when implementing benchmarking and most were able to relate this to the particular concerns of the volunteer staff of E5E.

(a) **The advantages and disadvantages of benchmarking for E5E are as follows:**

Advantages

- A better understanding of the firm's position
- Highlights particular areas that need changing
- Can identify problem areas in advance
- Can be integrated into target-setting, performance appraisal and bonuses
- Could highlight areas where other charities are much more effective so perhaps E5E should stop those activities
- Can be used to overcome complacency
- Should be particularly useful in improving economy and, to some extent, efficiency – all charities have financial constraints and benchmarking would highlight areas for improvement
- Enables better information to be provided to stakeholders – particularly useful in supporting applications for government funds.

Disadvantages

- Time consuming and expensive to implement
- Finding suitable comparisons can be difficult
- Not so useful in improving effectiveness as the stated objectives are very difficult to measure:

  'To fund world class research into the biology and the causes of heart disease.' What is 'world-class'?

  'To develop effective treatments and improve the quality of life for patients.' How do you measure 'quality of life'?

  'To reduce the number of people suffering from heart disease.' Cause and effect can be difficult to match – can reductions in mortality rates be traced directly to E5E's work?

  'To provide authoritative information on heart disease.' How to measure what is 'authoritative'?
- Not a competitive industry – does it matter if another charity is more effective in certain areas?
- Danger of information overload
- Problems gathering information when so many staff are volunteers – there may be a need for extra training here as well
- Can be demotivating if the organisation fails to meet benchmarks

In summary benchmarking may help the charity become more economic and efficient but will not aid effectiveness.

(b) **Stages in conducting a benchmarking exercise**

Tutorial note:

There is no universally agreed set of steps to follow when conducting a benchmarking exercise. The following is just one suggested answer.

E5E could use the following steps to conduct a benchmarking exercise:

1 *Planning*

- Decide what you wish to benchmark – for example, fund raising, % of funds passed on to recipients, % of funds raised from government, % of staff who are volunteers, funds raised per person, etc.
- Decide against whom you want to benchmark – this could include internal benchmarks (difficult), competitive benchmarks (e.g. other health research charities such as cancer research), activity benchmarks (e.g. universities to assess the educational aspects of E5E) and generic benchmarks (e.g. other communications organisations such as newspapers).
- Identify outputs required – e.g. a breakdown of funds collected, feedback on talks given.
- Determine data collection methodologies – e.g. should volunteers record information, should standard forms be prepared for talks, etc.

2 *Data collection*

- Secondary/background research – getting comparators.
- Primary research – from the benchmark.

3 *Analysis*

- Of the gaps – are they significant?
- Of the factors that create the gaps (enablers) – E5E would need to discuss findings with the relevant staff to understand why there are differences. For example, the benchmarking charity may have been much larger than E5E.

4 *Implementation of improvement programmes*

- Implementation planning – for example, visiting best in class and observing their methods.
- Roll-out of new modus operandi (changes) – for example, setting up new training programmes for volunteer staff, designing new advertising, training speakers, etc.

5 *Monitoring results*

- The process should be continuous.

(c) **Dealing with the concerns of staff**

In each of the above stages the concerns of voluntary staff should be taken into account:

- E5E should have meetings to explain to staff why benchmarking is being introduced, its benefits and potential problems.

- Staff should be reassured of senior management commitment to the process.
- They should be consulted when deciding what to benchmark and what measures to use.
- They should be asked to help design new forms if they will be using them.
- They should be asked if they have any experience of benchmarking – just because they are volunteers does not mean that they have not had jobs where such experience may be gained.
- Emphasis should be on improvements of the processes rather than criticising staff.

68 2B VALUE CHAIN (MAY 06 EXAM)

Key answer tips

Section (a) asks for a Porter's value analysis of the firm. This should be relatively straightforward as long as you justify how a given activity adds value. It is vital here that you use the information given rather than trying to cover every category in the value chain.

Part (b) is trickier and requires some thought to determine how the website will affect the value drivers. The best approach here is to work through each of the activities identified in part (a) and consider what customers expect from a store compared with a website when shopping.

(a) **Porter's value chain analysis**

Porter developed his value chain to help enterprises analyse their resources to see which activities contribute to the firm's competitive advantage and in what way – whether they gave rise to cost or quality advantages.

The value chain groups activities into primary and support activities:

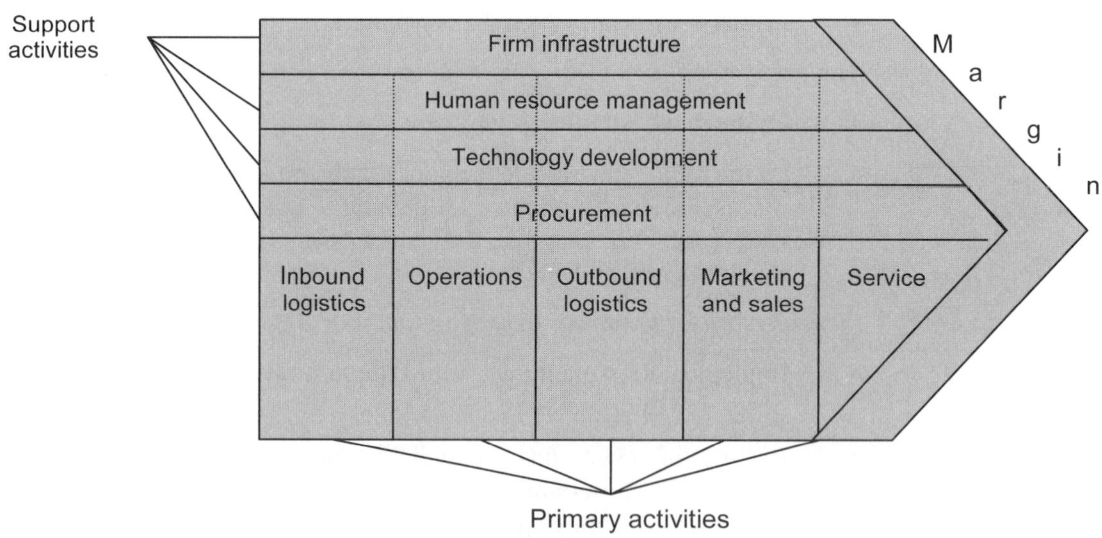

Applying this model to 2B, the company's competitive strategy of differentiation can be seen to be supported by the following activities:

Inbound logistics

- Procurement – good relationships with suppliers allow 2B to offer a wider range of products than competitors.

- Technology development – the computerised inventory system ensures that staff can verify stock availability quickly to be able to give customers accurate information about how long it will take to source items not in that particular shop.

Operations

- HRM – the policy of only recruiting sporting enthusiasts gives a quality advantage through excellent customer service.
- HRM – staff training results in very knowledgeable staff, again improving customer service.
- The store design allows customers to find products very easily, giving a quality advantage.

Marketing and sales

- Market research – the recent survey by store managers is indicative of a strong customer focus.
- Technology development – the current website is very basic and does little more than tell customers where stores are located and some details of products stocked.

(b) The main way e-retail investment will affect the value chain as follows:

Inbound logistics

- Procurement – the existing good relationships with suppliers will become even more important as 2B will want to offer a wide range of products on its website.
- Technology development – the computerised inventory system will become more important as 2B will want a facility on its website that allows customers to see whether an item is in stock and estimated delivery times.

Operations

- HRM – the existing policy of recruiting sporting enthusiasts will not add any value to online customers unless a help facility is available on the website for customers to ask questions.

  With many websites, customers' buying decisions are more likely to be influenced by online product reviews by other customers and links to trade reviews. When buying online, choice and price will become the new critical success factors.

  It may be that 2B can make some use of staff expertise by getting them to write detailed descriptions of products and their suitability for use on the website.
- HRM – existing staff training will not add value to online sales, except where staff need to be trained to process website inquiries.
- The store design will be of little relevance to online sales.
- Overall the operations value drivers will thus effectively contribute less to 2B's margin.

Marketing and sales

- Market research – the recent survey by store managers is indicative of a strong customer focus. This will continue to be important as feedback will be needed on the website. The website itself can be used to gain information on customers through the use of customer histories, profiling, cookies and surveys.
- Technology development – the greatest improvement will occur with the website for obvious reasons.

Summary

The main problem facing 2B is that its competitive advantage of differentiation through enhanced customer service and choice will count for little on the website.

Customers will compare prices between websites and buy the cheaper goods, once they know what they want. Even if 2B offers a very helpful online diagnostic service to help customers decide what to buy, there is nothing to stop customers then buying the product from a cheaper website.

2B will thus be under pressure to drop prices on the website to be competitive. This could seriously undermine shop sales as customers might go into the shop for advice and then expect 2B to match its web prices in store.

ACQUISITION AND DIVESTMENT STRATEGIES

69 DIVERSIFICATION POLICY

Key answer tips

Be sure to detail the three forms that related diversification might take, namely, backward, forward and horizontal integration. Remember that mergers and takeovers are well known for failing as a result of management inability to run the newly formed business combinations despite the benefits of increased resources being available. In Part (c) remember that there is much evidence to suggest that specialised companies who adopt the 'stick to the knitting' approach as observed by Peters and Waterman achieve better results than those with many diverse interests. Also, in a free capital market an investor can create his own diversified portfolio rather than relying upon those companies he is investing in doing the diversification for him.

(a) **Ansoff's product/market expansion grid** can be drawn as follows:

	Existing products	*New products*
Existing markets	Market penetration	Product development
New markets	Market development	Diversification

The grid is designed to reveal the appropriate strategic responses from different combinations of ideas to promote growth. The strategies are riskier when they involve new products or new markets.

For example, seeking to increase sales of one's current products in one's existing markets is low risk, but is unlikely to lead to sparkling growth. Diversification into new markets with new products offers the best growth prospects, but at the expense of higher risk.

(b) There are two broad types of diversification:

(i) related (or concentric) diversification

(ii) unrelated (or conglomerate) diversification.

Related diversification is development beyond the present product and market, but still within the broad confines of the industry. For example, Unilever is a diversified organisation with all of its interests in the consumer goods industry. Related diversification can take three forms:

(i) backward integration refers to development concerned with the inputs into the organisation, e.g. an oil company buying oil wells

(ii) forward integration refers to development into activities which are concerned with the organisation's outputs, e.g. an oil company buying filling stations

(iii) horizontal integration refers to development into activities which are competitive with, or directly complementary to, an organisation's present activities, e.g. an oil company buying another oil company with different interests.

Unrelated diversification is development beyond the present industry into products and/or markets which may bear no clear relationship to the present portfolio. An example of this in the past has been an organisation such as Hanson.

Diversification can be achieved by either internal or external means. Internal development uses existing resources of technical, marketing and managerial skills, while external development involves buying into new product-markets through licensing agreements, by joint ventures or by merger with or acquisition of another firm.

(c) The advantages of using the merger process to effect diversification are as follows:

(i) Acquisition and merger are the easiest way to grow rapidly. Organic growth needs careful stewardship over a number of years; in comparison the same growth can be achieved immediately by merger with an existing company.

(ii) The company merged with will have its own highly skilled employees already in place with experience of their market. This is much more efficient than having to recruit from outside or having to train existing employees into new skills areas.

(iii) There is a wide choice of possible targets to merge with, ranging in both geographical coverage and in business operations.

(iv) Diversification by merger can reduce the perceived risk of the company, since a wider range of markets and industries will be covered. This can have a positive effect on the share price.

(v) There are various financial accounting advantages associated with a merger. A company with static earnings can merge with a profitable company and report improved earnings. Sometimes it is possible for a company with a high P/E ratio to merge with a company with a low P/E ratio and impose its own higher P/E ratio on the whole of the new merged group. Finally there are advantages associated with accounting for a combination by using merger accounting, for example no need to set up an undistributable share premium account and no need to recognise goodwill arising.

The disadvantages of using the merger process to effect diversification are as follows:

(i) The merged company might have high costs with duplicated departments and lack of focus. Merger with an unprofitable company can only reduce profits in the short term.

(ii) The forecast benefits of a merger often do not arise in practice in the way that was forecast. In particular, the levels of synergy that were anticipated just do not occur.

(iii) Managers may be pleased with the bigger empires under their control and seek pay rises to match their new self-importance. There may therefore be some conflict of interest as managers push for more acquisitions and mergers while shareholders seek improvements in earnings per share and share price.

(d) In an economy with free capital markets, an individual investor can create his own diversified portfolio by buying shares in a number of different companies of his choice, rather than looking to the companies that he is investing in doing the diversification for him. There is considerable evidence that specialised focused companies in practice achieve better results than those with a ragbag of different interests, principally because the management in the focused company become specialists in their area of business and shareholders benefit from managers 'sticking to the knitting'.

In a diverse conglomerate, senior management attention is concentrated on whichever part of the business is having problems at any point in time, so the best is not squeezed out of the more successful parts. The trend in recent years is for conglomerates to unbundle themselves by demerging different interests in an attempt to avoid the conglomerate discount which reduces their share price. Companies such as Hanson hope that they can enhance shareholder value by splitting themselves up and that the sum of the parts will be greater than the whole.

In general therefore there is little validity in a company pursuing a policy of diversification in an economy which has free capital markets. Each company should stay focused and shareholders should protect themselves by creating diversified portfolios by holding shares in a number of different companies (or at least by holding shares in investment trusts or units in unit trusts).

70 OBJECTIVES

OB, at the start of its corporate existence

The development of OB is typical of many owner-managed enterprises. The success of the entity is entirely linked to the personality and drive of the founder. The management style of the founder is rarely based on a strategic outlook but on short-term opportunism based upon a series of good ideas, which have paid off rapidly. This type of small business culture is has an organisation structure, which could be modelled on Mintzberg's 'garden rake' in that there is one dominant personality supported by an infrastructure of a relatively few trusted subordinates. If organisational objectives were articulated they would focus on the need for profitability to generate the cash that would be utilised to reward the entrepreneur and pay off the persons who provided the start-up finance.

At the start of the life of the business, the founder would have probably deemed it sufficient to identify the roles and tasks of the various subordinates who would be expected to act as facilitators of the various business functions without any great autonomy of action. They would be expected to be satisfied by systems of financial reward which would recognise loyalty and industry. The organisational objectives would be short-termist in scope.

This 'free-wheeling' style of management will inevitably create problems as the business expands. The trusted subordinates are now managers who take risks and exercise judgement but are continually constrained by the highly personal management style of the founder. They are locked out of any true decision-making and, as the founder owns all the equity, they are probably locked out of any schemes to generate wealth in the long term.

As an expanding business entity OB will need to take a long-term view in establishing its organisational objectives.

Shareholder wealth. The founder may need to consider the possibility of parting with some of his equity in order to obtain the necessary funds for expansion. Specialist entities will provide both equity and loan capital to growing businesses. The drive to increase shareholder wealth must be underpinned by sound strategies to develop the business.

Market share increase. The entity must develop strategies to improve and consolidate its market position.

Product innovation. All growing organisations must seek to be innovative in developing new products and services.

Quality standards. Longevity depends on doing ordinary things excellently.

Social responsibility. The company cannot neglect the need for ethical business standards.

Managerial development. It is crucial to develop the skills and competences of human resources.

OB can monitor and control its progress by the following:

1 Identifying its corporate mission
2 Identifying objectives
3 Carrying out a SWOT analysis to appraise its business environment
4 Identifying the 'gaps' between objectives and achievable performance
5 Developing its strategies and action plans for the foreseeable future
6 Formulating a business plan which encompasses the above and defines the roles of the managers
7 Developing a culture which is less autocratic and based upon trust and responsibility
8 Implementing the business plan with regular reviews of progress
9 Identifying the necessary shifts in strategy in order to achieve objectives

71 DIVERSIFICATION

Key answer tips

As Part (a) of the question refers to the 'planning gap' it would be quite useful to include a diagram showing how the 'gap' might be filled. Note that since the question distinguishes between related and unrelated diversification then you should do likewise within your answer.

(a) **Gap analysis** involves the comparison of an entity's ultimate objective with the sum of projections and already planned projects, identifying how the consequent gap might be filled. The planning gap refers to the difference between the current objectives and the expected outcome from the current strategy and tactics. The diagram below from the CIMA *Official Terminology* shows how the gap can be filled.

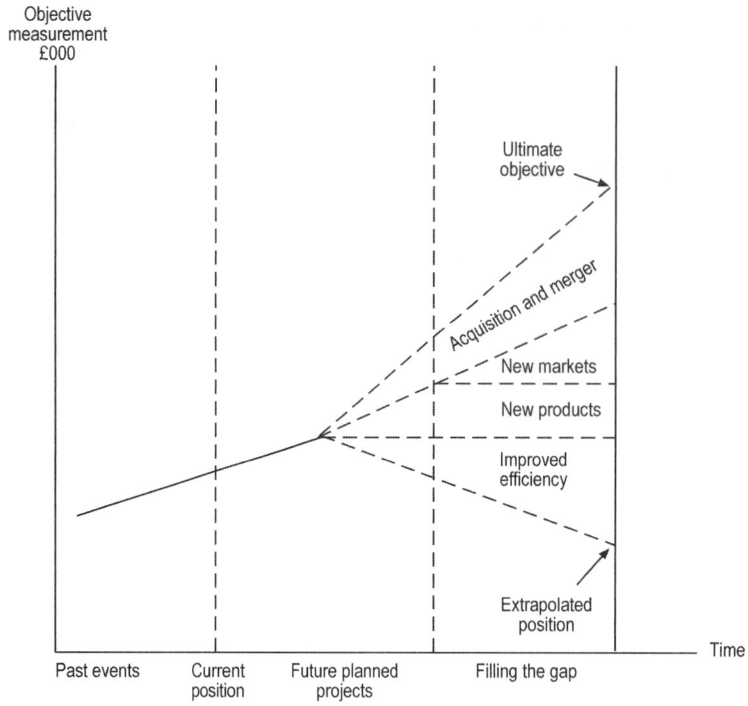

Improved efficiency is not something about which strategic decisions should be taken; such improvements should be constantly sought as part of the day-to-day running of the firm and are covered in the operations plan. The diagram therefore reveals the strategic possibilities available to fill a planning gap: new markets and/or new products.

These possibilities are normally displayed in **Ansoff's product/market growth matrix** as follows:

	Existing products	*New products*
Existing markets	Market penetration	Product development
New markets	Market development	Diversification

Diversification is a strategy that entails the deployment of a company's resources simultaneously into new products and new markets. If the current products and/or markets are in a declining stage of their life cycle, diversification will be an appropriate strategy to reinvigorate the organisation. However the lack of familiarity with the new environment is likely to increase the risk to which the company is exposed.

(b) Ansoff suggests three reasons why companies might choose to diversify their activities:

(i) **Objectives cannot be met without diversification**. If a gap analysis reveals the existence of a strategic planning gap that cannot be filled in other ways, diversification offers a route to rapid growth which offers the prospect of the gap being filled.

(ii) **The company is flush with cash**. If the return expected from diversification is higher than the return expected from other expansion strategies and management are comfortable with the risk, then diversification is an appropriate choice.

(iii) **Diversification offers high profit potential**. Even if the company's objectives could be met by staying within the current markets and products, a management may choose to diversify because it has identified high prospects of profits from such a path.

Whether diversification is an advantageous course of action therefore depends on the state of the market for existing products, and the prospects that can be identified in diversification opportunities. If the market for current products is highly competitive with nearly all the potential buyers already having been satisfied, sales of new products or to new markets may be the only possible way of increasing sales. Diversifying (i.e. *both* selling new products *and* entering new markets) has the potential of rapidly increasing sales.

Strategic advantage can be obtained by buying companies that own brands or leading edge technology or by acquiring competitors. Further advantage can be obtained by the economies of scale that may be available to the company simply by being bigger after having diversified. For example, access to new channels of distribution may be opened up, or overlapping service facilities may be stripped out.

In conclusion, diversification can improve the competitive strategic advantage of a company in a variety of ways. However there is risk associated with the strategy and competitive advantage is not automatic; it must be carefully managed after the diversification exercise has been agreed and implemented.

(c) It was stated in Part (a) that management's **lack of familiarity with the new environment** creates risk for the diversification strategy. Diversification can usefully be analysed according to whether the new activities are related or unrelated to existing activities.

Related diversification means that the expansion is made in the same industry as existing activities. This carries less risk than unrelated diversification, since management will have some feel for the new business area. Related diversification can be vertical (backwards or forwards) or horizontal (involving goods or services at a similar stage in production). Horizontal expansion would probably carry the least risk of all.

The argument could be made that unrelated diversification might in fact reduce risk, since with a spread of business activities it is likely that some businesses will do well while others do badly. However the lack of familiarity in the new environment presents a problem to the existing management.

This problem can be solved by diversifying through acquisition or merger rather than organically. Organic growth involves the existing management trying to expand the activities that it operates within its business. Growth by acquisition involves identifying a company already involved in the new business area and buying it, hopefully retaining the existing skilled and experienced workforce who can continue in the markets that they know best.

Thus there are many aspects to diversification as the chosen method of closing the planning gap; organic unrelated diversification is a high-risk expansion strategy while related diversification achieved by acquisition is less risky. For each possible diversification strategy that is identified as feasible, it is the responsibility of management to weigh up the risks and returns and select its strategy accordingly.

PROCESS INNOVATION AND RE-ENGINEERING

72 INVENTION AND INNOVATION

(a) It is difficult to distinguish between the two processes because they tend to be closely associated with each other. Both processes begin with the creativity and the generation of novel ideas. Invention is the creation of new and useful products and processes from a basic concept whereas innovation is the commercially successful application of an invention. The process of innovation includes the phases and stages that an idea needs to go through before it is commercially exploited and becomes an innovation. Product innovation applies to the products or services that the organisation produces or provides, whereas process innovation applies to the various business processes carried out in the organisation. Alvin **Toffler** argues that technical innovation has three main phases. The first phase is invention: someone has a creative idea. The second phase is exploitation: practical applications are developed. The third phase is diffusion; more people see the advantages of the new idea and apply it. This third phase then triggers more creative ideas.

(b) Invention is largely associated with **research and development** (R&D) departments but innovation involves people in every department. The job of the R&D department might involve:

- monitoring the scientific journals and new patent applications;
- developing new products or prolonging the lifespan of old products; as well as
- getting ahead of or catching up with the technology of the organisation's competitors

There are different types of innovation. **Incremental innovation** involves small changes built incrementally over time into a competitive advantage e.g. the various types of washing powder/liquids including biological, colour-safe and concentrated. Radical innovation is a step change, which represents a major departure from the established method. Examples of products in this category are Rolls Royce turbo fan engines and vertical take-off engines. Manufacturing techniques include the assembly line that was introduced by Ford to mass produce motor cars. By contrast, the introduction of robots into areas of car manufacture and steel works are a means of upgrading existing manufacturing techniques.

Innovation is the life-blood of a successful organisation and the management of innovation is central to this success. Strategic planning in some organisations results in targets being set for innovation, with successful achievements being rewarded through bonuses. New products and services can be developed following a major technical breakthrough in the field, or changes in society, or simply to copy existing products or services. None of this can happen without financial backing. Innovation means spending on R&D and market research and risking capital on new ideas. Certain managers can be made responsible for obtaining information about innovative ideas from outside and disseminating it throughout the organisation.

A successful company is one that is outward looking, has accepted the reality of constant change and the necessity to review its product-market policy continuously. It places emphasis on vigorous initiative, always looking to the future towards new markets, innovative products, better designs, new processes, improved quality and increased productivity. It has a management style and structure designed for innovation in which employees are stimulated to think and act innovatively, which recognises potential 'intrapreneurs' and ensures that everyone welcomes changes for the better. Management can encourage customers and employees to put forward ideas. The company might require people to work in cross-disciplinary teams with employees becoming more involved in the development of new products or processes, to move around and experiment with fresh ideas or to brainstorm various issues. It might adopt a 'suggestions box' for all interested parties to contribute to, with a reward scheme based on the best ideas per month/year.

Innovation demands a culture that focuses on the task, stimulates creativity, rewards ideas and supports individual and team abilities. Many companies, recognising the need, have embarked on ambitious cultural change programmes that have resulted in effective organisation arrangements facilitating new-product concept generation, evaluation and implementation.

It is widely accepted that **innovative organisations use all of the talents of their employees**. Getting the best from creative, inventive people means praising new ideas, encouraging them to explore off-beat possibilities, and giving them a high degree of autonomy. All companies can do more to encourage their employees to contribute to the creative processes. Declaring a culture of inventiveness and innovation will help to show employees that the company places emphasis on these aspects. Where appropriate, recruitment policy can be directed towards appointing people with the necessary skills for doing innovative work. Employees should be continually trained and kept up to date.

73 WOWR ORGANISATION

Key answer tips

For Part (a) a wide range of different systems and theories can be used (CSF and PI analysis; the value chain; SWOT; McFarlan; CBA) as long as they assess the priority for IT investment. Our answer below uses the framework proposed by Thomas Davenport in *Process Innovation: Reengineering Work Through Information Technology*, 1993, as in the official CIMA answer, since this seems most appropriate in the overall context of the question.

(a) Thomas Davenport, a leading writer on Process Innovation, suggests the following framework for assessing the priority for investment in competing IT systems:

- Identify processes that are suitable for innovation.
- Identify 'change levers' (enabling or transformation technologies).
- Develop 'process visions'.
- Understand and improve existing processes.
- Design and prototype new processes.

Processes that are suitable for innovation

Most of the basic transaction systems in the organisation have already been computerised, although it seems likely that the systems are nothing more than computerised versions of the previous manual system. It may be possible to establish closer links between the separate systems such as production, sales and finance. Production systems relate to books and magazines – in other words text and graphics – and these may well benefit from investment in newer technologies such as project management software and groupware for collaborative working.

Change levers

WOWR have made little investment in IT in recent years, during a time of great technological change, particularly in communications technology. It is likely that Internet-enabled systems, Enterprise Resource Planning systems and Customer Relationship Management systems could offer considerable benefits to a company such as WOWR. The company's products themselves (text and graphics) are perfect candidates for items that could be distributed on-line.

Process visions

This stage involves looking at processes as the means of achieving the company's mission. For instance WOWR may decide that, above all, it wishes to 'stick to the knitting' and not get involved in on-line publication. Nevertheless it is possible that its current products could be improved and better targeted and the company has a wealth of historical sales records that could be mined to identify hidden trends and other useful information.

Understand existing processes

This stage would look at the benefits and drawbacks of existing information flows and technologies. Any new process should not prevent the company from carrying out tasks that it can currently do, so long as those tasks add value. There may be some small steps that need to be taken before more radical process redesign is feasible, such as upgrading operating systems or cleansing of existing data stores.

Design and prototype new processes

This stage takes the change levers and uses them to alter the existing processes, for instance using ERP software to integrate production, sales and finance or creating subscription-based on-line versions of magazines.

(b) (i) **Process Innovation and Business Process Re-engineering**

Process Innovation (P1) and Business Process Re-engineering (BPR) are similar concepts that emerged in the early 1990s from the writings of various management gurus. BPR in particular has been interpreted in a wide variety of ways and was much criticised because in some interpretations it took no account of human issues.

- BPR is the fundamental re-thinking and rational re-design of the business processes to achieve dramatic improvements in critical contemporary measures of performance such as cost, quality, service and speed.
- PI emphasises the invention of entirely new processes, rather than tweaking existing ones. There is more emphasis on human resource management and the approach may involve rethinking the entire business and its mission rather than focusing on individual processes.

From this point of view PI is a more radical approach. It should be noted that there is no general agreement about the precise meanings of the terms or the difference between them.

(ii) **Why PI and BPR are important an organisation**

Changes in information and communications technology have come at an astonishing pace during the late 1990s and the early 2000s, and there is no sign of a slowdown. Each new development offers new opportunities to businesses and it is the businesses that embrace such change that are most likely to survive and thrive.

WOWR appears to be well-established in a mature industry, but its previous managers lacked the desire for change. From the limited information in the scenario it appears that the new management understand the importance of IT to the future of the business.

- At the very least WOWR need to invest to maintain its competitive position. If other publishers have amended their processes so that they can offer services such as on-line ordering, then WOWR will need to do the same.
- Preferably WOWR should attempt to gain competitive advantage. For example, innovation in products is a source of differentiation, which enables maintenance of this strategy: for example WOWR may be able to offer on-line supplements to its books and publications, adding value for purchaser and subscribers.
- However, innovation must be continuous because it is only a matter of time before competitors catch up with or improve upon another company's innovative ideas.

- Innovation in production processes might reduce production costs and hence support a cost-leadership strategy. Innovation in sales and marketing processes may lead to better decisions about which publications to target at which markets.
- Innovative organisations tend to attract and retain higher quality staff, who want to gain experience with the market leader and want the opportunity to contribute to the development of a forward-looking organisation. Or, from the opposite point of view, lack of change tends to demotivate staff, especially if they are aware that other companies have better systems and are able to produce higher quality products and give better service.

74 EXPERIENCE CURVE

Key answer tips

A relatively straightforward question, and remember the fundamental point that organisations that have experience are likely to possess a competitive advantage. You must relate your answer specifically to the life cycle concept.

The concept of the experience curve is well understood in manufacturing and service industries.

The simplest concept is that an organisation goes through a **learning process or learning curve**. It can be demonstrated that a manufacturing organisation can improve the quality of certain repetitive tasks so that the time for producing any given batch of output can be reduced, thus providing a considerable decrease in cost. The obvious advantage of lower cost with stable selling price generates value.

This phenomenon was extensively monitored in industries such as aircraft manufacture and is well evidenced in practice. This developed into the concept of being able to increase the scale of output without the increase in cost. The **concept of economies of scale** is particularly relevant in service organisations such as information technology services whereby output can be doubled or trebled without any great increase in marginal cost.

The third aspect of the experience curve phenomenon arises out of **the benefits of technology.** In manufacturing technology considerable cost advantages can be engineered by the development of advanced manufacturing methods which are relatively unaffected by the problems of irregular output levels. The falling cost of computer consumables and computer peripherals is an illustration of this point. Consider the reduction in selling prices of the diskette and the writable CD.

The **product life cycle concept** postulates that every product goes through various stages during a finite product life. These stages are start-up, growth, maturity and harvest and eventually, decline.

It can be observed that the experience curve phenomenon will enable management to make strategic plans so that **the maturity and harvest stage can be prolonged**. This is the period when contribution for the product is at its highest.

The interaction of the three factors that are inherent in the experience curve concept can have a significant effect on the ability to prolong the life cycle of products. In the pharmaceutical industry, the merger of Glaxo and Wellcome some years ago secured a global market advantage in the development and supply of the Zantac drug. The domination of the market effectively limited the ability of competitors to produce a substitute, which might be better than the Zantac drug. Their strategic alliance in effect prolonged the active life of the product.

The impact of the learning process in manufacturing can reduce product costs and give considerable competitive advantage to an organisation. The **process of continuous product improvement or value engineering** can lead to cheaper alternatives in terms of material cost and reductions in the time of the manufacturing cycle. This can be evidenced by the supply of cheap electronic devices like the pocket calculator, which is now so tightly value engineered so as to sell for a fraction of its original launch price in the 1970s.

Experience in the tastes of consumers has led to exploiting technology to extend product lives.

The change in the tastes of customers in the music and leisure business has been reflected in stable demand for the compact disc (CD) as opposed to the conventional vinyl disc. The improvements in technology will no doubt lead to the life cycle being extended so that it can compete with the digital video disc (DVD). Improvements in service provision are also affected by technological change to extend useful lives.

The experience phenomenon is implicit in the skills, attitudes and tasks of strategic management in developing the plans, ploys and positions of long-term growth and prosperity.

75 4D TEACHING HOSPITAL (MAY 06 EXAM)

Key answer tips

Part (a) is tricky because there are no universally accepted definitions of BPR and PI and some involve considerable overlap. If necessary the definition of PI could be invented!

In part (b) ensure that you explain and evaluate each benefit.

(a) (i) Business Process Re-engineering (BPR) is the fundamental re-thinking and rational re-design of existing business processes to achieve improvements in performance measures such as cost, quality, service and speed.

Process Innovation (PI) is the invention of entirely new processes.

The main differences between BPR and PI are as follows:

- BPR focuses on existing processes whereas PI emphasises the invention of new processes.
- There is a much greater emphasis on human resource management in PI. BPR has often been criticised for neglecting HR issues.
- PI may involve rethinking the entire business and its mission rather than focusing on individual processes as is the case with BPR.
- With BPR the role of IT is generally as an implementation tool, for example to improve the speed of information processing. With PI, IT is often a change trigger allowing the development of new processes due to technological advances.

  For example, improvements in the technology surrounding wireless LAN has allowed hospital consultants to refer to and update detailed patient records while doing ward rounds, completely changing the previous process of writing up notes later.

(ii) The new OTIS system could be viewed as an example of BPR on the grounds that:

- The new process is still one of linking students, lecturers and surgeons but on a larger scale. As such it is a development of an existing system.

However, it is more likely to be viewed as PI because:

- The inclusion of remote students to participate in the system could be argued to be an entirely new process.
- Developments in web technology have triggered the change.

On balance the new system should be viewed as PI.

(b) The benefits of OTIS are as follows:

To 4D

- The new system will improve 4D's already good reputation.This could be significant as it might result in greater success in raising funds and reduce the chance of closure if local government decides that it has too many hospitals.
- The new system will considerably reduce the training cost per student, freeing up funds for other areas.
- The new system could also allow 4D to raise additional funds by charging remote students to participate. This could be a significant injection into the hospital finances, facilitating further expansion of the teaching side.
- The extra possibilities that the new system presents could allow 4D to attract and keep the very best professors, lecturers and consultants. Given the existing excellence, this is unlikely to be a major benefit.

To society

- The improved training should mean that the level of expertise among surgeons will be higher, improving the likelihood of a healthy recovery of patients undertaking surgery. In the local community the standard of clinical excellence was already very high so the improvement will not be significant. However, the possibility of receiving high level training and supervision for surgeons in more remote locations could give a dramatic improvement in patient prognoses.
- The new system should also mean that surgeons can be trained more cheaply and efficiently. Given that some finance is likely to come from public sources, this should free up funds for other services (e.g. social care) to be provided. This benefit will be less significant due to the sums involved.

THE ROLE AND RESPONSIBILITIES OF DIRECTORS

76 MIELAIDE REMEDIES

Key answer tips

You will not have time to write down everything you know about corporate governance and the Combined Code, so it is important to concentrate on potential problems hinted at in the scenario, as in our answer.

Possibly relevant in this case is Richard Branson's flotation of Virgin in 1986 and then his repurchase of the company for £248 million in 1988, after only 20 months on the stock exchange. At the time he famously said "The delightful thing about not being a public company is that we don't have to worry about foolish analysts who say stupid things!"

REPORT

To: The Board, Mielaide Remedies

From: Consultant

Date:

Re: **Corporate governance implications of a listing on the London Stock Exchange**

Background

Fiduciary responsibilities

The term fiduciary means 'relating to, or founded upon, a trust or confidence'. In law a fiduciary relationship exists where a person (an individual or organisation) has an obligation to act on behalf of another person's interests in matters that affect the other person. Company directors are considered to hold a fiduciary position because they make contracts as agents of a company and they have control of its property.

In effect this means that the directors are answerable to the shareholders.

A fiduciary is obliged to act in the shareholders' best interests with total disregard for any personal interests. To date for Mielaide this may not have caused any problems since the chairman and managing director has been answerable only to members of his own family and ordinarily the interests of all those involved are likely to be similar.

Once a substantial proportion of the shares are listed many of the shareholders will be individuals and institutions and their interests may be very different from those of the family. The directors will now need to consider other interests and be able to show that they are acting responsibly.

Corporate governance

As a result of a number of high-profile corporate scandals and collapses it is now very widely accepted that organisations need systems and processes for ensuring proper accountability, probity and openness in the conduct of their business: this is what corporate governance means.

In the UK various sets of guidance as to how to do this were issued in the 1990s culminating in the Combined Code on Corporate Governance.

The Combined Code

The Combined Code on Corporate Governance is not actually mandatory for listed companies, but it is mandatory in effect because, as a condition of a listing, companies are required to explain in their financial statements the extent to which they have or have not complied with the code. Non-compliance without very good reason is likely to have an adverse impact on the share price, and that is clearly contrary to the interests of shareholders.

Points in the provisions of the Code that are of particular relevance to Mielaide Remedies in its current circumstances are as follows:

- *Board leadership and company leadership*

  Every company should be headed by an effective board, which is collectively responsible for the success of the company. However, the Combined Code requires that there should be a clear division of responsibilities at the head of the company between the running of the board and the executive responsibility for the running of the company's business (i.e. chairman and chief executive). No one individual should have unfettered powers of decision.

This means that Ian Candy is going to have to relinquish one or other of the positions of chairman and managing director.

- *Executive and non-executive directors*

  The Combined Code says that the board should include a balance of executive and non-executive directors (and in particular independent non-executive directors) such that no individual or small group of individuals can dominate the board's decision taking.

  At present Mielaide Remedies has no non-executive directors. The shareholding family members who currently attend board meetings can probably not be considered. It may be that some of them (for example Ian Candy's parents, if it is an old family business) have valuable experience, but they would not fit the definition of 'independence' given by the Combined Code. So other, properly independent non-executives would need to be sought elsewhere, perhaps using one of the specialist recruitment services that exist for this purpose.

  Depending on the size of Mielaide Remedies, the Combined Code recommends that from one third to a half of the board should be non-executive directors. This means that between three and five persons will need to be found.

- *Remuneration*

  The Combined Code says that a significant proportion of executive directors' remuneration should be structured so as to link rewards to corporate and individual performance. In particular it states that no director should be involved in deciding his or her own remuneration.

  It is unlikely that such stringent rules apply at present. A rewards scheme will need to be devised and procedures for deciding on remuneration will need to be drawn up.

- *Dialogue with institutional shareholders*

  The Combined Code says that there should be a dialogue with shareholders based on the mutual understanding of objectives. The board as a whole has responsibility for ensuring that a satisfactory dialogue with shareholders takes place.

  The significance of this change for the board of Mielaide Remedies should not be underestimated. They are used to dealing with shareholders who are well-known to them personally, or even related. Dealing with the City – stockbrokers, analysts and the like – is a very different matter. It requires experience and strong interpersonal skills, and it may be very difficult at first for executives to accept 'interference' from strangers who appear to know little about the business.

  This is a case in point of the usefulness of non-executive directors to strengthen the board – in this case a non-executive with a good track record of communicating with shareholders.

This outline will hopefully give you an initial impression of the consequences of a listing for board members. There are further provisions in the Combined Code regarding matters such as internal controls and audit committees, and I will happily provide further advice when I have the appropriate information regarding your company.

Signed

Management Consultant

77 CONFLICT

Pharmaceutical companies are commercial organisations, many with shares traded on the world's stock markets, and it is reasonable to assume that the long-term objective of these companies should be to increase shareholder wealth. Over the long-term, the aim would be to maximise shareholder wealth. Wealth is created through the provision of returns to shareholders, in the form of dividend payments, profit and dividend growth and increases in the share price. In the case of a pharmaceutical company, profitability comes from the sale of drugs to cure known diseases and ailments.

The hypothesis in the question is that developments in scientific research, particularly in the field of genetics, might eventually lead to a situation where the causes of disease can be removed, so that diseases are eliminated and the need for drugs will disappear. If the demand for drugs falls or even disappears, profits, dividends and shareholder wealth will all diminish.

In my view, the hypothesis as stated is false. If we accept that pharmaceutical companies seek to maximise the wealth of shareholders over the long term, this objective has always been within certain limitations or reservations. A company would not contemplate, for example, reintroducing a new disease in order to create new demand. For example, a company would not encourage the revival of bubonic plague simply in order to sell more drugs for dealing with it. There is a general acceptance that pharmaceutical companies operate within an environment in which the objective is to develop remedies for perceived illnesses and conditions. It could be argued that even if major advances are made in genetics, and even if many known diseases and ailments are eliminated, other conditions and ailments will take their place, for which new remedies will be needed. The market place is never static, and profits will be made from developments in genetics research.

It could also be argued that in a competitive environment, market forces will operate, whereby resources will always flow to the places they can be used most profitably. If pharmaceutical companies fail to embrace genetic research, other companies will take their place as long as they can see opportunities for good profits and returns. Pharmaceutical companies cannot attempt to 'stop the clock' or do more than slow the pace of change.

The pharmaceuticals industry faces a number of 'ethical dilemmas', and I would argue that there are other issues of more pressing concern than genetics research. In particular, there is the problem of the economic gulf between the richer countries and countries of the developing world. Drug research and development is expensive, and companies need to recover the costs of research and development through the prices they charge. Customers in Western economies can generally afford to pay the prices demanded. Potential users in a poorer country cannot. If pharmaceuticals sell their drugs to developing countries at a low price, the low price products will quite possibly be diverted back to the wealthier markets. Companies would not want this to happen, and are therefore reluctant to sell at low prices to governments of poorer countries. As a result of this, many individuals in poorer countries do not get access to drugs that might save their lives.

In practice, pharmaceutical companies, faced with a conflict between protecting their profits and providing help to poorer countries, try to negotiate agreements and arrangements with governments. The system is by no means perfect, but companies sometimes try to resolve the conflicts they face.

In summary, I would argue that the conflict described in the question is much less significant that it might appear. Pharmaceutical companies, rightly, seek to develop products that cure diseases. It is also in their commercial interests to develop techniques that prevent diseases and harmful physical conditions. In doing so, new marketing opportunities will inevitably open up. Indeed, it can be argued that in a world where governments have developed – and continue to develop – weapons for biological warfare, the market for drugs and other treatments will remain strong.

MEASURING PERFORMANCE

78 SCANDALOUS MEASURES

Key answer tips

Students are advised to apply the SMART and PRIME acronyms when answering Part (a). Part (b) is straightforward and requires a memory dump of the balanced scorecard key elements before evaluating its usefulness.

(a) **Discussion of the functions that organisational objectives should fulfil strategically**

The acronym SMART could be used as this shows how objectives aid the business in following its business strategy, as follows:

Specific

Measurable

Achievable

Realistic

Time-related

The acronym PRIME will prove useful in answering this section, as this highlights five main functions that objectives perform in the strategic functioning of an organisation.

Planning – Objectives must be put into tangible terms, meaning that the mission is translated into actionable terms. Providing the objectives are both formal and well explained then they should be capable of measurement.

Responsibility – In order to achieve objectives tasks should be assigned to individuals, divisions, business units and functional areas. This will mean that these groups know exactly what is expected of them. In this way strategic objectives are converted into operational objectives, offering the opportunity for increased visibility of accountability and control.

Integration – Objectives communicate business priorities to managers. Clear objectives will mean that goal congruence is achieved.

Motivation – By letting managers participate in the objective setting process and also by making sure the objectives are consistent and worthwhile.

Evaluation – Objectives act as a measure of success of a business strategy. This is because shareholders and other stakeholder groups can look at performance reports and form an opinion about whether the objectives are aiding the achievement of business strategy, by ensuring they are measured, corrected and controlled.

The main disadvantages of using only profit-related performance measures

Often there is an emphasis on the profit figure for private companies; this should mean that profit-based measures are the most useful measures of company performance. An example of this would be when a shareholder reads the annual reports of a plc. However, profit-based measures should only be used alongside other measures, as the use of these measures to run a business on their own has a number of disadvantages, as follows:

- They are only a snapshot of a single point in time; as such they ignore trends and other factors that may be crucial for the business to succeed.

- Profit is an accounting measure, which can result in a different decision being made than if an economic approach were used. For example in the valuation of intangibles.
- Profit is open to manipulation by creative accounting, and can also be manipulated, for example in the case of profit-related bonuses.
- Profit does not really tie in very well with strategic thinking; longer term strategic thinking should use both financial and non-financial performance measures.
- They encourage short-term thinking, for example the annual profit figure in the financial reports. For example in training the best policy long-term would be investment but short term it costs money so would lower the profit figure.
- The profit measure does not consider the cash position of a business; there have been many instances where profitable companies have failed as a result of not having adequate liquidity.
- Profit-based measures cannot be used in all businesses, for example non-profit making companies.
- To measure the performance of products/services measures like net profit are used; however, these ignore the capital assets used in the production of the good/service. This means that the net assets are ignored. These should be considered, as there could be opportunity costs if the assets are not been managed properly or could be used better elsewhere. Also they represent cash if they were sold, especially in situations where cash is in short supply.
- Overall objectives will not be aligned. For example, a manager may pursue an increase in profit at the expense of other divisions within the organisation.
- Not all functions within an organisation are financial, for example marketing and HR. Functions such as these are often cost not profit centres, and so the profit measure is of little value to these departments.
- Shareholders are not the only stakeholders in an organisation. These other stakeholders may have little or no use for the profit measures as a measurement of performance.
- A conflict of objectives can occur as the short-term views of shareholders will sometimes conflict with the long-term plans for the company.

(b) **Brief description of the balanced scorecard approach**

The balanced scorecard approach developed by Kaplan and Norton (1992, 1996) has four categories of measurement, as follows:

1 Financial performance

2 Customer perspective

3 Internal business processes

4 Learning and growth.

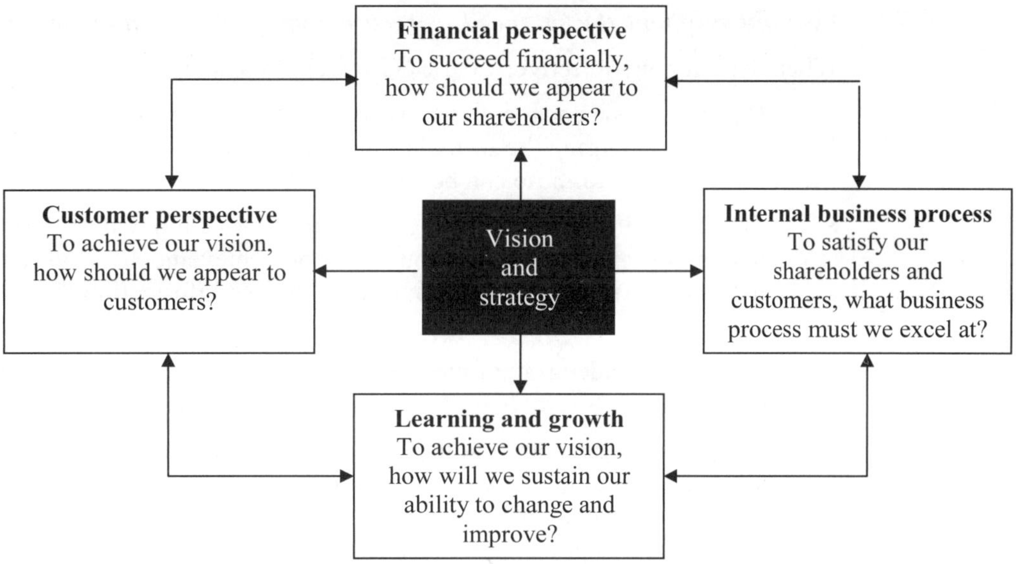

The balanced scorecard gives an outline to follow and is not intended to be followed exactly; instead prioritisation can be given to additional areas such as environmental and ethical concerns.

Evaluation of how the balanced scorecard meets stakeholder needs

Stakeholders could include shareholders, other investors, management, employees, suppliers and customers. In addition there are many other parties that could be considered as stakeholders.

Companies will have a large number of different types of stakeholder, and one of the best ways to ensure that company performance is aligned to the needs of all of these is to use the balanced scorecard approach. Instead of trying to simply prioritise the most important stakeholders, this approach looks at other non-financial performance measures in addition to financial measures.

- The balanced scorecard (BSC) encourages communication between stakeholder groups, as it provides a means for individuals, divisions and groups to get involved in the development of activity measures.
- The BSC gives owners more control through the use of performance targets, which will include both qualitative and quantitative measures, so supporting other performance measures present within the business. This means that through feedback behaviours can be modified in a positive way.
- The BSC acts as a mechanism of converting stakeholder expectations into performance targets, for example converting objectives into measures.
- As the BSC encourages the development of measures relating to corporate goals, this means that communication of corporate strategy occurs both within the company and to external stakeholders.
- When a company uses the BSC it produces something unique to its business. Reflecting the needs of its particular stakeholders.
- The BSC encourages stakeholders to focus on the strategy of the organisation; this means that they are in a position to make judgements on the effectiveness of this strategy. So meaning that stakeholders can form an opinion on the effectiveness of the firm, providing the results are reported externally.

Evaluation of how the balanced scorecard helps in determining objectives

When determining objectives the BSC can help in a number of ways:

- It encourages managers to choose relevant measures that tie into their objectives. During the formulation stage many ideas will be made and the most relevant of these can be selected.
- The BSC will provide management with information, which they can use to review objectives, policy formulation and achievements. If used properly it will provide users with objective and unbiased information that can be used to address all relevant areas of performance.
- It forces consideration of the question: What does our strategy mean in practice?
- It means that financial and non-financial objectives can be considered at the same time, as although the non-financial objectives are important in the short term, the financial measures should always be considered, in order to keep stakeholders happy in the long and the short term.
- It encourages decision-makers to think closely about many different areas of the organisation. These could be financial or non-financial, internal and external and short/medium and long term.
- It encourages the consideration of whether the organisational objectives are relevant, as it highlights factors that are crucial for the long-term success of the organisation.
- It can highlight conflicts between stakeholder groups, and aids in resolving these differences.
- It encourages an holistic view, by ensuring all objectives and their measures are considered together. This will highlight areas that conflict, for example investment in training will have a short-term negative effect on cash but a positive effect in the long term. The BSC will mean these conflicts are highlighted and the correct course of action embarked upon.

79 MULTINATIONAL AND LOCAL AUTHORITY

(a) The objectives of any organisation should relate to its mission. A **mission statement** is frequently formally stated, but this is not always the case. Sometimes this mission statement is informal i.e. it is not set out in unequivocal terms but is widely known and understood. The organisation's mission encapsulates the 'raison d'être' of the organisation and should focus on the demands of the principal stakeholders. Following from this the objectives of the organisation can then be stated within the framework of the rational planning model.

Within the MNC the **main stakeholder group** would be the shareholders whereas within the local administrative authority the main stakeholder group would probably be the local community.

It might well be that central government prescribes **objectives** for the local administrative authority, permitting some degree of freedom.

In order to determine in exactly what the strategic targets should be, those responsible for the local administrative authority must make a detailed assessment of the needs of the local community. Thus there exists the need to liaise with a number of other organisations with a local presence. Whatever strategic targets are set they will be set with the over-riding need to satisfy the objective that economic, efficient and effective services are provided by the local administrative authority. The targets should be set in a manner that enables performance measures to be made as to the extent to which the three Es have been attained.

It is quite conceivable that the needs of the local population will vary between different areas within the overall boundaries of the authority. Statistical information should be used in order to assess the actual level of service provision against the perceived level of need; for example, in assessing whether the provision of local housing in a particular location met the demand for such accommodation. This will assist in the setting of future objectives. Perhaps it may be necessary for housing to be established as the primary objective because there is a significant under-provision of locally administered housing. If this were to be the case then it is probable that other services would be affected.

By way of contrast, an MNC is likely to find its objectives much easier to establish. The shareholders are the major stakeholder group in the business. The primary objective of an MNC will be to maximise its long-term wealth and increase the value attached to its shareholding. It is probable that the MNC has secondary objectives relating to issues such as social responsibility, ethical trading practices and the quality of goods and services. These are usually set with the attainment of the primary objective, i.e. creation of long-term wealth for its shareholders in mind.

(b) The **measurement of performance levels** achieved by an organisation must relate to the nature of the objective that has been agreed. Objectives should be capable of being measured, and thus one that is non-specific in nature is likely to prove problematic as regards its measurement. Consequently, the extent of its attainment is difficult to quantify with any degree of exactitude. It is probable that the local administrative authority will establish targets, thereby enabling measurement of the extent to which objectives have been achieved. Carefully chosen performance indicators will be monitored. For example, with reference to locally administered housing, then appropriate performance indicators would be the number of residents waiting for accommodation and the average waiting time to be housed. In the event that a reduction were to occur in the number of residents awaiting housing due to the increased provision by the authority, this would indicate that the objective of effective service provision was being achieved with regard to housing in the area.

It is also possible for performance measurement to be made utilising the **'balanced scorecard'** approach. This would be applied in respect of the financial perspective, internal business processes, learning and growth and customer perspective. In order to determine how economically the local administrative authority is providing its services, it should not only compare its results with those of previous years, but also make detailed comparisons with the results of other authorities. The authority may review its business processes for the provision of various services and state how it has made changes to these processes as a consequence of learning from experience. The conduct of customer surveys will enable the measurement of the satisfaction of local residents to be measured.

As part of the **objective setting process**, it is appropriate for the representatives of the authority to determine how objectives will be measured. The appropriateness of performance measures will need to be reviewed in order to take into account the changing nature of the service provision in respect of the dynamic business environment.

The local administrative authority should give consideration to inviting members from within the local community to contribute to the measurement of its performance. For instance the local press, charity groups and other local interest groups would invariably seek a role in measuring the performance levels achieved by the authority. It would be much more positive for them to work in conjunction with the authority towards the attainment of agreed objectives as opposed to adoption of a more combative posture.

The MNC will probably have significantly lower levels of stakeholder participation in the measurement of its primary objective. Objectives defined in terms of profitability will be set within a given timeframe. The MNC will report on the levels of its earnings and the impact upon shareholder value. The financial markets will primarily determine the extent to which the MNC is successful in achieving its objectives. In contrast, the view of the local community will be the principal determinant as to whether the objectives of the local administrative authority have been attained.

Local vested interests will inevitably be visible within a local community, whereas the shareholders of the MNC will not have interests of such a nature. The shareholders will comprise a group with disparate interests. The MNC will therefore be subject to market pressures. The market will view the worldwide activities of the MNC, and the prevailing share price of the MNC will reflect the attitude of the market to those activities.

The 'balanced scorecard' approach could be used by the MNC in order to measure its overall performance. The principal aim of this approach is the quantification of how much shareholder value has been added. In essence, the market determines this value.

80 PUBLICLY FUNDED DEPARTMENT

Key answer tips

The scenario of this question relates to a publicly funded service, which has reduced its activity levels to meet more demanding budget constraints. Whilst this has been successfully achieved without making any staff cuts, the service is criticised for its inefficiency and lack of effectiveness. A consideration of the '3 Es' in discussing how the level of service can be improved, would be appropriate.

The advisory service has been criticised with reference to last year for overspending its budget, being inefficient as regards its methods of delivery, and wastage of resources that had been allocated to it. Each of these constitutes a severe criticism of the manager of the health advisory service and therefore it is imperative that changes are implemented if the service is to continue.

It is essential that the whole method of operation is re-examined. This will, of necessity, entail a review of its **economy, efficiency and effectiveness**. In order to determine a revised strategy, the nature of the costs of the organisation must be analysed. Since approximately **80% of expenditure is comprised of staff costs**, this aspect of the problem must be addressed as soon as possible. It seems obvious that the manager has 'protected the staffing levels' in order to avoid problems that might otherwise arise with the staff employed at the advisory service.

It is immediately apparent that major cost savings can only be achieved by tackling the area in which most of the resources are used. It appears that the manager is ineffective and not addressing the fundamental problems that arise as a direct consequence of the high staff costs borne by the organisation.

In order to address the problems being faced it is necessary that the **overall aims and objectives** of the advisory service are established. The expectations of the administrative authority as regards the publicly funded department need to be clearly understood by each respective party. It is vital that the aims and objectives of the managers of the advisory service are aligned with those of the authority. The managers need to ensure that the views of the stakeholders are understood and incorporated insofar as is practicable into the strategic planning process. Managers must also take steps to ensure that any performance indicators are appropriate to the advisory service. These will need to be reviewed periodically to ensure that they remain appropriate indicators of the performance of the advisory service.

Critical to the successful solution to the problems that have been experienced is the fundamental **need for a strategic plan** which is focused and co-ordinated on the attainment of the goals of health advisory service and the local administrative authority. There is a clear need to review present levels of the 'three Es', i.e. economy, efficiency and effectiveness. In order to establish the overall goals and the alternative courses of action that could be implemented at varying levels of funding, a zero-based budgeting exercise could be undertaken.

It is important that the **economy** of the operation is determined, to ensure that costs are under control. This will entail an assessment as to whether the organisation is currently using the minimum resources necessary in order to provide the present level of services. This will probably require comparisons to be made of costs with similar organisations in other regions; however, one must be careful to allow for regional variations which can and will inevitably exist. Another problem which can hamper comparisons lies in the fact that output in service organisations is extremely difficult to measure. The provision of advice is common to organisations such as the health advisory service but the time and resources needed per appointment can and will often vary considerably, and thus a performance measure such as the number of consultations may be inappropriate as the definitive measure of output.

The **efficiency** of the advisory service unit must also be measured and this will involve consideration as to whether the resources at the disposal of the advisory service are being used in an appropriate manner. The relationship between the inputs required to achieve the outputs of the advisory service unit will need to be reviewed and this too is a very subjective exercise, as the output of an advisory service cannot be measured in precise terms. In essence it is attempting to assess the impact of the advice provided by the health advisory service and this will invariably prove to be a difficult task. However, notwithstanding the difficulties involved, it is essential that output be assessed in relation to input.

Lastly, the **effectiveness** of the organisation requires consideration. The review must establish that outcomes are satisfying the objectives of the organisation. Much will depend on the very nature of the objectives that are identified at the beginning and this will impact upon the extent to which the organisation is considered to be meeting its objectives. Again, this will prove to be a difficult task as the quantification of objectives may well be problematic.

Only when these matters have been subject to detailed review and consideration will it be possible to review the alternative strategies that could be adopted. The potential effect of each alternate strategy will have to be assessed in terms of both the advisory service and the public who are the potential beneficiaries of the advice that is available from the advisory service.

It would be beneficial if managers were to undertake a benchmarking exercise in order to facilitate a comparison of the levels of costs and benefits with the inputs and outputs of providers of similar services to the public. This would enable the efficiency of the advisory service to be reviewed and necessary actions taken in order to meet the expectations of all stakeholders.

81 ROYAL BOTANICAL GARDENS (PILOT PAPER)

Requirement (a)

Board briefing

The concept of the balanced scorecard was introduced by Kaplan & Norton in the early Nineties to recognise what they considered to be two primary deficiencies in the implementation phase of many corporate plans.

First, they recognised that, although many organisations measure performance ratios these are primarily focused on historical figures and may have little to do with future success. Although such ratios are important they do not address important aspects of future strategy, particularly those concerned with the satisfaction of customers and their loyalty, organisational learning and the commitment of employees.

Additionally, they believed that, although strategic initiatives were formulated, these often had little impact on organisational behaviour or performance since they were not translated into measures which management and staff could understand and use.

Moving away from purely financial measures they claimed that what really mattered was the strategy implementation process and described three processes:

1 management – how the leader runs the organisation, how decisions are made and implemented

2 business – how products are designed, orders fulfilled, customer satisfaction achieved, for example

3 work – how work is operationalised, purchased, stored, and manufactured.

The balanced scorecard was developed to address any deficiencies in these areas and encompasses four key principles:

1 translating the vision through clarifying and gaining consensus

2 communicating and linking by setting goals and establishing rewards for success

3 business planning to align objectives, allocate resources and establish milestones

4 feedback and learning to review the subsequent performance against the plan.

They recognised that there should be, on every scorecard, four perspectives:

1 Financial perspective – 'To succeed financially, how should we appear to our shareholders?'

2 Customer perspective – 'To achieve our vision, how should we appear to our customers?'

3 Internal perspective – 'To satisfy our shareholders and customers, what business processes must we excel at?'

4 Future – the innovation and learning perspective. 'To achieve our vision, how will we sustain our ability to change and improve?'

For each perspective, a number of objectives, appropriate measures and target levels of performance together with initiatives for their achievement, would be defined. Thus the measures chosen under each perspective would reflect the strategic imperatives under which the organisation operates at the time.

Although the balanced scorecard was originally developed for commercial organisations, over the last few years it has found increasing use in the not-for-profit sector, where the same perspectives are equally important, but measured in a different way.

The Royal Botanical Gardens would benefit from the introduction of a Balanced Scorecard by:

- Placing the whole organisation in a learning process, aligning everyone to strategy in a single framework. The balanced scorecard has potential to improve itself over time by testing cause – effect hypotheses, refinement of the metrics selected, the measurement processes employed, resource allocation and identification of suitable initiatives.
- Encouraging more rational budgeting in a world of rapid change where resource allocations are based on performance and systematic, fact-based management replaces intuition.
- Encouraging and facilitating the anticipation of future outcomes and their impact on the organisation.
- Raising the visibility of what is happening, prioritising what most needs to be changed and helping to identify best practices.

In addition to the internal, managerial, benefits that the balanced scorecard can bring to the organisation it has the potential to demonstrate to external stakeholders that their mandates and objectives are being met. In this particular case, where the Government will need to be convinced to maintain, or even increase, the grant in aid, the measures incorporated can demonstrate that objectives over and above value for money are being achieved. It would make it easier for the Garden's negotiators to demonstrate the achievements in terms of assistance to education, industry, tourism and national prestige.

However, it must be recognised that it requires sustained effort to implement fully and requires a high level of organisational commitment. Its introduction may create fear and uncertainty since it raises both visibility and accountability. As with all other performance measurement techniques it will not solve problems – only strategy and initiatives and their successful implementation can do that.

Requirement (b)

It is important that the balanced scorecard is developed by a team of individuals and the commitment of the senior management is obtained. The team should be cross-organisational and contain representatives of all functional groups within the Gardens.

The main tasks of the teams are as follows:

- identify strategic themes
- define perspectives and desired outcomes
- create a strategy map
- define performance measures and targets
- develop strategic initiatives to achieve targets.

Once the team has been established the mission statement should be analysed to identify the strategic themes that are encompassed by the statement. This will provide a more specific focus for planning.

For instance the following themes, among others, might be distilled from the mission statement:

- knowledge and understanding through research
- knowledge and understanding through display
- conservation by living and preserved collections
- belonging to the Nation.

The next task will be to define the perspectives – the diverse ways of looking at the organisation from the perspective of different stakeholders. Also to define the meaning of mission success for each perspective and strategic theme. The different stakeholders for The Royal Botanical Gardens are many and would include, for example:

1 Financial perspective – government and research foundations that fund some of the work

2 Customer perspective – universities who use the facilities

3 Internal perspective – botanists using the facilities for research

4 Future – the innovation and learning perspective – educationalists attached to the Gardens.

Within the strategic theme of knowledge and understanding through research, these perspectives might lead to the following desired outcomes:

1 Financial perspective – government funders would look for value for money in the collection of novel plants and materials and the production of research papers.

2 Customer perspective – universities who deal with the Gardens would look for seamless access to any plants and materials they required in a cost-effective way.

3 Internal perspective – the botanists who work within the Gardens would look for support in their research so that they can work productively and advance the boundaries of science.

4 Future – the innovation and learning perspective – the educationalists might wish to raise the profile of the facilities and attract people to this area of study and would look to find innovative ways to bring people in.

For each strategic theme, the team would need to develop a chain of causes and effects that would be expected to lead to the desired outcomes. Each of these chains would be mapped onto a strategy map. Systems dynamics techniques would help in this area.

For instance considering the provision of samples to Universities from a future perspective:

This would mean enhancing information management, improving the employee climate and changing the skills gap. The botanists who work in the Gardens might see themselves in competition with the Universities. A co-operative approach would improve relationships, while seeking citation or acknowledgement in any research published. From the internal perspective looking for process efficiencies in picking and despatch would lead to more cost effective operations satisfying the financial perspective, while the enhanced service levels would, from the customer perspective, make them more likely to acknowledge assistance in research publications.

The definition of performance measures and targets would be achieved by answering the question 'How will we know if this theme/desired outcome is being achieved?' and deciding how each goal should be measured for example surveys or other means of data collection. If available, baseline data should be examined to set schedules and targets for improvement.

For instance, measures for the theme/outcome of provision of samples to Universities might include:

- financial – cost per sample provided, revenue generated from advice and consultancy
- customer – satisfaction surveys, amount of repeat business
- internal – citations in published research, published research
- future – new universities seeking samples; reduction in number of unsatisfied requests.

BUSINESS UNIT PERFORMANCE

82 TRANSFER PRICES

Key answer tips

Part (a) of this question requires a consideration of the reasons for having transfer prices determined centrally. In Part (b) you should draw a distinction between the tax avoidance (legal) and tax evasion (illegal) as a key issue in the ethical impact of transfer pricing.

(a) Many organisations are structured in semi-autonomous units, such as divisions, each one the responsibility of a divisional manager. To exercise control over divisions central management needs to be able to measure divisional performance. One problem that arises in this context is that of trading between divisions.

Where a division sells its output to external customers it is easy to measure the revenue earned. However, when a division transfers part or all of its output to another division within the organisation the problem is to determine the prices at which transfers are to be recorded. This is an important motivational factor for divisional managers and also helps the top management to ensure that decisions on output levels are made so as to benefit the organisation as a whole.

A variety of approaches to this problem is evident in practice. That adopted by P plc is for central management to decide unilaterally on transfer prices, their criterion being the minimisation of tax liabilities. There are several benefits to this approach:

(i) As the question states, 'the global position can be monitored effectively only from Head Office'. It is likely that central management are indeed in the best position to set prices so as to minimise tax.

(ii) Other fiscal barriers can also be negotiated most effectively from Head Office. For example, import duties can be minimised if the value of imports is set as low as possible. Similarly, this may be the most effective way to circumvent policies adopted by many countries to reduce the level of funds leaving the country.

(iii) The Head Office management is also best placed to calculate the transfer pricing policy which motivates divisional managers to produce at profit-maximising output levels.

(b) There is an important distinction between tax avoidance and tax evasion:

(i) **Tax avoidance** is the minimisation of tax liabilities by making intelligent, and legal, use of all features of a country's tax legislation. This is an accepted part of tax management, and shareholders have a right to assume that all legitimate tax avoidance is indeed carried out by company management.

(ii) **Tax evasion** is illegal – it involves bypassing or contravening legal regulations.

To the extent that P's management are engaged in tax avoidance it is difficult to criticise them. They have a responsibility to maximise returns to their shareholders by all legal and ethical means.

However, it is difficult to follow policies of this kind without overstepping the legal boundaries. If P plc falls into this trap, the short-term and long-term consequences could be very serious.

In the short term they could incur fines or other punishments levied by foreign governments.

In the long term they damage their reputation and endanger further dealings in the countries concerned.

Quite apart from the strict legal position, P plc must consider its ethical and social responsibilities. A growing weight of public opinion is hostile to 'anti-social' behaviour by large corporations. The concept of corporations acting as 'good citizens' has gained ground. P's policies hardly fit into this mould and the long-term damage caused by adverse publicity could be serious.

83 DIVISIONAL ACTIONS

Key answer tips

This question deals with the possibility of management manipulating financial performance measures. To ensure a focused answer (and economic use of time) consider the three suggestions under the four headings in the question. Group management action is required to ensure such proposals being implemented prior to forthcoming bonus calculations.

Each of the divisions' actions can be discussed as follows:

Division A

In financial accounting terms, the reduction in discretionary expenditure will lead to higher reported divisional profits than would have been the case if the original planned expenditure had taken place. Discretionary expenditure should be charged against profits as it is incurred. No provisions or accrual needs to be set up at the year end because the division is not compelled to make the expenditure.

There is some question as to whether the cut in training costs and repainting costs should be separately disclosed in the financial accounts in the overriding objective of giving a true and fair view. This depends on the materiality of the amounts involved, but is unlikely in the context of the group as a whole.

The ethical implications are more serious. The managers of Division A have deliberately manipulated the results in order to achieve the budget and be paid their bonuses. Their duty as managers is to serve the organisation, but they have served their own interests. Perhaps the two decisions can be distinguished from each other. The repainting of the premises is not important to the group; the timing of repainting is just the sort of matter than the group management should be happy to devolve to divisional management. The lack of training is more serious. It will probably lead to higher costs next year which the group managers would not be happy about.

Division B

In financial accounting terms, the decision to defer payment to the consultants should make no difference to the division's reported profits. If work has been carried out but not yet paid for at the balance sheet date, the division must set up an accrual for the amounts due. This will be charged against profits. So this idea should have no effect on the divisional managers' bonus payable.

The only way that the idea would increase reported profits would be if the division abandoned the accruals concept and tried to defer the charging of the expense until the consultants were paid. This would be contrary to established accounting practices, and would attract criticism from the auditors if the amounts were sufficiently material.

If the divisional managers were familiar with accounting practices, but decided not to accrue for the payments in order to be paid their bonuses, an ethical question arises. These managers have shown themselves to act unethically, and the group managers should warn the divisional managers about their conduct.

If no accruals were made this year, then next year's profits would be lower when the total cost of the contract has to be charged against profits. To avoid this kind of shock, and in the interests of giving a true and fair view, an accrual for the work carried out at the balance sheet date should be set up.

Division C

In financial accounting terms, the point of sale is the point when the purchaser starts to take responsibility for the risks and rewards of the goods. This is usually when the purchaser accepts delivery of the goods. So, by delivering goods which are accepted before the balance sheet date, the division has successfully moved the date of sale into the current financial year. The profit on such sales can therefore be included in this year's reported profits, which will help to trigger the bonus payments.

There would only be financial accounting implications to the scheme where it was decided that showing the higher profit this year, with next year's profit being lower than it would otherwise have been, destroys the true and fair view of the accounts. This is unlikely to be the case, particularly in the context of the group as a whole.

The nil stock at the year end could cause problems at the start of the next financial year. Any large order received early next year could not be satisfied out of stock; the purchaser might have to wait some time for the goods to be physically produced before they can be delivered. At best this is only an inconvenience to the purchaser. At the worst the sale may be lost altogether as the purchaser takes his custom elsewhere to a supplier who can deliver from stock. Thus a scheme that was designed to trigger bonus payments to the divisional managers in the current year could end up costing the group sales and consequent profits next year.

As in the other divisions, the divisional management have acted unethically. The possible loss of sales next year, and the pressuring of customers to accept early sales this year, simply so that managers can be paid bonuses this year, is not acceptable.

Group management action

The whole logic of establishing a divisionalised structure within a group is to allow local managements to manage their divisions as they think best, subject to meeting broad group criteria. Normally group management will adopt a hands-off attitude of observing procedures but not interfering. Interference would be resented by the divisional managers with adverse motivational consequences.

None of the proposals in the question is actually illegal, though division B's idea would be contrary to standard accounting practice, if an insufficient accrual were established. So, the group managers may feel unwilling to get involved and criticise the proposals.

However, there is a line to be drawn between legitimate 'income smoothing' (a good thing, since stock markets value highly companies with a smooth profit record) and manipulation of results to earn bonuses this year but which will depress profits next year. The idea of the bonus scheme is to reward good operational performance, not skills at profit manipulation.

So, however unwilling they may be to interfere unnecessarily, the group managers' responsibility to the stakeholders at large means that they must take up each of these issues with the divisional management, if only to prevent these proposals from being put in place every year as the bonus calculations are drawing near.

84 HOSPITAL

Key answer tips

Part (a) of your answer requires you to distinguish between long-term (strategic) and short-term (operational) target setting. In your answer to Part (b) you should discuss the separate objectives, which must be addressed by the new system. You should address ways of improving motivation among divisional managers, measuring performance within a not-for-profit organisation, and changing the culture in the management of the organisation.

(a) **Strategic targets** will be set following consideration of the mission statement. The mission statement sets out the overall aims of the organisation and why it exists. The mission statement can then be distilled into a series of specific objectives that become the strategic targets for the organisation. Actual performance can be measured against these long-term targets on a regular basis, for example, annually, to measure divisional performance.

Operational targets are short-term targets set in the budget to control the activities of an organisation. The idea is that, if the operational targets are met, then in the long-term the strategic targets will be achieved.

The key differences are therefore the purposes and timing of each set of targets. Strategic targets (e.g. market share achieved, quality of service offered) are set for the long-term by senior management in order to achieve the objectives of an organisation as a whole. Operational targets (e.g. wastage rate of material, number of units produced compared to budget) are set for the short-term by line managers to keep the organisation on-track.

Both sets of targets must be monitored regularly, and action taken if necessary to move activities closer towards what is required. However, strategic targets should be monitored much less frequently than operational targets, which may need to be examined daily or even hourly.

(b) There appear to be a number of separate objectives which must be addressed by the new system of performance measurement for divisional managers:

(i) improving motivation

(ii) measuring performance

(iii) changing the culture of management.

Since J is a not-for-profit organisation, whose objective is the provision of services rather than making a profit, any performance measurement system must include non-financial criteria as well as financial criteria. The importance of the non-financial criteria must be stressed to all involved. Outputs can be difficult to measure in not-for-profit organisations such as hospitals; for example the number of operations carried out by a surgeon may appear to be a useful statistic but, if half the operations are carried out poorly so that additional follow-up surgery is required, the absolute number of operations is not a valuable measure. Some depth of thought is therefore required in formulating appropriate statistics.

Motivation

The hospital board hopes that the performance measurement system will improve the motivation of divisional managers (and presumably all other staff members as well). It is important that all staff members identify with the targets that are set and believe that they are reasonable and attainable. It is generally agreed that this is more likely to be the case where staff representatives have participated in setting the targets, and have been convinced of the usefulness of the system as a control mechanism. It is also important that the goals of each manager are consistent and congruent with the goals of the hospital as a whole, so that every staff member is striving in the same direction.

However, it must be said that many workers in hospitals are principally motivated by the desire to heal sick people and the pleasure that seeing a patient recover can bring. So any scheme to motivate staff members must be seen as an opportunity to see more patients gets better, rather than a personal reward in cash terms that might be paid.

Measuring performance

The conventional way of measuring the performance of activities within a not-for-profit organisation is to look at the **value for money** (VFM) that the activity offers for the resources it has available. This entails in the present context looking at the economy, efficiency and effectiveness of each division of the hospital:

(i) **Economy** looks at the amounts of money spent by each division in providing its services. This could be compared over time and between similar divisions in other hospitals.

(ii) **Efficiency** looks at the relationship between the inputs and outputs of each division. For example, the cost per heart transplant operation carried out, or per X-ray taken, can be calculated and compared over time and between hospitals.

(iii) **Effectiveness** looks at the extent to which each division has succeeded in carrying out its objectives. These objectives are set at the start of each period, for example to carry out 500 hip replacement operations during the year.

The targets for economy, efficiency and effectiveness must not be imposed on the divisions by senior management. They should emerge as the consensus from a process of fair negotiation between line managers and senior managers. If the line managers view the targets as unreasonable, they will be less motivated to achieve them.

Changing the culture

In the previous functional responsibility organisation, the manager in charge of each function was responsible throughout the hospital for activities in that area. In the new system of devolved financial accountability, managers are only responsible for activities within a division. It is important that managers do not see this change as a demotion. The implementation of the change must be handled tactfully.

The new emphasis on input and output measures must also be explained carefully so that it is not misunderstood. Staff may be suspicious that 'the accountants are taking over'. They must be reassured that all medical decisions are still made by doctors, and that the purpose of the new system is to allow even more patients to be treated within the resources available.

LEAN SYSTEMS, R&D AND PRODUCT AND PROCESS DEVELOPMENT

85 INDICATORS

Key answer tips

This question requires you to consider the behavioural issues associated with performance indicators. In addition, it requires you to consider how managers' behaviour is affected by the use of performance indicators, and also how important it is that operational managers' are committed to the organisational aims of achieving total quality.

(a) In simple terms a manager might be assumed to be working in order to earn money and he/she will be paid more money if they are promoted on the basis of satisfactory performance appraisals. **A manager might therefore concentrate attention on whatever indicators are used in measuring his or her performance**.

For example, one manager might be told that his salary bonus will be calculated from the short-term profits earned by his area of the business over the forthcoming year. The temptation might be to stop replacing staff who leave, slash the advertising budget and scrap the research and development department, knowing that these actions would all increase reported profits. Or a manager who is told that her bonus will depend on sales volumes might push for overtime to be worked every day in order to boost production volumes, regardless of the costs incurred.

In practice, the situation is not so clear-cut. A manager is seeking a long-term career in a company, so more than one year's results will be important. There is no point in earning a significant bonus one year if the company goes bust soon afterwards due to a lack of investment. Managers know that quality of output has to be maintained at a high level, otherwise customers will go elsewhere and the company will run into difficulties. So even if managers are not appraised on the basis of quality, one will still find quality being a priority, since without quality the company will have only a limited future.

The personality of individual managers will also be a factor here. Some people by nature are perfectionists, who will automatically strive for high quality standards regardless of whether they will be given any direct monetary reward. Other people by nature are happy to make do with lower quality as long as the required output is achieved on time. Both sorts of people are valuable in their own niches and it is one of management's tasks to fit people into jobs for which they are suitable.

The safest approach to performance appraisal is to include in the appraisal exercise all the factors which are considered important by senior managers, including costs, volumes, qualities, disputes, etc. That way managers will be motivated to achieve all the objectives set for them which are congruent also to the goals of the company.

(b) **Total quality management** is the continuous improvement in quality, productivity and effectiveness obtained by establishing management responsibility for processes as well as outputs. Every process has an identified process owner and every person operates within a process and contributes to its improvement.

The establishment of performance indicators in a TQM exercise will set hoped-for standards against which actually achieved standards of performance can be compared. TQM standards are set ambitiously to improve processes, so it is likely that most reported variances will be adverse. This should not be taken as reflecting badly on the employees responsible. There is a danger of employees becoming demotivated and just giving up if they believe that their efforts are being criticised in the adverse variances. Sensitive management will be able to encourage the employees into even greater efforts in the next reporting period.

Traditionally set standards emphasise the costs and quantities of resources used; using less quantity than expected gives rise to a favourable variance. TQM variances must not replicate this situation; for example if quality can only be improved by using more materials, this is a favourable outcome and should be encouraged since it should lead to long-term prosperity.

The definition of TQM emphasised that it is a philosophy which should be applied throughout the whole organisation. In the past there has been a belief in some companies that quality is only the responsibility of certain employees such as line supervisors. Once all employees have recognised their quality responsibility, indicators should be built into each employee's appraisal to assess the quality of their work. These indicators should be seen to be fair and objective, and standards should be set at an attainable level.

The introduction of TQM as a method of achieving competitive advantage should therefore lead to a higher quality of performance from all employees throughout the whole organisation.

(c) The **successful implementation of change** is becoming a more and more important skill for a manager as the pace of change continues to accelerate in the modern business environment. **Implementation of a TQM programme** is an example of such a change which has been applied in many organisations in recent years. Basic principles which can increase the chances of a successful change are planning, communication, commitment and training.

Planning the change is vital, with a timetable laid down for when each department is expected to join the programme. A choice will be possible between a Big Bang approach with all departments joining at the same time, and a gradualist approach with the departments following one after the other. Careful planning should instil a sense of structure into the implementation, so that everyone knows what is meant to be happening. The new performance indicators relevant to quality should be devised and discussed with line managers.

Communicating the reasons behind the change and the timetable for the change to the workforce is an important factor in whether the workforce accepts the change or not. Human nature is to be suspicious of the unknown, so employees must be convinced of the benefits of the TQM approach if it is to be successful. Pinning notes on notice boards is not enough; senior managers must take time to explain the benefits to line managers, and line managers to operatives. If senior managers do not present a convincing argument to line managers, then the success of the overall programme is jeopardised.

Commitment to the TQM programme is therefore vital, for each employee from the top to the bottom of the company. Each employee will be taking responsibility for the quality of the work that they do, perhaps for the first time. If senior managers are seen as uncommitted to the programme, it is unlikely even to get off the ground.

Training employees for their new responsibilities may be necessary and resources must be planned for training time before and during the implementation process. The new performance indicators upon which employees will be appraised must be introduced so that they are accepted by workers as being fair and logical. It should be possible to convince employees that today's markets require quality products, and without quality nobody will have a future because the company will cease to exist.

86 HOT-SPOTS MULTIMEDIA

Key answer tips

ISO 9000 is not mentioned specifically in your syllabus, but it is very relevant to many businesses worldwide in the context of quality management, so it is worth practising a question on it. You may be able to use knowledge of ISO 9001 in an answer to a more general question on quality issues.

REPORT

To: Bob Ball, Hot-Spots Multimedia

From: Management accountant

Date:

Re: **ISO certification and quality management issues**

Certification

To become certified an organisation needs to develop a quality management system that meets the requirements specified by ISO 9001:2000. These are set out under five main headings:

- Quality management system
- Management responsibility
- Resource management
- Product realisation
- Measurement, analysis and improvement.

Once the quality system has been fully developed and implemented, the organisation must ask an independent Registrar to audit it.

Hot-Spots Multimedia is clearly capable of delivering high-quality work, but it would appear from the information available that it does not have formal explicit knowledge of how it does this. In other words there is relatively little that needs to be changed to achieve ISO 9001 certification, but current ways of working will need to be documented, and documented in such a way that flexibility is not lost and new ideas are actively encouraged.

The point of documentation is not merely to satisfy an auditor. Ideally it should be helpful for staff – especially new staff – because it will add certainty to what is to be done in specific circumstances.

Quality management system

Quality system documents consist of a quality manual, forms and checklists, external documents such as customer specifications, and records such as accounting records, timesheets, production schedules, correspondence – anything, in fact, that provides evidence of the processes being carried out.

The information is probably available in some form already in Hot-Spots existing records; it simply needs to be organised. Here are some examples.

- A database of in-house skills, experience and performance. This would be organised by staff members and would include details of past and present projects and work allocated for the future, available dates and whether each project was delivered on time. Full details of past projects may not now be available but it should be collected in future. A timesheet system would suffice, but staff will need to be convinced of the need to maintain timesheets. An intranet-based system, completed largely by selecting items from menus, would make this easy for them: an off-the shelf system may be suitable or Hot-Spots could possibly develop their own, given that they have in-house experience of this type of work.
- A database of freelancers including their skills, contact details, rates, any information known about availability, and information about past performance, such as known deficiencies in their work that will need in-house editorial attention, late delivery or unusually quick delivery.

Management responsibility

ISO 9001 stipulates that the initiative to implement a quality management system needs to come from the very top of the organisation and be communicated to everyone within the organisation. A positive attitude towards quality management needs to be so deeply ingrained that it is an expectation: something so fundamental that staff would never even consider approaching their work in any other way.

Within Hot-Spots this is likely to be the major difficulty. It is clear that past experience has prejudiced senior management against 'procedures' and that they are only willing to consider a more formal system if it will help them to obtain work, not for its own sake. The implication is that they will only pay lip-service to a system for the purpose of an audit. Attitudes will need to change: the development of a system that will not stifle creativity should be seen as a challenge, not an impossibility.

Resource management

Hot-Spots major resources are its staff. An organisation's staff should have the right experience, education, training and skills to do the job that they do. Under ISO 9001 Hot-Spots will need to define acceptable levels of competence for each job, and maintain records of competence (typically this would be part of an individual's personnel record). It also needs to be able to show that it takes measures to identify individuals' training needs and then delivers training programmes to meet those needs.

ISO 9001 requires organisations to identify, provide and maintain infrastructure needs. Infrastructure consists of buildings, workspace and associated utilities, hardware/equipment, software and support services. Little information is available about Hot-Spots infrastructure except that it uses the very latest technologies available.

An area for particular attention in an organisation such as Hot-Spots may be the work environment: it is possible that this is contributing to the problem of missed deadlines. Some aspects of the work environment are merely practical (for example, ergonomic workspaces) while others are social, psychological and cultural: auditors might be able to observe, for example, whether staff willingly co-operate with their colleagues: quite possibly not given that writing is an individualistic process.

Product realisation

A product starts out as an idea which is then made real by following a set of product 'realisation' processes. Hot-Spots management will be pleased to know that the latest version of ISO 9001 allows organisations to ignore or exclude any requirement in the product realisation section if they cannot apply it because of the nature of the organisation or the nature of the product.

One particularly relevant requirement, in Hot-Spots' case, is to plan and develop product realisation processes in the light of *both* the organisation's quality objectives and its customers' requirements. Customers' requirements are being met in terms of the product itself, but not in terms of delivery and this is likely to be due to problems in the planning process. For example:

- Does the company take on more work than it can realistically handle?
- Does it take proper account of the availability of staff?
- Do staff do more work than the customer requires, merely for personal gratification?

Measurement

The final section of ISO 9001 is about 'remedial processes'. The requirements are intended to ensure that the organisation makes the effort to find out whether it is conforming to its quality objectives and takes appropriate action if not. The answer in Hot-Spots case is clearly 'No' in terms of customer deadlines, so this is a key area to address.

Hot-Spots should use suitable methods to monitor and measure its processes and take action when the processes fail to achieve planned results. A product delivered late is regarded as a 'non-conforming product' under ISO 9001, no matter how good it is.

It seems most likely that Hot-Spots is not monitoring the progress of its products towards completion closely enough, and therefore not taking action – for example, re-deploying resources – early enough to overcome the problem.

87 RUS PLC

Key answer tips

This is a straightforward question about the relevance of implementing a TQM strategy, its financial and organisational implications, and the contribution that a company could expect from the strategy. A good answer will bring out knowledge of the 'value chains' involved in the TQM system, and focus on the specific 'slant' adopted by the examiner.

(a) CIMA defines **Total Quality Management (TQM)** as 'the continuous improvement in quality, productivity and effectiveness obtained by establishing management responsibility for processes as well as outputs. In this every process has an identified process owner and every person in an entity operates within a process and contributes to its improvement.'

Quality is a term often used to signify 'excellence' of a product or service. However, if we are to define quality in a way which is useful to the management of RUS plc, then we must recognise that quality is simply meeting the requirements of the people who use the hotels. This means that the company needs to start its assessment of quality by understanding the true requirements of its various customers. The company's stated policy is to provide 'a high-quality service for the discerning guest' and presumably meeting its customers' requirements has wide implications which include dealing with initial enquiries, availability of accommodation, prices charged for the various services provided, level of customer service, facilities offered, standard of food and overall reliability, amongst many other features.

TQM will emphasise the importance of RUS plc's **'marketing' function**. It must take the lead in establishing the quality requirements for the services. This will determine service features such as the grade, quantity, facilities, timing, etc. For example, prior to opening a new hotel or refurbishing an existing one, the company's management will need to consider its location and accessibility, before deciding whether it will be principally a budget, first-class, business or family hotel. This may, of course, involve the use of market research techniques.

TQM, and the way it is organised (which is discussed in (b)), gives people throughout the organisation a **common language for improvement**. It enables all the people working in the hotels, with different abilities, needs and priorities, to relate readily with one another, in pursuit of the common goal of quality. A hotel is so complex and employs so many different specialist skills that everyone has to depend on the activities of others in achieving their own quality standards. TQM provides the vitally important chain which links the 'users' and 'providers'.

TQM involves the **continual examination** of the requirements and RUS plc's ability to meet them. After all, the needs of both 'internal' and external customers change over time. This alone will lead to a 'continuing improvement' philosophy. The benefits of making sure that requirements are met at every link of the chain are very great in terms of improved customer satisfaction, increased competitiveness and market share, improved productivity, elimination of waste and reduced costs.

Relevance of a strategy needs to be evaluated in terms of costs and benefits. A TQM programme for RUS plc will be costly. The staff may need to be increased substantially to provide the quality levels required, and training will also have a prominent role. However the benefits could be enormous.

(b) The ability of the company to meet its 'upgrading' objective will depend on its staff and organisation. Throughout the group as a whole, and within each separate hotel, there is a series of quality chains which may be broken at any point by one person or one service not meeting the requirements of the customer.

The **key to TQM is for everyone in the organisation to have well-defined customers** – an extension of the word 'customer' beyond the customers who use the hotel, to anyone to whom an individual provides a service. Thus the 'Room Service' staff would be the customers of the kitchen staff, who would themselves be the customers of the purchasing staff. These relationships form a chain of customers and suppliers. Areas of responsibility will need to be identified and a manager allocated to each, and then the customer/supplier chain relationships established. True to the principle outlined above, the quality requirements of each 'customer' within the chain would be assessed, and meeting these would then become the responsibility of the 'suppliers' who form the preceding link in the chain.

Quality has to be managed – it will not just happen. To meet the requirements of TQM, RUS plc will probably need to recruit more staff, particularly managers, and may also need to change the level of services on offer to its customers, which includes the 'internal' customers. This will involve costs in terms of the re-design of systems, recruitment and training of staff, the purchase of equipment and the refurbishment of existing facilities. These costs need to be estimated and included in cost-benefit assessments, and in the strategic plan that is being formulated.

(c) The contribution of the management accountant breaks into three distinct aspects: (i) providing information, (ii) analysing and interpreting the information, and (iii) advising managers on the basis of the analysis. This contribution can be related to the needs of RUS plc's new TQM strategy.

(i) **Provision of information**

The vital need of TQM is to first **find out what the customer requirements are**. The internal supplier/customer relationships are often the most difficult to establish. To achieve quality, data needs to be obtained, sifted and analysed to provide information on: working or 'chain' relationships, requirements of the people involved, measurements that will be used for performance assessments, capabilities, availabilities, and reporting lines. The management accountant's participation in 'quality circles' would be very useful.

Also there must be a **corporate understanding of the company's quality position** in the market place. Information regarding the company's competitive position in terms of locations, services, prices and facilities will be required. Market research techniques using both secondary and primary data collection methods will be appropriate.

A **formal 'position audit'** of RUS plc's existing resources of people, equipment, facilities and services will provide data that will enable the company's needs to be matched with capabilities. This will particularly help in identifying the major areas of existing quality weaknesses. **Performance assessment** and the **competitive appraisal** already referred to will be extremely useful in this regard.

The management accountant would also become responsible for designing the **information systems** required by the new TQM system, at the centre of which will be the budget system.

Data will also be required to provide for the cost estimation of investments envisaged by the strategic decision.

(ii) **Analysis of the information**

The management accountant will use an arsenal of techniques included in the tasks of cost estimation, capital investment appraisal, cost-benefit analysis, management and systems auditing to produce report information for management, which can be used to decide on the extent of the changes required, how these changes should be effected, and the cost-benefit aspects. Statistical methods can be applied effectively in an analytical role.

(iii) **Advice for management**

Management will reasonably look to the management accountant for advice on the strategy. The management accountant's attributes of knowledge of the situation, professional competence and flair for imagination and creativity would provide useful inputs into the strategic decision. Also, of course, the management accountant would be heavily involved in the decisions relating to the implementation of the new TQM system.

KNOWLEDGE MANAGEMENT

88 XYZ PARTNERSHIP

Key answer tips

Don't provide an excessive amount of information about the Internet itself (history of development, number of users, and so on), without relating this to the question requirement. Explain the issues of sharing of information and providing a user-friendly interface; but do not provide too much detail on these areas leaving little or no time to move onto other relevant points.

In Part (b), although not considered in detail in this answer, students could discuss the problems associated with resistance to change.

(a) The deficiencies in the current system are identified in the scenario.

- Lack of standard software which means that partners and staff cannot use the computer systems in offices other than their own.
- No modern communications technology.

The partners' Internet experience and knowledge will have had a considerable impact on their appreciation of the advantages of modern communications technology for sharing information and inter-office co-operation.

- Communication between offices is currently limited to typed memos, whereas the partners will know from their Internet experiences that it is possible to communicate almost instantly across the world via e-mail.
- The partners will also be aware that communication with customers, suppliers, and other third parties such as planning authorities could be considerably enhanced using e-mail.
- Files can also be shared over the Internet almost instantly, either by distributing them as e-mail attachments or by allowing access to shared folders on an Internet or intranet server. The only alternative for separate XYZ offices at present is to place the files on floppy disks or CD-Rs and to distribute them by post.
- Common formats in use on the Internet such as PDF will have helped the partners to appreciate that information can more easily be shared if it is created by a package that is freely available to all. For instance a partner in Office A may not presently be able to view and amend a CAD drawing created by a partner in Office B because they do not use the same CAD package. If they were to do so, and make the files available for download over the Internet or a WAN, it would be possible for partners to work from home or at least avoid travelling so much between offices.

(b) **Problems involved in implementing a suitable information sharing system in XYZ**

Is it really necessary?

Although it seems, on the face of it, that more information sharing is a good idea, the matter has arisen because partners and staff find themselves working from more than one office. There may be other ways of avoiding the problem, for instance by expanding the size of some offices, or amalgamating just two offices, or relocating staff. These options do not appear to have been considered so far.

If a new system is to be implemented, XYZ need to make out a clear **business case** for doing so in preference to other options.

What systems should be implemented?

The least disruptive option is presumably to find out what systems are in use throughout XYZ and to roll out the most common technologies across all offices. This may not be ideal, however, because it is driven by the technology rather than by the current and future needs of the business.

It is inevitable that some data will have to be transferred into a new common format and this can lead to errors, omissions and inconsistencies if not done with great care.

It may be that not all information actually needs to be shared, or at least not in the short-term. The partners will need to make a decision about this and draw up a timetable for the changeover.

Legacy systems

The nature of the information used by XYZ – in particular complex CAD drawings – means that it will be difficult or even impossible to transfer all data into a common format. It is likely that older information will not be held in digital form at all. A decision is needed about how to archive this material. Will individual older systems be maintained or will it be accepted that such material has to be recreated from paper records if it is ever needed? Will archives be held locally or centrally?

Human issues

For some staff the notion of making their information available to other staff in other offices may be difficult. They will have their own established and familiar methods of organising their information and may even refuse to change their current practices to fall in line with a centrally imposed system.

At the very least there is likely to be some demotivation amongst staff. Some may resent having to give up a system that they know and like and learn a new one, especially if they are not given adequate training and adequate time to adapt. Beyond this there may be political issues and inter-office rivalries: information is power and some staff may fear that their own status within the organisation will be impaired if they have to share the source of their power with others.

Budget

The new system will have cost implications and these could be significant in offices whose systems are very different from the new standard. Costs will include the costs of changeover, training and re-training costs, and the costs of new hardware and software where necessary. A budget needs to be agreed, and some way of sharing the costs must be devised so that offices that require heavy investment are not unfairly penalised because of a centrally imposed decision.

Practicalities

There are various methods of achieving an information sharing solution, for instance connecting offices via a Virtual Private Network or via the public Internet. The solution chosen will have implications for set-up costs, for ongoing management and maintenance and for the technologies employed. XYZ will probably need to employ a consultant to advise them on all the options.

89 VNS CHARITY

Key answer tips

In Part (a) make sure that you **evaluate** the use of the extranet – in other words your answer should consider both positive and negative aspects. Be sure to include sufficient detail to show how the points you make relate to the charity. In Part (b) some candidates made the mistake of discussing systems that are not normally used for sharing knowledge such as expert systems and EDI and others focussed on systems that are used to share information within an organisation (such as workflow and intranets) but would not be used to share information with third parties.

(a) **Evaluation of the VNS charity's proposed extranet**

The extranet has been proposed in an attempt to alleviate the problems of over-worked staff, neglect of database maintenance, late delivery of information to hospitals and information hogging.

This solution should certainly help to relieve the burden upon staff of dealing with telephone calls, assuming the online version of the database is easy enough to use and provides information in the form required by callers.

Not all callers will have Internet access, of course, so it will still be necessary to provide a telephone option, though there is probably a good case for making this available only during normal working hours.

The extranet may also need to be offline for short periods to allow for updating and maintenance of the online database, but downtime can probably be kept to a minimum – say one hour in every 24.

Assuming re-inputting of the data is not too problematic or time consuming, and assuming the technology works as expected, staff should soon be able to attend to more important activities without the diversions they are experiencing at present.

There is a more fundamental issue to be considered, however. The charity was established 'to provide hospitals with detailed statistical information … and to recommend treatments', but it seems unlikely that this is the kind of information that is now being provided over the telephone, especially as calls are from members of the public, not just from hospitals.

It is possible that the extranet could generate new income for the charity if it is run on a subscription basis. This opportunity should not be ignored.

Demand for information has already reached 250 enquiries per day. An extranet will need to be able to cope with at least this volume of traffic, or probably a good deal more, since enquirers are likely to spend more time searching for peripheral information that they might not ask for on the telephone, and there will be sundry casual visitors who might not have considered bothering the charity with a telephone call but will feel perfectly free to explore the database online.

In principle, since the database already exists and will continue to be maintained whatever the case, it should be cheaper to provide the extranet than to have staff deal with calls, but a suitable interface will have to be devised and it must be easy enough for a non-expert to use. This may not be easy to achieve and it is liable to require some kind of support service. Some staff may find that, although they are no longer answering the telephone, they are now offering a computer helpline service rather than focusing on matters that are really important to the charity.

Copyright will also have to be carefully considered. In making the material available in this way the charity is allowing free access to its own copyright material and could be breaching the rights of others if material is also collected from other sources.

The issue of vetting applications for access is mentioned almost as an afterthought in the scenario but it could be fraught with difficulties. If telephone calls from members of the general public are currently receiving responses then it is hard to see why access needs to be restricted at all, subject to the confidentiality issues discussed earlier.

Finally, regarding the problem of information hogging by some staff, it is unlikely that an extranet will make any difference: information can just as easily be withheld from a computer system as it can from colleagues. This is a people management problem and it needs to be addressed by negotiation with, or at worst, disciplinary action against, the people concerned: their current attitude hardly seems compatible with the charitable purposes of the organisation they work for.

Conclusion

In conclusion the charity urgently needs to decide what business it is in and what market it wishes to serve. If it decides that provision of information is part of that business, then an extranet seems to be a sensible way of addressing many of the problems it is currently experiencing.

(b) **Alternative ways of providing information to third parties**

Some or all of the database could be made available as a general public website, while telephone calls are only accepted from registered users who could provide, say, an account number. The website might be sufficient to cater for the most common enquiries from the general public and, if such telephone calls were eliminated, that might free up enough staff time to enable them to concentrate on their main job of serving hospitals. The charity would have to develop some web expertise, and maintain and update the site periodically, or else it could contract out this work to a third party.

The charity could restrict its telephone service to registered and verified users such as hospitals, and only provide information to others via e-mail. This would help staff to manage their workload (for instance, they could spend the last hour of each day replying to e-mails, and otherwise get on with other activities). However, it generally takes longer to type a reply to an e-mail than it does to give a spoken response: the overall workload would increase but the speed of response would decline. Backlogs could very quickly develop.

The information could be provided in a downloadable format for use offline (either via a simple web page or on CD-ROM). There would be no need to invest in and maintain elaborate web-hosting services with significant bandwidth, secure on-line databases, log-in systems and the like, so this option may be cheaper.

If CD-ROM is used, however, there will be the costs of disks and replication and regular updating costs. There is the danger that enquirers will rely on a version that is not the most up-to date. There would inevitably be some users who would need help in using the database, so some kind of telephone support would still be required.

Conclusion

Assuming the charity decides that it wishes to share information, the best solutions appear to be either the extranet as proposed, or else some more limited version of it on a public website.

90 AHM COMPANY

(a) **Barriers to sharing knowledge and their impact on the efficiency of information transfer**

Organisational

The directors consider that there are strong benefits to be gained from local control and have not perceived the need to encourage communication between the factories. This policy is now being questioned by research staff, who feel that a company-wide strategy for information systems – in particular for its communication infrastructure – would be more appropriate.

The research department is regarded as the only source of innovation, but this is not the case. Other managers and shop floor workers have also had useful ideas but because of the culture of local control these have not been implemented since they were not brought to the attention of the appropriate people.

Although systems are 'replicated' in each factory, this does not necessarily mean that they are operated in the same way. For instance the research department in factory A may use terminology and report formats that are perfectly adequate for its own purposes but may be quite different from those in factory B, and therefore difficult to understand outside of factory A.

The three factories are geographically separate, so there is little opportunity for informal sharing of information. Formal meetings are extremely rare: there has only been one in the last five years. The outcome of this meeting indicates that the company has been neglecting a valuable means of identifying improvements to its products.

Research staff are now very much aware that lack of communication has resulted in duplication of effort, and failure to take advantage of the synergies to be gained from group thinking and knowledge sharing. This will be frustrating for them and may give rise in the future to a variety of informal information sharing systems. This may be an improvement, but with no overall control it may create further confusion.

Social

It is somewhat surprising that the research department has not previously understood that there may be benefits to be obtained from sharing information with their colleagues in other factories. It is also evident that they have not previously seen any necessity to seek the views of staff in other areas of the company such as shop floor workers, perhaps indicating a degree of arrogance.

Given the culture of local control it is possible that there is some rivalry between separate factories. Individual departments may be jealously guarding their own new ideas and/or they may be dismissive of ideas from other locations.

The fact that staff from different locations rarely meet face to face will also create barriers. In five years it is likely that the majority of members of each research department will have changed, so all will be strangers. This does not encourage a culture of trust, and allows no opportunity for taking advantage of specialist knowledge in other factories, simply because staff will not know that specialist knowledge exists.

Technological

Although systems are replicated at each location (so in theory there should be no problems of compatibility) there are no direct computer links between locations. If information is shared at all this will be by post or by telephone. The postal system is relatively slow and it is relatively easy for the recipient to ignore or overlook letters, and paper documents are not conducive to further analysis (unless documents are provided on floppy disk). Telephone conversations are not suitable for sharing complex information, technical drawings and so on.

As a bare minimum the company would benefit from establishing e-mail links between the three factories. This will require some investment in communications hardware such as mail servers and enhanced LAN hardware and software. Given the highly competitive nature of the motor industry and the commercial sensitivity of research data in particular a high degree of security will be advisable.

(b) **Systems to facilitate the sharing of knowledge**

The most radical solution would entail establishing central functions for common services that are likely to benefit from information sharing. On the evidence in the scenario it seems likely that the company could benefit from a centralised R & D department, serving all three factories, although it might be argued that R & D needs to be close to the factory floor in order to understand and solve *ad hoc* problems that arise.

Failing that the company could consider various systems:

- more regular meetings and/or conferencing in various forms
- e-mail links between locations via the Internet, or a private network
- a bulletin board and shared data stores on an intranet
- groupware.

Most of these solutions assume that each factory already has a Local Area Network, but if this is not so LANs within each factory are a pre-requisite.

More regular meetings and/or conferencing in various forms

The recent joint staff meeting mentioned in the scenario appears to have been a spectacular success from the point of view of information sharing. Whatever developments occur in the future it is certainly a good idea in the short term to hold further discussions on a much more regular basis.

Regular face-to-face meetings may be impractical because of travelling time and the expenses involved in arranging a venue and accommodation. If this is the case a useful and relatively cheap alternative is the conference call, which enables live discussion and any number of participants in each location, although they cannot see each other. Documents for this kind of meeting can either be distributed in advance or made available via a WAN, as described below.

A further option is video conferencing, although this is much more expensive and some participants may find it quite inhibiting.

E-mail links between locations, via the Internet, or a private network

Such links would facilitate fast company-wide communication, where appropriate, or communication to specific interest groups or expert individuals throughout the company. Assuming the different locations use the same applications software, documents could be exchanged as e-mail attachments.

This is fine for sharing of simple factual information but, if the intention is that each recipient of an attached document should be allowed to make changes to it and offer them up for consideration by others, then very strong controls will be needed to keep track of which is the most up-to-date version, and which changes are accepted and which not. It may be possible for the originator of the document to keep a master copy and collate it with proposed amendments as they arrive, but this will be more and more difficult to manage the more suggested changes there are.

A bulletin board and shared data stores on an intranet

Under this system staff would post messages to an electronic notice board which could be organised under a variety of headings. They could also upload documents for consideration (but not amendment) by others to a central place (an intranet, say), accessible by authorised staff within the company.

This is very similar to the e-mail alternative, except that participants need to opt in rather than receiving e-mails automatically (whether or not they are of interest) and except that there would only ever be one 'official' copy of a document. Once again, however, it would be necessary for someone to maintain a master copy of any document up for comment and to collate suggestions manually, and this may be difficult to manage.

There are also security considerations: the company would need to ensure that the intranet was suitably protected from the prying eyes of competitors.

Groupware

Groupware products such as Lotus Notes or (to some extent) an Office suite can be set up so as to track changes made to a centrally stored document. In theory all readers of the document can see any changes made to it but only the 'owner' of the document can accept or reject them as he or she sees fit.

In practice there are still problems. Reader A may make a change and reader B may make a change, but there is no guarantee – at least in the short-term – that reader A will be aware of reader B's change, or vice versa. Reader B may not have made their change, or may have made a completely different change, if he or she had been aware of reader A's change. Once again this requires very careful management by the owner of the document. One option is to ask for comments on a rota basis – for instance not ask for reader B's comments until reader A has completed their review of the document – but this could create an endless loop, unless strict time limits are set as to when comments will and will not be taken into account.

There are also political issues when all comments are visible to all others. If a reader's suggestions are ignored, or another reader's suggestions are preferred, without explanation, then conflict and resentment may be the result.

91 JN INTERNATIONAL BANK

Key answer tips

The official CIMA answer to Part (b) makes it clear that the examiner was actually thinking of shared databases, messaging systems, decision support systems and the like, not 'groupware', which is usually intended to help groups collaborate on specific projects by co-ordinating work and exchanging project-specific information.

(a) **Explicit and tacit knowledge**

- **Explicit knowledge** is formal and standardised and can be easily shared and communicated. For example, knowing the basics of how to drive a car is explicit. You could explain it to someone else.

- **Tacit knowledge** is personal and rooted in a specific context. Once you learn how to drive a car and have been doing it for some time, you develop certain techniques (and bad habits) and driving becomes second nature. However, this phase is more difficult to articulate.

Within an organisation explicit knowledge is knowledge that has been captured and held in an information system. Typically, however, an organisation will not know what tacit knowledge it possesses.

Sharing knowledge

It is not always necessary to invest in expensive technology to address problems in information sharing: often the problem will arise because of organisational matters such as an inappropriate organisation structure. The solution may be simply to expand the size of a department or merge departments or relocate departments or individuals, so that those who need to share knowledge actually in the same physical place.

There may be some technological barriers to overcome, such as the need to roll out a suitable modern network across an organisation, if one is not in place already.

There will be situations in which problems arise because of incompatible systems and working methods in different parts of the organisation. It is inevitable that some data will have to be transferred into a new common format and this can lead to errors, omissions and inconsistencies if not done with great care.

The main problem with tacit knowledge is recognising that it exists in the first place. One sales person may be more successful than others at gaining new customers but may have no idea what it is about the way he or she goes about the job that leads to this success. Meetings, brainstorming sessions and role-playing sessions may be held, and information is likely to be shared in the form of anecdotes about work at social gatherings, but in every case the attempt to release the knowledge is hit and miss: it may depend on someone else just happening to ask the right question.

Above all there are social barriers to information sharing. For some staff the notion of making their information available to other staff may be difficult. They will have their own established and familiar methods of organising their information and may even refuse to change their current practices to fall in line with a centrally imposed system.

Beyond this there may be political issues and inter-office rivalries: information is power and some staff may fear that their own status within the organisation will be impaired if they have to share the source of their power with others.

(b) **Groupware**

Groupware is a term that is usually used for software that helps work groups to collaborate on specific projects, but the Director of Information Systems at JN International Bank appears to be using it in a broader sense.

A typical groupware system will have the following features that would assist information transfer and sharing.

- **Messaging**. In other words e-mail facilities for exchanging messages with others. Messages can be sent on a round trip to individuals, who can add their own comments before passing it on to the next person, or it can be sent to everyone involved at once.

  Where a global product is being developed, or a local version of a product already developed in another country, this will allow the staff involved to discuss and resolve problems, irrespective of time differences and distance.

Messaging will also facilitate the use of expert knowledge by the whole organisation rather than that knowledge being limited to the country in which the expert individual happens to live. On the other hand, specific banking rules may vary from country to country, so caution is needed in applying the knowledge.

- **'Public' folders** to store files and share them with others involved in a project throughout the organisation.

  In the case of JN a groupware solution could incorporate worldwide access to databases for sharing of knowledge, although staff in Country A probably do not need access to information about regulatory changes in Country B or customers in another country (in fact it may be illegal to share such information between countries due to data protection legislation).

  From the point of view of the Board, however, such access should enable them to obtain more timely information on the company as a whole and help them to get an overall picture.

Other typical features of groupware such as workflow management, task assignment, group scheduling and so on will be very useful for managing individual projects but are not really relevant to information sharing across the company as a whole. It could be argued that groupware generated project management records will help those implementing similar projects to learn from others' experience, but the information will need to be organised in such a way that others are made aware of it or can find it if needed.

Groupware is unlikely to facilitate the sharing of tacit knowledge unless this happens indirectly as a result of sharing of anecdotes.

Groupware will not overcome language barriers. It is likely that English would be used and staff in non-English speaking countries may resent this. Misunderstandings could arise and mistakes occur as a result of mistranslation.

Groupware will not overcome prejudices that some individuals may have against 'foreigners'.

There is a limit to the extent that groupware can overcome time differences. There may be a company expert on a particular topic but he or she will not be available 24 hours a day, and therefore possibly not when needed by someone in a different time zone.

INFORMATION STRATEGY AND IMPLEMENTATION

92 SYSTEMS, TECHNOLOGY AND MANAGEMENT STRATEGY

Key answer tips

'IT' is pretty clearly about technology, but in current usage there is not really any agreement over what is 'IS' strategy as opposed to 'IM' strategy … or 'KM' strategy, or whatever the latest buzz words happen to be when you come to read this.

The official CIMA answer is waffly and somewhat confused, and it makes IT strategy the link between IS and IM. This is putting the cart before the horse in our opinion and is well out of touch with modern thinking: the technology is just one of the resources used by the manager.

Part (b) is difficult because you are given very little information about the MG organisation and it is scarcely credible that an organisation could take such a head-in-the-sand approach to business. The points to make are obvious, but you may well have struggled to find 15 marks worth of material. You are specifically told to recommend changes, so don't ignore this part of the requirement.

(a) **Information strategies**

Information Systems strategy

The term information systems (IS) refers to the interconnected organisational activities that gather and process data and provide **information**. Some of these activities may be carried out by technology, but many may be human processes achieved by human interactions.

A strategy for information systems is concerned with identifying what information is needed by the organisation to enable it to achieve its business objectives. This includes considering the information needed at strategic, tactical and operational levels and the ways in which those levels of information should interconnect and interact.

Because the term 'systems' is often associated with tangible things (a central heating system, the Underground system, etc,) it might better to refer to this part of the chain simply as 'Information Strategy'.

Information Management strategy

Information management strategy is the next step. Information management is a highly complex activity, concerned with identifying the sources of information needed, collecting that information in appropriate formats, storing information, facilitating existing methods of using information and identifying new ways of using it, and ensuring that information can be accessed by all who need it (but only by those people).

Information Technology strategy

Information technology (IT) refers to the resources used to manage information: basically **hardware and software** used for everyday data processing, communication, office automation and production automation: IT describes any 'kit' concerned with the capture, storage, transmission, presentation or interpretation (e.g. by a robot) of information.

Relative importance

In spite of the above, in many organisations technology has, until relatively recently (that is until the early to mid 1990s), been allowed to dictate information strategy as a whole. Because the initial investment in computers was such a large expense and the possibilities were not well understood by senior managers, organisations simply equipped themselves with the best they could afford and were then limited in what they could do with their information by the capabilities of the technology they had locked themselves into, and the imagination, or lack thereof, of technology suppliers.

Clearly business goals should come first and managers should be able to choose what resources they use to achieve those goals, but this has only really become possible in the last four to five years thanks to rapidly falling costs of hardware, the rise and rise of the Internet and associated technologies and long-overdue co-operation between hardware and software suppliers to develop open standards.

(b) **Information systems strategy of MG Organisation**

MG is a case in point of an organisation whose information strategy is principally driven by technology and the cash that happens to be available rather than by genuine information needs to fulfil business objectives.

The IT budget

There appears to be simple acceptance that costs will rise every year and upgrades will be necessary every year.

No doubt this thinking is partly due to the marketing methods of the computer industry itself, which still encourages users to think of IT as a fashion accessory rather than as a business tool. In all probability MG has very few systems that need to be upgraded on a yearly basis. There are exceptions such as payroll software, which is dependent upon legislation changes, but for most packages this will not be true. For instance Word 2003 is not actually significantly better at its basic function (word processing) than much older versions.

In future it is recommended that the IT budget is set by reference to the overall business objectives for the coming year and the information that will be required to help fulfil those objectives. If extra spending on technology is required to extract or process the necessary information then that should be the basis of the budget.

User expectations

User expectations appear to be extremely limited (day-to-day transaction processing, tactical information, etc). This suggests a lack of imagination on the part of management: no consideration appears to be given to new possibilities such as using information systems and technologies to develop different ways of carrying out business functions, perhaps to reduce costs or to offer an enhanced service to customers.

It is recommended that a study be undertaken, probably with the help of external consultants with some knowledge of practices in other companies in the same industry, to look into ways in which better use can be made of MG's information systems.

Environmental scanning

So far as we can tell from the question, MG only concerns itself with internal information: no information appears to be collected about competitors' activities and performance or about developments in the markets that MG serves. There is no executive information system (which would typically provide such information) and no attempt to benchmark with other companies.

A certain amount of environmental scanning could be undertaken immediately by Board members or senior managers, simply by spending some time looking at relevant websites on the Internet, and the company could subscribe to information services for its industry to keep itself up to date with new developments.

Again, a study by external consultants such as market researchers would help MG to understand its position in its market more clearly and identify upcoming threats and opportunities.

Focus on the tactical level

It is difficult to see how tactical reports (which are typically used by relatively junior managers and are concerned with current and recent past performance), can supply the information actually needed by the Board to steer the organisation into the future and make long-term decisions.

A proper EIS is clearly needed to help give the Board a better overview of the business as a whole and the market it operates in. The development of such a system as soon as possible should be the main focus of the IT budget: this is far preferable to spending on unnecessary upgrades to operational systems.

Errors and omissions

Errors and omissions in reports are regarded as mere annoyances and it appears that no attempt has been made to identify the reasons for them or to rectify them. It is possible that many of the decisions made by the Board are sub-optimal because they are based on bad information.

Since it is recognised that reports contain errors and omissions (and many more may go unnoticed), in the short term reports should be carefully reviewed by senior managers before submission to the Board, and in the longer term the reasons for errors and omissions should be identified and eliminated, either through better training of staff or modifications to software or hardware.

93 DS

(a) **Information problems facing DS**

Packages

Instead of real-time processing, the central database is updated from each warehouse every three hours on average. This means that the system is unable to provide current information about packages within the system for DS. Only the individual warehouses have up-to-date details, e.g. size, weight, destination, of the packages they hold. The warehouses do not have accurate data about what is to be delivered to them. If the journey time is less than three hours, goods from another warehouse may arrive unexpectedly.

There should be an overall system/manual reconciliation of all packages but no information seems to be available either on urgent deliveries or on packages that may have been lost during sorting.

Routes

DS does not have a system to inform them of the most economical way of satisfying delivery requirements. The company maintains 27 warehouses, uses lorries to forward to the appropriate or intermediate distribution warehouse and has a fleet of vans for local delivery. The computer indicates the optimum method of transferring the package to the warehouse which is closest to the delivery address but, for the lorry drivers, lack of information about the final destination of the package means that they cannot deliver directly 'en route' to a customer to minimise handling costs. The drivers of the local delivery vans are expected to organise their own route, without any guidance on the quickest, shortest or cheapest routes available. Because of the inherent inefficiency in this procedure, the system should assist in sorting the packages and preparing delivery schedules for local deliveries.

Warehouse operations

Packages are tracked through the system at each warehouse. The transfer list is attached to the package and is input to the computer as each package is dispatched or arrives at the warehouse. Because there could be a delay of three hours before the local LANs are updated with the information about what packages are likely to arrive, the warehouse faces potential storage problems. Local sorting, by area code, could also be frustrated by this time delay as delivery vans could leave half-full and then have to make a repeat journey later the same day.

Drivers appear to be allocated to fixed areas. Local routing information would allow vans to be switched to other areas to handle peak traffic.

Procedures

There are no details on how the list of expected collections for the day are drawn up and the fact that non-collections are 'noted' suggests that this is a manual procedure and very prone to loss of information. The information about the packages is input by keyboard to each local database at each point throughout the system. This re-input of information may cause problems because of discrepancies that may arise through miscoding, omission or incorrect input.

(b) **Critical Success Factors (CSFs)**

Critical Success Factors (CSFs) are those necessary for the organisation to flourish. DS's CSFs are likely to focus on it's core activities, as there is no mention of new markets or new products being sought or developed. Possibilities include the following:

(i) getting the package safely to its correct destination

(ii) time sensitive, early morning and same day delivery service

(iii) delivery to remain competitively priced

(iv) retaining and/or increasing market share through customer satisfaction.

The data sources to ensure each CSF is met include:

(i) Getting the package safely to its correct destination

Accurate data concerning proof of delivery with package undamaged is required. The systems analyst can obtain this data by interrogating the existing system or by standard routine reports to indicate DS's failures, such as packages lost or undelivered and damage to packages in transit.

(ii) Time sensitive, early morning and same day delivery service

When the package is collected the time will be entered onto the receipt set and when it is delivered the customer should sign for the package and record the time of delivery. Routine reports, obtained by the analyst, can identify where excess time is taken and provide the information to ensure that the delivery time is as promised to the customer.

(iii) Delivery to remain competitively priced

Competitors' price lists and their delivery promises can be monitored regularly to ensure that DS remains competitive.

(iv) Retaining and/or increasing market share through customer satisfaction

The company's marketing department will provide data about the take up of DS's services by new customers and how systems can strategically affect marketing prospects. Warehouse staff and drivers will be able to identify problems ranging from handling of packages to the customer receipt.

Customers can be asked about those aspects of the service that are good and those that require improvement. This can be done through regular customer surveys and also through appropriate market research bodies that provide an interfirm comparison service.

By using consultants/independent advisors who have the necessary experience, it may be possible to identify important issues that DS should be considering to improve/expand its services by using its computer systems to full advantage.

94 PR UNIVERSITY

Key answer tips

There are some positive points that can be made about current data use within the University, for instance staff appear to be happy with what they have, so beware of suggesting change just for the sake of change. Be sure to link your CSFs to the overall mission of the University or to the performance indicators needed to enable appropriate information systems to be developed. In Part (b) some candidates discussed centralised systems in general: however, the question is about data warehousing.

(a) (i) **Data use within the University**

Although the data needs of individual departments are being met there are a number of problems that make information systems in the University as a whole cumbersome and expensive.

Above all the problem is duplication, both of effort and of data. The same data has to be input separately to the system of each department in which a student studies. This is a waste of time and there is a possibility of inconsistency between the records held by different departments.

The various systems are incompatible so information cannot be transferred between them and it will be difficult to develop the proposed integrated database.

Incompatible systems and diversity of applications also mean that it will be difficult for administrative staff to transfer between departments: they will need retraining each time. This may limit career opportunities within the University.

On the other hand staff will be used to their own systems and may resent or resist any centrally-imposed change that requires them abandon a working system and learn new skills.

(ii) **Critical Success Factors for revising the system**

Critical Success Factors (CSFs) are the limited number of areas in which results, if they are satisfactory, will ensure successful performance. They are the vital areas where 'things must go right' for the organisation to flourish.

There is no indication in the scenario of any respect in which the University as a whole is not flourishing or individual departments are performing unsuccessfully. This is not to say that there are no improvements to be made, however, especially as the systems are becoming expensive to operate.

The aims of individual departments are likely to be broadly similar – for instance, to attract sufficient numbers of students, provide X number of teaching hours per week, achieve certain standards in terms of exam results and future employability of graduates. Some departments may also have research interests and goals.

An overriding aim of the University's Board of Management will be to ensure that the entire organisation is on a sound financial footing and its activities are properly funded, and therefore any means of reducing costs (or getting better value from new investment in information systems) will be important.

The Board of Management can establish CSFs in each of these areas and then identify suitable performance indicators that will show whether CSFs are being met. This in turn will help to define what information will be needed in the future to monitor whether CSFs are being achieved.

It is likely that this analysis will reveal a gap between current information provision and required information provision, and appropriate revisions to the current information system, to close the gap, can then be specified.

(b) **Disadvantages of data warehousing**

A data warehouse supports information processing by providing a solid platform of integrated, historical data from which to do analysis. It is a database, data extraction tool, decision support system, or other analysis tool or procedure that extracts data from one or more of the organisation's existing databases, reformats it and loads it into a database designed for querying with an on-line analytical processing systems (OLAP). OLAP allows users to dynamically extract pertinent summary information.

Although the concept of data warehousing appears to offer considerable advantages, especially to organisations such as RR University with a large number of disparate legacy systems, there may be considerable problems when trying to implement such a system.

The systems used in different departments of the RR University are incompatible, and that is likely to mean that data is in a wide variety of different formats. As noted earlier there are also likely to be inconsistencies between different databases where duplicated items of data should, in theory, be identical, but in practice are not.

The data will either need to be analysed and 'cleansed' before it can be integrated into a warehouse, or else some kind of middleware will be required, probably converting all data to a common format such as XML. Whichever option is chosen, with 34 different departments this will not be easy, quick or cheap to achieve.

Incompatible systems will also mean that most of the departments will need to be furnished with new hardware and software before they can use the data warehouse. This is likely to expensive and disruptive to the day-to-day work of each department.

Moreover almost all staff who want to use the new system will need training, both in the use of the data warehouse itself, and probably also in the use of new hardware, operating systems and applications software.

Individual departments may use data in widely different ways and require all manner of different reports. It could be very difficult to create a common interface that is capable of delivering information in every format that may be required. Report formats that are only needed in a single department may not be catered for, and this will cause resentment.

Even if the above problems are overcome, scalability is a key issue. As the new system proves its worth more and more demands will be made of it, so ongoing maintenance, adequate network bandwidth, sufficient storage space, and highly flexible upgrade capability are all essential.

Finally it is worth pointing out that with all the University's data in a single main source it is vital to ensure that effective backup arrangements are made and strictly adhered to. Depending on how the data warehouse is implemented, loss or serious corruption of data could be disastrous.

95 PRECISION PARTS

Key answer tips

This question which focuses upon position appraisal, requires you to assess the validity of management accounting data for strategic planning purposes. You must also suggest how benchmarking could be applied to information for strategic planning purposes. As a general point, it is worth noting that the examiner regularly shows an interest in the role of the management accountant in strategy.

(a) The management accounting reports which are currently provided to the management of W comprise monthly cost variance reports covering direct materials, direct labour, variable and fixed production overheads, and regular sales price and volume variance reports. These will help management in its control of the company's operations, by focusing on areas where results actually achieved are materially different from those expected.

But **controlling activities is only one aspect of management accounting**. Other important responsibilities are the formulation of strategy and optimising the use of resources. The inward-looking reports currently produced focus only on what is happening within the company by reporting internally generated numbers to internal managers who are expected to adjust their internal actions.

A successful business must react to changes in its external environment and be outward looking. The current reports are inward-looking and appear to have no strategic content. However punctually and comprehensively they are produced, they are still inadequate as information to assist the board's strategic decision making.

(b) Effective strategic planning starts with the **setting of objectives** and a **position audit** of the company. W appears to want to increase its profits, but it is unclear whether objectives exist in terms of earnings per share, products/markets, productivity, etc.

A position audit examines the current situation of the company in terms of resources, products, markets, operating systems, internal organisation, current results and returns to stockholders. The audit should be carried out now as a matter of urgency and repeated regularly to keep the information up to date. Planning is not an activity that can be carried out once a year and then forgotten about during the rest of the year; to be valuable it must be a regular ongoing process.

Environmental analysis considers the environmental conditions within which the company will be operating, looking at product demand, production technology, competition, etc. This analysis is particularly lacking from the management information that the management accounting department has previously provided.

Specific reports are recommended to be prepared as follows:

(i) Statement of objectives

(ii) Position audit

- Resources (people, fixed assets, finance)
- Products and markets
- Operating systems (including use of technology)
- Organisation
- Results (segmental analysis of profits, returns to shareholders)

(iii) Environmental analysis

- Product demand: what market share is currently achieved and forecast for the future?
- Customers: why do the existing customers buy from W? Perhaps the company possesses specific skills or technology, or prices its products keenly. Whatever it is, the source of competitive advantage must be identified and built upon.
- Workforce: numbers and skill levels of existing employees. Why is so much work being turned away? If there is a shortage of skilled employees, new people must be trained or recruited.
- Technology: if it is a shortage of machines that is leading to so much work being turned away, then the cost of new machines should be compared with the forgone profits.

The **segmental analysis of results** recommended in the position audit should show the profits currently achieved on each of the company's existing products. Often profits can quite easily be improved by stripping out loss-making lines and shifting resources to the highest-profit products. Similar segmentation can be carried out by customer and by market. Without this information managers cannot make correct decisions about the products that the company should choose to make.

The **current budgetary control system could be improved** by calculating planning and operational variances rather than the traditional variances now reported. Line managers could then concentrate on improving operational matters for which they are genuinely responsible. The disadvantage of planning and operational variances is that too often all adverse variances are explained away as being planning errors.

The **standard costing system could be improved** by setting standards on the basis of activity-based costing (ABC) rather than any other method. This will identify the cost drivers for each process and is particularly important if the standard cost plus pricing basis is to be persevered with. A market-based pricing method would be preferable since it offers the prospect of maximising profits.

Finally, **information on current and future cash flows** must be reported regularly to managers. Companies fail because they run out of cash, not because they are unprofitable, and cash control will become important if any expansion plan is implemented. A monthly statement of current and forecast cash flows would be a valuable source of information to managers.

(c) **Benchmarking** is a continuous, systematic process for evaluating the products, services and work processes of organisations that are recognised as representing best practices for the purpose of organisational improvement.

Essentially you compare your organisation with another in the hope of identifying ways of improving your output, organisational structure, etc.

The exercise will be most useful if the companies benchmarking each other are in the same industry and have similar technology. Thus W should look for another small-scale engineering company with a similar cost structure to its own. It is likely that this will be a competitor to W who might be unwilling to co-operate with the exercise so, if both parties are to benefit without endangering their commercial secrets, it is usual that benchmarking is limited to specified non-sensitive areas and that the exercise is mutual. Thus each company agrees to co-operate with the representatives of the other company in showing their operations.

Since W knows that its management information system is currently less than excellent, it could seek to benchmark MISs between companies to learn what system a successful company is operating. This may however prove difficult to agree, since the information in any MIS will be highly commercially sensitive. Perhaps proformas and document flow charts can form the basis of the benchmarking exercise rather than the actual MIS schedules and numbers.

It may be more realistic to try and benchmark the MIS of a company which is not in direct competition with W but which does have a reputation for excellence concerning its strategic planning. The disadvantage is the possible lack of relevance to W of the information generated in the other company; for example, a much larger company might have more tiers of management which have no counterpart in W's structure.

In conclusion, if W Ltd has appreciated that its current system for developing information for strategic planning needs improving, benchmarking the MIS of a similar company with a proven excellent MIS could bring benefits to W. However, a relationship of trust must be established between two companies before benchmarking can be implemented, and such mutual trust may not be possible between two rival companies in direct competition.

96 Q

Key answer tips

Your answer should clearly show why the points stated in the scenario would result in the system not being used by the representatives. You should use the scenario information effectively and make sure that your answer to Part (b) doesn't repeat points made in Part (a).

(a) **The reasons why representatives may have stopped using the system**

Difficulty of using system

The usefulness of the initial involvement of user input in setting up the system will have been limited due to fact that last-minute changes and amendments by programmers were performed without user involvement. It is highly probable that users find the system more difficult to use because the primary aim of the late amendments was focused on enhancing the system for programmers as opposed to users. Their exclusion from involvement in these changes is also likely lead the users to consider that the system does not belong to them and thus they will fail to take ownership of it. As a direct consequence of this system use will inevitably decrease.

Not wanting to share information

Since representatives are paid commission on sales made there is no incentive to share information because this could lead to another sales representative taking a customer telephone enquiry using sales information obtained by another representative. Such systems can lead to sales representatives working in an 'insular' manner and, consequently, information which should be input into the new system (which after all belongs to Q!) will not be input to the new system because this will mean that the representatives could lose commission.

Good manual system

Prior to the implementation of the new system the sales representatives used a manual system that they considered satisfied their requirements and, therefore, there was little or no incentive to move away from this system since it was working so well. As the sales representatives perceive that the new system has some distinct disadvantages, there is very little incentive for staff to adopt the new system.

Lack of time to learn or be trained in new system

From the viewpoint of the users the system implementation and changeover was badly planned. Whilst implementation during a holiday may have been useful for the IT support department since it minimised disruption, it was ill-timed because the potential users of the system could not receive adequate training by virtue of the fact that they were on holiday. This lack of training would make the system much more difficult to use. If the users encountered initial difficulties with the system, which appears to have been the case, then this would raise the probability of the system failing to gain their acceptance. The management of Q should recognise that the intended users of the system are sales representatives with different levels of IT expertise, and that lack of training will serve as a major barrier to the adoption of the new system.

(b) **The actions to try ensure system used in future**

In view of their bad experience of the system to date, any action to try to get sales representatives to use the new system will be difficult to implement. However, it is essential that some action is taken and staff in the company may need to persevere with the new system to obtain any of the expected benefits.

Consult with the sales representatives to find out exactly why the system is not being used

In the absence of information to the contrary the assumption was made in Part (a) that the new system was not being adopted owing to problems in allocating commission between the different sales representatives. However, before taking any remedial action, the representatives should be interviewed to ascertain the precise reasons why the system is not being used. If this is not practicable due to the number of sales representatives, a carefully chosen sample from across the business should be selected for interview. Only when this has been done should an action plan be formulated.

'Sell' the benefits of the new system

The new system was implemented 'in some hurry'. It is probable, therefore, that very little information was given to staff concerning it and, consequently, staff were not made aware of the potential benefits of the system. The provision of information regarding the system in the form of memos, messages on bulletin boards, etc would have provided a more meaningful insight into and pave the way for the adoption of the new system.

Amend the remuneration structure of staff

A major hindrance to use of the new system lies in the existing remuneration system of providing commission to individual sales representatives. This is primarily due to the fact that it does not facilitate sharing of information. Consideration should be given to amending the remuneration structure so that staff work in teams, and commission is paid to each team. This will precipitate the sharing of information within each team. Another major benefit that will arise from 'team-working' will be the improvement in customer service levels that will result from customers not having to wait to speak with a specific sales representative.

Check that user requirements are included in the new system

User requirements were included in the initial systems specification. However, a number of these may have been lost as a result of the last-minute changes and amendments that were made by the programmers. Another review of the system is required to ensure that it meets the original specification. If the system is deficient or lacking in any respect then appropriate amendments should be made. These further amendments will make the system far more acceptable to the users.

Agree revised implementation plan, including appropriate training and transfer of data on to new system

A new implementation plan, including appropriate training of users, should be determined when the amendments to the system have been agreed. User involvement in the plan will ensure that they 'own' and, therefore, willingly accept the revised system. Appropriate training checks that users know how to use the system should be made while also selling the benefits of the new system.

Review new system after a few months, refine system and organise additional training as necessary

Since user requirements are likely to change with time, the system should be reviewed every few months to ensure that any revised requirements are catered for. Thus, the checking and review of the system should be part of a continuous review process. Where shortcomings are identified additional amendments should be made to the system as required. The mere fact that a programme of ongoing amendment is seen to be in operation will help retain staff motivation and belief in the system because they will observe that it is being updated to satisfy their requirements.

CHANGE MANAGEMENT

97 GVF – ORGANISATIONAL CHANGE

(a) There are a number of generic turnaround strategies that can be used in combination at GVF. Slatter's list of generic strategies is:

- change of management
- strong central financial control
- organisational change and decentralisation
- product-market reorientation
- improved marketing
- growth via acquisitions
- asset reduction
- cost reduction
- investment
- debt restructuring and other financial strategies.

The change of management has already taken place and the new Chief Executive Officer believes that the company has too many layers of management, narrow functional attitudes, a controlling bureaucratic head office culture and no longer responds to customer needs. She needs to initiate a strategic review to identify the key problems and formulate a clear image of the future, which should raise confidence in the turnaround. The other strategies that can be included are:

- strong central financial control to strengthen disciplines and drive down costs
- organisational change and decentralisation which can include re-structuring, reducing the layers of management, outsourcing head office departments and adopting a system of performance measurement linked to pay increases. This should help to stimulate employees to re-double and re-focus their efforts
- continuation of the development work on the new stores and initiatives to improve synergy and competitiveness
- respond to customer needs by conducting a survey and examining business processes – possibly leading to process re-engineering
- debt restructuring to replace debt with increased equity. A rights issue has already been suggested.

(b) (i) The following sources of resistance can be expected:

- fear of the unknown
- need for security
- vested interests threatened
- contrasting interpretations
- poor timing
- lack of resources.

Resistance to organisational change can come from anywhere in the organisation:

- Managers may interpret the problems differently and feel that the radical actions proposed are inappropriate. They will probably dislike implied criticism of past performances.
- Influential individuals may feel threatened, or may have been sidelined for showing resistance, and may try to build wider support through the 'grapevine'.
- Employees working in administrative jobs will feel threatened because they are likely to be redundant.
- Long-serving employees who see themselves as guardians of the corporate tradition may resist change even though it affects them least dramatically.
- Groups of employees may be awkward and de-motivated. Some of the resistance will manifest in the form of collective action such as trades union grievances.
- Some external parties (customers, suppliers, joint venture partners, etc) might also see dramatic change as a threat to their settled relationships and the smooth operation of their businesses.

(ii) Lewin's force field analysis of the conflicting tensions in organisations undergoing rapid change might be of help to the new Chief Executive Officer at GVF. It is a general purpose diagnostic and problem-solving technique that shows managers how to consider any change situation in terms of the factors encouraging and facilitating the change (the driving forces), as well as the factors that hinder change (the restraining forces).

The force field model suggests two ways of dealing with change. The first is by strengthening your own side and the second is by weakening the opposing forces.

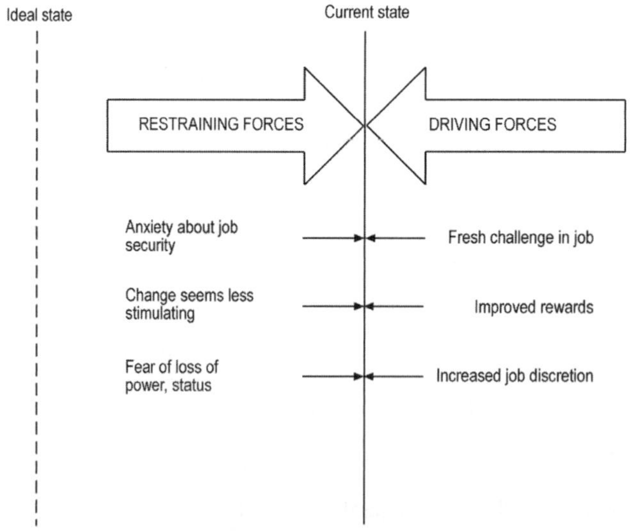

If the forces offset each other completely, it results in equilibrium and status quo. Change can be brought about by either increasing the driving forces or by reducing the restraining forces. New pushing forces can also be added. Reducing the restraining forces is often easier because to increase driving forces without attention to the restraining forces may increase pressure and tension in the system to the point that creative problem solving becomes impossible. Lewin's model allows for radical change that can only go on for so long before the health of the organisation requires a period of stability/slower change. This is implicit in the emphasis the model puts on there being a long-run equilibrium.

Mrs Bilder could use the model to list the driving forces and restraining forces at play at GVF and explain to the employees why it is natural for them to be cautious about committing to her vision of change. She can assure them that, even after a majority have been won over, others may choose to put up robust obstruction. Nothing must deter her from driving through change against strong bastions of inertia, but she must be astute and sensitive enough to spend time winning people over. She must also be ruthless enough to realise that she will come across some employees in GVF who will need to be removed because the time and effort needed to win them over is too great.

98 CC PLC

Key answer tips

Your answer should consider the effect of placing an intranet into an organisation as well as the effect on information usage that this system ought to provide.

The organisational and human reasons why information may not become more widely available

Organisational reasons

There is a clear need for investment in better equipment because current hardware only just meets specifications. The creation of an intranet would otherwise prove pointless, as the service would not function in an efficient manner.

Other than the associated costs of the investment, the organisation cultural issues that CC plc would have to face need to be considered. Since it is the intention to provide such facilities to all staff, then management need to place their trust in the staff. Management may find it difficult to accept such a degree of 'openness' that will arise as a consequence of the planned changes as they have a background in a more traditional industry.

The strategic nature of this investment makes it vital for the management of CC plc to give detailed consideration as to whether the organisation is ready for this investment. They must be confident that they will be able to fully exploit the advantages that can be derived from the investment. CC plc would undoubtedly be able to operate more effectively and could create a competitive advantage by making these provisions for staff.

Overall the organisation needs to support a more open management style with a particular emphasis upon improving communications within the organisation and providing an environment wherein employees become empowered. This is essential if the full potential of the investment is to be realised.

Human reasons

The provision of an intranet does not of itself ensure that information will become more available in CC plc. This may arise due to the fact that individuals choose not to disseminate information as they view it as a source of power. In such circumstances, other personnel i.e. staff have to make requests to view the information and this confers a sense of power and control upon the 'keeper' of the information.

The extent of duplication conveys the impression that staff like to create and maintain their own individual records and may be unwilling to share information as part of a team. Unless the staff at CC plc are willing to operate on a team basis, it is most unlikely that information will be shared more widely. Management should as a matter of urgency initiate a communications exercise in order to improve the levels of trust and co-operation within the company. In this regard staff training and education will be a vital aid to 'selling the benefits' of improved trust and co-operation within the organisation.

The communication facilities that exist at the moment, e.g. e-mail, should promote the sharing of information among offices. However, the fact that information is not shared by staff indicates that the creation of an intranet may not improve this. Management should institute a programme of activities focused upon Organisational Development in order to ensure that information becomes a more widely shared resource. A vital part of any such programme lies in the need to address the cultural issues by the provision of staff training relating to the new working practices of the company.

Whether or not the creation of an intranet is the most appropriate solution for the company is largely dependent on what shape it will take in the future. It might well be the case that a more traditional information system would be more appropriate.

99 CITYGO

Jim Ryan's belief that organisational culture is important to the success of his plans is well founded. Charles Handy describes culture as 'the way we do things round here'. This brief definition could be expressed more fully as being the sum total of the belief, knowledge, attitudes, norms and customs that prevail in an organisation. Schein emphasises that it is the pattern of basic assumptions that a given group has invented, discovered or developed in learning to cope. This pattern will have worked well enough to be considered valid and, therefore, to be used to influence the type of people who are keen to join such an organisation and who are recruited and trained. The culture becomes embedded in an organisation because it is seen as the correct way to perceive, think and feel in relation to any problems. **Peters and Waterman**, in their book *In Search of Excellence*, found that the 'dominance and coherence of culture' was an essential feature of the 'excellent' companies they observed. Jim Ryan seems to think that the prevailing culture is not driven towards excellence, because the staff have not had any experience of innovation, customer care, quality and competitive advantage.

Handy identified four cultural types: the power; role; task; and person culture. CityGo's culture will probably be similar to those found in bureaucracies (role culture) with formal rigid structures of rules, organisation, job descriptions and procedures, where position in the structure is far more crucial than personality. Unfortunately, bureaucracies are very slow to adapt to change and this is a company in a hurry to change to a situation where there is limited formalisation, and where decision-making centres on key people. Mintzberg would argue that CityGo will be moving from a machine-based organisational form toward an entrepreneurial form. The prevailing culture dictates the way in which management functions of planning, organising, controlling, staffing and leading are carried out. However, privatisation means an essential change in direction. CityGo will need re-positioning within its environment. This will force change onto the management team and require it to develop a strategy for creating and maintaining the culture changes needed for organisations which are competitive, customer-led and innovative. Change can be gradual and small or it can be on a significant scale as in CityGo, involving changes in the environment, working methods, management and working relationships and changes to the core values, structure and systems, requiring organisational transformation and re-structuring.

Inevitably these changes will cause resistance from those wishing to preserve the existing state of affairs and the way that the changes are put forward and implemented will be crucial to CityGo's success. Reactions to change can range from acceptance through indifference to resistance. The worst scenario is of active resistance which could include deliberate spoiling or errors, go-slows, sabotage, absenteeism or strikes.

Cultural resistance tends to occur in different ways and at different levels of an organisation. It can be organisation-wide, at a level of management, in a particular department, by particular individuals or a trade union group. Resistance to cultural change can be managed or reduced with total, genuine and visible support for the change by top management and good communication/participation systems associated with the change. Kurt Lewin has also demonstrated that behaviour change is more likely to occur and persist when commitment is on a group basis rather than an individual one and, in this respect, Jim Ryan's involvement of Rita Moran will be helpful as she is already experienced in working in a different environment. The first step for her will be to analyse the reasons why people resist change. At CityGo it is most likely because the changes will create an unknown future. This causes fear and resistance. People like to feel secure and have an influence on the events of their lives. Also, not knowing the reason for the change will cause resistance. Change could pose a threat of reduction in status and power, loss of security or removal of challenging, interesting work.

Lewin suggests that managers should recognise that there exists a current state of equilibrium with forces pushing for change on the one hand and, equally, forces resisting change aiming to maintain the present situation. The tendency is to increase the pressure of the driving forces, which is often counter-productive because it causes increased pressure from the restraining forces. It is better practice to analyse the restraining forces with a view to reducing or eliminating their pressures. The company can then move more smoothly to the new state of equilibrium The process of change includes unfreezing habits or standard operating procedures, changing to new patterns and refreezing to ensure lasting effects:

- **unfreezing** – where management convince staff of the undesirability of the present situation, creating the initial motivation to change
- **the change process itself** – which will often involve new information, new attitudes, and new concepts
- **refreezing** – which reinforces the new pattern of work or behaviour by rewards, developing the belief that the changed situation satisfies organisational and personal values.

The strategies for managing change include participation, education, communication, coercion and negotiation. CityGo would probably choose a combination of strategies to bring about the desired changes. Participation strategy aims to involve the staff, usually by allowing some input into decision-making or by a share ownership scheme. Employees are more likely to support changes made and give positive commitment if they 'own' the change or have a stake in the future of the company. Another advantage of participation is the improved utilisation of employee expertise. Newsletters, suggestion schemes and quality circles are all examples of refreezing activities carried out by co-operative, motivated workers. An education and communication strategy relies upon the hopeful belief that communication about the benefits of change to employees will result in their acceptance of the need to exercise the changes necessary. The challenge to the management team at CityGo would be to communicate Jim's vision of the future and show how each employee can contribute to it. The obvious advantage is that any changes could be initiated easily. However, employees may not agree about the benefits of proposed changes as being in their best interests. Also, the process of education and persuasion can be lengthy to initiate and exercise unless there is a firm mutual trust. Coercion as a strategy involves the compulsory approach by management to implement change. When there is a state of high unemployment, management enjoys greater power and is therefore able to use this strategy with more success. The advantage of this method is that changes can be made with speed; however, the lack of commitment of the workforce resulting in weak motivation, low morale and performance and the determination to reverse policy when times change can be a problem. A negotiation strategy is often practised in unionised companies where the process of bargaining leads to a situation of compromise and agreement. The advantage of a negotiation strategy is that it offers the company the opportunity to note possible conflict and allows it to be dealt with in an orderly fashion. This hopefully prevents such problems as industrial action. Also, when an agreement has been made, the outcome can be to encourage commitment, preserve morale and maintain output.

Section 5

MAY 2007 EXAM QUESTIONS

SECTION A – 50 MARKS

[The indicative time for answering this section is 90 minutes]

Answer this question

QUESTION ONE: AFR FURNITURE

Introduction

AFR is a large retailer of furniture, based in an Asian country. It has three strategic business units (SBUs) which specialise in office, bedroom and lounge furniture. Each SBU is responsible for the design, procurement and retailing of its own range of furniture. AFR sells all its product ranges through a chain of large 'furniture superstores' throughout its own country. Each store sells all three furniture ranges.

AFR has been in existence for over 20 years, and has always been profitable. Recently, the organisation's profitability has been slightly higher than average for the furniture retail sector.

All the furniture that AFR sells is designed 'in-house'. Design staff from each of the three SBUs work in a centralised research and development (R&D) department, where all designs are developed. Production of the designs is outsourced to a number of small local manufacturers. This ensures that AFR can keep close control of product features, style and quality, while negotiating down the unit cost of production.

Segmental analysis

The following figures are extracts from the report and accounts of AFR for 2006. AFR reports its performance in the local currency, the dollar.

		$ million
Sales revenue	Office furniture	4.23
	Bedroom furniture	3.20
	Lounge furniture	6.04
	TOTAL	13.47

		$ million
Contribution	Office furniture	0.81
	Bedroom furniture	0.44
	Lounge furniture	0.75
	TOTAL	2.00

Market conditions

The market for office furniture is estimated to be growing at a rate of about 15% each year. The market leader is DS with a reported sales revenue from this sector of $6.35 million. DS sells a much narrower range of 'basic' office furniture than AFR, through a chain of specialised office furniture stores. Most of its products are mass produced in large factories elsewhere in Asia, and it is therefore able to sell at much lower prices than AFR.

The market for bedroom furniture is considered to be declining by about 5% each year. AFR is market leader in this segment, ahead of NKO (with sales revenue of $2.85 million) and MK ($2.14 million). AFR has a good reputation for the style and quality of its bedroom furniture, and customers report very high satisfaction levels.

The market for lounge furniture, such as sofas and easy chairs, is growing at a rate of about 2% each year. AFR is a relatively small player in this market which is dominated by MK with its sales revenue of $14.25 million. The second placed competitor is TSC ($11.96 million), closely followed by NKO ($8.94 million). Despite having tried to increase its market share in this segment, AFR has had little success. Much of AFR's lounge furniture is made to order, with customers allowed to choose from a wide range of styles and fabrics.

The following information has been provided by the Government bureau of economic statistics:

		$ million
Market volumes	Office furniture	23.60
(2006)	Bedroom furniture	12.80
	Lounge furniture	70.00

Dining furniture

The research and development (R&D) manager of AFR has noticed that the market for dining furniture, such as dining tables and formal dining chairs, is growing at a rate of about 10% a year. Furthermore, he is aware that neither DS nor MK has any dining furniture products. This market segment is served by many small retailers, each of whom sells a similar range. Most of the dining furniture currently on sale originates from a few large manufacturers.

The R&D manager has proposed to the Board of AFR that the organisation develops its first ever range of dining furniture. The R&D manager has provided the following estimates of project cost and revenue.

	$
Depreciation (per year)	24,000
Other fixed costs (per year)	80,000
Variable cost (per unit*)	560
Average sales price (per unit*)	800

* *A unit is one table and six chairs.*

The R&D manager has calculated that, to break even, AFR must sell just over 400 units per year. He believes that such a level of sales is almost certain due to the stylish designs he has been working on.

The marketing manager is not sure. She feels that sales need to be closer to 500 units each year if AFR is to make a profit. The marketing manager also believes that demand is unlikely to exceed 500 units for such unusual designs. She is also concerned that the new dining furniture may be overpriced at $800 per unit.

The managing director asked the R&D manager how much investment in new capital equipment would be required, and the R&D manager said that the investment cost of $120,000 was already taken into account in the depreciation figure.

AFR evaluates projects over a five-year period.

Required:

(a) Evaluate the existing product portfolio of AFR.

Note: There are up to 7 marks available for calculations in this requirement.

(15 marks)

(b) Recommend an appropriate strategy for each existing product range.

(9 marks)

(c) Advise the Board whether to invest in the new range of dining furniture. You should assume a cost of capital of 10% for this project, a project life of five years and no taxation.

Note: There are 6 marks available for calculations in this requirement.

(14 marks)

(d) Recommend appropriate control measures, assuming none are currently in place, for

(i) the three existing product ranges

(6 marks)

(ii) the project to develop the new range of dining furniture should it go ahead. (The project, for the purpose of this question, may be assumed to be the design of the new product range and production of prototype products **ONLY.**)

(6 marks)

(Total for Question One = 50 marks)

(Total for Section A = 50 marks)

SECTION B – 50 MARKS

[The indicative time for answering this section is 90 minutes]

Answer TWO questions from four

QUESTION TWO: B MEDIA COMPANY

B is a media company, publishing lifestyle magazines for the consumer market. These lifestyle magazines contain articles and advertisements about fashion, health and beauty products, homes, furniture and hobbies and are bought by people aspiring to a high standard of living.

Increasingly, consumers are turning to other media for the information and entertainment traditionally provided by this type of magazine.

Traditionally, 60% of B's revenue has been derived from selling advertising, the balance being provided by the cover price of each magazine. Over the last four years both the revenue and profits have declined as there has been a steady reduction in the sale of both advertising space and the number of magazines sold.

The industry is very dependent upon the level of discretionary disposable income. If this income is at a low level, fewer luxury goods are advertised. However, people still buy the magazines to read about these goods.

The company has tried to expand abroad but has failed, expensively, to achieve this. Similarly, attempts to enter other segments of the home market, particularly teenage magazines, have failed. Both of these failures have come as a surprise to the Board of Directors who thought that they understood the respective markets well enough to make the appropriate decisions.

New technology, in the form of digital media, has also affected the magazine industry. These changes have been felt in both production methods, such as broadband distribution of proof copies, and the choice of media, such as the Internet, available to consumers. To a large extent, the speed of these developments was a surprise to the directors of B.

Required:

As Management Accountant, you have been seconded to work with the organisation's forecasting and planning function, to improve its long-range planning.

(a) Evaluate the benefits to B of implementing a process of systematic environmental analysis.

(12 marks)

(b) Describe the essential stages that should be included in a scenario planning process that could be introduced by B.

(13 marks)

(Total for Question Two = 25 marks)

QUESTION THREE: C PHARMACEUTICALS MANUFACTURER

C is a major pharmaceutical manufacturing company producing and supplying a variety of prescription drugs in its home market. C currently uses its own fleet of vehicles to deliver to the wholesalers. There are six competitors who supply drugs that can be used to treat the same diseases as those produced by C.

Up until three years ago, the supply chain for the industry consisted of the manufacturers, and a group of ten wholesalers which covered the whole country and which supplied approximately 4,000 independent pharmacies. These independent pharmacies are all small companies which source their drugs from the wholesalers.

Traditionally, patients would see a doctor who would write a prescription for the correct dose of the required drug which the patients had to take to the pharmacy to get their supply. This was the only way they could obtain their medication. Because of a government subsidy, regardless of the medication prescribed, all prescriptions are charged at a fixed rate.

Three years ago, the legislation changed and for the first time supermarkets were allowed to employ a qualified pharmacist and to supply prescription drugs. Because of their size and buying power, the supermarkets are now refusing to deal with the wholesalers and are insisting on being supplied directly by the pharmaceutical manufacturers.

These changes have not been well received by the independent pharmacies. There has been a significant volume of comment in the press about pressure groups which see this as another encroachment by 'big business' on the small independent traders. Some government ministers have also expressed concern about the increasing market power of the supermarkets.

C is considering changing its distribution network so that it no longer supplies the wholesalers but will sell directly to all the independent pharmacies and will share the wholesalers' margin with them.

Although the transport manager has said that he believes the arrangements can be dealt with in-house, some of the Board of Directors feel that it might be better to outsource all the transport function.

The Board of Directors recognises that there would need to be significant changes in the way the company operates were either, or both, proposals to be implemented. These changes would also have a significant effect on the stakeholders of the business.

Required:

(a) Discuss the advantages and disadvantages, to C, of the proposal to supply directly to the pharmacies.

(10 marks)

(b) Discuss the advantages and disadvantages, to C, of the proposal to outsource the transport function should the proposal to directly supply pharmacies be adopted.

(8 marks)

(c) Advise the project team how C might best communicate the decision, to directly supply independent pharmacies, to each of its principal stakeholders.

(7 marks)

(Total for Question Three = 25 marks)

QUESTION FOUR: D MANAGEMENT CONSULTANCY

D is a management consultancy partnership providing complex computer modelling services to utility companies. Three partners started the business ten years ago but rapid growth in the past four years has seen it increase to fifteen partners. Each partner has a team working exclusively for, and reporting directly to that partner. Competition between the teams is fierce and sometimes heated. The loyalty of each team to its respective partner is very strong.

Members of each team are rewarded with an annual team bonus based on the amount of new business they bring in each year. However, recently it has been discovered that teams have been competing with each other for the same potential new client.

Partners recruit all consultants as trainees, usually after they have obtained a doctorate in pure mathematics or economics. After a six months' probationary period they are either confirmed in post or asked to leave. The rewards for those who stay are high with at least 60% of income derived from the team bonus. Typically a basic salary of $40,000 would be boosted to $100,000 if the team has worked aggressively and found new clients.

The service that the partnership provides is highly specialised and at the forefront of available technology. Each team will write computer simulations to address its clients' problems. These models are not made available outside the company and, on some occasions, have not even been shared with other teams in the consultancy.

At a recent partners' meeting, it was agreed that the inter-team rivalry was not working in the partnership's best interest, since teams were competing in such a way as to damage the firm's reputation, profitability and its prospects for growth. Recognising that the current performance measurement system encouraged this behaviour, the partners agreed that an appropriate performance measurement system should be introduced which was less one-dimensional. The partners believed this would encourage better practice in terms of knowledge sharing and a co-ordinated approach to their existing clients and potential clients. They have recognised that the introduction of a multi-dimensional performance measurement system will involve a significant training programme for their teams to redirect their current focus away from only finding new business.

Required:

As a first stage in this process, you have been appointed as management accountant and practice manager.

(a) Advise the partners of the functions that an effective performance measurement system will perform for D.

Note: You are NOT required to describe, in detail, any particular system.

(10 marks)

(b) Recommend the process that should be used in developing the performance measurement system to be used within D.

(15 marks)

(Total for Question Four = 25 marks)

QUESTION FIVE: E DEVELOPING COUNTRY

E is a developing country in a group of islands where each island is a separate country. A number of the islands formed a trade bloc five years ago and co-operate economically and in their terms of trade.

Those countries that are in the trade bloc impose no tariffs on imports and exports between member countries but impose a common rate of import duty on any goods or services brought into the group. The trade bloc jointly advertises the attractiveness of the area for inward investment, exports and tourism, and this has been reasonably successful recently. At present, each island has a different currency but full monetary union has been proposed for the future.

E does not belong to the trade bloc at this point in time and is the least developed of the islands in the group although, geographically, it is one of the largest.

There is a fairly large volume of trade between the islands and the majority of E's exports of agricultural products and light engineering products go to other countries in the group of islands. Since the other islands are more industrialised than E, they are not self-sufficient for foodstuffs.

The school system of E produces well-educated children, many of whom go to a nearby industrialised country, F, to take degrees. F is not part of the trade bloc. Only 10% of those students return to E and usually work in their parents' business or other small firms. The average age of the population of E is some ten years higher than that of the islands in the trade bloc.

Although E is an attractive location, there is a limited tourism industry in E and there is very little in the way of service industry, although the government has recently received a grant from the World Bank to improve the telecommunications infrastructure of the island.

Required:

(a) Identify those internal and external stakeholders who would be interested in E's decision to join the trade bloc and discuss the nature of their interest.

(12 marks)

(b) Discuss the advantages and disadvantages that could be experienced by the stakeholders based in E if the country were to enter the trade bloc.

(13 marks)

(Total for Question Five = 25 marks)

(Total for Section B = 50 marks)

Section 6

ANSWERS TO MAY 2007 EXAM QUESTIONS

SECTION A

1 AFR FURNITURE

Key answer tips

The obvious framework to use in parts (a) and (b) is the BCG matrix analysis. However, it is important that you consider the specific details of each SBU and are willing to contradict the conventional BCG wisdom where appropriate.

In part (c) make sure you conclude your discussion with recommendations.

In part (d) the term 'control measures' could be interpreted as meaning both systems/processes and KPIs.

(a) **Product portfolio evaluation**

The product portfolio can be assessed using the BCG matrix framework as follows:

Diagram (see W1 for details)

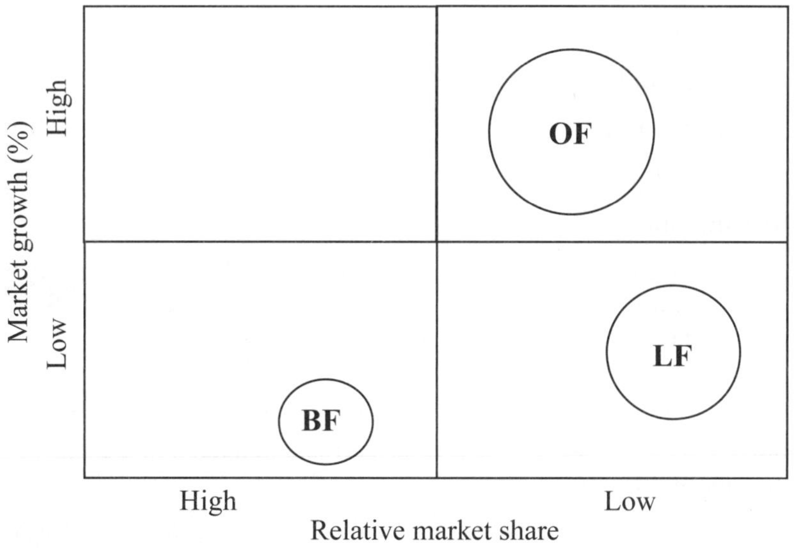

Commentary

According to the BCG matrix, office furniture would be classified as a problem child, having a relatively low share of a high growth (and hence attractive) market. This would normally imply that it is receiving investment in excess of any cash flows generated by itself and hence requires cash subsidisation by other SBUs. This seems unlikely in this case as office furniture provides the largest share of contribution and has the highest C/S ratio (W2).

Bedroom furniture would be classified as a cash cow, having a relatively high share of a low growth (and hence unattractive) market. Conventional BCG analysis would suggest that this SBU should be cash rich and able to provide funds for financing other SBUs. With AFR it appears that bedroom furniture generates the lowest contribution, so again does not fit with the BCG 'wisdom'.

Lounge furniture would be classified as a dog product, having a relatively low share of a low growth (and hence unattractive) market. This would normally imply a product with few prospects and a cash neutral or even cash negative position. The relatively low C/S ratio of 12.4% (W2) would indicate the lack of a clear competitive advantage, but lounge furniture does provide 37.5% of the firm's contribution suggesting a cash positive position.

Summary

AFR has three major SBUs, each of which generates a positive contribution to fixed costs. Lounge and bedroom furniture have the lowest C/S ratios, due to competitive pressure and/or cost efficiency.

The fact that AFR's profitability has been higher than average for the sector would reinforce the view that it has a healthy, balanced portfolio.

BCG matrix analysis, however, would suggest that the portfolio is not balanced due to the lack of star products.

Workings

(W1) **SBU**

	Market growth	*Relative market share*	*Contribution (gives circle size)*
Office furniture	+15%	4.23/6.35 = 0.67	0.81
Bedroom furniture	–5%	3.20/2.85 = 1.12	0.44
Lounge furniture	+2%	6.04/14.25 = 0.42	0.75

(W2) **C/S ratios**

Office furniture:	C/S ratio	= 0.81/4.23	= 19.1%
Bedroom furniture:	C/S ratio	= 0.44/3.20	= 13.8%
Lounge furniture:	C/S ratio	= 0.75/6.04	= 12.4%
Overall:	C/S ratio	= 2.00/13.47	= 14.8%

(b) **Office furniture**

According to BCG, office furniture is a 'problem child' and hence the choice is to 'double or quit'. Given it has the highest growth prospects and C/S ratio within the portfolio, the best approach is to 'double' or invest.

The BCG remedy assumes a competitive strategy of cost-leadership and relies on gaining market share to achieve economies of scale. However, DS appears to be following a cost-leadership approach so it would make more sense for AFR to pursue a strategy of differentiation.

This will involve a process of value analysis to determine which aspects of furniture design and manufacture could be the source of a quality advantage. Investment should also be targeted at marketing and branding to enhance a quality reputation/image.

Bedroom furniture

According to BCG, bedroom furniture is a 'cash cow', so the prescribed strategy is to cut back on investment and harvest cash for reinvestment in other SBUs.

However, bedroom furniture produces the lowest contribution in the portfolio. It may also be a mistake to cut back all investment as AFR is currently the market leader with a good reputation.

Some investment will be required to defend this position from NKO and MK. As with office furniture, a strategy of differentiation would be recommended.

Lounge furniture

Lounge furniture is a 'dog' and so should be phased out according to BCG.

This is clearly wrong in this case as lounge furniture generates 45% of AFR's revenue and 37.5% of its contribution.

However, BCG are correct in their assumption that a dog product like this lacks the economies of scale to compete on a cost basis. AFR should look to develop a differentiation with a focus strategy for tailor-made furniture.

(c) **Dining furniture**

The proposal to move into dining room furniture can be assessed using the 'suitability, feasibility, acceptability' framework of Johnson and Scholes:

Suitability

The market for dining room furniture appears to be growing at about 10% a year and has the advantage that none of AFR's existing major competitors are currently present. Given that most existing retailers source from the same few manufacturers, there may be an opportunity for AFR to offer something new to the market.

Feasibility

AFR's existing distribution network could be used for the new range and AFR's reputation for quality for bedroom and lounge furniture should transfer to the dining room sector well.

Acceptability

The R&D manager has estimated the breakeven point at just over 400 units per annum. Incorporating the time value of money, the correct figure is 466 units (see W2 below). Given that the marketing manager believes that sales of 500 units are unlikely, this would suggest that the proposal carries a high risk of failure.

Conclusion

The proposal is certainly worth further investigation. More extensive market research would be advisable to try to get a better idea of customer requirements, gaps in the market and more accurate sales figures before proceeding.

Workings

(W1) **BEP using accounting figures**

Total fixed costs = 24,000 + 80,000 = $104,000 a year

Contribution per unit = 800 – 560 = $240 per unit

BEP = Fixed costs/Contribution per unit = 104,000/240 = 433 units a year

(W2) **BEP using discounted cash flows**

Assuming sales of S unit's p.a.

Time	Narrative	CF	DF@10%	PV
		$		$
0	Investment	(120,000)	1	(120,000)
1 – 5	Contribution (S × 240)	240S	3.791	910S
1 – 5	Fixed costs	(80,000)	3.791	(303,280)
	NPV			910S – 423,280

Setting NPV = 910S – 423,280 = 0 gives a breakeven volume of S = 466 units

Tutorial note: The BEP can also be found by calculating the NPV for both sales of 400 and 500 units and then interpolating.

(d) **Control measures**

(i) **Existing product ranges**

A conventional system of budgeting, target setting and variance reporting should be set up for each store and product range. Within this critical success factors should be identified and corresponding key performance indicators monitored. These could include the following:

- C/S ratios
- sales targets, with commissions linked to whether sales targets are met
- cost variances
- % discounts given.

Given that it is recommended that each SBU pursues a competitive strategy of differentiation, quality assurance systems should be put in place to ensure quality is maintained and enhanced. Specific KPIs could include:

- % customer returns / warranty claims / complaints
- customer satisfaction surveys
- staff turnover.

This could be structured within a move to implement TQM or to encourage manufacturers to achieve ISO 9000 status.

Marketing campaigns should be subject to rigorous appraisal, authorisation and review to ensure that the advertising budget is used effectively.

(ii) **Dining furniture**

The plan to develop the new range should be controlled like any other project:

- A project manager, project team and a steering committee should be set up and clear responsibility allocated.
- The project manager should have regular meetings with the steering committee to report and assess progress.
- Key project variables are time, scope and cost. A detailed project specification will be required to set out the scope and budgets should be prepared for time and cost control. Detailed figures should be calculated for both design and prototype stages. Project planning tools such as network analysis, work breakdown structure and Gantt charts will help here.
- Milestones should be set to help monitor progress.
- There should be a post-project review or audit to ensure that target deliverables have been achieved. This will allow lessons to be learnt for future developments.

2 B MEDIA COMPANY

Key answer tips

Section (a) asks you to **evaluate** benefits rather than simply list them.

Part (b) is standard bookwork but needs to be related to B to get full marks.

(a) **Environmental analysis**

Systematic environmental analysis would benefit B in the following ways:

- More comprehensive information available for decision making

  A number of B's recent strategic decisions, such as overseas ventures have failed due to insufficient information. A more detailed environmental analysis would have helped B identify key factors to consider. This is perhaps the most important aspect – systematic environmental scanning will improve the planning and decision-making process.

- Anticipating opportunities and threats sooner

  B seems to have been slow to appreciate the growing importance of the Internet for advertising and, more specifically, as a media type with the development of online magazines. As a consequence, this appears to have become a threat to B's business model rather than an opportunity to exploit. A PEST-style analysis would have revealed this technological development sooner.

- Be able to evaluate opportunities more thoroughly

  B recently failed in an attempt to enter the domestic teenage magazine market. A PEST style analysis would have indicated the extent and drivers of growth in this segment and a Porter's five forces analysis would have revealed key competitive forces. This information may have resulted in a decision not to enter the market or a different strategy for entry. Either way, the considerable costs of failure would have been avoided.

- Quicker response to changing customer needs

  The directors of B are being forced into a reactive style of management as they are being surprised by the rate of change in some markets. Systematic market analysis would allow them to identify changes sooner and hence change products to more quickly match customer needs.

- Lower risk

  The net result of all of the above is that systematic environmental analysis will reduce B's downside risk exposure but should increase its ability to exploit opportunities.

- More accurate budgeting

  A greater awareness of forecasts regarding the advertising industry and the mix of paper versus e-advertising would allow B to budget its future advertising income more accurately.

(b) **Scenario planning**

Scenarios are detailed and plausible views of how the business environment might develop in the future based on groupings of key environmental influences and drivers of change about which there is a high degree of uncertainty.

Scenario planning involves the following steps:

1 ***Identify high-impact, high-uncertainty factors in the environment***

Relevant factors and driving forces could be identified through a strategic analysis framework such as a PEST analysis. Once identified, factors need to be ranked according to importance and uncertainty.

For example, for B three key factors could be the speed of development of e-magazines, consumers' attitudes to e-magazines and the cost of paper.

2 ***For each factor, identify different possible futures***

Precision is not possible but developing a view of the future against which to evaluate and evolve strategies is important. For example:

Factor	*Possible futures*
Development of e-magazines	• Rapid • Slow
Consumer attitudes to e-magazines	• Good substitute • Poor substitute
Cost of paper	• Rising • Stable

3 ***Cluster together different factors to identify various consistent future scenarios.***

This process usually results in between seven and nine mini-scenarios. For example,

- *Scenario 1:*

  Consumers still prefer conventional magazines, partly because of the limited growth in e-magazines offered to the market.

  However, the future does not look positive, due to rising paper costs. If these are passed on to customers, then it might encourage them to consider e-magazines more seriously.

- *Scenario 2:*

  Rapid growth in the availability of e-magazines and associated marketing costs.

  Together with increasing acceptance of e-magazines as an alternative to paper-based products, this has resulted in many potential customers switching to electronic media.

4 ***'Writing the scenario'***

For the most important scenarios (usually limited to three), build a detailed analysis to identify and assess future implications.

As part of this, planners typically develop a set of optimistic, pessimistic and most likely assumptions about the impact of key variables on the company's future strategy.

The result of this detailed scenario construction should include:

- financial implications – anticipated net profits, cash flow, and net working capital for each of three versions of the future

- strategic implications – possible opportunities and risks
- the probability of occurrence, usually based on past experience.

5 ***For each scenario identify and assess possible courses of action for the firm***

For example, possible strategies for the two alternative scenarios outlined above:

- *Scenario 1:* A possible strategy would be to cut paper costs by the increased use of recycled products.
- *Scenario 2:* A possible strategy would be to develop ranges of titles aimed at older customers, who will (presumably) be slower to accept e-magazines.

Some strategies make sense whatever the outcome, usually because they capitalise on or develop key strengths of the firm. For example, B could look to strengthen its relationship with key advertisers.

However, in many cases, new resources and competencies may be required for existing strategies to succeed. Alternatively, entirely new strategies may be required. For B this could be the development of on-line versions of its magazines, accessible by subscription.

6 ***Monitor reality to see which scenario is unfolding***

7 ***Revise scenarios and strategic options as appropriate***

3 C PHARMACEUTICALS MANUFACTURER

Key answer tips

Parts (a) and (b) ask you to discuss pros and cons, so ensure that you explain your points, rather than simply listing them.

When discussing communication in part (c), you need to give details of the methods you suggest.

(a) The advantages and disadvantages of supplying directly to pharmacies are as follows:

Advantages

- By avoiding wholesalers' margins, C will be able to charge more for its products. Subject to the cost increases detailed below, this will result in greater profits.
- C can build goodwill and customer loyalty directly with pharmacies by being seen to be responsive to their worries and concerns regarding supermarkets.
- C might also build greater brand awareness among end-users who may also be concerned about supermarket growth. This could give C an opportunity to differentiate itself from its six main competitors.
- By dealing directly with pharmacists, C will be 'closer to the customer' and thus better positioned to understand customer needs and respond accordingly.
- The move may win C some influence in government with ministers who are also concerned about supermarket power.

Disadvantages

- Pharmacists may be used to dealing with a single wholesaler who can provide all of their product needs – drugs, cosmetics, food and drink, for example – and may be unwilling to switch to C who can only supply drugs. C may thus lose customers.
- In order to meet pharmacists' needs, C will probably have to hold higher inventories of drugs. Previously wholesalers would have held buffer inventories.
- There will be much higher administration costs managing relationships with 4,000 pharmacies rather than 10 wholesalers. There is also the greater risk of irrecoverable debts.
- C may well incur higher packaging costs. Previously it would have supplied wholesalers with large boxes of drugs and relied on them to disaggregate. Now it may have to supply lots of small boxes to individual pharmacies.
- Unless outsourced (see below), distribution costs are likely to be much higher as C will have to deliver to 4,000 independent shops, rather than 10 wholesalers. This may mean, for example, that C will need more trucks.
- By focusing on supplying pharmacies directly, C could be missing out on the opportunity to supply supermarkets. This could be a major error should the supermarkets gain significant market share.
- If the supermarkets do gain market share, then it will be at the expense of the pharmacies that C is targeting.

(b) The pros and cons of outsourcing transportation are as follows:

Advantages

- The external supplier will have greater logistics expertise to handle deliveries to 4,000 pharmacies more efficiently than C.
- The external supplier may benefit from economies of scale allowing it to bid for C's contract at a lower price than the cost if C kept distribution in-house.
- Outsourcing avoids C having to buy more trucks for distribution to the 4,000 pharmacies. Completely outsourcing all deliveries would allow C to sell its existing trucks.
- C would be able to focus on its core skills of pharmaceuticals manufacturing without being distracted by distribution issues.

Disadvantages

- Outsourcing would make it more difficult for C to control its distribution function. Any problems with delays, for example, would impact on C's goodwill.
- The inevitable redundancies could damage C's reputation.
- Even though distribution is not considered core to C's business, outsourcing will result in lost competences and skills that may subsequently be useful.
- C is unlikely to have the skills required to manage subcontractors so may need to acquire these.

(c) If C decides to supply pharmacies directly, then it should ensure that key stakeholders are informed as follows:

Stakeholder group	**Communication methods**
Independent pharmacies	• A letter or an article in a trade magazine informing pharmacies of the proposed strategy and reasoning. Most pharmacists should be sympathetic to the reasoning concerning supermarkets. • Sales representatives should then arrange meetings with individual pharmacists to discuss their concerns and try to get customers signed up.
Wholesalers	• Senior staff from C should arrange a face-to-face meeting with wholesalers to explain their plans. This will minimise disruption in the period up to existing contracts ending.
Distribution staff	• Senior staff should arrange a meeting with all transportation staff as soon as a decision is made to discuss plans and outline the assistance that C may be able to offer (retraining, relocation, etc). Given that many staff will lose their jobs it is important that C acts responsibly as a caring employer.
The local community	• C should seek to generate good PR by trying to get articles in local newspapers, communicating with local chambers of commerce and business watchdogs. Throughout these the message should focus on protecting local businesses.
Doctors	• Letters should be sent to GP surgeries explaining the changes. Hopefully the doctors will support C's stand to support local businesses and may be willing to allow posters to be put up on notice boards to communicate to patients.

4 D MANAGEMENT CONSULTANCY

Key answer tips

Part (a) is tricky as it asks for the **functions** a performance management system would provide, rather than asking for a description of an optimal system. Make sure you answer the question!

Part (b) should detail a process with each step explained and justified. The main problem faced by many students was that they felt that they did not have enough to say for the 15 marks available. Some time spent planning would have helped here.

(a) An effective performance management system should perform the following functions for D:

- Establishing current position

  A broader set of measures will allow the partners of D to gain a more comprehensive picture of how the consultancy is performing against the measures chosen. These should include not only financial performance but also knowledge management, learning and reputation.

This can be made more useful by benchmarking between teams and against competing consultancies.

- Communicating direction

  An effective performance measurement system can be used to communicate performance to key stakeholders. For D these will include partners and senior managers / team leaders. Depending on the level of detail disclosed, managers will be able to see the local performance of their teams and the overall performance of the partnership, together with future targets and plans.

- Changing the culture of the organisation

  The current system of targets and bonuses has encouraged a culture where teams try to undercut each other and are reluctant to share knowledge. Suitably chosen measures and remuneration schemes should help to change the culture towards one where greater co-operation is the norm.

- Confirming priorities

  The performance management system should inform all employees of the partners' priorities. Currently this is assumed to be new business development, but should be expanded to include knowledge sharing.

- Influencing behaviour

  Particularly if bonuses are linked to a new set of measures, then the new system will change employee priorities and, hence, performance. The single-minded approach currently seen needs to be replaced with a broader set of measures.

(b) The following process should be adopted in developing the new performance management system for the consultancy service:

- Stakeholder participation

  While the partners may be convinced of the need for a new system, many consultants who currently receive large bonuses may be less willing to embrace change. It is important therefore that partners arrange meetings with consultants to communicate plans and gain 'buy-in'.

- Identify the key outputs required from the service

  Key outputs are what different stakeholders want from the service. In the case of clients this could be effective computer simulations delivered on time. By considering partners this can be extended to include delivering solutions within budget and achieving target profits.

- Identify the key processes to deliver the outputs

  Effective control follows the rationale of quality assurance rather than quality control so focuses on the inputs and processes as well as the eventual outputs. Partners need to understand the whole process from a client enquiry to delivering a possible solution.

  This will be accomplished by:

  - discussions with management and staff involved in providing the product
  - observation and 'walk-through' of the process
  - investigation into instances of client dissatisfaction
  - examination of background to decisions and structures of authorisation.

- Identify the interfaces in D's value network

  These are the outside persons or other processes on which D relies to do its work. This will include suppliers, customers and co-workers in other processes. The quality of this interface may have an impact on the service quality.

  For D this could include examining the relationships partners and consultants have with clients and with each other.

- Develop performance indicators for key processes

  A range of key performance indicators (KPIs) needs to be established for each critical success factor (CSF) identified. Most consultancy firms emphasise profit and chargeable hours. However, D should seek to incorporate a wider set of measures, such as those developed by Fitzgerald et al:

  - financial performance
  - competitiveness
  - resource utilisation
  - quality of service
  - innovation
  - flexibility.

- Identify data sources

  These will vary enormously according to what is being measured and many will not be readily quantifiable. Internal sources could include timesheets, and external sources could include client satisfaction surveys and peer review ratings.

- Develop the reporting system

  This will depend on the management style and systems being used. In D this will focus on empowering teams.

- Review effectiveness

  Initial control systems will have faults. Therefore:

  - pilot the system on a limited scale, say to one team, before a 'big bang' introduction
  - record the improvements to KPIs through time
  - review the adequacy of the system as the work of the firm changes.

5 E DEVELOPING COUNTRY

Key answer tips

Part (a) is a straightforward stakeholder analysis. Try to include as many groups as possible.

In part (b) make sure you discuss points, rather than simply listing them. One of the main problems with this question lies in distinguishing your points between parts (a) and (b) and avoiding duplication.

You may be aware of the arguments currently surrounding enlargement of the EU. Many of these can be repurposed for this question.

(a) The different stakeholders who would be interested in E's decision include the following:

'Internal' Stakeholders based in E

- The government of E will be interested in making the best decisions for its country in terms of economic growth and jobs. On a more individual note, the ministers concerned will be interested in the possible increase in their workload and any gain prestige from greater exposure on the world stage.
- Businesses in E that export to trade bloc countries will be interested in eliminating import duty on their products and the consequences of this for demand and profitability.
- Businesses in E that import goods from countries outside the trade bloc countries will be interested in the additional import duty that will be charged on imports and the consequences of this for their costs and profitability.
- Many businesses will be interested in the extra advertising carried out by the trade bloc and the implications of this in terms of greater demand from around the world for exports.
- Businesses involved in the tourist industry will be interested in the likely increase in the number of tourists visiting E.
- Citizens of E will be interested in the likely implications of cheaper goods and more jobs. They will also be interested in whether this will mean that more students return to find jobs in E after graduating.

External Stakeholders based outside E

- Businesses exporting to E from other trade bloc islands will be interested in the opportunities for greater trade with E.
- Businesses importing from E will be interested in how the elimination of import duties, and hence lower prices in the market place, will affect demand from consumers.
- Citizens of other trade bloc countries should see a reduction in the price of goods imported from E.
- Global firms seeking to invest in the region will be interested in whether the move would make E a more attractive target for investment.

(b) The main advantages and disadvantages for stakeholders within E of entering the trade bloc are as follows:

Advantages

- The removal of trade barriers between member countries should result in a greater volume of trade between E and its co-members as goods effectively become cheaper for consumers. This should lead to economic growth and more jobs within E.
- Being part of the trade bloc will make E more attractive to foreign firms considering investing in the region. Such foreign direct investment (FDI) should also result in greater economic growth.
- The government should receive higher tax revenues allowing greater investment in infrastructure and tertiary education. This may reduce the current trend for students to go overseas for degrees.
- Additional well-paid jobs may encourage more young people to stay and work in E, reducing the current skills drain.
- The government of E will gain extra status by being part of a larger group and by presiding over a period of economic growth.
- The advertising carried out by the bloc should benefit E's growing tourist industry and the businesses involved in it.

Disadvantages

- Businesses in E may suffer due to import duties being imposed on imported goods not currently subject to such tariffs. This will make imported goods from outside the bloc more expensive.
- The government of E may face some restrictions over economic policy relating to interest rates and government spending, particularly if it subsequently wishes to join a single currency.
- The lack of trade barriers with other bloc countries may result in local firms facing more competition from other member firms.
- Global firms attracted to invest in E may not share gains with local businesses, seeing E as simply a gateway to the trading bloc with low labour costs.
- Some citizens may object to changes to traditional lifestyles that result from economic growth, such as greater industrialisation and more tourists, for example.

Section 7

NOVEMBER 2007 EXAM QUESTIONS

SECTION A – 50 MARKS

[The indicative time for answering this section is 90 minutes.]

ANSWER *THIS* QUESTION

QUESTION ONE

Introduction

AA is a large food manufacturer, making a range of basic canned and bottled foodstuffs. With a turnover of almost €500 million, AA is a major employer throughout Western Europe. While a few AA brands are recognisable market leaders, notably a range of canned fish and a 'household name' tomato ketchup, most of AA's products are in the second tier of food products. The company also produces a wide range of 'own brand' products for major supermarket chains (these are products in packaging bearing the name of the supermarket retailer, rather than the producer).

Financial performance (2007/8)

The following information is taken from the October 2007 management accounts of AA. It relates to the budget and latest forecast for the full financial year ending 31 March 2008.

	Year to date € million	*Latest full year forecast* € million	*Full year original budget* € million
Sales revenue from major supermarket chains	177.0	357.0	
Sales revenue from wholesalers	42.9	89.4	
Gross sales revenue (after returns)	219.9	446.4	495.6
Discounts given	(9.9)	(20.1)	(15.6)
Net sales revenue	210.0	426.3	480.0
Gross profit*	36.2	68.2	99.0

* The prices charged to customers are calculated to generate a gross profit margin, before any discount, of 20% (that is, 495.6 × 20% = 99).

After much discussion about the possible causes of this year's poor performance, the most recent board meeting of AA discussed possible solutions. The following initiatives were identified, which should increase forecast sales revenue in the five remaining months of the current financial year.

- The Marketing Director stated that the effects of a major advertising campaign, aimed at wholesalers, had been omitted from the most recent forecast. This would be launched shortly, and should result in an increase in sales revenue from wholesalers of 8% for the remainder of the year.

- The Business Development Director proposed that a new product line, planned for launch in 2008/9, should be launched early. The new products are already in stock, and should generate gross sales revenue of €8.4 million by year end, without affecting the sales of other products.
- The Sales Director announced that a new wholesale customer had just been won, in an Eastern European country. This new customer should generate about €12 million of net sales revenue in the remaining five months of the year. This revenue was not included in the latest forecast, as the Sales Director had not expected to win the contract.

Customer strategy

The directors of AA are concerned about the high cost of servicing some of its major supermarket customers. During a recent brainstorming session, they identified the following possible strategies to deal with the least profitable of these customers:

(1) Stop selling to them. This will mean that the customers, if they wished to sell AA products, would have to buy them through a wholesaler.

(2) Persuade the customers to reduce the number of cost-generating activities (as identified in the forecast data below).

(3) Introduce new technologies to reduce the cost of the cost-generating activities.

The Sales Director of AA has provided the following information relating to three of AA's major supermarket customers:

Forecast for 2007/8

	S1	*S2*	*S3*
Sales revenue (before discounts and returns)# (€million)	58	24	108
Average discount given (%)	3	2	8
Number of sales visits made	12	15	218
Number of purchase orders processed*	59	26	760
Number of 'standard'** deliveries made	104	318	602
Number of 'rush'*** deliveries made	7	2	158
Damaged products returned (% of sales revenue)****	2.1	2.0	3.4

Notes:

The prices charged to customers are calculated to generate a gross profit margin, before any discount, of 20%.

* Purchase orders are paper documents, specifying items and quantities required, and the expected date of delivery.

** A 'standard' delivery is one that is ordered and scheduled in the normal way, that is, at least 24 hours before the delivery is required.

*** A 'rush' delivery is one that is ordered and scheduled for delivery on the day of order. This normally happens as a result of unexpectedly high demand causing a supermarket to run out of stock, or due to a customer error in calculating order quantities.

**** Customers are given a full refund for all damaged goods. These goods cannot be re-used or re-sold.

The Operations Accountant has provided the following costing information:

Forecast averages for 2007/8

	Cost (€)
Making a sales visit	685
Processing a purchase order	148
Making a 'standard' delivery	2,250
Making a 'rush' delivery	6,475

Required:

(a) (i) Briefly explain what is meant by 'gap analysis' in the context of strategic analysis. **(4 marks)**

(ii) Briefly explain the use of the Ansoff product/market growth strategies model in strategic planning, providing examples relevant to AA to illustrate your explanation. **(6 marks)**

(b) (i) Calculate the effect of the three initiatives (identified at the board meeting) on the full year net sales revenue gap. **(4 marks)**

(ii) Categorise each of the three initiatives in terms of the Ansoff growth strategies. **(3 marks)**

(c) Calculate and analyse the forecast net customer account profitability of each of the three major supermarket customers of AA, during the 2007/8 financial year.

Note: There are 18 marks available for calculations in this requirement. **(25 marks)**

(d) Evaluate the three alternative strategies proposed for the least profitable of AA's major supermarket customers and recommend which of these strategies you believe AA should adopt. **(8 marks)**

(Total: 50 marks)

(Total for Section A: 50 marks)

SECTION B – 50 MARKS

[The indicative time for answering this section is 90 minutes.]

ANSWER *TWO* QUESTIONS FROM FOUR

QUESTION TWO

D is an international logging company, which cuts down timber and supplies sawmills where the timber is seasoned and then cut to appropriate sizes for use in a range of industries. D will work with any timber, ranging from softwoods used in construction or paper manufacture to exotic hardwoods used in expensive furniture. Its usual approach is to secure the rights from a landowner, or in some cases a national government, to cut timber. This can often involve the payment of large initial cash deposits to these suppliers, money which D usually borrows. A logging team then cuts down the trees as quickly as possible and hauls the timber to a convenient river where it is floated to a sawmill. Moving on rapidly to the next site, the loggers usually leave considerable surface damage behind them.

Since an increasing proportion of the company's work has been in the tropical rainforest, it has recently come under pressure from environmental groups protesting that it is not socially responsible to act in this way. Whilst the softwood forests can be regenerated in a couple of decades by replanting, hardwoods in tropical forests take far longer to mature.

The Chief Executive of the company has argued that he is not concerned about these protests since, as far as he is concerned, the company always acts ethically as it has the agreement of the national government in any country in which the company operates.

A recent development in the timber industry has been the harvesting of timber from the bottom of reservoirs which have been created by flooding valleys. Although the capital equipment required for this approach is significantly more expensive than that used in conventional logging, the operating costs are lower. Waterlogged trees in reservoirs have balloons attached, are cut, float to the surface and are towed to a sawmill. The underwater process is quieter and less disruptive to wildlife and the environment.

It has been estimated that there are over half a billion trees, or 20 years' supply, submerged in reservoirs across the world, but it can take considerable research and expense to find them. As long as the timber has remained submerged deeply enough, it is of the same quality as timber harvested from the land. There is currently only one company conducting underwater logging, although a number of other companies are also considering this development.

Some of the Board of Directors feel that D should pursue this underwater approach and abandon land-based logging. The Chief Executive and one other director feel that the underwater approach carries too high a risk.

Required:

(a) (i) Briefly explain the differences between business ethics and corporate social responsibility (CSR). **(5 marks)**

(ii) Discuss the CSR issues relating to D's business and how the company might improve its CSR position. **(8 marks)**

(b) With reference to D, evaluate the two approaches to logging and recommend which you think is most appropriate for D. **(12 marks)**

(Total: 25 marks)

QUESTION THREE

F is a leading manufacturer of plastics. Its major products are beer crates and small containers for food sold in supermarkets. Together these two product ranges constitute 90% of F's business, the remainder coming from selling more technologically sophisticated products.

The company is faced with a number of difficulties and may have to issue a profits warning in the coming year. Although the profit levels have been uneven for the past five years, this is the first time that F will have to report significantly reduced profits.

F has been adversely affected by the aggressive marketing of foreign companies importing beer crates into the market, such that F's market share has fallen from 80% to 60% in the past three years. Consolidation in the brewery industry has meant that profit margins for crate manufacturers have been squeezed.

The company is heavily dependent upon the home market, which accounts for 75% of its total sales. Exports have been mainly of food containers for supermarkets in neighbouring countries.

F has invested heavily in research and development (R&D) and, although there is one exciting proposition in electro-plastics, most expenditure has been on projects selected by R&D managers who have little commercial awareness. There is the possibility that some new products may be developed from the electro-plastics research.

F is highly centralised, with many decisions taken by the 20 members of the Board of Directors. The workforce is highly unionised, with a number of different unions represented. Each factory has several negotiating committees set up to agree pay and conditions. Negotiations are often time-consuming and confrontational. This has resulted in very precise job definitions, which are strictly adhered to. This has further resulted in considerable inflexibility, together with a complicated system of labour grades.

The Directors have had little communication with stock market analysts and investors, who have little knowledge of the company other than what is shown in the published accounts. An informal group of institutional shareholders has asked for a strategic review and has suggested that F should withdraw from the beer crate market.

Required:

(a) (i) Discuss the main difficulties faced by F. **(5 marks)**

(ii) Identify and evaluate alternative strategies that F could adopt to address its difficulties and recommend those that are most appropriate. **(12 marks)**

(b) Explain why the failure to keep the shareholders more informed is a significant weakness for F. **(8 marks)**

(Total: 25 marks)

QUESTION FOUR

B is a multinational company with more than 20 divisions operating in various light engineering industries supplying automobile and aircraft manufacturing companies. Each division is managed by a Chief Executive Officer (CEO) reporting directly to the Board of Directors of B.

B has recently acquired C, a smaller company with only five divisions, which also operate in light engineering and supply similar customers to B's existing businesses. Each division is managed by a CEO reporting to the Board of Directors of C.

In the previous acquisitions that B has made, the acquired companies have been allowed to continue operating independently. This is despite the fact that there are overlapping or competing divisions in the combined enterprise. There is no certainty that this approach will continue.

Using Goold and Campbell's classification, B operates a system of 'strategic planning', and C operates a system of 'strategic control'.

B has announced that the Board of Directors of C will retire and each of the former divisions of C will report directly to the board of B.

The Board of Directors of B recognises that this will represent a considerable change in culture, working practices and expected behaviour for the CEOs of the divisions of C. It is concerned that there may be problems in ensuring the commitment of those CEOs to both B and its 'strategic planning' style.

As part of the acquisition team you are responsible for the transition to the new structure.

Required:

(a) Discuss the differences between 'strategic planning' and 'strategic control'. **(4 marks)**

(b) Discuss the impact that the change in planning culture is likely to have on the CEOs of the former divisions of C. **(11 marks)**

(c) Explain how the changes to the reporting arrangements could be implemented to ensure the commitment of those CEOs to B. **(10 marks)**

(Total: 25 marks)

QUESTION FIVE

G supplies electronic components to the automobile industry by exporting from the home country in which it is currently based. The company has recently set up a research facility in the home country to develop hydrogen fuel cells. The concept of hydrogen fuel cells has attracted a great deal of interest from the environmental lobby since it offers the prospect of very environmentally friendly vehicles. The market for these vehicles is in the development stage and there have been relatively few sales so far for this new technology. G hopes that the current pressure from environmental groups and governments will lead to large volume sales.

Increasingly, electronic component manufacturers are under pressure to manufacture close to the locations of their customers, the automobile manufacturers.

The research and development (R&D) director has decided that there is a need to open a research facility abroad, to work in partnership with the facility in the home country and capitalise on the benefits that a foreign base could offer. If this venture were successful, G would open a manufacturing facility next to the proposed overseas R&D base.

The Board of Directors recognises that different countries will offer different potential advantages and disadvantages. It has been decided that the ideal characteristics and factors for the chosen country should be determined, so that potential choices can be screened effectively before a final decision is made.

Required:

(a) Advise what ideal characteristics and factors should be present in the chosen country. **(15 marks)**

(b) Recommend the nature and sources of information that G should use when evaluating potential countries. **(10 marks)**

(Total: 25 marks)

(Total for Section B: 50 marks)

Section 8

ANSWERS TO NOVEMBER 2007 EXAM QUESTIONS

SECTION A

1 AA FOOD MANUFACTURER

Key answer tips

This is a fairly straightforward question with clear guidance about what is required. The main problem would be the need for good time management to ensure that the whole question is answered in the time available.

(a) (i) **Gap analysis**

Gap analysis is the comparison of an entity's ultimate objective with the sum of projections and already planned projects, and identifying how the consequent gap might be closed.

Gap analysis thus takes a key corporate objectives (e.g. revenue) and looks at the difference between

- Where an organisation is expected to be at a future date, assuming that existing strategies are continued
- Where the organisation wants to be.

For example, a profit gap could be analysed as follows:

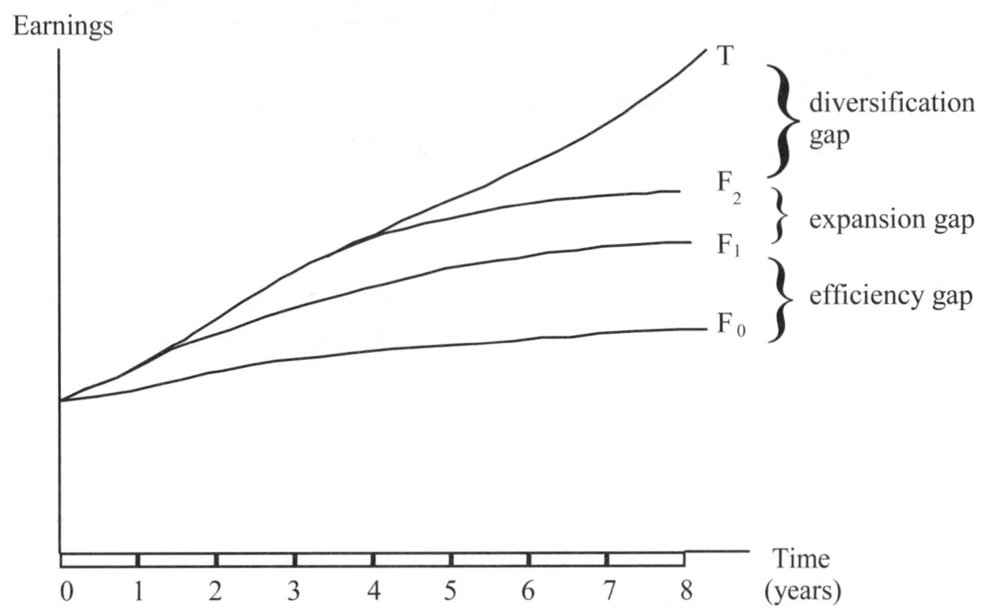

In the diagram showing the gap:

T = target

F_0 = initial forecast

F_1 = forecast adjusted for improvements in internal efficiency

F_2 = forecast adjusted for product-market expansion

Analysis of the gap reveals that in this instance the objectives cannot be achieved beyond year 4 without diversification. This gap is significant if the lead time for diversifying exceeds four years.

(ii) **Ansoff's matrix**

Ansoff's matrix is a useful way of classifying existing and potential strategies according to

- Does the strategy involve existing products or new ones?
- Does the strategy involve existing markets or new ones?

Depending on the answers to these two questions there are four possible strategy types:

	Existing products	**New products**
Existing market	Focussing on existing operations, there are two options available: • Internal efficiency gains could be made by better use of IT, for example • Market penetration involves gaining market share, for example by expanding the sales team to target smaller supermarket chains.	Product development involves making new products to sell to existing customers. • For AA this could include developing a range of drinks to sell to supermarkets.
New market	Market development involves developing new markets for existing products. • For AA this could include starting operations in the US and/or Asia	Diversification involves moving into new products for new markets • For AA this could involve forwards vertical integration by selling direct to the public via a website.

(b) **Initiatives**

(i) **Impact of new initiatives**

Existing gap in net sales revenue = 480.0 – 426.3 = €53.7 million

Impact of new proposals:

		€m	€m
• Advertising (note)	– 8% × (89.4 – 42.9)		3.7
• New product line	– Additional gross sales	8.4	
	– Expected discount (8.4 × 20.1/426.3)	(0.4)	
			8.0
• New customer			12.0
			23.7

(Note – we have assumed that the figures given for advertising are net of discounts)

The overall impact is that the revenue gap should fall to 53.7 – 23.7 = €30 million.

While the gap is smaller, there is still a shortfall to be made up.

(ii) **Classification of initiatives**

- The advertising campaign would be classified as market penetration as it aims to increase market share of existing markets with existing products.
- The new product line is aimed at existing customers so would be a product development strategy.
- The question does not state precisely where AA's customers are based but, given AA's manufacturing facilities are in Western Europe, it is reasonable to suggest that the Eastern European customer is in a new market for AA. The initiative would thus be a market development strategy.

(c) **Customer account profitability (CAP) analysis**

Analysis of customer profitability shows the following issues:

- Despite S3 generating more revenue, S1 is the most profitable customer and generates the highest net margins of the three customers.
- The main area of improvement for S1 would be to encourage them to cause as many rush orders.
- S2 has the highest gross margin of 16% but the net margin is only 12.9%. This is due mainly to the excessive number of deliveries needed - S2 has the smallest deliveries as measured by revenue per delivery.
- AA need to investigate whether this is a problem with S2 (for example, are orders made centrally but they have a large number of small stores requiring delivery) or with AA (e.g. inefficient delivery scheduling or unavailability of certain product lines).
- AA's main problem is with S3. It gives the lowest margins (6.2% net margin), the greatest percentage of rush deliveries (20.8%), the lowest value per order (€142,000), the highest level of returns (3.4%) and is given the greatest discount (8%).
- Despite this AA still makes €6.6 million profit each year from the S3 account. AA need to investigate why S3 makes so many smaller orders (e.g. ordering may be decentralised to local stores) and why so many deliveries are rush (e.g. S3 may be trying to minimise store inventories relying on AA to deliver at short notice).

Customer profitability calculations	***S1***	***S2***	***S3***
	€000	€000	€000
Sales revenue before discounts and returns	58,000	24,000	108,000
Returns	(1,218)	(480)	(3,672)
Gross sales revenue after returns	56,782	23,520	104,328
Discounts	(1,740)	(480)	(8,640)
Net sales revenue	55,042	23,040	95,688
Cost of sales = 80% × sales revenue	(46,400)	(19,200)	(86,400)
Gross profit	8,642	3,840	9,288
Cost of sales visits @ €685	(8)	(10)	(149)
Cost of processing orders @ €148	(9)	(4)	(112)
Cost of standard deliveries @ €2,250	(234)	(716)	(1,355)
Cost of rush deliveries @ €6,475	(45)	(13)	(1,023)
Net profit	8,346	3,097	6,649

Further analysis			
Gross margin	14.9%	16.0%	8.6%
Net margin	14.4%	12.9%	6.2%
Average revenue* per order (€000)	983	923	142
Total number of deliveries	111	320	760
% of total deliveries that are "rush"	6.3%	0.6%	20.8%
Average revenue* per delivery (€000)	522	75	142

(*before discounts and returns)

(d) **Evaluation**

Strategy	**Advantages**	**Disadvantages**
Stop selling to the least profitable customers	• Supermarkets would buy through wholesalers reducing AA's costs in dealing with them	• Potential lost sales as supermarkets go elsewhere • Reduced margin if sell via wholesalers
Persuade customers to reduce cost generating activities	• Would help streamline the business and save costs, improving margins. • Could help build stronger relationships with supermarkets reducing the risk of them switching suppliers • An obvious move, given AA's competitive strategy of cost leadership	• Customers will need encouragement to make any changes as they will perceive the costs to be AA's problem – for example, supermarkets could be offered additional discounts if they hit targets on, say, rush deliveries.
Introduce new technologies	• Greater efficiency processing orders • Could smooth production reducing inventory levels • Could enable better relationships with customers – for example, AA could set up an extranet allowing customers to order electronically.	• Cost of hardware, software and training could undermine AA's compctitivc advantagc.

It is recommended that in the short term AA seek to encourage customers to reduce the number of cost generating activities – for example, the number of rush deliveries could be reduced by better planning by the supermarket.

In addition AA should look at further investment in IT to improve production efficiency and build stronger links with customers.

SECTION B

2 D LOGGING

Key answer tips

This is a reasonably straightforward question on ethics and corporate social responsibility. To generate enough issues in part (a)(ii), ensure that you consider a wide range of stakeholder interests.

(a) (i) **Ethics and CSR**

Ethics is the study of determining right from wrong behaviour. Business ethics relates to the application of ethical values to business behaviour. In the same way that individuals have ethical values and are expected to follow those values, so organisations are now also expected to have ethical values.

As with individual ethics, business ethics goes beyond legal requirements indicating a higher moral standard than simply "following the law". There will be situations where an organisation follows the law, but ethical action means doing something more than this. This indicates that ethical actions are to some extent discretionary, in that the organisation does not have to take ethical action. However, expectations on the organisation from other sources (e.g. customers, suppliers and employees) also indicate that ethical action is normally expected of a company.

Many ethical dilemmas involve a conflict of interest between stakeholder groups. For example, a firm could increase profits for shareholders by exploiting the workforce in a third world country where human rights legislation is less stringent. This may not be illegal but would be considered by many to be unethical.

Corporate social responsibility is one aspect of business ethics and is concerned specifically with the ways in which an organisation exceeds the minimum obligations to stakeholders specified through regulation and corporate governance. Organisations are encouraged to produce a CSR report detailing their behaviour in this respect.

(ii) **D's CSR issues**

The Chief Executive of D is wrong to suggest that as long as D operates within the law, then this means that it is acting ethically. The main CSR issues relating to D are as follows:

Deforestation

- Deforestation can have a dramatic negative effect on local wildlife, the lifestyle and livelihood of indigenous tribes as well as increasing the risk of mudslides when it rains.
- On a global level the loss of tropical rainforest reduces the planet's ability to absorb $C0_2$, thus increasing the rate of global warming.
- It is thus unethical for D to make profits at the expense of local residents without making any attempt to clean up or rectify the mess created.
- Even though D may be acting within the law it could suffer from the adverse publicity being generated, so should implement plans for some regeneration post logging – for example, working with the local government to replant areas.

Use of hardwoods

- While the use of hardwoods is not illegal, there is widespread concern that forests will not have time to recover and that, ultimately species will be lost.
- D should investigate which hardwood trees are considered most at risk and see if it is feasible to leave them unfilled when logging an area.

Use of rivers for transportation

- The use of rivers for transporting the logs could cause pollution and erosion, threatening riverside settlements and local wildlife.
- D should investigate the impact of different volumes of logs on local rivers and consider staggering moving the logs if necessary.

Winning contracts

- While making large initial payments to Governments may be normal business practise, some may consider this to be tantamount to bribery and thus unethical.
- D should disclose amounts paid to ensure full transparency.

(b) **Logging strategies**

Arguments in favour of switching to the underwater approach

- D's ethical reputation will be greatly enhanced if it is seen to be taking a moral lead in this respect.
- At some stage in the future legislation regarding logging may be tightened. A move into underwater logging counters this threat and starting to switch now allows D to develop expertise and gain critical mass ahead of competitors.
- Once the machinery has been bought, operating costs will lower. In any case the machinery can potentially be used for up to twenty years in which to generate a return.
- There will be less damage to local wildlife, other than perhaps to fish.
- There will be considerably less disruption to local citizens as any major environmental damage would have already occurred when the reservoir was created in the first place.
- There will be a reduced impact on global warming as the trees concerned are no longer removing greenhouse gasses from the atmosphere.

Arguments in favour of continuing with land-based logging

- The existing method is probably much cheaper. A switch to underwater logging may make D's wood too expensive unless an environmental premium can be charged.
- Only a limited range of woods may be available underwater. The current scheme allows D to meet all market needs.
- A switch to underwater logging would necessitate considerable investment in the required machinery and training.

- The outflow of water from many reservoirs is carefully controlled. It may not be feasible to try to transport the volume of logs involved downstream via controlled gates and sluices.

Recommendations

- It is recommended that D takes a lead in investigating underwater logging and starts to switch methods where particularly exposed to negative criticism, such as the felling of tropical hardwoods.

3 F PLASTICS

Key answer tips

In part (a)(i) you only have 5 marks for discussing F's many difficulties so be careful not to exceed the time allocation.

For part (a)(ii) you need to generate a range of strategies to discuss. This could either involve a framework such as Ansoff's matrix or you could brainstorm different possibilities for each of the current products mentioned.

In part (c) the main problem lies in generating ideas but enough to pass should be fairly easy.

(a) (i) F has a deteriorating financial position as seen by falling market share and reduced profits. This is due to the following underlying difficulties:

Narrow product portfolio.

- F is over-reliant on two product ranges and heavily dependent on its domestic market. Any threats to these products thus have a much bigger impact on F as a whole.

Lack of a clear competitive strategy

- F's main emphasis seems to be competing in markets where products are fairly standardised such as beer crates. This would suggest that a cost leadership competitive strategy is needed. However, it also sells more technologically sophisticated products and invests heavily in R&D, indicating a differentiation strategy.
- This lack of a clear strategy could ultimately undermine both approaches, leaving F stuck in the middle.

Threat from competitive forces

- The combination of an increasing threat from cheap crate imports and industry consolidation is forcing down margins on crates.

Cultural deficiencies

- F has a mechanistic, bureaucratic culture that has resulted in a lack of flexibility and confrontations with unions.

Lack of focus in R&D

- F is not directing its R&D spend efficiently.

(ii) F should consider the following strategies to address its difficulties:

Enhance a low cost strategy for crates by cost-cutting

- F could try to enhance its competitive advantage by cutting back on unnecessary expenditure, such as R&D. This would improve margins and may discourage new entrants to F's domestic market.

- The main disadvantage of this option is that F would have to give up its high technology products, thus limiting its future prospects to an even smaller portfolio.
- On these grounds this proposal is rejected. As a compromise F should analyse its crate operations to see where efficiencies can be gained without compromising other product ranges.

Withdraw from the beer crate market

- Some shareholders have suggested withdrawing from beer crates. The main argument in favour of such a move is that the current trend is of increasing competition and falling margins.
- However, crates are one of F's main products. Profit may be falling but management need to see if F is still making positive contribution. If it is then closure should be rejected at least in the short run.
- In the longer run it is recommended that F reduce its reliance on crates. This may involve a phased withdrawal but widening the product range would offer more opportunities for growth (see below).

Look for new markets for crates

- Given that foreign competitors are exporting to F's domestic market, there may be scope for F to export to those foreign markets.
- The main advantages of this are that it would enable F to utilise spare capacity lost over the last few years. There may be scope for F to use existing distribution channels for the crates.
- The main problem is whether F can compete with foreign competition on cost once distribution costs have been incorporated. This is a major concern given F's experience in its domestic market. It is recommended that the directors assess neighbouring countries to see if the plan is viable.

Increase the development of electro-plastics and other high-technology products

- F does currently sell more technologically sophisticated products and could seek to develop these further.
- The main arguments in favour of this move are that
  - this could be a high growth area with less competition,
  - F already has a well established R&D function,
  - F is ahead of the competition in the use of electro-plastics and
  - F may be able to command higher margins through a strategy of differentiation.
- The main problem is that R&D is currently lacking focus. This should be straightforward to rectify so this strategy is recommended.

(b) Failure to keep shareholders informed is a serious weakness for the following reasons:

- A lack of information will make shareholders feel that their investment in F is more risky, resulting in a lower share price. The directors of F will thus be failing in their main objective of maximising shareholder value.
- At some stage F will be seeking to raise additional finance for investment. A failure to build good relationships with shareholders now will make them more reluctant to invest further. This will limit F's opportunities for raising finance.

- Any new ventures are likely to result in share price falls as shareholders will not have sufficient information to understand new proposals fully. Even if information is disclosed investors may be suspicious due to a history of a lack of details. This may discourage the directors of F from seeking new growth opportunities.
- Without regular detailed press releases, investors will place too much reliance on the published financial statements. There could thus be an over-reaction to the fall in profits and widespread selling of the shares with a corresponding fall in the share price.
- A combination of all of the above will result in F's share price being more volatile.
- Should a takeover bid be made for F, then shareholders will be less loyal to the current board and more willing to accept an offer. While a bid may be beneficial in terms of shareholder wealth, a lack of loyalty would be a concern for the directors.
- If profits continue to fall, then at some stage there may be a motion at the AGM to replace all or some of the directors. Failure to develop strong relations with major shareholders would make the likelihood of dismissal greater.
- The lack of disclosure may well be in breach of governance guidelines and relevant Stock Exchange regulations.

4 B MULTINATIONAL

Key answer tips

Many students avoided this question as they were unfamiliar with Goold and Campbell's classification so felt unable to tackle part (a). This was probably a wise move as those students may also have struggled to generate enough ideas for part s (b). Part (c) is more straightforward if viewed as a change management question.

Overall this is a difficult question to score well on.

(a) Goold and Campbell identified generic parenting styles to running divisionalised conglomerates, two of which are "strategic planning" and "strategic control".

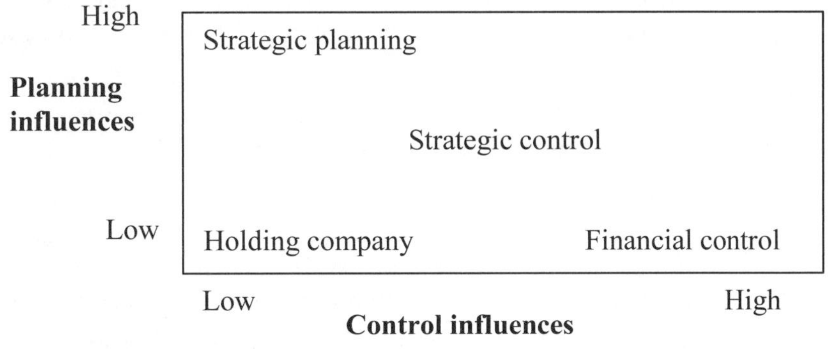

The main differences between them are as follows:

Planning influence

- The strategic planning style has a more centralised approach to planning than strategic control. Head office (or "the centre") is seen as the "master planner". This involves prescribing detailed plans and roles for business units, whose role is limited to the operational delivery of those plans.

- The strategic control style involves a fairly low degree of planning influence, preferring to allow business unit heads to develop plans, but then review them for acceptability.

Control influence

- The strategic planning style sets performance targets in broad terms with an emphasis on long-term strategic targets.
- In contrast, as its name would suggest, the strategic control style uses much tighter strategic control with firm targets for a range of KPIs.

(b) The change in planning culture is likely to have the following impact on the CEOs of the former divisions of C:

Potentially negative impacts

- The CEOs will have had established relationships with the board of directors of C. Given that the latter will be retired off, the CEOs will lose those relationships and may feel resentment and an enhanced state of anxiety and stress regarding their own security.
- CEOs will previously have had significant autonomy to develop business plans. The loss of this autonomy to the "centre" may result in managers who feel little commitment to the strategies handed down to them.
- CEOs may feel that they have lost the status that they once enjoyed as they will no longer be seen as the "boss" of their division. Some may thus want to leave B to find new challenges elsewhere.
- CEOs will feel that they have less impact than previously. Again this could be viewed as the loss of a key motivational factor.
- The information needs of the centre under a strategic planning style will be much greater than under strategic control. CEOs may resent the pressure to supply information for the board of B to make decisions previously made by them.
- In summary, the main negative impact is a potential loss of motivation with key staff looking for new opportunities outside of the group.

Potentially positive impacts

- CEOs may feel that the switch from detailed financial targets to longer term strategic ones gives them more freedom with respect to operational management issues.
- CEOs of "difficult" divisions with high risk and uncertainty may welcome greater input into the planning process from the Board of B.
- Some CEOS may have been too risk averse to suggest and implement high risk strategies in their divisions under the strategic control model for fear that they would be held personally responsible when short term targets were missed. Under the strategic planning approach they would feel more able to suggest such strategies to the "centre" without being held responsible should the strategy be accepted and then fail

(c) To ensure the commitment of CEOs to B, the cultural change associated with the reporting arrangements needs to be handled carefully. In particular, Effective cultural change needs:

- To be done slowly as values and attitudes have to change.

- To be planned to prevent poor performance.
- To be controlled to ensure that the objectives are achieved.

In particular, arrangements should be changed as follows:

Education and communication

- The directors of B should arrange meetings with the CEOs of former C divisions to communicate to them the pros and cons of the two parenting styles, why B has adopted the strategic planning model and the implications for the CEOs.
- There should be scope within the meeting for CEOs views to be aired to ensure that they feel heard and for suggestions to be incorporated.

Participation in systems design

- Given that CEOs will fear a major loss of status and autonomy, it is important that they are invited to participate in discussions to determine how best to apply B's parenting style to their divisions, which are the most appropriate long term targets and so on.

Participation in target setting

- Some of the CEOs' loss of autonomy can be mitigated by inviting them to participate in target setting. This should ensure greater commitment to targets set.

Discussion of results and subsequent action

- The CEOs should be invited to discuss the reasons why their divisions have / have not hit strategic targets and to help determine appropriate responses.

Phased changeover

- Rather than a sudden switch to more centralised planning, B may wish to consider a phased changeover where existing CEOs have some input into strategy planning but with their input gradually reduced.

Unfreezing and refreezing the culture (Lewin)

- Lewin suggested that cultures need to be unfrozen, changed and then refrozen.
- The existing culture can be unfrozen by, for example, explaining the disadvantages of a strategic control model compared with a strategic planning model.
- Once changes have been made, the new culture can be refrozen by linking remuneration to performance under the new scheme. In particular, B could arrange it so the CEOS have a reasonable expectation of higher bonuses under the new scheme than under the old.

Power/coercion

- As a last resort, B could consider replacing CEOs who are unwilling to embrace the new system.

5 G ELECTRONICS

Key answer tips

In part (a) frameworks such as PEST, Porter's five forces and Porter's diamond can be useful for generating ideas but they need to be applied correctly to the scenario. For example, using Porter's diamond, strong domestic rivalry is viewed as a positive factor as it can result in highly competitive domestic firms but this would not make the market attractive to a new entrant such as G. In part (b) you need to be careful to avoid repeating your answer to part (a).

(a) Given that G is planning to set up both research and manufacturing facilities, the ideal characteristics of a country are as follows:

Macroeconomic factors

- Strong growth in GDP and disposable income should ensure growth in demand for cars with a corresponding increase in demand for components.
- A stable currency reduces the perceived risk of the project and should facilitate better planning.
- Low inflation will also reduce the risk associated with the investment as well as generating consumer confidence.
- Low interest rates will give low cost finance for G, its potential customers and car purchasers.

Political environment

- A stable political environment will reduce the risk of the investment. For example, what is the likelihood of armed conflict, civil war or of employees being kidnapped by terrorist groups?
- The political attitude towards foreign firms is extremely important. For example, will G face protectionist measures regarding ownership structures and repatriation of funds?
- On the other hand some governments may be keen to encourage FDI via incentives such as soft loans and tax breaks.
- If the country is a member of a regional trade union such as the EU or NAFTA, then exporting components into neighbouring countries will be much easier and cheaper.

Social factors

- High standards of local education, especially to degree level and beyond, will ensure a good supply of suitable candidates to recruit locally for both the research facility and the manufacturing plant.
- Availability of labour and wage rates would be key factors for the manufacturing facility. Ideally G would want a developing country where education and skills levels are high but average wage levels have yet to catch up with its home country.
- A shared spoken language between G's home country and the target country will make communication easier.

Technological factors

- Is the communications infrastructure of the target country sufficiently developed? For example, some African countries still have very limited high speed internet access, which would make communication between the two research facilities more difficult.

Ethical issues

- G would want to check the country's record on human rights to avoid attracting negative publicity as investing there could be considered to be supporting the incumbent regime.

Competitive/market issues

- G would want to choose a country with a high number of major automobile manufacturers present. As well as providing potential customers for components, there may be scope for collaboration over research.
- Ideally there would also be neighbouring countries that are reasonably close with major car manufacturers.
- The presence of many rival components manufacturers could be a deterrent to G as it would make it much harder to earn high margins there.

(b) G could use the following sources of information when evaluating potential countries:

- There are likely to be many publications regarding the state of the economy, GDP, average earnings, growth estimates and so on. The target country government is likely to produce many of these but international organisations such as OECD and the World Bank should also be contacted.
- Government departments in the target country could be contacted to determine government policy, both locally and nationally – for example, to see attitudes towards encouraging foreign firms to invest and/or what protectionist measures are in place.
- The published accounts of competitors and customers in the target country could indicate changes in the industry, growth profiles and provide useful information for benchmarking.
- Given the global nature of the automobile industry, there are likely to be many industry publications detailing the state of the industry in different countries and growth opportunities.
- Details regarding security risks and terrorism can be obtained from UN Departments and from the foreign offices of most developed countries. The latter will normally classify and assess the risks concerned.
- A country's environmental and human rights records can be assessed using Amnesty International and Greenpeace reports respectively.
- A target country's educational and skills standards will be the subject of UNESCO surveys and investigations.
- More specifically related to a potential research facility, G could contact local universities and examine their websites to see which areas of research they are involved with.
- The Internet can be an n invaluable source of desk research with many websites, particularly US-based, who specialise in assessing country risk.